THE EU BETTER REGULATION AGENDA

Better Regulation in the EU is a perennial and topical question which has important implications for the future direction of EU law. While actions directed at improving the quality and accessibility of EU regulation are not novel, in recent years the Better Regulation Agenda has significantly affected the structural organisation and day-to-day operation of the EU legislative process. Yet, many questions about the future of the Agenda remain, not least in light of Brexit. Exploring the Better Regulation Agenda (and its relation to the overall EU legal and political order) necessitates an integrated, interdisciplinary approach. This edited volume presents insights from economics, political science and legal scholarship. Furthermore, to allow full understanding, it examines institutional practice, where the Agenda is made and shaped on a daily basis. Hence, the book features contributions from the perspective of the work of the main EU institutions: the European Commission, the Parliament, the Council and the Court of Justice. This results in a seminal overview of the subject, of interest to scholars and practitioners alike.

Volume 87 in the Series Modern Studies in European Law

Modern Studies in European Law

Recent titles in this series:

EU Liability and International Economic Law
Armin Steinbach

The EU and Nanotechnologies: A Critical Analysis
Tanja Ehnert

Human Rights Between Law and Politics:
The Margin of Appreciation in Post-National Contexts
Edited by Petr Agha

The European Union and Social Security Law
Jaan Paju

The Rule of Law in the European Union: The Internal Dimension
Theodore Konstadinides

The Division of Competences between the EU and the Member States:
Reflections on the Past, the Present and the Future
Edited by Sacha Garben and Inge Govaere

Unity in Adversity: EU Citizenship, Social Justice and the Cautionary Tale of the UK
Charlotte O'Brien

The Use of Force and Article 2 of the ECHR in Light of European Conflicts
Hannah Russell

Environmental Crime in Europe
Edited by Andrew Farmer, Michael Faure and Grazia Maria Vagliasindi

Questioning EU Citizenship: Judges and the Limits of Free Movement
and Solidarity in the EU
Edited by Daniel Thym

The European Union under Transnational Law: A Pluralist Appraisal
Matej Avbelj

Illegally Staying in the EU: An Analysis of Illegality in EU Migration Law
Benedita Menezes Queiroz

Social Legitimacy in the Internal Market: A Dialogue of Mutual Responsiveness
Jotte Mulder

For the complete list of titles in this series, see
'Modern Studies in European Law' link at
www.bloomsburyprofessional.com/uk/series/modern-studies-in-european-law

The EU Better Regulation Agenda

A Critical Assessment

Edited by
Sacha Garben and Inge Govaere

•HART•
OXFORD • LONDON • NEW YORK • NEW DELHI • SYDNEY

HART PUBLISHING
Bloomsbury Publishing Plc
Kemp House, Chawley Park, Cumnor Hill, Oxford, OX2 9PH, UK

HART PUBLISHING, the Hart/Stag logo, BLOOMSBURY and the Diana logo are trademarks of Bloomsbury Publishing Plc

First published in Great Britain 2018

A catalogue record for this book is available from the British Library.

Library of Congress Cataloging-in-Publication data

Names: Garben, Sacha, 1982-, editor. | Govaere, Inge, editor.

Title: The EU better regulation agenda : a critical assessment / Edited by Sacha Garben and Inge Govaere.

Description: Portland, Oregon : Hart Publishing, 2018. | Series: Modern studies in european law ; volume 87 | Includes bibliographical references and index.

Identifiers: LCCN 2017058062 (print) | LCCN 2017058397 (ebook) | ISBN 9781509917358 (Epub) | ISBN 9781509917334 (hardback : alk. paper)

Subjects: LCSH: Administrative agencies—European Union countries. | Trade regulation—European Union countries. | Foreign trade regulation—European Union countries.

Classification: LCC KJE5794 (ebook) | LCC KJE5794 .E9 2018 (print) | DDC 342.24/06—dc23

LC record available at https://lccn.loc.gov/2017058062

ISBN: HB: 978-1-50991-733-4
ePDF: 978-1-50991-734-1
ePub: 978-1-50991-735-8

Typeset by Compuscript Ltd, Shannon

To find out more about our authors and books visit www.hartpublishing.co.uk. Here you will find extracts, author information, details of forthcoming events and the option to sign up for our newsletters.

Contents

Part I: Introduction and State of Play

1. The Multi-faceted Nature of Better Regulation.....3
Sacha Garben and Inge Govaere

2. Integrating Regulatory Governance and Better Regulation as Reflexive Governance.....13
Colin Scott

Part II: A Critical Assessment of the Main Elements of the Better Regulation Agenda

3. Improving the Quality of EU Legislation: Limits and Opportunities?.....29
Helen Xanthaki

4. Cost-Benefit Analysis and EU Policy: Limits and Opportunities.....49
Andrea Renda

5. The Better Regulation Agenda and the Deactivation of EU Competences: Limits and Opportunities.....63
Robert Zbíral

Part III: Views from EU Institutional Practice

6. The European Commission and its Better Regulation Agenda.....79
Ben Smulders and Jean-Eric Paquet

7. The European Parliament and the Better Law-Making Agenda.....105
María José Martínez Iglesias

8. The Council: Some Historical and Practical Aspects to the Better Regulation Agenda.....119
Jenő Czuczai

9. The Member States and the Better Regulation Agenda: The Case of Belgium/Flanders.....137
Jan de Mulder

10. From Better Regulation to Better Adjudication? Impact Assessment and the Court of Justice's Review.....185
Julian Nowag and Xavier Groussot

Part IV: Broader Perspectives on the Better Regulation Agenda

11. Eurolegalism and the Better Regulation Agenda 205
R Daniel Kelemen

12. An 'Impact Assessment' of EU Better Regulation 217
Sacha Garben

Index 243

Part I

Introduction and State of Play

1

The Multi-faceted Nature of Better Regulation

SACHA GARBEN* AND INGE GOVAERE**

A SEMI-PERMANENT YET DYNAMIC FEATURE OF EU LAW AND POLICY

THE EU BETTER Regulation Agenda has been around for quite some time, although it has known various different manifestations.[1] As Colin Scott sets out in Chapter 2, like many national governments around the world and supported by international organisations such as the Organisation for Economic Co-operation and Development (OECD), over the past few decades, the EU has consistently engaged in such regulatory review exercises, examining the quality and quantity of EU regulation, generally with a view to increasing the former and decreasing the latter. As it should therefore by now be considered a semi-permanent feature of the EU legal and political landscape, it merits an in-depth and comprehensive discussion, which is what the present book aims to offer. At the same time, the Better Regulation Agenda is not a static institution but instead a recurring phenomenon that develops dynamically over time, making it a challenging subject of study. It is in many ways a 'moving target': a fluid phenomenon that adapts itself to evolving political circumstances and to the powers that be. This finds illustration in the rather different interpretation and follow-up given to the Better Regulation Agenda by the current European Commission headed by President Juncker, as compared to the previous Barrosso Commission. The latter could be argued to have followed a 'self-flagellating' line, to borrow Daniel Kelemen's expression, who addresses this in Chapter 11, which largely gave

* Sacha Garben is Professor of EU Law at the College of Europe and is on leave from the European Commission. Nothing in the present contribution represents the views of the European Commission.

** Inge Govaere is Professor of European Law, Jean Monnet Chair in EU Legal Studies and Director at the Ghent European Law Institute (GELI) at Ghent University, and Director of Studies of the College of European Legal Studies Department. We wish to thank Mrs. Valérie Hauspie for her invaluable assistance in the organisation of the workshop on which this book is based, as well as her excellent editorial assistance.

[1] See earlier initiatives such as the Commission Staff Working Document, 'Making Single Market Rules More Effective, Quality in Implementation and Enforcement' SEC(1998) 903, 3–5, 'Better Law-Making' in the early 2000s: European Commission Communication, 'European Governance: Better Law-Making' COM (2002) 275 final; and 'Smart Regulation' in the late 2000s: European Commission Communication, 'Smart Regulation in the European Union' COM (2010) 543 final.

in to the perception in some Member States that the EU's rule-making was out of control and had to be reined in, therefore operating the Agenda to cut existing EU standards and to curb the adoption of new ones. However, the current Juncker Commission has instead demonstrated that a different interpretation of Better Regulation may very well lead to new legislative initiatives and thus to more regulation, rather than less, if this is warranted by the outcome of evaluation exercises and coincides with political priorities.[2] It thus seems that each political leadership will have its own specific agenda in relation to Better Regulation. Furthermore, while the European Commission is certainly the *chef de file* on the issue of Better Regulation in the EU, as the contributions in Part III of this volume also address, the Agenda equally impacts the other institutional actors, which may yet have a different interpretation, or version, of Better Regulation. For instance, as can be seen from María José Martínez Iglesias' discussion in Chapter 7, while generally subscribing to Better Regulation's objectives, the European Parliament has a rather different view from the Commission on some of the concrete requirements that it entails, or should entail, for the legislator, such as the obligation to conduct Impact Assessments and to take the Commission's assessment as a starting point in this regard. All this means that we have to be very careful, as our collected authors have endeavoured to be, in drawing any firm conclusions about the features and consequences of 'Better Regulation' in general, and to refer to its specific 'incarnations' where appropriate.

DEMOCRATIC AND CONSTITUTIONAL LEGITIMACY QUESTIONS

However, the fact that the content and direction of the Better Regulation Agenda is fundamentally influenced by the political authority in place does not mean that it is simply a policy tool that can be fully moulded and adapted by the governing power to its wishes. Over time, several features of Better Regulation have become entrenched in the EU institutional framework, its policy and its law. As such, it has started to 'live its own life' and operates—at least to a certain extent—independently from the political powers of the day. Autonomous institutions, such as the Regulatory Scrutiny Board discussed by Ben Smulders and Jean-Eric Paquet in Chapter 6, have been created. Whereas Xavier Groussot and Julian Nowag point out in Chapter 10 that Impact Assessments have become an important tool for the Court of Justice of the European Union (CJEU) to examine the validity of EU legislation, particularly on the grounds of subsidiarity and proportionality.

[2] For instance, in the context of the recently launched European Pillar of Social Rights, an important new legislative initiative to revise and strengthen Written Statement Directive 91/533 builds on the findings of an earlier REFIT evaluation. The proposal is to amend the Directive, introducing minimum standards applicable to every employment relationship and prohibiting the abuse of precarious workers. See European Commission, *REFIT Evaluation of the 'Written Statement Directive'*, SWD(2017) 205 final. The Commission has launched the first-phase consultation of the Social Partners required on the basis of Art 154 TFEU, C(2017) 2611.

In its growing independence from political authority in the EU through its institutionalisation and in its potential to actually limit the exercise of that authority, the Better Regulation Agenda inevitably raises questions about its democratic legitimacy. Certain of the Agenda's objectives are conducive to that legitimacy, such as its commitment to participatory government through public consultation and to transparency, but others are instead about curbing political discretion in pursuit of the 'regulatory paradigm' of evidence-based policy. If the Agenda were only a political instrument of the reigning powers, it could arguably directly derive its authority from those powers. Especially since the use of *Spitzenkandidaten* in European elections, it could be argued that the European Commission has stronger political legitimacy, and then so would a deliberate policy choice such as the Better Regulation Agenda—at least to the extent that the Commission applies it to its own activities.[3] However, since the Agenda partially operates independently from the Commission's political level and because the Commission seeks to also apply it to the European Parliament and Council, as well as to national governments and parliaments, the Agenda needs a different, additional source of legitimacy.

This could potentially be found in the EU Treaties. Certain pointed provisions, such as those on EU environmental and social policy, refer to the need to take into account the 'potential benefits and costs of action or lack of action'[4] and the need to 'avoid imposing administrative, financial and legal constraints in a way which would hold back the creation and development of small and medium-sized undertakings'.[5] Both the EU Better Regulation Agenda and the Regulatory Fitness and Performance Programme (REFIT) exercise[6] which is part of it, could arguably be defended in reference to these stipulations in EU primary law itself, precisely in the areas where it has proven most controversial politically. But also applicable in a horizontal manner and, more generally stated, Article 5 of the Treaty on European Union (TEU) provides that EU action ('the use of Union competences') shall respect the principles of subsidiarity and proportionality. This further supports the constitutional mandate of the Better Regulation Agenda, which contains an explicit subsidiarity component in its Impact Assessment and could overall be conceived as a proportionality assessment of EU legislation: considering whether the measure in question is necessary, effective and whether no less 'restrictive' action is possible. Furthermore, Declaration 18 annexed to the Treaty of Lisbon explicitly provides for the option of repeal of legislation, particularly in view of

[3] For a comprehensive discussion of the tension between the regulatory and political paradigms of Better Regulation, see M Dawson, 'Better Regulation and the Future of EU Regulatory Law and Politics' (2016) 53 *CMLR* 1209.

[4] Article 191(3) TFEU stipulates that 'in preparing its policy on the environment, the Union shall take account of … potential benefits and costs of action or lack of action'.

[5] Article 153(2)(b) TFEU on social policy provides that the European Parliament and the Council may adopt, by means of directives, minimum requirements for gradual implementation: 'Such directives shall avoid imposing administrative, financial and legal constraints in a way which would hold back the creation and development of small and medium-sized undertakings.'

[6] European Commission Communication, 'EU Regulatory Fitness' COM (2012) 746 final.

subsidiarity and proportionality.[7] This therefore endorses aspects of the Agenda by a 'basic constitutional rule expressly entrenched in primary law after the Lisbon Treaty reforms', as Robert Zbíral discusses in Chapter 5. Finally, the Better Regulation Agenda's constitutional legitimacy could be supported by Article 2 TEU, which refers to the Rule of Law as one of the EU's founding principles. As the Rule of Law demands a clear, enforceable regulatory framework in which individuals can ascertain what rights and obligations they have as well as dispose of means of enforcement thereof, the Better Regulation Agenda's commitment to improve the quality and enforceability/enforcement of EU legislation can be seen to contribute to it.

At the same time, however, there are some constitutional arguments against certain aspects of the Better Regulation Agenda. For instance, the Agenda's at times hostile stance towards higher national regulatory standards in areas of EU regulation, qualifying these as 'gold-plating' and generally discouraging them,[8] is constitutionally questionable. It would seem that either such national provisions are incompatible with the harmonised EU standards (or other Treaty provisions)—in which case the problem is not 'gold-plating' but instead an infringement of EU law that can be taken up before the Court—or it concerns an issue that is not fully regulated by EU law—in which case the principle of conferral entails that the remaining regulatory capacity falls within the powers of the Member States. The 'gold-plating' critique is particularly problematic in areas such as the environment, consumer protection and social law, where the Treaty on the Functioning of the European Union (TFEU) explicitly lays down the principle of minimum harmonisation and thus recognises the Member States' right to provide higher levels of protection, and where such higher national levels are instead to be encouraged from the perspective of the policy areas' objectives.

[7] This provides: 'When the Treaties confer on the Union a competence shared with the Member States in a specific area, the Member States shall exercise their competence to the extent that the Union has not exercised, or has decided to cease exercising, its competence. The latter situation arises when the relevant EU institutions decide to repeal a legislative act, in particular better to ensure constant respect for the principles of subsidiarity and proportionality. The Council may, at the initiative of one or several of its members (representatives of Member States) and in accordance with Article 241 of the Treaty on the Functioning of the European Union, request the Commission to submit proposals for repealing a legislative act. The Conference welcomes the Commission's declaration that it will devote particular attention to these requests.'

[8] According to the European Commission: 'Member States also often go beyond what is strictly required by EU legislation when they implement it at national level ('gold-plating'). This may enhance the benefits but can also add unnecessary costs for businesses and public authorities which are mistakenly associated with EU legislation.' It urges Member States to 'avoid unjustified "gold-plating"' and that Member States should be invited to explain the reasons for any such gold-plating. Commission Communication, 'Better Regulation for Better Results—An EU Agenda' COM (2015) 215 final. The European Parliament has adopted a different line, stating that 'in the case of directives, it is the prerogative of the Member States to decide whether to adopt higher social, environmental and consumer protection standards at national level than those minimum standards of protection agreed upon at EU level, and welcomes any decision to do so; reaffirms that such higher standards must not be regarded as "gold-plating"'. European Parliament, *Report on Regulatory Fitness and Performance Programme (REFIT): State of Play and Outlook*, 24 June 2015, 2014/2150(INI), para 44.

The application of the Agenda to the Social Partners, as happened under the previous Commission, in the case of the Collective Agreement in the Hairdressing Sector[9] similarly poses problems from the perspective of the TFEU, in particular as it is stated in Article 155 TFEU that: 'Agreements concluded at Union level *shall* be implemented either in accordance with the procedures and practices specific to management and labour and the Member States or, in matters covered by Article 153, at the joint request of the signatory parties, by a Council decision on a proposal from the Commission' (emphasis added). The mandatory language suggests that the Commission does not have a discretionary choice in submitting the proposal to the Council, whether or not it considers that the Agreement complies with the Better Regulation Agenda. While the General Court held in *UEAPME* that after the joint request of the Social Partners, the Commission 'resumes control of the procedure and determines whether it is appropriate to submit a proposal to that effect to the Council',[10] the General Court (GC) referred in particular to the Commission's responsibility to assess the representativeness of the organisations that have concluded the agreement.[11] Therefore, provided that the procedural conditions of valid social dialogue as set out in the Treaties are fulfilled, it is doubtful whether the agreement can be rejected on political grounds. Indeed, as the GC also held in *UEAPME*, in resuming control of the procedure, the Commission must act in conformity with the principles governing its action in social policy, in particular the obligation under Article 154(1) TFEU to promote the consultation of management and labour at the EU level and to take any relevant measure to facilitate their dialogue by ensuring balanced support for the parties.[12] To refuse proposing a successfully concluded agreement for adoption to the Council on political or 'better regulation' grounds does not sit easily with that obligation and adds (perhaps unnecessary) grist to the mill of those that accuse the Better Regulation Agenda of being inspired by deregulatory ideology.

Furthermore, while, as Ben Smulders and Jean-Eric Paquet point out in Chapter 6, it would be ill-informed to paint a picture of EU Better Regulation as an unequivocal drive towards deregulation in the interests of businesses, many scholars have argued that certain elements of the Agenda carry a risk of systematic bias against

[9] This Agreement, aimed at improving the health and safety of workers in the hairdressing sector concluded by workers and employers, was publicly denounced by the European Commission as an example of bad regulation and was not put forward to the Council. See REFIT '"Fit for Growth": Examples How EU Law is Becoming Lighter, Simpler and Cheaper', http://europa.eu/rapid/press-release_MEMO-13-833_en.htm. As Schindler notes, former Commission President Barroso polemically declared in a TV interview that Europe does need to regulate hairdressers' 'high heels', even though the agreement primarily concerns the use of chemicals in the sector where workers are most at risk of work-related skin diseases. Interview by D Krause, *Tagesschau*, 2 October 2013, https://www.tagesschau.de/ausland/interview130.html, as reported by S Schindler, 'The Social Chimera of the Economic and Monetary Union, Social Policy in the Context of European Economic Governance', *LUP Student Papers* (2014), available at https://lup.lub.lu.se/student-papers/search/publication/4460811.

[10] Case T-135/96 *UEAPME v Council of the European Union* ECLI:EU:T:1998:128, para 84.

[11] ibid paras 85–88 of the judgment.

[12] ibid para 85 of the judgment.

regulatory standards, particularly to pursue non-economic interests. One of the main methodologies used in Impact Assessment and Evaluations is cost-benefit analysis, which—as Andrea Renda explores at length in Chapter 4— poses a number of problems in terms of its reliance on certain doubtful economic assumptions and the quantification of non-quantifiable benefits. It was out of concern for the expected negative consequences of the EU Better Regulation Agenda in this sense that in 2015, more than 50 civil society groups joined forces in the setting up of a 'Better Regulation watchdog'.[13] Even if, as Robert Zbíral's empirical analysis in Chapter 5 also shows, their fear of a grand repeal of the *acquis* has not come to pass, it may be a more difficult challenge to measure opportunity cost in terms of 'initiatives not taken'. After all, the administrative resources spent on the various *ex ante* and *ex post* evaluation exercises, and the expected burdens and difficulties of passing an Impact Assessment, may have deterred certain Commission Directorates General from developing new proposals from the outset, which is most likely to have occurred in the non-economic policy areas. In any event, without coming to a final verdict on whether or not the Better Regulation Agenda ultimately leads to an economic bias in EU law and policy-making, it seems justified to be at least vigilant about the risk thereof. Such a bias would be problematic from a constitutional point of view: Article 7 TFEU implies a duty on the EU institutions to ensure 'consistency between its policies and activities, taking all of its objectives into account', which should be read in keeping with the broad range of objectives listed in Article 3 TEU, as well as several 'mainstreaming' provisions, suggesting that market-making policies should be conditioned by a number of non-market objectives, from social exclusion to environmental protection, non-discrimination and animal welfare.[14] An application of Better Regulation that would systematically hold back the promotion of EU non-market objectives, whether through a flawed methodology or an express political commitment, would be hard to justify constitutionally.

THE VARIOUS NARRATIVES UNDERLYING THE EU BETTER REGULATION AGENDA

From the brief discussion above, it already clearly emerges that the EU Better Regulation Agenda has a very complex, multi-faceted nature. It has seen many incarnations over time, has many different features and furthermore seems to have many different objectives. This makes an assessment of its legitimacy, or of any other aspect, more difficult, as the answer will invariably depend on what precisely the Agenda's aims and concrete elements in support thereof are. Yet, there is remarkably little conceptual consensus on these issues. As Sacha Garben explores

[13] See www.betterregwatch.eu/about-us.

[14] Dawson, above n 3, 1227.

in more detail in Chapter 12, at least five different rationales can be distinguished: (i) improving the quality of EU legislation';(ii) reducing the quantity of EU legislation; (iii) increasing public participation in the legislative process; (iv) promoting science-based governance; and (v) enforcing the subsidiarity and proportionality principles. It becomes clear from the various contributions to this book, and is systematically analysed in Chapter 12, that all these different rationales for/of Better Regulation have their (constitutional, democratic, substantive) merits, but also their inherent challenges, not in the least because many of them are, to a certain extent, contradictory and because they are sometimes based on unproven assumptions.

A clear distinction between the competing strands informing the EU Better Regulation Agenda provides a better basis to analyse and discuss the topic. Importantly, it provides us with guidance on how to tackle the legitimacy question. Every separate rationale necessitates its own justification in reference to its underlying 'problem definition', its feasibility and to the Treaties' constitutional and democratic principles. To the extent that the Agenda would be about reducing the quantity of EU regulation in the interest of business, it would seem to be a political choice and thus need a clear democratic validation. To the extent that it would be about improving the quality of EU regulation, it expresses a commitment to the Rule of Law and thus its concrete features need to be assessed against that background. Reflexive and participatory governance are both about democracy in a non-representative, 'throughput'[15] sense, and thus need to be judged against that yardstick. On the other hand, technocratic, or science-based, governance is about output legitimacy or mitigating 'raw political power', as Ben Smulders and Jean-Eric Paquet put it in Chapter 6. Subsidiarity in turn encompasses federal concerns about national identity, autonomy and diversity. Apart from allowing each different aspect of Better Regulation to be judged against its own standard, this conceptual framework will also facilitate a better understanding of the trade-offs in the competing overarching interests involved in mediating the conflicting elements of the Agenda.

THE QUALITY OF THE BETTER REGULATION DEBATE

This book aims to contribute to an improved quality and integration of the public, political and academic debates on Better Regulation, which currently appear somewhat disparate and impoverished. More than perhaps EU regulation itself, the feverish *public* debate on (the need for) Better Regulation can be said to suffer from an inflated quantity of often deplorable quality. Outlandish, fact-free claims about the EU's regulatory zeal have dominated tabloid headlines in

[15] Term as used by V Schmidt, 'Democracy and Legitimacy in the European Union Revisited: Input, Output and Throughput' (2010) 21 *KFG Working Paper*, http://userpage.fu-berlin.de/kfgeu/kfgwp/wpseries/WorkingPaperKFG_21.pdf.

some Member States, which is likely to have had an important influence on public attitudes towards EU integration more generally and, as such, may—tragically—have some part in explaining the UK's Brexit vote. Certain national political actors may see (short-term) political gain in condoning the largely unsubstantiated discourse of a rule-sick, power-hungry EU and to tag calls for national regulatory autonomy on the back of that discourse. But, in addition, the somewhat more reasonable *political* debate does not sufficiently engage with the complex, multi-faceted nature of the Better Regulation Agenda and its manifold objectives. For businesses and the right side of the political spectrum, Better Regulation should be about 'bonfires of red tape', and the EU can never do enough to quench this thirst, while for public interest organisations and 'the left', Better Regulation is seen as a neoliberal drive to dispose of important public interest rules and should be given as limited an interpretation as possible. Sharply contrasting with this polarised discussion, the EU institutions, on the other hand, seem to prefer a depoliticised approach, presenting Better Regulation as an objective policy that simply seeks to ensure that regulation is 'rational', based on scientific facts and methodology, but thereby risking glossing over the Agenda's important political implications. *Academia* in turn has mostly focused on the technicalities of Better Regulation and its various aspects, often from a disciplinary perspective, without sufficiently integrating the important polemics that shape the Agenda and its perception, and leaving somewhat under-explored the way in which the Agenda relates to constitutional principles and the EU legal and political order as a whole.[16]

STRUCTURE OF THE BOOK

Part I of the book, including the present chapter, introduces the Better Regulation Agenda as it currently stands and how it has developed over the years. In particular, Colin Scott sets out the emergence of Better Regulation policies in the era of the neoliberal Reagan and Thatcher governments of the 1980s, and the subsequent emphasis on a need for EU legislation to demonstrate compliance with the doctrines of subsidiarity and proportionality. The chapter links better regulation and regulatory governance in a reflexive and iterative process of experience, review and enhancement. By providing insights into the Agenda's historical roots and the current state of play, this first part of the book serves as a launchpad for the analysis of the specific elements of the Agenda as set out in Part II.

In Part II, the ins and outs of the Better Regulation Agenda authors are analysed in detail, to a certain extent from an inter-disciplinary perspective. Each chapter focuses on a specific element of the Better Regulation Agenda, subjecting it to an

[16] There are, of course, notable exceptions, such as (non-exhaustively) Dawson (above n 3), the various contributions in the special issue of *European Public Law* on Better Regulation ((2011) 17 *European Public Law*) and S Weatherill, *Better Regulation* (Oxford, Hart Publishing, 2007).

in-depth and critical assessment, particularly reflecting on the limits and opportunities of these elements to achieving the Agenda's objectives. Helen Xanthaki presents the current picture of EU legislative quality, takes stock of the intricacies of legislating for the EU, and recommends conceptual reform in the task of EU legislating and transposition. Andrea Renda reviews current practices and the academic debate on cost-benefit analysis, and proposes a new framework for assessing the impacts of major policy interventions in the EU, oriented towards the overall coherence rather than the 'efficiency' of new policy interventions. Finally, Robert Zbíral explores the link between the Better Regulation Agenda and the deactivation of EU competences. The aim of Better Regulation is to constantly review the fitness of all EU measures, which may naturally result in the repeal of those measures that no longer meet the strict conditions, but his analysis indicates that the deactivation of EU competences is not treated as a viable option.

Part III of the book shifts the focus from the specific content of the Better Regulation Agenda to an institutional perspective. Each chapter discusses the role of a key institutional actor in the Better Regulation Agenda, usually by an author with unique practical insights into that role. Ben Smulders and Jean-Eric Paquet set out and explain the relevant aspects of the Better Regulation Agenda from the perspective of the European Commission, paying special attention to dispelling some of the persistent myths about its impact and intentions. María José Martínez Iglesias looks at the relevant aspects of Better Law-Making for the European Parliament, paying special attention to the actual practice of the institution, against the backdrop of the Interinstitutional Agreement on Better Law-Making and the positions defended by the Parliament in the negotiations. Jenő Czuczai gives a historical overview of Better Regulation, a summary of the new Interinstitutional Agreement and practical examples of better law-making in recent years from the perspective of the Council. Jan de Mulder addresses the role of Member States in the EU's Better Regulation Agenda's follow-up and implementation, using Belgium as a case study. Finally, Xavier Groussot and Julian Nowag address the role of the Better Regulation Agenda in form of legislative Impact Assessments in the CJEU's review on proportionality and subsidiarity, suggesting that it can provide an avenue for a positive feedback loop where 'better regulation' leads to 'better adjudication' and vice versa.

The fourth and final part zooms out to provide a broader contextual, normative assessment of the Better Regulation Agenda. R Daniel Kelemen casts a sceptical eye, emphasising the Better Regulation Agenda's failures as a substantive reform agenda and as a public relations exercise. He argues that EU regulation remains characterised by a mode of governance labelled as 'Eurolegalism', and that Better Regulation fails substantively in its effort to change these core attributes of EU regulation because they are deeply rooted in the project of continent-wide market integration and in the EU's fragmented institutional structure. Better Regulation will also fail as a public relations exercise designed to combat criticisms that the EU suffers from onerous regulations that strangle businesses. Such critiques are ultimately grounded in Eurosceptic and sometimes anti-government ideologies, and cannot be swayed even by successful reforms. Finally, Sacha Garben's chapter provides an 'Impact Assessment' of the EU Better Regulation Agenda, evaluating the validity of its implicit assumptions, its effectiveness, its costs and benefits and, more generally, its impact on the EU legal and political order in relation to already-existing asymmetries and democratic deficiencies in the integration process. This final part of the book therefore invites readers to reflect on the Agenda beyond its technical and specific features and implications, so that taken together, the four parts provide a comprehensive multi-dimensional analysis of a topic that is dynamic, complex and multi-faceted.

CONCLUSION

This edited volume aims to contribute to an increased quality of the debate on Better Regulation by: (i) attempting to provide a better conceptual understanding; (ii) promoting an integration of the academic, political and public discussions; (iii) exploring the topic in its manifold manifestations and from a variety of perspectives, with an honest attempt to address and weigh up both advantages and disadvantages, challenges and opportunities; and (iv) placing the analysis within the broader framework of European integration. This is of course a tall order, but is a necessary endeavour considering the importance of the issues which go to the core of the future of the European integration process, as several of our authors have pointed out. While it is difficult to establish with certainty the exact role that perceptions of EU regulation have played in the Brexit vote and continue to play in other strands of Euroscepticism, it shall be clear that, wrongly or rightly, many citizens perceive EU rule-making to be somehow deficient.[17] For all the flaws and inherent limitations of the Better Regulation Agenda, it thus seems that the EU needs to address these pressures and perceptions. This book intends to provide the crucial actors and those who influence them directly or indirectly with some analytical tools to reflect and decide on how to best meet that challenge. In this, the diversity of the views expressed by our authors, which are at times in disagreement, should be seen as a particular strength, illustrating that while everybody agrees that 'Better Regulation' is—in principle—a good thing, no one agrees on what that actually means. As such, while at times criticising and at other times defending the status quo, the very diverse views of our collected authors are united in having been expressed in a genuine commitment to the good functioning of the EU legal and political order, keeping in mind—above all—the interests of its citizens.

[17] As H Xanthaki notes, 'a depressing (or is it impressive?) 74 percent of Europeans believe that the EU generates too much red tape', citing Eurobarometer Question QA 16.4 on p 59: https://ec.europa.eu/public_opinion/archives/ec/eb79/eb79_anx_en.pdf. Of course, it is a different question what they would precisely consider to be such 'red tape' and whether they would still feel that way if it were better explained what the objectives and benefits of particular rules are.

2

Integrating Regulatory Governance and Better Regulation as Reflexive Governance

COLIN SCOTT*

INTRODUCTION

POLICIES OF BETTER Regulation originate from the Reagan and Thatcher governments whose small government agendas led them to become concerned that there might be a tendency to ratchet up the obligations and costs on businesses associated with regulation with little by way of countervailing mechanisms to curb the urge to increase regulatory burdens (as they saw it).

Whereas early policies on both sides of the Atlantic set down the objectives of lifting regulatory burdens and deregulation, the language and ethos changed over time. An early foray for the EU in the 1990s targeted simplification of legislation in the internal market (the Simplification of Legislation in the Internal Market (SLIM) programme) and by the late 1990s, the Organisation for Economic Co-operation and Development (OECD), the EU and many of the OECD states were talking about Better Regulation. The EU programmes was briefly restyled as SMART regulation (2010–14), but soon came back to Better.

There is a large body of scholarly and policy work concerned with regulatory governance, conceptualising what it is (and is not), how regulatory norms are made, scrutinising the variety of mechanisms through which feedback and compliance occurs and seeking to better understand when behavioural correction is likely to be effective.[1]

The policy and practice fields of Better Regulation, which take as their focus the improved efficiency of regulation, has almost completely passed by the scholarly

* Colin Scott is Vice-President for Equality, Diversity and Inclusion, Dean of Social Sciences, Principal UCD College of Social Sciences and Law and Professor of EU Regulation and Governance, University College Dublin.

[1] R Baldwin, M Cave and M Lodge, *Oxford Handbook of Regulation* (Oxford, Oxford University Press, 2010); D Levi-Faur, 'Regulatory Networks and Regulatory Agencification' (2011) 18 *Journal of European Public Policy* 810.

field of regulatory governance, which is concerned with both understanding and enhancing regulatory governance. These two policy and scholarly fields have in common a substantial degree of scepticism concerning the capacity and appropriateness of states to regulate businesses wholly through forms of command, anchored in the enforcement of binding legal rules. The trend in both fields is towards seeking to understand better the limits of command and control regulation and the range of alternative mechanisms of steering behaviour. In this chapter I focus on the big picture trends in Better Regulation and regulatory governance, and propose a way of integrating the scholarly and public policy fields through elaborating the concept of reflexive governance. A key point of focus for this evaluation is the reforms to Better Regulation initiated by the Juncker Commission (which took office in November 2014) and which were launched in May 2015.[2]

BETTER REGULATION: REGULATORY GOVERNANCE AND REFLEXIVE GOVERNANCE

Better regulation policies originated with the deregulation movement initiated by the Reagan and Thatcher governments in the US and the UK in the early 1980s. The impetus of these reforms was clearly liberalising in approach, seeking to review and remove unnecessary regulatory demands. Deregulatory policies were a key aspect of political agendas to shrink the state.[3] In the UK, for example. policies were initiated by papers on 'Burdens of Business' and 'Lifting the Burden', published in 1985.[4] There was an initially a polarising tendency for political actors to express themselves as being in favour of or opposed to regulation. This unhelpful dichotomy was resolved progressively through reshaping the programmes to review and reduce regulatory burdens with a focus on Better Regulation, expressed for example in the five principles put forward in the UK: proportionality, accountability, consistency, transparency and targeting.[5]

The principal focus of Better Regulation policies has been on rule-making. Thus, the application of the principles in the UK has been concerned with ensuring that rules are proportionate to the objective being sought (and in particular do not apply a disproportionate cost for achieving the objective sought) and that they should be targeted to the particular objective and should not generate a wide range of costs relating to matters which are not within the objectives. A high degree of

[2] European Commission, 'Better Regulation for Better Results—An EU Agenda' in *Communication from the Commission to the European Parliament, the Council, the European Economic and Social Committee and the Committee of the Regions* (Brussels, European Commission, 2015).

[3] H Feigenbaum, J Henig and C Hamnett, *Shrinking the State: The Political Underpinnings of Privatization* (Cambridge, Cambridge University Press, 1999).

[4] J Froud, R Boden and A Ogus, *Controlling the Regulators* (London, Macmillan, 1998).

[5] Better Regulation Task Force, *Principles of Good Regulation* (London, Cabinet Office, 1998).

emphasis has been placed in many programmes on the application of forms of cost-benefit analysis to proposed rules. Such processes have involved both consultation on particular proposals and also wider consultation with industry-led taskforces and the like. Arguably there has been insufficient emphasis within such programmes on consideration of alternatives to rules, which include doing nothing, self-regulation and market-type measures such as information provision taxation and subsidies.[6]

National trends on Better Regulation were picked up by the Public Management team of the OECD. Since the mid-1990s, the OECD has used its surveillance, benchmarking and engagement capacities to identify and to advocate for the development of best practice Better Regulation policies across all the OECD Member States.[7] As part of this role, the OECD was commissioned by the European Commission to review the implementation of Better Regulation policies across the EU Member States.[8]

EU policies on Better Regulation originated in the process to complete the Single Market in the early 1990s. Their focus was not directly on reducing burdens on business, but rather on defining the appropriate relationship between EU-level and domestic-level measures, with an attempt to give priority to the latter. In his report on the working of the Internal Market, published in 1992, Peter Sutherland recommended that the EU address the risk that 'future Community legislation may be too heavy-handed'.[9] Avoiding this risk entailed a renewed emphasis on the doctrine of subsidiarity,[10] with a particular focus on acting at the Community level only when national measures threaten the four freedoms and such national measures are inappropriate, and a Community level solution is 'demonstrably better'.[11] Where Community measures were to be proposed, the most effective solution, ranging from self-regulation to total harmonisation, should be identified and adopted, all subject to the principles of proportionality, consistency and communication.[12] This approach underpinned the SLIM programme adopted by the European Commission in 1996.[13] This programme involved both a review and cull of new measures and a review of existing measures against the five principles set down. This was followed up with the recommendation that the European

[6] Regulation Taskforce, *Rethinking Regulation: Report of the Taskforce on Reducing Regulatory Burdens on Business* (Canberra, Productivity Commission, 2006).

[7] OECD, *Regulatory Impact Analysis: Best Practices in OECD Countries* (Paris, OECD, 1997); OECD, *Regulatory Reform* (Paris, OECD, 1997).

[8] OECD, *Better Regulation in Europe: Ireland* (Paris, OECD, 2010).

[9] High-Level Group on the Operation of the Internal Market, *Report of the High Level Group on the Operation of the Single Market* (Brussels, European Commission, 1992) 3.

[10] G de Búrca, 'Subsidiarity and Proportionality as General Principles of Law' in J Nergelius and U Bernitz (eds), *The General Principles of EC Law* (Rotterdam, Kluwer, 2000).

[11] Above n 9.

[12] ibid.

[13] Council Resolution of 8 July 1996 on legislative and administrative simplification in the field of the internal market OJ C 224 1 August 1996, 5–6.

Commission develop machinery for reviewing legislation which was developed in the early 2000s.[14] The 2002 Better Regulation Programme carried forward the emphasis on better and simpler legislation and was underpinned by an inter-institutional agreement which focused on better law-making.[15] The 2002 programme included new instruments for reviewing new legislative proposals in the form of regulatory impact analysis and also machinery within the Commission for overseeing the undertaking of these evaluations. Thus, the scope and focus of Better Regulation in the EU gave priority to legal rules at the expense of other aspects of Better Regulation programmes which include, centrally, giving consideration to doing nothing and to promoting self-regulation and co-regulation as alternatives to formal legal rules. The commitment in the SLIM programme to review not only new legislation but also existing legislation was revived with the adoption of the REFIT programme in 2013.[16]

Whereas Better Regulation policies generally and in particular within the EU have tended to focus on the making of legal rules, scholarly research has emphasised two distinctly different dimensions to regulation. First, there has been an emphasis on alternatives to legal rules[17] and, perhaps to an even greater extent, on processes of monitoring and enforcing compliance with regulatory rules.[18] This research has emphasised trends towards drawing in a wider range of actors and instruments into regulatory governance,[19] and has attempted to show the benefits of more nuanced approaches to the steering of businesses and others towards public interest goals, and, related to this, the benefits of taking responsive approaches to enforcement which take into account limited resources and also the motivational posture of those being enforced against.[20] Thus, scholars conceive of regulation as a field of control involving some norms, some mechanisms for monitoring compliance with the norms and some processes for correcting behaviour which deviates from the norms.[21] As Figure 2.1 shows, we look beyond rules to also embrace principles, soft law, contracts, and private and self-regulatory norms such as technical standards. Mechanisms for monitoring include self-reporting duties, inspection as well as information from third parties in the

[14] Mandelkern Group on Better Regulation, *Final Report* (Brussels, European Commission, 2001).

[15] European Parliament, European Council, and European Commission, 'Inter-Institutional Agreement on Better Law-Making' (Brussels, 2003).

[16] Commission Communication, 'Regulatory Fitness and Performance (REFIT): Results and Next Steps' COM (2013) 685 final Brussels 2 October 2013.

[17] Neil Gunningham and Peter Grabosky, *Smart Regulation: Designing Environmental Policy* (Oxford, Oxford University Press, 1998).

[18] I Ayres and J Braithwaite, *Responsive Regulation: Transcending the Deregulation Debate* (Oxford, Oxford University Press, 1992); C Parker, 'Twenty Years of Responsive Regulation: An Appreciation and Appraisal' (2013) 7 *Regulation & Governance* 2.

[19] C Scott, 'Regulation in Age of Governance: The Rise of the Post-regulatory State' in J Jordana and D Levi-Faur (eds), *The Politics of Regulation* (Cheltenham, Edward Elgar, 2004).

[20] J Braithwaite, 'Rules and Principles: A Theory of Legal Certainty' (2002) 27 *Australian Journal of Legal Philosophy* 47.

[21] C Hood, H Rothstein and R Baldwin, *The Government of Risk* (Oxford, Oxford University Press, 2001).

form of consumer or competitor complaints, and also whistleblower information. Mechanisms of correction include education and advice, and the more stringent mechanisms of administrative penalties, criminal sanctions and licence revocation. The focal points on norms, monitoring and enforcement mechanisms are captured in Figure 2.1.

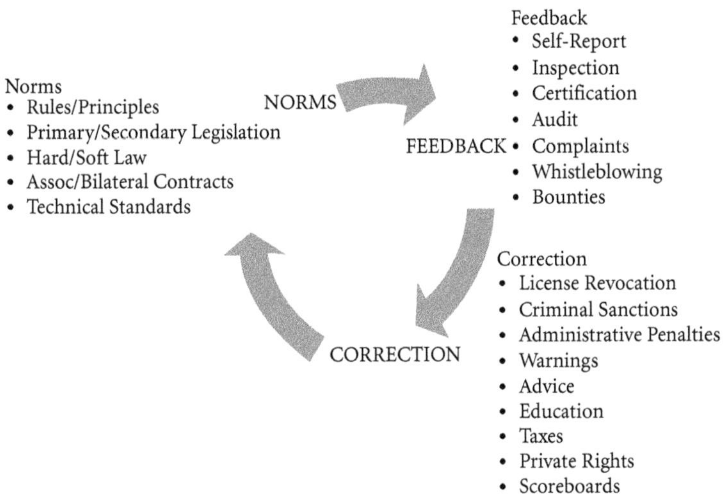

Figure 2.1: Aspects of regulation

A very influential approach to regulatory enforcement emphasises that most regulators tend to operate not through stringent and punitive enforcement, but rather through educating and advising where they find infractions, reserving more stringent enforcement capacity for circumstances where because of deliberate, persistent or egregious wrongdoing, escalation up an enforcement pyramid is deemed necessary.[22]

The focus of EU measures on rule-making may be explained, in part, by the limited range of instruments available to the EU institutions. There are examples where the Commission has sponsored more thinking about alternative instruments, for example, with self-regulatory strategies in advertising,[23] and more recently with a community of practice on self-regulation and co-regulation, and with the establishment of a scheme of tradeable permits to address pollution control.[24] Much of the implementation is the responsibility of the Member States,

[22] Ayres and Braithwaite, above n 18.

[23] European Commission, 'Self-Regulation in the EU Advertising Sector: A Report of Some Discussion among Interested Parties' (Brussels, European Commission, 2006).

[24] R Baldwin, 'Regulation Lite' (2008) 2 *Regulation & Governance* 193.

and less formal modes of regulating would create challenges for the European Commission concerned with ensuring transparent compliance.

There has been insufficient effort to draw together the scholarly and public policy streams such that, first, we may focus more on the alternatives to regulation through legal rules in the policy-making phase and, second, to a wider range of strategies for steering behaviour in the monitoring and enforcement stage. There is, of course, more opportunity for interchange between the policy focus (largely on rule-making) and the scholarly focus (largely on implementation). The scholarly literature would be enhanced by a stronger focus both on *ex ante* policy-making and *ex post* evaluation of the kind to which Better Regulation policies aspire. Better regulation policies would be enhanced by paying more attention to the variety of norms which are available in regulatory regimes and also to the challenges of monitoring and enforcement.

Such an integrated approach to Better Regulation and regulatory governance would recognise the potential for learning both amongst policy-makers and scholars, but also within policy processes.[25] It requires an openness to reflecting on and sometimes recasting the problem which is to be addressed, as well as the mechanisms which will be developed to address it. In brief, such an approach could be described as reflexive in its approach to governance because of that openness to other experiences and learning.

There is some evidence within recent EU reforms of Better Regulation, introduced by the Juncker Commission, of a greater openness to a wider range of oversight mechanisms for Better Regulation and of considerable innovation (also noting that the reforms are not without their critics).[26] In the next section of this chapter I briefly set out the case for analysing Better Regulation policies in the context of reflexive governance and then, in the following section, provide an evaluation of the state of the art in Better Regulation generally and in the EU in the context of the opportunities for more reflexive styles of regulation.

REFLEXIVE GOVERNANCE AND BETTER REGULATION

Regulation is a key instrument of contemporary governance, but it is also challenging. In particular, the aspiration to exert control through rules has tended to be frustrated by the behaviours both of regulators and those subject to regulation. These departures from expectation and examples of counterproductive

[25] N Gunningham, 'Regulatory Reform and Reflexive Regulation: Beyond Command and Control' (Louvain-la-Neuve, Centre for Philosophy of Law, 2009); J Lenoble and M Maesschalck, 'Renewing the Theory of Public Interest: The Quest for a Reflexive and a Learning-Based Approach to Governance' and C Scott, 'Reflexive Governance, Regulation and Meta-regulation: Control or Learning? in O de Schutter and J Lenoble (eds), *Reflexive Governance: Redefining the Public Interest in a Pluralistic World* (Oxford, Hart Publishing, 2010).

[26] A Alemanno, 'Assessing the Impact of the Better Regulation Package on the European Union: A Research Agenda' (2015) 6 *European Journal of Risk Regulation* 344.

regulation and regulatory failure might be predicted and better anticipated if there were more opportunities for mutual learning and innovation within regulatory policy-making and implementation.[27] The development of more reflexive modes of regulatory governance offers a partial solution to some of the challenges and weaknesses in conceiving of regulation as control.[28]

The concept of reflexive governance in regulation centres around the idea of the multiple parties involved in a regulatory regime having the opportunity to shape not only the targets and instruments associated with the regime, but also in some cases the purposes and broad objectives. It embraces the practice of joint problem-solving between government and stakeholders and, in particular, governance is said to be reflexive when the actors involved are learning from each other—to the extent that evidence of cognitive reframing can be identified. In this sense, we can distinguish reflexivity from traditional bargaining such that the parties actually *change* their thinking or position on certain issues, as distinct from simply accepting a compromise solution or outcome that, even though it may take into account their interests, their actual preferences do not necessarily shift. In reflexive governance, preferences and interests can and do shift, principally as a result of shared learning through interaction.[29]

Evaluating regulatory governance generally and Better Regulation policies in particular it is possible to identify a number of different kinds of reflexive governance measures, drawn from a study of experience in three countries:[30]

- *Evaluation measures*: processes which focus chiefly on the evaluation of current or new rules against criteria, such as costs imposed relative to expected or actual benefits.
- *Dialogic measures*: processes which engage stakeholders in exchanges over such issues as appropriate instruments, targets or objectives within a regime.
- *Oversight measures*: processes which involve those who make or apply rules being subject to oversight or control by others, for example, in a central government unit.
- *Information/communication measures*: processes through which the sharing of information about a regime and other transparency measures create greater knowledge and engagement.

This method of categorising different aspects of reflexive governance in Better Regulation may be coupled with an approach that looks at where in the policy cycle innovative and reflexive approaches occur, and this is elaborated in the next section of this chapter.

[27] P Grabosky, 'Counterproductive Regulation' (1995) 23 *International Journal of the Sociology of Law* 347.

[28] Scott, above n 25.

[29] C Brown and C Scott, 'Reflexive Governance in Better Regulation: Evidence from Three Countries' (Louvain-la-Neuve, Reflexive Governance Programme, 2009).

[30] ibid.

BETTER REGULATION AS REFLEXIVE GOVERNANCE IN THE EU

The context for evaluation of the state of the art for Better Regulation in the EU is the rejuvenation of the Better Regulation programme signalled by President Juncker on his taking office with the appointment of Frans Timmermans as First Vice-President with Better Regulation amongst the named aspects of his portfolio. New Better Regulation measures were adopted in May 2015 which developed and expanded prior measures in new Better Regulation Guidelines (the current version at the time of writing).[31] The new measures were accompanied by a draft revised Interinstitutional Agreement on Better Law-Making, adopted in April 2016, which commits the European Parliament and the Council to the integration of Better Regulation instruments into their processes.

The new Better Regulation Guidelines emphasise that Better Regulation addresses the entire policy cycle and not just rule-making. This includes the preparation and adoption stages, with associated Impact Assessment, consultation, implementation and application stages with both evaluation and consultation.[32] The implementation stage is to be supported with an implementation plan shared with Member States and close attention to implementation and enforcement issues in drafting policies and legislation.[33] Thus, the 2015 package offers quite a lot of promise from the Commission to change the way it works and, perhaps, in a way that is more inclusive and reflexive. At a rather fundamental level, this creates a potential tension between legitimating regulation in the more traditional way through claims to technical correctness, as compared with what is hinted at in the new approach, which is that regulation will be legitimated through the inclusion of and engagement with stakeholders.[34] Arguably this tension can be resolved through pointing out that a more reflexive governance approach has potential to reach technically better solutions *because* of the wider engagement of stakeholders. At the same time, such an approach must steer clear of risks and perceptions that policy processes are captured by dominant private interests.

The 2015 package foregrounded transparent commitment to potentially more reflexive governance through adopting stronger consultation with stakeholders at all levels as a key aspect of policy-making with both information/communication measures and dialogic measures. In particular, the Commission committed to push consultation back to the very start of the policy cycle through publishing roadmaps at the outset and encouraging consultation on 'inception Impact Assessments'.[35] Consultation was also extended to the draft texts of delegated implementing acts,

[31] European Commission, 'Better Regulation Guidelines' (Brussels, 2017).

[32] ibid 5.

[33] ibid 9.

[34] M Dawson, 'Better Regulation and the Future of Regulatory Law and Politics' (2016) 53 *CMLR* 1209.

[35] European Commission, 'Better Regulation for Better Results: A European Agenda' (Brussels, 2015) 5.

which had hitherto been regarded as technical and not open for consultation. The roadmaps were initially published together on the Commission's website,[36] but are now collated on a 'have your say page' on better law-making.[37] There is no doubt that these measures contribute to greater transparency in relation to proposed measures and at an earlier stage. Furthermore, there is an aspiration to reflexivity through a requirement that: 'Feedback should be given to respondents about how their information and views were used.'[38] This last aspect has not been fully implemented. While comments are invited, there is not yet a systemic commitment to publishing comments and signalling their impact in the policy process. Consequently, the opportunity for a proper dialogue between the Commission and stakeholders, a point recognised as important in the Guidelines, is missed. The one-way nature of communication from the Commission is also emphasised in the commitment to better explanation of policy initiatives.[39]

Amongst the evaluation measures, regulatory impact analysis has been a key tool since the early 2000s. The Commission further committed to evaluation processes which include consideration of 'both regulatory and well-designed non-regulatory means as well as improvements in the implementation and enforcement of existing legislation'.[40] Extensive guidance on the conduct of Impact Assessment is provided in the Better Regulation Guidelines.[41] The guidance is quite reflexive in its orientation, instructing Commission officials to give proper consideration to the policy problem, the rationale for acting, the outcomes sought and the various options for achieving the objectives. It is too soon to tell whether this guidance together with scrutiny will allow the Commission to overcome its commitment to legislating rather than properly considering alternatives.

In relation to oversight measures, the oversight of assessment and evaluation was beefed up with a new Regulatory Scrutiny Board, named to signal the somewhat broader remit than the Impact Assessment Board, which has been established in 2006 and which it replaced.[42] The new Board was to evaluate and feedback on both draft Impact Assessments on new legislation and retrospective fitness checks on existing legislation (under REFIT). The inclusion of both *ex ante* and *ex post* evaluation within the remit gives the Regulatory Scrutiny Board the potential to evaluate the whole policy cycle for regulation, recognising that the ambition of 'closing the policy cycle' is very challenging.[43] The inclusion of outsiders as three

[36] http://ec.europa.eu/smart-regulation/roadmaps/index_en.htm.
[37] https://ec.europa.eu/info/law/better-regulation/have-your-say_en.
[38] European Commission, above n 31, 8.
[39] European Commission, above n 35, 5.
[40] ibid 6.
[41] European Commission, above n 31, ch III.
[42] J Wiener and A Alemanno, 'Comparing Regulatory Oversight Bodies: The US Office of Information and Regulatory Affairs and the EU Regulatory Scrutiny Board' in S Rose-Ackerman, P Lindseth and B Emerson (eds), *Comparative Administrative Law* (Cheltenham, Edward Elgar, 2017).
[43] C Dunlop and C Radaelli, 'If Evaluation is the Solution, What is the Problem?' (Exeter, Exeter University, 2016).

of the seven members of the new Board was designed to enhance both expertise and accountability.

Looking at the policy cycle overall, as noted above, Better Regulation practitioners have focused chiefly on *ex ante* and now to a greater extent *ex post* evaluation, whereas the regulatory governance scholars have focused more on implementation, notably enforcement, but also monitoring of regimes and rule types and alternatives to rules. Figure 2.2 below puts forward a model for joining these concerns up in a complete modelling of the regulatory policy cycle to include the five components with a (not comprehensive) listing of the kinds of choices which need to be made (and engaged) within each stage.

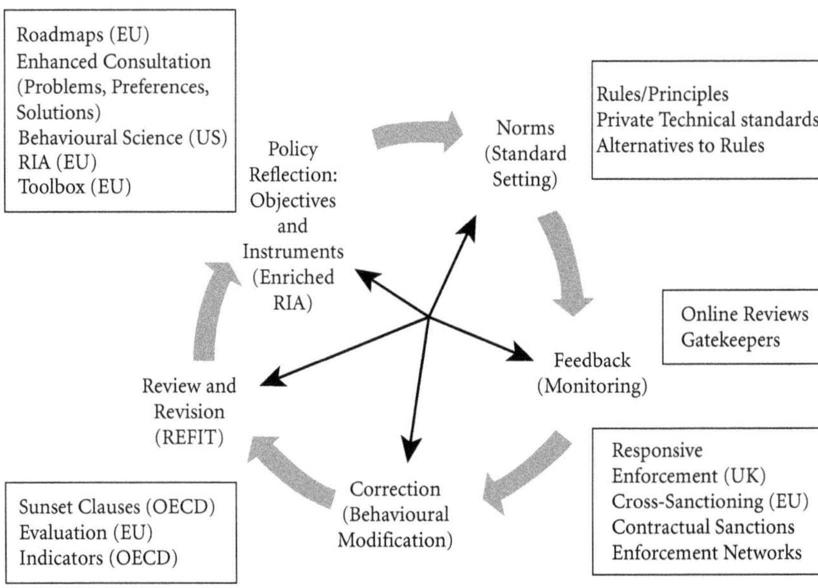

Figure 2.2: Reflexive model integrating Better Regulation and regulatory governance

In what I refer to as the policy reflection stage are located the commitment to enhanced consultation (taking in not only preferences and solutions but also, as the Commission sets down in the Better Regulation Guidelines, engagement on the problem being addressed), the Roadmaps, (Regulatory) Impact Analysis (including oversight of the Regulatory Standards Board) and the European Commission Regulation Toolbox more generally. I note here that the US President has determined that all policy-makers are required to engage with the insights of behavioural sciences in designing policy solutions, and which is likely to lead to a wider range of interventions, beyond classical regulation. No similar imperative has been laid down by the European Commission which continues to struggle with the proposal of measures other than legal rules.[44]

[44] Alemanno, above n 26.

This takes us to the next phase of the policy cycle: the setting down of norms through legislated rules or principles or through private instruments such as technical standards (which are often adopted within EU legislation, but do not fall within the remit of Better Regulation scrutiny in the EU) and alternatives to rules such as tax and subsidy measures, and soft law instruments such as guidance. There are many choices here concerned with the shaping of norms. For example, the setting down of principles, rather than rules, challenges regulated organisations to take more responsibility for thinking about what compliance means, whether through following some more detailed public or private standards or through devising their own internal management systems to elaborate and promote compliance.[45] Where rules are adopted, there are choices about specificity and precision which affect both compliance and enforcement opportunities.[46]

In the next phase, feeding back the extent to which the norms are being complied with, we noted above many choices for detecting behaviours within a regulatory regime. Additional instruments include online reviews and the assignment of monitoring (and reporting) functions to gatekeepers (such as the role taken on by banks to report suspicious transactions in money laundering regulations).

In the correction or behavioural modification phase, we find traditional enforcement approaches, but also responsive enforcement models of a kind that have been developed in a number of countries, including in the UK through first guidelines[47] and more recently a statutory Regulators' Code.[48] These kinds of policy instruments, overseeing regulatory enforcement, together with a stronger commitment to variation in enforcement measures more generally, have a strong but neglected capacity to contribute to Better Regulation.[49] Within the EU, there is some experience of cross-sanctioning, under which, for example, equality and environmental rules, which are the responsibility of particular Directorates General, are enforced in inspections of other Directorates General, for example, in respect of structural funds expenditure.[50] We also recognise here the potential for the application of sanctions through contracts, where private rules have been incorporated into contracts. Amongst regulators, both public and private, networks have become increasingly important for sharing operational and strategic knowledge about enforcement, with a strong degree of reflexivity and learning in such arrangements.[51]

[45] J Black, 'Forms and Paradoxes of Principles-Based Regulation' (2008) 3 *Law & Policy*; Braithwaite, above n 20.

[46] J Black, '"Which Arrow?": Rule Type and Regulatory Policy' (1995) *Public Law* 94.

[47] Department of Trade and Industry, *Enforcement Concordat: Good Practice Guide for England & Wales* (London, Department of Trade and Industry, 1998).

[48] Regulatory Enforcement and Sanctions Act 2008.

[49] K Yeung, 'Better Regulation, Administrative Sanctions and Constitutional Values' (2013) *Legal Studies* 312.

[50] C Hood, C Scott, O James, G Jones and T Travers, *Regulation inside Government: Waste-Watchers, Quality Police, and Sleaze-Busters* (Oxford, Oxford University Press, 1999).

[51] Levi-Faur, above n 1.

The last phase of the policy cycle is review and revision, which is strongly represented in the EU REFIT programme. The EU not only reviews its own measures, but also the Better Regulation policies and their implementation in the Member States (with OECD assistance noted above). More generally, the OECD and other international organisations are increasingly developing indicators of competitiveness which include evaluations of regulatory burdens as barriers to competitiveness.[52]

How reflexive is the EU Better Regulation policy in its aspirations and its implementation? The 2015 package is clearly a significant enhancement of the evaluation measures, with the extension of evaluation from *ex ante* to *ex post* and more rigorous oversight. As regards dialogic measures, the strong commitment to consultation at earlier stages and throughout the policy cycle is very promising, yet carries with it the risk that this represents greater transparency but not more effective dialogue, unless the feedback runs in both directions. Thus, the information/communication measures are significant. The capacity for oversight is enhanced with a more independent Regulatory Scrutiny Board and some evidence of greater stringency.[53] As to overall reflexiveness, much depends on continuing implementation and a willingness to engage more seriously through these processes not only with how policy problems are conceived and addressed in policy-making, but also in terms of a willingness to deploy other kinds of norms and to revisit both feedback and correction mechanisms. Because of the variety in implementation capacity and modes within the Member States, it is difficult to conceive of the EU making very extensive use of less legalistic and more reflexive governance modes for the core regulatory implementation measures. The tendency towards legalism is somewhat hardwired, for reasons which are understandable, but which need to be overcome for a more reflexive approach to Better Regulation to reach beyond rule-making to the stronger potential for alternative instruments of meeting policy objectives.

CONCLUSIONS

Policies on Better Regulation have become a key part of the central architecture for overseeing legislative policy and implementation generally, and the deployment of regulatory instruments more particularly. The extent to which Better Regulation policies have focused on the promulgation of legal rules is striking. Within the EU, this is explicable both by reference to a preference for legal rules as being more readily comparable in their implementation across Member States and because the stages beyond rule-making, concerned with implementation, are

[52] World Bank, *Doing Business: Equality for All* (Washington DC, World Bank, 2017).
[53] Regulatory Scrutiny Board, 'Annual Report 2016' (Brussels, 2017).

substantially within the responsibility of the Member States themselves. But this pattern, under which the wider opportunities for Better Regulation to consider alternative instruments and to reach into implementation processes are missed, is almost equally present in domestic Better Regulation processes amongst the Member State governments and elsewhere in the OECD. Better regulation does not always signal smarter regulation.[54] This fact is suggestive of a great opportunity both for the EU and the Member States to develop more reflexive capacity for enhancing regulation. Stronger engagement with the concerns of scholarship in regulatory governance, which prioritises the evaluation of alternatives to rules and the effects and effectiveness of implementation processes, would provide a creative challenge to policy-makers to engage more strongly with these opportunities. If accompanied by a commitment to greater reflexiveness and learning in policy-making more generally, the opportunity would be greater still. By the same token, scholars in the field could learn to reflect more on the *ex ante* agenda-setting stages and also the *ex post* evaluation stages of regulatory governance that are a particular focus of Better Regulation programmes.

A more reflexive approach, integrating public policy and scholarly concerns, could valuably review the potential for stronger transparency and communication, enhance dialogic measures, and provide more extensive evaluation and a strong commitment to oversight of the practices for agenda setting, the making of regulatory policy, the development of regulatory instruments, the processes for monitoring compliance, enforcement processes and evaluation and review. Thus, reflexive governance of Better Regulation could take in the whole policy cycle and engage all the knowledge, both procedural and substantive, that might serve to make regulation better.

[54] R Baldwin, 'Is Better Regulation Smarter Regulation?' [2005] *Public Law* 485.

Part II

A Critical Assessment of the Main Elements of the Better Regulation Agenda

3

Improving the Quality of EU Legislation

Limits and Opportunities?

HELEN XANTHAKI*

AMIDST A BOMBARDMENT of national legislation thrown at citizens from their national legislatures and international fora, the EU finds itself accused of failure as a legislator: too much EU legislation[1] and bad EU legislation is at the core of neo-scepticism. However, little time is devoted to what constitutes good EU legislation, how good EU and good implementing laws can be drafted, and what constitutes best practice in EU legislating and transposing.

The objective of this chapter is to identify the main problem with EU legislation and to suggest possible ways of addressing it adequately. The chapter begins with the definition of good EU legislation as a theory and the identification of its constituting elements. It continues with the analysis of the expression of good EU legislation in institutional instruments, mainly in the post-Lisbon era, and assesses the extent to which the institutions have grappled with legislative quality as a product. Having applied legislative quality to the EU, the chapter attempts to identify legislative quality in the transposing/implementing national laws. Finally, it collates the gaps identified at the EU and the national levels and suggests possible solutions.[2]

WHAT IS GOOD EU LEGISLATION: THE THEORY

Defining good EU legislation is no easy task. And much of the answer depends on the angle from which the question is asked. My functional definition of good

* Helen Xanthaki is Professor of Law at UCL and Director of International Postgraduate Laws, University of London; Senior Fellow at the Sir William Dale Centre for Legislative Studies of the Institute of Advanced Legal Studies of the University of London; and President of the International Association for Legislation.

[1] See 'How Much Legislation Comes from Europe?', House of Commons Research Paper 10/62, 13 October 2010.

[2] See H Xanthaki, 'Emerging Trends of Legislation in Europe' in U Karpen and H Xanthaki (eds), *Legislation and Legisprudence in Europe* (Oxford, Hart Publishing, 2017).

legislation defines good legislation as legislation that manages to achieve the desired regulatory results.[3] In other words, good EU laws are laws that contribute to the achievement of the policy aims pursued by the EU regulators, to the extent set by these regulators and within the timeframe imposed by them.

There is a direct link between EU regulation and EU legislation. Their precise relationship is mainly identified within an academic, non-functional[4] context. Mousmouti and Voermans distinguish between legislative quality as an issue closely linked to the constitutional principles of legality, effectiveness and legal certainty, and regulatory quality as an issue related to the success of legislation in promoting economic development.[5] Thus, legislation is not synonymous with regulation. EU regulators, like all regulators, use legislation as a tool of successful governing,[6] a tool for putting into effect policies that produce the desired regulatory results[7] or as the qualitative measure of successful legislation, which is the extent of production of the desired result[8]—provided of course that the regulators' choice can indeed put a policy into effect rather than only on paper.[9]

Within this context, EU regulation is the process of putting EU policies into effect to the degree and extent intended by government.[10] EU legislation, as one of the many regulatory tools available to the regulators,[11] is the means by which the production of the desired regulatory results is pursued. In the application of

[3] See H Xanthaki, *Drafting Legislation: Art and Technology of Rules for Regulation* (Oxford, Hart Publishing, 2014) ch 1.

[4] See ST Trautmann, 'Empirical Knowledge in Legislation and Regulation: A Decision-Making Perspective' (2013) 1 *Theory and Practice of Legislation* 533, 538–39.

[5] See M Mousmouti, 'Operationalising Quality of Legislation through the Effectiveness Test' (2012) 6 *Legisprudence* 191, 194; see also W Voermans, 'Concern about the Quality of EU Legislation: What Kind of Problem, by What Kind of Standards?' (2009) 2 *Erasmus Law Review* 59, 223 and 225; and R Baldwin and M Cave, *Understanding Regulation: Theory, Strategy and Practice* (Oxford, Oxford University Press, 1999) 85.

[6] See OECD, 'Recommendation of the Council on Improving the Quality of Government Regulation', 9 March 1995, C(95)21/Final.

[7] The executive branch of government is no longer expected to confine itself to the mere making of proposals: it has to see them through. See J Craig Peacock, *Notes on Legislative Drafting* (Washington DC, REC Foundation, 1961) 3.

[8] See N Staem, 'Governance, Democracy and Evaluation' (2006) 12(7) *Evaluation* 7, 7.

[9] And the choice is that of the governments, not the drafters: see P Delnoy, 'Le rôle des légistes dans la détermination du contenu des norms', 2013 Report for the International Cooperation Group, Department of Justice, Canada, http://section15.gc.ca/fra/pr-rp/sjc-csj/pji-ilp/norm/norm.pdf, 3.

[10] See National Audit Office, Department for Business, Innovations and Skills, 'Delivering Regulatory Reform', 10 February 2011, para 1.

[11] Tools for regulation vary from flexible forms of traditional regulation (such as performance-based and incentive approaches) to co-regulation and self-regulation schemes, incentive and market-based instruments (such as tax breaks and tradable permits), and information approaches. See Better Regulation Task Force (BRTF), 'Routes to Better Regulation: A Guide to Alternatives to Classic Regulation', December 2005; see also J Miller, 'The FTC and Voluntary Standards: Maximizing the Net Benefits of Self-Regulation' (1985) 4 *Cato Journal* 897; OECD Report, 'Alternatives to Traditional Regulation', para 0.3; and OECD, *Regulatory Policies in OECD Countries: From Interventionism to Regulatory Governance* (Paris, OECD, 2002).

Stefanou's scheme on the policy, legislative and drafting processes,[12] legislative quality is a partial but crucial contribution to regulatory quality.[13] This promotes the synergetic approach to legislation eloquently expressed by Richard Heaton, former First Parliamentary Counsel and Permanent Secretary of the Cabinet Office in London:

> I believe that we need to establish a sense of shared accountability, within and beyond government, for the quality of what (perhaps misleadingly) we call our statute book, and to promote a shared professional pride in it. In doing so, I hope we can create confidence among users that legislation is for them.[14]

This approach feeds into the below diagram of elements of regulatory and legislative quality.[15]

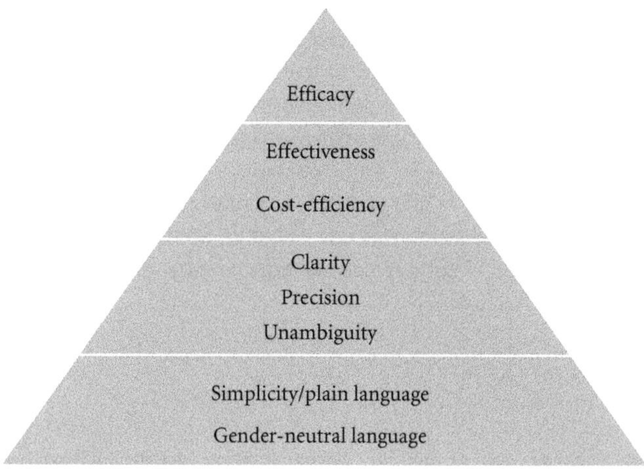

Figure 3.1: Pyramid of drafting qualities

The ultimate goal for regulation is efficacy. Efficacy is the extent to which regulators achieve their goal.[16] It is often misnamed 'effectiveness', especially by non-English speakers or experts outside the legislative field. From the point of view of drafting, efficacy is the capacity of EU laws to achieve the regulatory aims that

[12] See C Stefanou, 'Legislative Drafting as a Form of Communication' in L Mader and M Travares-Almeida (eds), *Quality of Legislation Principles and Instruments* (Baden-Baden, Nomos, 2011) 308; and see also C Stefanou, 'Drafters, Drafting and the Policy Process' in C Stefanou and H Xanthaki (eds), *Drafting Legislation: A Modern Approach* (Aldershot, Ashgate, 2008) 321.

[13] In fact, there is an emergence of public interest in the good quality of rules: see M De Benedetto, M Martelli and N Rangone, *La Qualità delle Regole* (Bologna, Il Mulino, 2011), 23.

[14] See R Heaton, 'Foreword' in Cabinet Office, Office of Parliamentary Counsel, *When Laws Become Too Complex*, 16 April 2013.

[15] See H Xanthaki, 'On Transferability of Legislative Solutions: The Functionality Test' in Stefanou and Xanthaki, above n 12, 1.

[16] See ibid 126; see also Mousmouti, above n 5, 200.

they are designed to address.[17] Efficacy, as a measure of quality of legislation for the purposes of achieving the desired regulation, is not a goal that can be achieved by the drafter alone.[18] A wonderful draft may be capable of producing the desired regulatory effects, but bad implementation[19] and bad judicial application may interfere with its actual results.[20] Of course, one has to accept that the extent of the margin for incorrect implementation and judicial application is directly linked to the quality of the draft,[21] but it is quite possible that the error in the draft may be attributed to a fault in the content of the pursued policy or in the calculations of the regulatory Impact Assessment made for the allocation of resources for implementation.

Within the umbrella of efficacy, the drafter pursues effectiveness in legislation.[22] The term 'effectiveness' is used widely but often without a definition: the EU calls for accountability, effectiveness and proportionality as a means of achieving better law-making, but the term is not defined at all.[23] Similarly, the UKs Office of Parliamentary Counsel repeats its aspiration to effectiveness as a contribution to or in balance with accuracy, but does not define the term.[24] Mader defines effectiveness as the extent to which the observable attitudes and behaviours of the target population correspond to the attitudes and behaviours prescribed by the legislator.[25] Snyder defines effectiveness as 'the fact that law matters: it has effects on political, economic and social life outside the law—that it, apart from simply the elaboration of legal doctrine'.[26] Teubner defines effectiveness as a term encompassing

[17] See N Gunningham and D Sinclair, 'Designing Smart Regulation', www.oecd.org/dataoecd/18/39/33947759.pdf, 18; and R Baldwin, 'Is Better Regulation Smarter Regulation?' (2005) *Public Law* 485, 511.

[18] See JP Chamberlain, 'Legislative Drafting and Law Enforcement' (1931) 21 *American Labor Legislation Review* 235, 243.

[19] See D Hull, 'Drafters Devils' (2000) *Loophole*, www.calc.ngo/sites/default/files/loophole/jan-2016.pdf.

[20] See U Karpen, 'The Norm Enforcement Process' in U Karpen and P Delnoy (eds), *Contributions to the Methodology of the Creation of Written Law* (Baden-Baden, Nomos, 1996) 51, 51; see also L Mader, 'Legislative Procedure and the Quality of Legislation' in Karpen and Delnoy, ibid, 62, 68.

[21] See G Teubner, 'Regulatory Law: Chronicle of a Death Foretold' (1992) 1 *Social Legal Studies* 451.

[22] See C Timmermans, 'How Can One Improve the Quality of Community Legislation?' (1997) 34 *CMLR* 1229, 1236–37.

[23] See Communication from the Commission, 'European Governance: Better Law-Making', COM (2002) 275 final, Brussels, 5 June 2002; see also High Level Group on the Operation of Internal Market, 'The Internal Market After 1992: Meeting the Challenge—Report to the EEC Commission by the High Level Group on the Operation of Internal Market', SEC (92) 2044.

[24] See Office of Parliamentary Counsel, 'Working with OPC', 6 December 2011 and 'Drafting Guidance', 16 December 2011.

[25] See L Mader, 'Evaluating the Effect: A Contribution to the Quality of Legislation' (2001) 22 *Statute Law Review* 119, 126.

[26] See F Snyder, 'The Effectiveness of European Community Law: Institutions, Processes, Tools and Techniques' (1993) 56 *MLR* 19, 19; see also F Snyder, *New Directions in European Community Law* (London, Weidenfeld & Nicolson, 1990) 3.

implementation, enforcement, impact and compliance.[27] Muller and Ulmann define it as the degree to which the legislative measure has achieved a concrete goal without suffering from side-effects.[28] In Jenkins' socio-legal model, effectiveness in the legislation can be defined as the extent to which the legislation influences in the desired manner the social phenomenon which it aims to address.[29] Voermans defines the principle of effectiveness as a consequence of the Rule of Law, which imposes a duty on the legislator to consider and respect the implementation and enforcement of legislation to be enacted.[30] Mousmouti describes effectiveness as a measure of the causal relations between the law and its effects, and so an effective law is one that is respected or implemented, provided that the observable degree of respect can be attributed to the norm.[31] For the purposes of drafting in its narrow sense, therefore, effectiveness is the ultimate measure of quality in legislation.[32] It simply reflects the extent to which the legislation manages to introduce adequate mechanisms capable of producing the desired regulatory results.[33] If one subjects the effectiveness of legislation to the wider semantic field of efficacy of regulation, effectiveness manages to hold true even with reference to diverse legislative phenomena, such as symbol legislation, or even the role of law as a ritual. If the purpose of legislation is to serve as a symbol, then effectiveness becomes the measure of achieved inspiration of the users of the symbol legislation. If the legislation is to be used as a ritual, effectiveness takes the robe of persuasion of the users who bow down to its appropriate rituality.

In its concrete rather than abstract conceptual sense, effectiveness requires a legislative text that can: (i) foresee the main projected outcomes and use them in the drafting and formulation process; (ii) state clearly its objectives and purpose; (iii) provide the necessary and appropriate means and enforcement measures; and (iv) assess and evaluate real-life effectiveness in a consistent and timely manner.[34]

Leaving cost-efficiency aside,[35] effectiveness can be achieved through clarity, precision and unambiguity. Clarity, or clearness,[36] is the quality of being clear and

[27] See G Teubner, 'Regulatory Law: Chronicle of a Death Foretold' in L Lenoble (ed), *Einfuhrung in der Rectssoziologie* (Darmstadt, Wissenschaftliche Buchgesellschaft, 1987) 54.

[28] See G Muller and F Uhlmann, *Elemente einer Rechtssetzungslehre* (Zurich, Asculthess, 2013) 51–52.

[29] See I Jenkins, *Social Order and the Limits of the Law: A Theoretical Essay* (Princeton, Princeton University Press, 1981) 180; see also R Cranston, 'Reform through Legislation: The Dimension of Legislative Technique' (1978–79) 73 *Northwestern University Law Review* 873, 875.

[30] See Voermans, above n 5, 230.

[31] See Mousmouti, above n 5, 200.

[32] See H Xanthaki, 'On Transferability of Legal Solutions' in Stefanou and Xanthaki, above n 12, 6.

[33] See Office of the Leader of the House of Commons, *Post-legislative Scrutiny: The Government's Approach*, March 2008, para 2.4.

[34] This is Mousmouti's effectiveness test: Mousmouti, above n 5, 202.

[35] See R Posner, 'Cost Benefit Analysis: Definition, Justification, and Comments on Conference Papers' (2000) 29 *Journal of Legal Studies* 1153.

[36] See Lord H Thring, *Practical Legislation: The Composition and Language of Acts of Parliament and Business Documents* (London, John Murray, 1902) 61.

easily perceived or understood.[37] Precision is defined as exactness of expression or detail.[38] Unambiguity is certain or exact meaning:[39] semantic unambiguity requires a single meaning for each word used,[40] whereas syntactic unambiguity requires a clear sentence structure and the correct placement of phrases or clauses.[41] Clarity, precision and unambiguity offer predictability to the law. Predictability allows the users of the legislation, including enforcers,[42] to comprehend the required content of the regulation. Predictability of effect is a necessary component of effectiveness and indeed of the Rule of Law.[43] Thus, compliance becomes a matter of conscious choice for the user rather than a matter of the user's subjective interpretation of the exact content of the legislation and, ultimately, the regulation.

At the third level of the hierarchy of goals for the drafter comes plain language and gender-neutral language.

Thus, good EU laws are laws that, provided there is synergy among the other actors in the legislative process, are capable of producing the desired policy results. This presupposes that EU regulators have set a realistic achievable and sound policy aim, with equally achievable and sound mechanisms for its achievement. If this is in place, a good EU law can express the aim, the mechanisms and ultimately the demands made to citizens in a manner that can communicate the regulatory message adequately. A good EU law facilitates the user's understanding on what they have to do, for what reason and in what way. This incites compliance, at least amongst those citizens who are inclined to comply. It also enhances accountability on the basis of the visibility of the legislative aim, the reasoning behind the mechanisms chosen and the legislative quality: citizens know what is to be achieved by when and can therefore question if that has happened or if it has not.

WHAT IS GOOD EU LEGISLATION: EU INSTRUMENTS?

The EU started its engagement with regulatory and legislative quality back in the early 1990s. However, it was in the 1998 Commission Staff Working Paper entitled 'Making Single Market Rules More Effective, Quality in Implementation and Enforcement'[44] that the Commission clarifies the necessity for and the

[37] See *Compact Oxford English Dictionary of Current English* (Oxford, Oxford University Press, 2005).

[38] ibid.

[39] ibid.

[40] J MacKaye, AW Levi and W Pepperell Montague, *The Logic of Language* (Hanover, NH, Dartmouth College Publications, 1939) ch 5.

[41] For the distinction between semantic and syntactic ambiguity, see R Dickerson, *The Fundamentals of Legal Drafting* (Boston, Little, Brown, 1986) 101 and 104; for an application of rules of logic to resolve syntactic ambiguities, see LE Allen, 'Symbolic Logic: A Razor-Edged Tool for Drafting and Interpreting Legal Documents' (1956–57) 66 *Yale Law Journal* 833, 855.

[42] See A Seidman, R Seidman and N Abeyesekere, *Legislative Drafting for Democratic Social Change* (The Hague, Kluwer Law International, 2001) 255.

[43] See Sir S Laws, CALC Conference 2009, Hong Kong.

[44] See SEC(1998) 903, 25 May 1998, 3–5.

purpose and the content of quality in legislation. Clear and simple legislation helps businesses and citizens to comply with the law without excessive burdens. It facilitates its enforcement. Moreover, it addresses complaints for excessive red tape often leading to cases for damages, such as *Francovich*. All this can be achieved by the use of legislation that is easy to transpose and apply and that takes into account the views of interested parties expressed in consultation under the 1998 Regulatory Policy Guidelines of the Commission and the 2002 General Principles and Minimum Standards for Consultation of Interested Parties by the Commission. Accountability, effectiveness and proportionality were put forward as the main elements of better law-making in the 2002 Communication on 'European Governance: Better Lawmaking'.[45] Moreover, the Commission Communication to the European Council 'Legislate Less to Act Better: The Facts' emphasised the need to concentrate on policy priorities through the strict application of the subsidiarity and proportionality principles (legislate less), the need for improved consultation procedures, and the need for clearer, simpler and more accessible legislation (act better). These aims are achievable through the reduction of legislative proposals; the use of alternatives to legislation as a regulatory tool; the quality of legislative drafting through the introduction of drafting guidelines for clear, coherent and unambiguous legislation; the simplification of legislation through the SLIM programme; the appropriate use of formal consolidation (or codification in today's terminology), recasting and informal consolidation; easier access to information; proper transposition; shared responsibility amongst institutions; and the rationalising of national legislation.

The culmination of rules for legislative quality came with the 1998 Interinstitutional Agreement on common guidelines for the quality of drafting of Community legislation,[46] as supplemented by the 2003 Interinstitutional Agreement on Better Law-Making[47] and consolidated into the Interinstitutional Style Guide on 22 April 2015:[48] Community acts must be clear, simple, precise, concise and with homogeneous content. Drafting must be appropriate to the type of act concerned and to the audience to whom it is addressed. Terminology must be internally and externally consistent. The standard structure of title/ preamble/enacting terms/ annexes (if necessary) applies. The title offers a full indication of the subject matter. Citations set out the legal basis of the act. Recitals set out concise reasons for the chief provisions of the enacting terms without paraphrasing or reproducing them. Only clauses of normative nature can be included in legislation. Internal and external references must be kept to a minimum. Repeals must be introduced expressly. Dates of transposition or enforcement must be introduced clearly as day/month/year.

[45] See Communication from the Commission, above n 23.

[46] See OJ C 73, 17 March 1999, 1.

[47] See Parliament, Council and Commission Interinstitutional Agreement on Better Law-Making [2003] OJ C321/01.

[48] See http://publications.europa.eu/code/en/en-000500.htm.

The Interinstitutional Style Guide binds drafters in the institutions, but continues to take the form of a formalistic, fragmented and incomplete manual on legislating for the EU. As a result, it fails to address the elements of legislative quality and continues to promote a formalistic and technical approach to drafting.

The fury of action for the achievement of legislative quality in the EU ended at some point in 2003. Numerous policy documents continued to refer to Better Regulation, which continued to be at the forefront of the EU's governance debate, but a closer look at them shows beyond doubt a transfer from legislation as an autonomous product to legislation as a regulatory tool. This is of course exceptionally insightful as legislation is indeed a tool for regulation. However, rather unfortunately, this conceptual move in the EU led to the sidelining of legislation. One could trace the conceptual framework behind this movement as far back as 2001 and the Mandelkern Group Report on Better Regulation. It is notable that since 2001, the Better Regulation Reports are pursuant to and therefore limited to proportionality and subsidiarity, whereas from 2007, even the title of Better Regulation reports has been usurped by subsidiarity and proportionality, thus excluding the scope for legislative quality conventions and innovative assessments. The 2008 Second Strategic Review of Better Regulation in the EU focuses solely on administrative burdens, legislative scrutiny, reducing the number of legislative instruments, and emphasising the shared responsibility of the EU and its Member States. Similarly, the 2009 Third Strategic Review of Better Regulation in the EU is another prime example of this move from legislation to regulatory agendas: although clear, precise and accessible legislation lies at the heart of regulatory reform, none of the recommendations addresses it: pre- and post-legislative scrutiny are the only focus.

The most recent innovation in the field comes with the Smart Regulation Agenda,[49] now revamped as the Better Regulation Agenda. The October 2010 Commission Communication on Smart Regulation constitutes the formal passing from the old Better Regulation Agenda to the new Smart Regulation Agenda.[50] The Commission identified three key messages in the Agenda: first, Smart Regulation is about the whole policy cycle and thus touches upon the design of a piece of legislation, its implementation, enforcement, evaluation and revision; second, Smart Regulation remains a shared responsibility between the EU institutions and the Member States; third, the views of users of regulation have a key role to play in Smart Regulation, as consultation is an element of democracy. In other words, the novelty of Smart Regulation refers to three main themes: smart regulation throughout the policy cycle; shared responsibility; and stakeholder engagement.[51]

[49] See H Xanthaki, 'The Regulatory Reform Agenda and Modern Innovations in Drafting Style' in L Mader (ed), *Regulatory Reform* (Baden-Baden, Nomos, 2013) 128.

[50] See European Commission, 'Smart Regulation in the European Union' COM (2010) 543, 8 October 2010, http://eurlex.europa.eu/LexUriServ/LexUriServ.do?uri=CELEX:52010DC0543:EN:NOT.

[51] See H McColm, 'Smart Regulation: The European Commission's Updated Strategy' (2011) 9 *European Journal of Risk Regulation* 9.

There is no doubt that Smart Regulation is revolutionary. The reaction of the experts to the Commission's agenda has been positive, although the need for further action has already been identified. This includes the need to carry out Impact Assessments for every new regulatory proposal; to improve the informative value of roadmaps; to make the Commission's Impact Assessment Board more independent; to conduct systematic *ex post* evaluations from the end user's perspective; to strengthen the role of the High-Level Group; and to consult the public.[52] Smart Regulation presents obvious positive points. It follows Stefanou's identification of the drafting process as a part of the legislative process, which is a part of the policy process.[53] It confirms that EU regulation is a shared responsibility of the institutions and Member States. In addition, it affirms the need for in-depth consultation. Focus is placed on the simplification of EU law via the reduction of administrative burdens past the expected 25 per cent cuts in red tape by 2012; the evaluation of law effectiveness and efficiency *ex ante* via fitness checks on key areas (for example, the environment) and via strategic general policy evaluations; the selection of the 'the best possible' legislation through Impact Assessment; the improvement of implementation records, via post-legislative scrutiny, SOLVIT and EU Pilot; and achieving clearer and accessible legislation via simple language, codification, recasting and e-access. These are worthy aims. In addition, the Commission can show considerable success in this field. For example, the EU's Impact Assessment system has been praised as first class.[54] The question is how these noble aims are going to be achieved.

The simplification of EU law is indeed a wonderful goal. A depressing (or it is impressive?) 74 per cent of Europeans believe that the EU generates too much red tape.[55] In addition, the Commission has responded to this via Impact Assessments and stakeholder consultation, and via regular fitness checks undertaken within the Regulatory Fitness and Performance Programme (REFIT) of December 2012. These initiatives have contributed to a reduction of red tape of well above the 25 per cent target set out in the Administrative Burden Reduction programme:[56] the precise figures correspond to a decrease of 25 per cent in administrative burdens

[52] See 'Common Position Paper of the Five European Independent Advisory Boards for Cutting Red Tape and Better Regulation', Adviescollege toetsing regeldruk (ACTAL), The Netherlands; Nationaler Normenkontrollrat (NKR), Germany; Regelrådet, Sweden; Regulatory Impact Assessment Board (RIAB), Czech Republic; Regulatory Policy Committee (RPC), UK, www.regelradet.se/wp-content/uploads/2012/09/2012-Reaction-on-consultation-Smart-Regulation.pdf.

[53] See C Stefanou, 'Drafters, Drafting and the Policy Process' in Stefanou and Xanthaki, above n 12, 312.

[54] See OECD, 'Sustainability in Impact Assessments—A Review of Impact Assessment Systems in Selected OECD Countries and the European Commission', 2011; European Parliament, 'Comparative Study on the Purpose, Scope and Procedures of Impact Assessments Carried out in the Member States of the EU', 2011; CEPS/University of Exeter, 'Regulatory Quality in the European Commission and the UK: Old Questions and New Findings', 2012.

[55] See Eurobarometer Question QA16.4 on p 59: http://ec.europa.eu/public_opinion/archives/eb/eb79/eb79_anx_en.pdf.

[56] See SWD (2013) 401 final.

in 13 priority areas equivalent to savings of €30.8 billion, with a further €5 billion still pending adoption by the co-legislator. However, simplification cannot be taken to mean simply a streamlining of legislation and a reduction of administrative burdens. In fact, the Smart Regulation agenda neglects to address a number of crucial aspects of simplification without which reduction of administrative burdens cannot be achieved. What about the simplicity of the chosen policies? If a policy choice is complex in itself, then the reduction in red tape will not suffice to make it accessible to citizens. What about simplicity in the selected regulatory means? Is the notoriously user-unfriendly legislation not a most complex regulatory tool? As such, reducing administrative burdens via legislation brings with it inherent complexity, which may well endanger the end result. What about the chosen drafting style as a means of simplifying the expression of a simply policy when a simpler regulatory tool is considered ineffective? A complex legislative style would diminish the actual effect of any simplification effort irrespective of what the percentage of administrative burdens in the simple policy chosen may be: if the users cannot understand the language of the law, how can they benefit from the opportunities created by a policy of reduced red tape? What about straightforward enforcement methods? And could one rely on a reduction of administrative burdens within the EU text if the national implementing measures are complex and seize on any opportunity for discretion in the EU text in order to add further burdens? Finally, could EU law be considered simple when the methods of pre- and post-legislative scrutiny utilised are inherently complex and therefore inaccessible for its users?

Similarly, evaluation of law effectiveness and efficiency *ex ante* is a fantastic initiative in theory. It is defined as a judgement of interventions according to their results and impacts, and the needs they aim to satisfy.[57] However, can it be achieved simply via fitness checks and general policy evaluations? In a legislative environment where the definition of effectiveness has not been provided conclusively, the goal that the regulatory team is supposed to be trying to achieve becomes a moving target, a vague and ambiguous goalpost, which carries a different meaning for the different actors in the regulatory process, particularly between the EU and the national levels. However, even where the concept of effectiveness appears clear, what are the specific criteria of effectiveness by way of successful regulation that must be used in reference to a specific piece of legislation? The application of the generic elements of the semantic field of the concept of effectiveness in the specific context of a piece of legislation as applied in the specific legal system that serves a specific society in a specific time is not an easy task and should not really be ignored or left to chance. There is a dire need to ensure that the criteria for effectiveness of any piece of legislation are agreed between policy-makers, law experts and legislative drafters, and that they are clearly expressed in the legislation itself, perhaps via their inclusion in a purpose clause or an objectives article. These can

[57] See G Luchetta, 'Impact Assessment and the Policy Cycle in the EU' (2012) *European Journal of Risk Regulation* 561, 572–73.

then be carried through to post-legislative scrutiny and then utilised to confirm effectiveness, thus allowing the text to continue its legislative life.

But how will ineffectiveness be addressed? What if the effectiveness criteria are not met by the piece of legislation at the pre-set time of post-legislative monitoring: will the legislation die an automatic death via perhaps a sunset clause, will it continue to plague the statute book as it stands until an enlightened decision-maker decides to address the problem or will it lead to an automatic exercise of fine-tuning, perhaps via an amending piece of legislation?

Moreover, Smart Regulation fails to identify the way in which, if at all, evaluation will take place at the Member State level. Here other considerations should also come into play. Will national scrutiny be compulsory or could the Member States be offered discretion based on national sovereignty in the legislative-making process? Moreover, Smart Regulation fails to address the extent of any national scrutiny process, namely whether it must relate strictly to the national implementing measures or whether it can refer to the original EU text. This is crucial, especially in reference to national legislation, which departs from the policy and law of the EU by means of either a direct or an indirect breach, or even legitimately by means of an acceptable exercise of discretion, as would be the case with the implementation of a directive. And what if the national scrutiny exercise identifies a flaw in the EU policy? Can this be reported back to the EU and will this result in any action at the EU level?

Moreover, the initiative fails to define efficiency. It is unclear whether this refers to a mathematical exercise involving financial cost or whether social and other impact must be calculated towards the reduction of burdens, or indeed how these can be calculated.

The improvement of the implementation record is a third worthy point of reference for Smart Regulation. But once again one has to distinguish between the aim and the proposed methods for its achievement. Can implementation be improved solely via post-legislative scrutiny, the availability of SOLVIT and EU Pilot on clarification and assistance with the application of EU legislation? What about clear guidance on the definition of complete transposition for new, older and aspiring Member States? What about clear guidance on the definition of quality in legislation for the purposes of EU drafting and also EU transposition? What about the establishment of national drafting offices with trained specialist drafters vetting (if not drafting) implementation measures based on the UK model for drafting national primary legislation (the Office of Parliamentary Counsel)? What about extending the scrutiny of implementation beyond substantive transposition to technical quality of transposition?

Finally, who would disagree with the election of the 'the best possible' legislation? However, is this really achievable simply via Impact Assessments, clearer and accessible legislation, simple language, codification, recasting and e-access? What about opening the debate for a holistic approach to effectiveness in the sense of the use of legislation as a tool for regulation? What about setting a hierarchy of goals for the drafter? What about training drafters to achieve these goals? What about considering a central drafting office with trained drafters within EU institutions, including the Commission, the Council and the Parliament? What about training national drafters to contribute to the effort?[58]

Therefore, even post-Lisbon EU legislative quality continues to face challenges that have remained unaddressed for the most part. The analysis of the relevant EU initiatives, namely the Better Regulation agenda, identified a pause somewhere around 2003. Despite the flurry of activity in the field of legislative quality up to then, all initiatives from the EU after that date refer to legislative quality as an aim, but have transferred the focus of attention to holistic regulatory quality, thus leaving legislative quality aside.[59]

The move towards regulatory quality as the focus of the EU's better governance campaign is by no means a negative development in the field. Indeed, legislative quality is an intrinsic part of regulatory quality: without regulatory quality, one cannot perceive the notion of legislative quality. As legislative drafting can only aspire to effectiveness, namely to the production of a legislative text that, with the cooperation and synergy of all other actors in the policy process, can achieve the regulatory aims, one cannot possibly expect it to produce quality legislation when the regulatory aims are erroneous or illegal, when the choice of legislation as a regulatory tool is inappropriate or, indeed, when the implementation of the legislation has not been thought through. However, at the same time, one cannot possibly perceive regulatory quality without legislative quality in cases where legislation is the appropriate regulatory tool. To me, this is the great error of the EU's current strategy. By turning its focus of attention from legislation to regulation, the EU seems to have forgotten about legislation altogether, somehow trying to simply wish away the continuing problems of legislative quality.[60] The same conclusion was reached by the analysis of Smart Regulation, the 2010 EU initiative constituting the successor of Better Regulation. This conclusion is confirmed by an analysis of the new Interinstitutional Agreement on Better Law-Making between the European Parliament, the Council of the European Union and the European Commission on Better Law-Making made on 13 April 2016. Once again, the institutions re-affirm their common goal for effectiveness of legislation, but fail to address their drafting altogether: the emphasis is on procedural issues (such as planning and monitoring) and on pre- and post-legislative scrutiny. However, the actual drafting is ignored, and therefore the criteria by which legislation as a product is to be assessed remain vague and, as such, inapplicable in practice.[61]

[58] For a full presentation of my critique on Smart Regulation, see H Xanthaki, 'Implementation of EU Legislation', Oral Evidence, Public Hearing at the Legal Affairs Committee of the European Parliament 'Better Regulation' Hearing, Brussels, 21 June 2011.

[59] See M Mousmouti, 'The Effectiveness Test' (2012) *Legisprudence* 191, 196.

[60] See C-H Montin, 'Smart Regulation in the European Union', 29 November 2012, http://montin.com/documents/smartregulation.pdf.

[61] See also Communication from the Commission to the European Parliament, the Council, the European Economic and Social Committee and the Committee of Regions, 'Better Regulation for Better Results—An EU Agenda', 19 May 2015, COM (2015) 215 final.

What is even more disappointing is the 2020 Agenda for Europe, where not only Better Regulation but also Smart Regulation is ignored. The question is why the EU felt that it could move from Better Regulation to Smart Regulation, and then to a strategy for growth and competitiveness. From the perspective of legislative studies at least, none of the two moves makes sense. Why would the EU decide to leave Better Regulation and Smart Regulation aside when neither of these agendas has borne the desired fruits? Surely, one could not seriously support the argument that EU legislation and national implementing legislation or indeed the EU regulatory environment have reached perfection. One is tempted to attribute this move to an underlying policy of competitiveness for businesses rather than a policy for better legislation in Europe. Perhaps the legislative and then regulatory quality agendas are viewed by the EU solely as a means of pursuing the policy aim of growth and competitiveness. It is precisely this aim that is repeated, and even more clearly expressed, in the 2020 Agenda for Europe.

In view of this, where is Europe going with reference to legislative quality and quantity? What the EU has clumsily missed here is a unique opportunity to finally balance its focus of attention to both businesses and citizens. While the first enjoy the fruits of Better Regulation, Smart Regulation and the 2020 Agenda for Europe, citizens are still facing the same issues of confusion stemming from the multitude of bad EU laws (not tackled by SLIM as they did not relate to small and medium-sized enterprises (SMEs)) and bad regulation (not tackled by Smart Regulation since administrative burdens were not applicable). This imbalance may well be intentional. However, it remains unjustifiable within the focus on citizen and citizenship expressed clearly in the Treaty of Lisbon. And it cannot be accommodated within the emphasis on social equity for EU citizens so eloquently professed in the Treaty of Lisbon, which declares the passage from the Internal Market to a forum of citizenship, international justice and peace.

Therefore, it appears that the new challenge for Europe in the field of EU legislative studies is to apply Better Regulation, Smart Regulation and the 2020 Agenda for Europe to citizens, along with businesses, thus showing that the Treaty of Lisbon is not a list of good political intentions, but an accurate reflection of the new EU for its citizens and peoples. The challenge is to go back to Better Regulation and Smart Regulation, and assess their success from the point of view of the citizens using the Treaty's citizenship concept as a focus. Transferring the focus from businesses to citizens would tint the picture of the effectiveness of these three regulatory initiatives with much darker colours because the amount of work that remains in order to make EU legislation and EU regulation palatable is daunting, but absolutely necessary.

Does this mean that there is only doom and gloom ahead for Europe and its legislation? Far from it. The EU as a regional organisation is lagging behind whilst a number of groundbreaking initiatives are being pursued within the Member States: this is where inspiration is plentiful and, conveniently, tried and tested. The Timmermans team are already seeking to learn from Member States, and their work is admirable, albeit not focused on legislation as a product—or at least not just yet. At the same time, the academic discipline of legislative studies is enriching Europe with innovative concepts for better legislative quality: the EU is in the enviable position of harvesting European talent to pick the most effective legislative solutions, but only if it has the political inclination to do so and the boldness to be radical.

What the EU needs to address its legislative gridlock is a radical and ruthless critical review of its own practices and processes. The starting point can only be a principled approach to legislative quality. Departing from the current dry formalistic approach to legislative dilemmas, which often serves tick-boxing exercises well, is not an easy reform. It would require less hierarchy in the performance of *fonctionnaires*' duties, thus allowing enlightened drafters to approach legislation in a creative manner. For example, instead of checking which national instrument transposes each of the provisions of EU legislation, those undertaking a transposition check could identify the regulatory efficacy sought by the text and assess the effectiveness of the national transposing instrument on a holistic principled basis. This may seem like a subjective exercise, but the law is subjective. And, in any case, is Impact Assessment not a subjective exercise anyway?

The subjectivity of the proposed creative approach to legislative scrutiny at the EU and Member State levels would be balanced by the identification of objective, clear policy goals to which the legislative text contributes. However, policy goals cannot possibly continue to be expressed in the political context currently present in most recitals: policy goals must be set in a concrete and measurable manner in order to ensure that the contribution of the EU and national texts can be assessed as objectively as possible. For example, introducing money laundering as a criminal offence can no longer be presented as a measure contributing to the Single Market and to the safety and security of EU citizens. Although this supergoal is obviously relevant, for the purposes of legislative drafting, more concrete goals can be used as thresholds of effectiveness that can and will be applied in the post-legislative scritnuty of the legislative text. Succeeding in the prosecution or conviction of a minimum set number of money launderers, saving the EU and its citizens a minimum set amount of money, serves both as a concrete legislative objective and as a measure of legislative success within a period of a set number of years. Perhaps most importantly, it offer EU citizens a tangible, concrete and plausible rationale for the EU legislative text, thus quietening the populist voices attributing the text to an alleged fearsome EU need for more control over citizen activities or to rather mundane policy aims. If the bananas directive included as an objective the aim to eradicate disease in banana crops within a set period of time, those populist voices will have lost the opportunity to distort the regulatory aims of the EU, which may well have gained increased support from farmers and consumers as their champion against disease.

Of course, expressing EU legislative texts in a manner that reflects clear tangible policy objectives in a creative structure that reaches EU citizens as well as Member State authorities is a task that can only be performed adequately by professional drafters. Trained lawyers and non-lawyers, aware of the theory of legislative drafting and experienced in the practice of achieving effectiveness, do not grow on trees, and of course they are not available to the EU right now. This is even more so since Commission *fonctionnaires* lack the independence to express policy without vested policy agendas: given that policy formulation, legislative drafting, and transposition vetting are all collected on the same person, there is little guarantee of independent legislative verification of the draft and, perhaps most importantly, little respect for the constitutional principle of separation of powers.

The lack of external verification of draft EU laws is exacerbated by a lack of trained parliamentary personnel. In order to perform its duty as a learned and able European Parliament, its staff and members must be trained in legislative scrutiny. Without knowing what the quality elements of effective laws are, surely they cannot be expected to perform their scrutiny duties at any level other than the political one. At a time when, post-Lisbon, national parliaments are actively seeking to inform and train their staff and members, it makes little sense to deprive the European Parliament of the privilege of strengthening its voice in legislative quality.

Finally, within the context of a stronger European Parliament, the choices offered to its members can be clarified further. What can they do if draft laws are ineffective or are now obsolete? Fine-tuning and repealing can become an initiative of MEPs, in addition of course to the current Commission staff.

One wonders whether these requirements are utopian under the current realities of an enlarged and at times chaotic EU. Much as I welcome the polyphony and multi-culturalism of a now richer EU, as a drafter I share these doubts. With a richer selection of diverse voices, it is becoming a triumph to pass any piece of legislation, let alone a quality one. The pressure is increased for the Commission and the other EU institutions to manage to achieve agreement on legislative instruments, whilst the task is becoming all the more difficult.

But if this is the case, is there not a mismatch between the legislative capacity of the EU institutions and the type of legislative instruments produced? It is not possible to change the legislative process and the customs created after almost 60 years of European integration. In addition, one can only rejoice at the great diversity of policy approaches, jurisdictions, legal cultures, languages and legislative styles contributing to EU instruments. Given this wonderful status quo, which one would not want to change, it seems that the task of passing effective EU laws has reached a level of impossibility. In order to unblock this dead-end, one could simply embrace the new reality and accept that binding, final and complete legislative texts that are effective in all national legal orders are not feasible. Regulations are doomed to fail as regulatory tools simply because, irrespective of the greatness of talent and skill of EU drafters, it is impossible to create a law that is effective when parachuted into the political, legal and financial environments of 28 Member States. When weighing up the understandable delight of passing a regulation against the great probability of its eventual ineffectiveness, perhaps the EU can begin to seek legislative quality as a means of regulatory efficacy as opposed to the now banal joy of the *droit diplomatique* of olden times.

In practice, this means that regulations should be sought in the very rare cases where both the text agreed and the receiving national legal orders are identical—in which case, one wonders whether the regulation is necessary anyway. It is time for the EU to embrace its crucial role as a goal regulator and legislate solely via directives, thus ensuring that national drafters have the space to intervene legislatively and offer effectiveness in the national transposing measures as their national legal and legislative style directs. This move from the EU as a legislator to the EU as a regulator is no simple decision. It requires trust in national drafters to achieve effectiveness of the EU/Member State regulatory package by means of national transposing regulatory (not necessarily legislative) measures. In addition, it requires a shift of mentality, which places the responsibility but also the willingness to achieve full implementation on the Commission rather than on Member States. However, this mentality overlooks the fact that Member States remain within the EU because they share its ideals and its values, not because of fear of infringement procedures by the Commission. Of course, the task and responsibility of scrutinising the level of national implementation remains with the Commission and ultimately the European courts. However, checking whether implementation has been achieved is completely different from assuming the role of the only responsible drafter of legislation. After all, the Commission itself identified EU legislation as a shared responsibility with the Member States as long ago as the 1990s.

WHAT IS GOOD TRANSPOSING LEGISLATION?

Good transposition legislation is legislation that achieves effectiveness at two levels: the EU level and the national level. National drafters pursue the achievement of the desired regulatory results as introduced in the EU legislative text and as translated within the national legal order. Drafting transposition legislation is one of the most difficult drafting tasks because the drafter serves two masters: two sets of regulatory goals, two texts, two sets of legal concepts, two sets of common and legal languages, and two drafting styles.

These difficulties are exacerbated by the inherent lack of freedom in the performance of the transposition task. Currently, transposition remains chained to the choices of the EU legislator. The tests of necessity, proportionality, adequacy, synergy, adaptability and subsidiarity have been passed, albeit at the EU level. The choice of legislation as the appropriate regulatory tool has already been made and alternative regulatory choices have been rejected. The type of legislative instrument has been decided, at least for the EU text. And the model law has been drafted. It is quite possible for national drafters to simply copy and paste the EU text. Equally explicable is the safety sought by national drafters in the faithful repetition of the EU text: within a formalistic scrutiny exercise, the Commission is expected to accept the text drafted by its staff as a plausible legislative solution.

However, effectiveness as a value of legislative quality demolishes the image depicted above. Effective transposition requires that the national drafter repeats all the tests of necessity, proportionality, adequacy, synergy and adaptability. The repeating of these tests is necessary because the national drafter does not conduct them against the policy, legislative, financial, administrative or cultural environment of EU law, but rather against the national environment. It is possible that national law already provides for the desired EU regulatory aims rather successfully. What is necessary at the EU level may not be necessary at the national level. What is adequate at the EU level may require a more forcible legislative message in Member States where culture or societal values are adverse to the desired regulatory reform. Of course, national reservations on synergy, subsidiarity or proportionality have little role to play here, as one would have expected them to arise at the level of passing of the EU text. Nevertheless, proportionality against existing national legislation may well be relevant where EU legislation offers a level of discretion above the required minimum.

In the transposition process, the choice of legislation as the appropriate regulatory tool must also be assessed against national laws. It is plausible for the national drafter to demote the regulatory tool for the achievement of the desired regulatory result in jurisdictions where legislation is not communicating with citizens adequately and non-legislative tools are successful in regulating behaviours. The UK is one of those jurisdictions where legislation is reserved as a solution of last resort and regulatory results have been achieved by means of labour agreements or by means of self-regulation. If the EU departs from its formalistic box-ticking scrutiny of transposition, the national drafters' arguments for effective transposition by alternative means of regulation can be truly effective. Of course, agreed monitoring mechanisms and agreed regulatory goals within set review times would be required, but the option is there and is quite plausible.

The same approach applies to the type of legislative instrument selected for transposition. It is not always necessary to provide a national implementing text whose type corresponds to that of the EU text. Regulations may require further legislative intervention. Directives may require transposition by means of a national law or even by a selection of diverse national texts of diverse types for the various regulatory parts of the EU text. Judgments of the European courts may well require legislative transposition. At the end of the day, the choice is one of effectiveness, not of formal correspondence between the EU and transposing laws.

Finally, the EU text is not a model law whose role is to be copied and pasted. Effectiveness demands that EU laws are used by the national drafters as legislative instructions, not model laws. They are there to state the desired regulatory result, to identify the policy tools promoted as most appropriate to achieve them, to draw the drafter's attention to the elements that must be transposed compulsorily, and to alert the drafter to discretion in the transposition process. Although currently these elements are not easily identifiable by the existing legislative structure of EU texts, these are nevertheless the elements that the national drafter must extract in order to transpose effectively. This process, if conducted adequately, can lead to an effective national text, which in turn can lead to correct implementation and ultimately to true regulatory success for the EU and national legislators.

CONCLUSIONS: WHAT ON EARTH IS REALLY WRONG AND HOW TO CHANGE IT

Having identified effectiveness as the value of legislative quality and having juxtaposed it against current EU texts, policies and practices, one can see the problem of EU legislation. It is not technical in nature. It is an expression of an inherent clash between the legislative procedures and customs developed over the last 60 years of European integration and the legislative needs of the EU. For quite a few years in its development, the EU produced a diplomatic law addressed to Member States and requiring sporadic intervention in the national legal orders. But the EU has changed and so have its legislative needs. EU law is now also addressed to its citizens, who acquire rights and obligations as a direct result. It is not a diplomatic law—it is a law that regulates the everyday life of natural and legal persons. It is now a law that has direct effect and very often direct applicability. It is now a law that applies to the richness of its diverse cohort of 28 Member States. It is now a law that, as is the case with national laws, is read by its constituents who demand to understand it in order to apply it, all the more so at a time when most national authorities simply copy and paste it into the national statute books. And this success is at the root of its failure. EU legislation, as a process and a product, is no longer fit for purpose. It continues to be passed as the old *droit diplomatique*, yet it has succeeded in becoming much more than that. It is a binding, strong regulatory tool that achieves EU and national regulatory reforms, whose legislative expression is communicated exclusively via its texts.

This legislative deficit cannot possibly be addressed by means of formalistic guides or meticulous form-focused pre- or post-legislative scrutiny. Just as legislative needs have changed, the EU's legislative mentality must change to match them. There are two policy options open to the EU. The first requires a change in the regulatory and legislative processes in order to align them with national legislative structures and processes. This option seems unfeasible: the EU is not a state and its processes are a wonderful compilation of political consensus that serves a fragile unique political balance. The second requires a change in legislative mentality. The EU must accept its role as a goal regulator and must embrace its potency as a goal legislator. Without releasing any responsibility of creative legislative and implementation scrutiny, the EU must legislate solely via directives, thus offering national drafters the space and opportunity to bring effectiveness to EU law through effectiveness in the national implementing measures.

Does this shift of drafting prerogative signify a shift in regulatory power? Absolutely not: under the proposed framework, the EU remains as the policy-maker, the original drafter, and the scrutiniser of transposition and implementation. In fact, the EU retains the opportunity to draft complete binding provisions, where

Member States 'must' take set actions. But national drafters regain the responsibility, and the consequent liability, for discretion on the choice of national regulatory tool, national legislative tool and national legislative expression.

This is not a paradigm that does not affect the way in which EU legislation is drafted. Far from allowing EU legislation to lag behind, it creates new opportunities for EU drafters. Under this paradigm, EU legislation must share the goal and supergoal of the required regulatory results. Citizens acquire a clear and accurate vision of the required reforms, of which they have ownership. This shuts down the populist voices and avoids misunderstanding of the reasoning behind EU regulation. It also allows the EU to explain and persuade EU citizens that EU action is more effective than national action. In other words, it relays subsidiarity to non-specialists, thus demolishing the myth of useless or unilaterally passed EU laws. Finally, it conveys a list of clear binding obligations for national transposition and allows national drafters to diversify for increased effectiveness where this is considered useful.

What is wrong with EU legislation? It is a victim of its own success. Much as political success required bold and radical thinking and actions, so does legislative success. The hope of this author is that this chapter is the start of a radical debate for real EU legislative quality.

4

Cost-Benefit Analysis and EU Policy

Limits and Opportunities

ANDREA RENDA*

THE DEBATE ON the use of cost-benefit analysis (hereinafter CBA) to support public policy decisions, and in particular regulatory initiatives, is far from new, but still rages in many international fora, as well as in academia.[1] The debate on CBA and public policy dates back almost three centuries, and the use of this method to support regulatory reform has since then made important inroads in many governments around the world. A preliminary map of the debate leads to identifying three main attitudes towards CBA: the *CBA enthusiasts* support the extensive, pervasive use of CBA to improve the rationality, transparency, accountability and efficiency of public policy;[2] the *constructive sceptics* try to modify the existing practice of CBA to reflect a number of methodological and ethical concerns;[3] and the *opponents* of CBA consider that the methodological flaws and distortions generated by this method warrant the search for alternatives, such as multi-criteria analysis, trade-off analysis, a focus on minimising compliance costs, or simply a qualitative assessment of the prospective or retrospective impacts of public policies.[4]

All these opinions have some theoretical and empirical support, as will be discussed in more detail below. At the international level, the more enthusiastic

* Andrea Renda is Senior Research Fellow at CEPS, Duke University.

[1] CBA is also used for public investment projects, tax transfer reforms and social expenditures; see R Boadway, 'Cost-Benefit Analysis' in M Adler and M Fleurbaey (eds), *The Oxford Handbook of Well-Being and Fair Distribution* (New York, Oxford University Press, 2016). This chapter focuses in particular on regulation.

[2] eg, RW Hahn, *In Defense of the Economic Analysis of Regulation* (Washington DC, American Enterprise Institute, 2005).

[3] eg, MD Adler, *Well-Being and Fair Distribution: Beyond Cost-Benefit Analysis* (Oxford, Oxford University Press, 2012); MD Adler, 'A Better Calculus for Regulators: From Cost-Benefit Analysis to the Social Welfare Function' (2017) *Duke Law School Public Law & Legal Theory Series* 19; MD Adler and E Posner, *New Foundations of Cost-Benefit Analysis* (Cambridge, MA, Harvard University Press, 2006).

[4] A Sinden, 'Cost-Benefit Analysis, Ben Franklin, and the Supreme Court' (2014) 4 *UC Irvine Law Review* 1175; L Heinzerling and F Ackerman, 'Law and Economics for a Warming World' (2008) 1(2) *Harvard Law and Policy Review* 331.

position has been dominant, especially since the early 1980s, thanks to the widespread promotion of CBA in policy-making by institutions such as the Organisation for Economic Co-operation and Development (OECD) and national administrations in the US, Canada, Australia and the UK. Against this background, in adopting and implementing its Better Regulation Agenda since 2002, the European Commission has consistently but not exclusively endorsed the use of CBA as an overarching methodological framework for assessing and evaluating the economic, social and environmental impacts of proposed new EU major policy initiatives. This occurred despite the fact that the EU policy appraisal system features a much broader scope, and thus possibly more methodological complications, compared to homologous systems such as the US one.[5] Such difference led to tensions in the consistent application of CBA in the European Commission.

This chapter explores the pros and cons of using CBA in support of public policy, and discusses the specific case for relying on this method in the EU Better Regulation Agenda. The first section looks at the academic debate on CBA and its possible alternatives. The second section describes the place occupied by CBA in the EU Better Regulation Agenda and identifies a number of peculiar aspects of the EU Impact Assessment system, which inevitably led EU institutions to depart from a fully fledged, orthodox adherence to the use of CBA. The third section briefly concludes by discussing the potential for partly diverging from a CBA-oriented approach to improve the salience and usefulness of the EU Better Regulation toolbox and process.

CBA AND PUBLIC POLICY: A NEVER-ENDING ACADEMIC DEBATE

The desirability of using CBA as a decision-making tool has long been recognised in public policy. It has been traced back to the letter Benjamin Franklin wrote in 1772 to his friend Joseph Priestley, recommending that Priestley address a challenging decision by explicitly listing and comparing the pros and cons.[6] Since then, the method is associated with the practice of identifying, listing and assessing the positive and negative consequences of alternative courses of action, and then choosing the alternative that maximises net benefits. In public policy, CBA is seen as an instrument aimed at the maximisation of social welfare and as such is often traced back to the seminal work of Jeremy Bentham. Bentham's vision of the role of public policy, described in his *Fragment on Government* in 1776, was one aimed at maximising 'happiness' for the 'greatest number'.[7] He defined happiness as the

[5] A Renda, *Impact Assessment in the EU: The State of the Art and the Art of the State* (Brussels, CEPS, 2006); A Renda, *Law and Economics in the RIA World* (Amsterdam, Intersentia, 2011).

[6] JB Wiener, 'The Diffusion of Regulatory Oversight' in MA Livermore and RL Revesz (eds), *The Globalization of Cost-Benefit Analysis in Environmental Policy* (Oxford, Oxford University Press, 2013) ch 8.

[7] See *A Fragment on Government*, in which Bentham describes as a fundamental axiom: 'it is the greatest happiness of the greatest number that is the measure of right and wrong'.

sum of all pleasures and pains, implicitly introducing a net benefit concept in the measurement of the impact of public policies. CBA was then formalised by economists like Jules Dupuit and Alfred Marshall during the nineteenth century and has been used in the US at the federal level since the 1930s, having been initially developed by the Army Corps of Engineers. It is now used widely by government agencies and international institutions around the world. However, the road from Bentham's utilitarian view to the current version of CBA used in public policy has been more tortuous than often acknowledged. While an exhaustive account would fall outside the scope of this chapter,[8] the main methodological disputes are summarised below.

A first problem that emerged in operationalising Bentham's original view is the difficulty of directly measuring happiness and well-being. While the economics literature has made important progress in this respect,[9] early neoclassical economists did not come out with a fully satisfactory way of comparing inter-personal utility without relying on an imperfect proxy such as income,[10] and ended up incorporating utility into their models without paying 'much attention to its doubtful philosophical and psychological foundations'.[11] More specifically, neoclassical economists have come to rely on individual willingness to pay (WTP) as a measure of the intensity of happiness or utility associated with future states of the world. In other words, regulatory impacts are appraised by asking individuals how much they would in theory be willing to pay to realise specific future outcomes, whereas scenarios associated with negative WTP are considered to be associated with a worsening of the individual's perceived utility.

As observed inter alia by Boadway,[12] this preference-based approach has both advantages and shortcomings. On the positive side, it appears non-paternalistic as it takes a bottom-up view of what individuals consider to be an improvement; in other words, it does not incorporate any normative agenda set by the policy-maker, but exclusively relies on the observation of what affected people would prefer ('willing to pay for'). However, this approach has several limitations. First, for marketed goods it incorporates all the behavioural biases and imperfections featured by market outcomes, including imperfect information, bounded rationality, externalities and many more. Second, by considering WTP in the absence

[8] See, eg, Renda, *Impact Assessment*, above n 5.

[9] D Fujiwara and R Campbell, *Valuation Techniques for Social Cost-Benefit Analysis: Stated Preference, Revealed Preference and Subjective Well-Being Approaches. A Discussion of the Current Issues*, Report for the UK Government, HM Treasury and Department for Work and Pensions, July 2011; M Fleurbaey and D Blanchet, *Beyond GDP: Measuring Welfare and Assessing Sustainability* (Oxford, Oxford University Press, 2013); Adler and Fleurbaey, above n 1.

[10] Bentham himself suggested that happiness could be proxied by money. See J Bentham, *An Introduction to the Principles of Morals and Legislation. In Utilitarianism and Other Essays* (Harmondsworth, Penguin, 1789).

[11] K Binmore, 'Interpersonal Comparison of Utility' in D Ross and H Kincaid (eds), *The Oxford Handbook of Philosophy of Economics* (Oxford University Press, 2009).

[12] Boadway, above n 1.

of income constraints, it only considers the preferences of those on the demand curve who end up participating in the market: if a person does not have a sufficient ability to pay for a specific good or service, CBA will consider that person as having insufficient WTP and thus no specific preference for that good or service. Third, for non-market goods such as environmental quality or fundamental rights, the only way to incorporate monetary value in the analysis is to infer some measure of WTP and build shadow prices: this has been criticised as utterly arbitrary and leading to 'knowing the price of everything, and the value of nothing',[13] as exemplified in particular in the debate over the value of a statistical life[14] and on pricing environmental goods.[15] Fourth, economists have long debated the need to differentiate gains from losses in the individual perception of preferences and regulatory outcomes, and this has led to estimating values of WTP for gains, and willingness to accept compensation (WTA) for losses, which are wildly diverging; practical experience in the application of CBA has shown that obtaining reliable WTA measures is a nightmare and that in most cases the figures obtained are greatly exaggerated. Fifth, and relatedly, the need to use income as a proxy for utility and the need to avoid difficult comparisons between heterogeneous measures (WTP and WTA) have led economists to largely ignore distributional issues when using CBA: this was mostly done by implicitly assuming that income has constant marginal returns, an assumption that is both intuitively and empirically found to be unfounded. Finally, these problems are also exacerbated by the fact that CBA is based on methodological individualism, ie, it assumes that individual preferences are dependent on each individual's specific condition and not on external constraints. More precisely, under a methodologically individualist approach, marginal utilities—and thus individual preferences in market and non-market contexts—do not depend on what society as such has, but on what individual members have.[16] All inter-dependencies between individuals are necessarily ruled out.

In summary, the fully fledged version of CBA assumes that income is a good proxy for happiness (wealth equals welfare); that individuals behave rationally and

[13] F Ackerman and L Heinzerling, *Priceless: On Knowing the Price of Everything and the Value of Nothing* (New York, The New Press, 2004).

[14] WK Viscusi and JE Aldy, 'The Value of a Statistical Life: A Critical Review of Market Estimates throughout the World' (2003) 27(1) *Journal of Risk and Uncertainty* 5.

[15] D McFadden and K Train, *Contingent Valuation of Environmental Goods: A Comprehensive Critique* (Cheltenham, Edward Elgar, 2017).

[16] Following Schumpeter, 'nobody values bread according to the quantity of it which is to be found in his country or in the world, but everybody measures the utility of it according to the amount that he has himself, and this in turn depends on his general means'. See J Schumpeter, 'On the Concept of Social Value' (1908–09) 23 *Quarterly Journal of Economics* 2013. See, eg, H Hovenkamp, 'The Limits of Preference-Based Legal Policy' (1994) 89 *Northwestern University Law Review* 4, 6; L Udehn, 'The Changing Face of Methodological Individualism' (2002) 28 *Annual Review of Sociology* 479, 484, GM Hodgson, 'Meanings of Methodological Individualism' (2007) 14(2) *Journal of Economic Methodology* 211; and RB Ahdieh, 'Beyond Individualism in Law and Economics' (2009) *Emory Public Law Research Paper* No 9-78; *Emory Law and Economics Research Paper* No 9-48.

are unconstrained, and thus market outcomes are efficient; that (almost) everything can be priced based on observed or stated WTP; that income has constant marginal returns and as such distribution is irrelevant; and that happiness does not depend on context, but only on what individuals have. All these assumptions are at least questionable, but does this make CBA a bad tool for policy-making? The answer is not straightforward and would necessarily have to take into account available alternatives to CBA, and in particular their level of complexity. Authoritative Chicago School economists such as Milton Friedman (1957) explicitly rejected any further sophistication of neoclassical economics, which would have undermined its phenomenal predictive power. And Richard Posner followed this approach in proposing an economic analysis of the law, which would basically draw on neoclassical economics to create a fictional world in which individuals always express their preference through market acts. Putting a price on non-market benefits thus ironically became the price to pay to preserve the power and primacy of economics among social sciences—a price that can be considered as very high, in particular when CBA is applied to sensitive issues from the standpoint of fairness, distribution and social justice.[17]

Not surprisingly, the idea that CBA should permeate all aspects of public policy, advocated by scholars like Richard Posner during the 1970s, met with significant resistance across the academic community. Already in the 'Symposium on Efficiency as a Legal Concern' culminated in two issues of the *Hofstra Law Review* in 1980, the use of efficiency criteria (in particular, the Kaldor-Hicks potential Pareto-superiority criterion) in all areas of policy-making, advocated inter alia by Posner, was heavily criticised.[18] While Posner argued that Kaldor-Hicks efficiency (which implies the adoption of net beneficial solutions with no concern for distributional impacts) would be the preferred one by individuals under a 'veil of ignorance' as a guiding principle for governing society as a whole, many other scholars resisted this view by highlighting the major limitations of CBA and potential Pareto superiority, especially in terms of fairness, distribution and justice.[19] More recently, Cass Sunstein used the term 'cost-benefit state' to denote the widespread use of CBA in all aspects of public decision-making.[20] However, in the US, where this debate has reached the highest level of sophistication,

[17] G Calabresi, *The Future of Law and Economics: Essays in Reform and Recollection* (New Haven, Yale University Press, 2016).

[18] Renda, *Impact Assessment*, above n 5.

[19] Posner's 'pre-constitutional view' implied that in all areas of common law, including legal adjudication and government regulation, the real objective should be wealth maximisation; that economic efficiency is the natural way to achieve wealth maximisation; and that this goal is justified on moral grounds as it is a measure (or, better, an 'ancillary paradigm') of justice. The direct consequence of the Posnerian view of efficiency was that efficiency criteria *à la* Pareto (including potential Pareto efficiency or Kaldor-Hicks efficiency) could be justified on ethical grounds. See Renda, *Impact Assessment*, above n 5.

[20] CR Sunstein, 'The Cost-Benefit State', University of Chicago Law School, John M Olin Law & Economics, Working Paper No 39, May 1996.

academics are still debating the issue: the last opportunity for debate was offered by the US Supreme Court's decision in *Michigan v EPA*, in which the Court argued that the Environmental Protection Agency had failed to adequately consider regulatory costs when deciding whether to regulate hazardous air pollutant emissions from power plants. This decision led to enthusiastic statements by the supporters of CBA and to more dismissive replies by the CBA opponents in what became, once again, a debate over the merits of the whole CBA approach.[21]

Since then, the debate has moved forward, mostly in the direction of modifying CBA to incorporate more methodologically and normatively agreeable arrangements, at the same time possibly increasing the complexity of the method (eg, utilitarian social welfare functions and accounting for inter-individual effects), radically simplifying it to allow for its application by civil servants[22] or entirely replacing it with allegedly better alternatives (eg, fair allocation approaches and equality of opportunities approaches). Most notably from a methodological perspective, the direct measurement of subjective well-being and happiness made significant progress,[23] but its operationalisation in public policy-making would probably require its simplification in many government contexts. At the same time, research on distribution and inequality[24] has eventually become more applied and has spurred a discussion on possible alternative social welfare functions, for example in the context of the World Bank's Shared Prosperity agenda and more recently in the debate on the Sustainable Development Goals.[25]

That said, it is fair to state that a very limited number of practical alternatives to the use of CBA in regulatory policy have emerged to date. All of them have pros and cons, of course. For example, cost-effectiveness analysis (CEA) is often preferred by the critics of CBA, as it does not imply the monetisation of benefits. Benefits can be quantified in other metrics, and then CEA will compare alternative options based on the cost per unit of benefit (for example, the monetary cost of every life saved or the cost per quality-adjusted-life-year (QALY)).[26] But in most circumstances, CEA is less appropriate than CBA as it does not imply a calculation of the net addition to well-being and it can then lead to choosing alternatives that are less beneficial for society if it displays a higher benefit-cost ratio. Likewise, feasibility analysis has been proposed, especially in the US, as a more 'moral'

[21] https://www.theregreview.org/2016/09/26/debate-cost-benefit-analysis.

[22] C Carrigan and S Shapiro, 'What's Wrong with the Back of the Envelope? A Call for Simple (and Timely) Benefit-Cost Analysis' (2017) 11 *Regulation & Governance* 203.

[23] Adler and Fleurbaey, above n 1.

[24] A Atkinson, *Inequality: What Can Be Done?* (Cambridge, MA, Harvard University Press, 2015).

[25] World Bank, *Policy Research Report 2014: A Measured Approach to Ending Poverty and Boosting Shared Prosperity: Concepts, Data, and the Twin Goals*, available at http://www.worldbank.org/en/topic/measuringpoverty/publication/a-measured-approach-to-ending-poverty-and-boosting-shared-prosperity.

[26] The QALY is a generic measure of disease burden, used in economic evaluation to assess the value for money of medical interventions. One QALY equates to one year in perfect health. See, eg, PJ Neumann, *Using Cost-Effectiveness Analysis to Improve Health Care* (New York, Oxford University Press, 2005).

alternative to CBA, particularly for those statutes in which Congress directs the agency to reduce a risk to the extent 'feasible', or to the 'maximum' extent, with no mention of costs;[27] this method operates mostly with technology-based assessments and was criticised for being unable to offer consistent methodological guidance.[28] Other alternatives include the measurement of macroeconomic impacts and general equilibrium analyses, the application of prioritarian social welfare functions, capabilities-based approaches and more generally various blends of multi-criteria analysis, in a debate that parallels that occurring at the more macro-level on possible alternatives to GDP measurement.[29]

All these methods have advantages and disadvantages: the debate on their possible introduction is mirrored by slow but significant adjustments in the economic analysis of regulation and by a progressive blurring of the boundaries between CBA and alternative, often simpler methods for justifying regulation. More specifically, in the US, the Trump administration seems to be focusing almost exclusively on cost minimisation, despite the administration's efforts to show continued interest in regulatory benefits.[30] In the UK, emphasis on CBA in *ex ante* Impact Assessment and *ex post* evaluation have been gradually accompanied, and almost replaced, by a renewed attention for regulatory budgeting and cost-focused stock-flow linkage rules such as 'one in, three out'. In Australia, Mexico and Canada, similar trends are observed, with CBA gradually losing ground to red-tape reduction strategies.[31]

CBA AND THE EU BETTER REGULATION AGENDA

The European Commission has endorsed CBA as a method to assess the impacts of new EU policy initiatives since the early days of its Better Regulation Agenda.

[27] A Sinden, DA Kysar and DM Driesen, 'Cost-Benefit Analysis: New Foundations on Shifting Sand' (2009) 3 *Regulation & Governance* 48; and DK Kysar, *Regulating from Nowhere: Environmental Law and the Search for Objectivity* (New Haven, Yale University Press, 2010).

[28] MIT Professor Nicholas Ashford proposed an alternative termed 'trade-off analysis', which however meaningful has not been implemented to date in federal agencies. N Ashford, 'The Legacy of the Precautionary Principle in U.S. Law: The Rise of Cost-Benefit Analysis and Risk Assessment as Undermining Factors in Health, Safety and Environmental Protection' in N de Sadeleer (ed), *Implementation the Precautionary Principle: Approaches from the Nordic Countries, the EU and the United States* (London, Earthscan, 2007). See also JS Masur and EA Posner, 'Against Feasibility Analysis' (2010) 77 *University of Chicago Law Review* 657; University of Chicago Law & Economics, Olin Working Paper No 480; University of Chicago, Public Law Working Paper No 274.

[29] D Philipsen, *The Little Big Number: How GDP Came to Rule the World and What to Do about it* (Princeton, Princeton University Press, 2015); P Schreyer, 'Cost-Benefit Analysis' in Adler and Fleurbaey, above n 1.

[30] See the letter from 95 economists and legal scholars, critiquing EO13771 for focusing only on costs, at https://www.eenews.net/assets/2017/05/24/document_gw_07.pdf. And see also N Ashford, 'Trump Rejects Science, Technology, Economics, and the Constitution with His Two-for-One Executive Order' *Huffington Post* (1 February 2017).

[31] See A Renda, 'Introducing EU Reduction Targets on Regulatory Costs: A Feasibility Study' (2017) *Study for RegWatchEurope*, forthcoming.

The 2002 Communication on Impact Assessment took a relatively cautious stance on the method to be used to perform the analysis of alternative policy options, stating that 'a number of analytical methods can be used to assess impacts. They differ in concept and coverage (eg cost-benefit analysis, cost-effectiveness analysis, compliance cost analysis, multi-criteria analysis and risk assessment)' and that 'the choice of method and the level of detail will vary with the nature of the problem and judgments about feasibility'.[32] Interestingly, the Commission also added that 'when assessing impacts, strict cost-benefit analysis may not always supply the most relevant information; for example, the degree of irreversibility should also be considered'; the Communication went on to advocate the use of the precautionary principle when appropriate[33] and the impact on established policy objectives where available.[34] However, already in 2004, in relaunching the Impact Assessment system, the Commission clarified that the analysis of prospective economic, social and environmental impacts should occur first qualitatively, and possibly with monetisation of impacts, covering 'not only the costs associated with the proposal but also its expected benefits over time'.[35] However, the revised 2009 guidelines attached more importance to CBA by mandating that for the most important (so-called cross-cutting) initiatives, after an initial qualitative analysis, a quantitative/monetary estimate of expected benefits and costs be provided where feasible. At the same time, methodological guidance remained open to the use of other methods such as CEA and multi-criteria analysis (MCA): the Commission clarified that 'full cost-benefit analysis should be used when the most significant part of both costs and benefits can be quantified and monetised, and when there is a certain degree of choice as regards the extent to which objectives should be met … a measure is considered to be justified where net benefits can be expected from the intervention'.[36]

The new 2015 Better Regulation Toolbox led to a more nuanced approach of the Commission towards CBA, which is featured as one of many methodologies that could be used to assess the impacts of prospective policy initiatives. CBA is described as having 'significant potential to identify and inspire efficient regulatory choices, but is subject to several weaknesses, related to its relative ignorance of distributional impacts, its reliance on income as a proxy for utility and happiness, and a number of other underlying assumptions, which can prove detrimental for the accuracy of the whole exercise'.[37] As also recommended by an ad hoc

[32] http://eur-lex.europa.eu/legal-content/EN/TXT/?uri=CELEX:52002DC0276.

[33] On the compatibility between CBA and the precautionary principle, see, eg, D Driesen, 'Cost-Benefit Analysis and the Precautionary Principle: Can They Be Reconciled?' (2013) *Michigan State Law Review* 771.

[34] ibid.

[35] http://ec.europa.eu/smart-regulation/impact/key_docs/docs/sec_2004_1377_en.pdf.

[36] See http://ec.europa.eu/smart-regulation/impact/commission_guidelines/docs/iag_2009_en.pdf.

[37] See http://ec.europa.eu/smart-regulation/guidelines/docs/br_toolbox_en.pdf.

study that contributed to the new guidelines,[38] CBA is indicated as an appropriate method only under specific circumstances, in particular when at least all direct benefits and direct costs can be monetised, the magnitude of impacts justifies the effort and time needed to perform CBA, and distributional impacts are unlikely to be substantial. In all other circumstances, CEA, least-cost analysis or MCA is indicated as preferable to CBA.

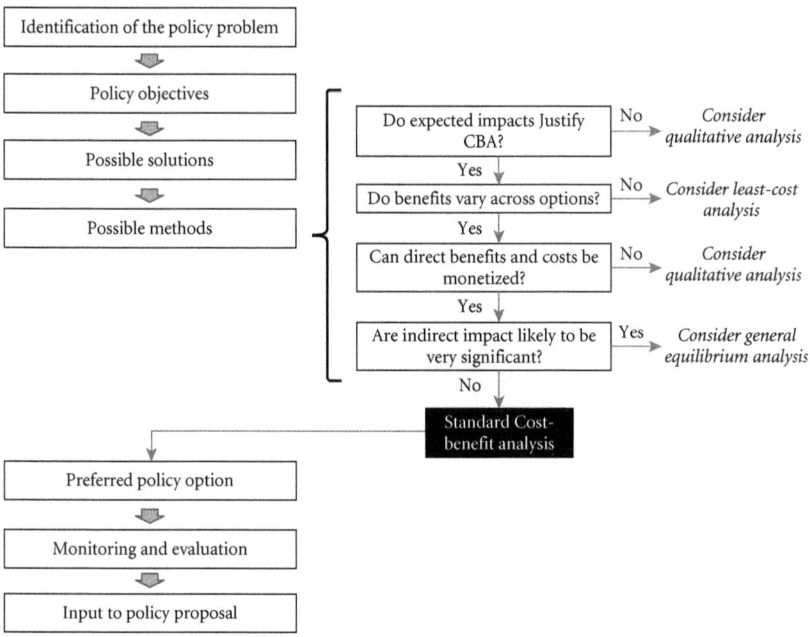

Figure 4.1: CBA within the Impact Assessment process

Source: A Renda, G Luchetta, L Schrefler and R Zavatta, *Assessing the Costs and Benefits of Regulation*, Study for the European Commission's Secretariat General, 2013.

Over the past few years, and even more so after the adoption of the Better Regulation package in May 2015, emphasis has been increasingly placed on the need to quantify both benefits and costs where possible, as also demonstrated by the recent Annual Report of the new Regulatory Scrutiny Board, which shows relatively encouraging data on the degree of quantification of costs and benefits in the Commission.[39] On the other hand, the system has become more fragmented and multi-dimensional, with operational guidance issued on a widely diverse set

[38] A Renda, G Luchetta, L Schrefler and R Zavatta, *Assessing the Costs and Benefits of Regulation*, Study for the European Commission's Secretariat General, 2013.

[39] See https://ec.europa.eu/info/sites/info/files/2016-rsb-report_en.pdf.

of impacts (fundamental rights, competitiveness and micro-enterprises, employment etc), and with increased pressure on the Commission to go in widely different directions, such as adopting net reduction targets for compliance costs and mainstreaming the sustainable development goals into the policy process.[40]

In summary, the Commission has never officially endorsed CBA as the key method to be used in *ex ante* Impact Assessment of policies, contrary to what has happened in the US for many types of federal regulation. The Commission has made more systematic use and reference to CBA in the appraisal of spending programmes and investment projects, and even more in specific fields such as regional policy and transport.[41]

The European Commission has completed more than 1,000 Impact Assessments since 2003. Looking at these documents, the use of real fully fledged CBAs seems to have been relatively limited. Some of the available empirical literature on this issue is summarised below:

- A comparison of the US Regulatory Impact Analyses (RIAs) produced between 1982 and 1999 and EU Impact Assessments completed between 2003 and 2007[42] found that US RIAS monetised at least some benefits in 51 per cent of cases, whereas only 34 per cent of EU ones did, and that 68 per cent of US RIAs calculated net benefits or cost-effectiveness compared to 26 per cent of EU ones (although for the most important binding initiatives, the EU percentage went significantly up to 64 per cent).
- A comparison between EU and UK IAs completed in the period 2005–10 showed that the extent to which IAs assessed net benefits or cost-effectiveness was greater for the EU in 2005, and after peaking in 2008 declined significantly in 2009–10, contrary to what occurred in the UK.[43]
- Overall, a quick glance through all Impact Assessments completed in the 2002–17 timeframe reveals that the Commission often and increasingly engages in the quantification of at least some benefits and costs, but quite systematically refrains from calculating net benefits. Even less common is the calculation of the net present value of alternatives, which lies at the core of CBA. Only a few Directorates General in the European Commission actually engage in such an exercise.
- The European Commission also displays a tendency to use CEA in lieu of CBA, which is in many cases inappropriate from a methodological perspective, especially if benefits calculated in the CEA are monetised. These two

[40] See Renda, above n 31.

[41] https://www.eufunds.bg/archive/documents/1295270958.pdf; http://www.tide-innovation.eu/en/upload /Results/ T495_ TIDE-Assessment-Handbook-Lite.pdf.

[42] C Cecot, RW Hahn, A Renda and L Schrefler, 'An Evaluation of the Quality of Impact Assessment in the European Union with Lessons for the US and the EU' (2008) 2(4) *Regulation & Governance* 405.

[43] O Fritsch, CM Radaelli, L Schrefler and A Renda, 'Comparing the Content of Regulatory Impact Assessments in the UK and the EU' (2013) 33(6) *Public Money & Management* 445.

techniques, normally considered as substitute methods by Impact Assessments guidelines (including the EU ones), yield very different results in reality. While CEA can be considered preferable to the calculation of net benefits since it avoids the substantial problems created by the monetisation of benefits, the Commission actually uses it to compare monetised costs with monetised benefits, actually defeating its advantages. This can lead the Commission to express a preference for more conservative policy options, which entail very small compliance costs compared to the baseline.[44]

In summary, the use of CBA in the European Commission is neither systematic nor frequent. Both the official guidance documents and the practice of IA suggest that CBA is not the reference method used by the Commission to reach its decisions on future policies. Rather, the Commission uses a variety of methods (with certain Directorates General more inclined to using specific methods instead of others)[45] and very often relies on the quantification/monetisation of costs and benefits as a step towards the determination of these policy alternatives that appear most effective in achieving the stated goals of its proposals. In other words, the approach adopted by the European Commission in its *ex ante* Impact Assessment system appears to be de facto converging towards the framework used for *ex post* evaluation (where efficiency is given the same weight as effectiveness, relevance, coherence and EU added value) more than towards a CBA framework. In this respect, the Commission has developed a specific multi-criteria analysis framework, which awaits further specification and is very far from the original CBA model.

The reasons for supporting a departure from CBA in the European Commission are many. First, the scope of the Commission's Impact Assessment system is very different, and much broader, compared to the scope of Impact Assessments completed in the US, Australia, Mexico or the UK. As a matter of fact, the recent extension of the Impact Assessment system to implementing and delegated acts, together with the Impact Assessment practice of some agencies (in particular in the financial sector) has created more overlaps between these systems.[46] But CBA may be worth pursuing only for a subset of the implementing and delegated acts

[44] Suffice it to recall two recent examples: the impact assessment of the Directive on periodic roadworthiness tests (2012) and the impact assessment on the Proposal for a Regulation on Requirements relating to Emission limits and Type-approval for Internal Combustion Engines for Non-road Mobile Machinery (2014). In both cases, the Commission ended up choosing on the basis of CEA (benefits/costs) an option that would have been discarded under CBA (benefits—costs), with negative consequences for the stringency of the resulting rules. More generally, while using these alternative techniques can provide some flexibility in accepting policies otherwise rejected under a strict net benefits approach, they suffer from several problems, including monetising conventions of questionable validity and time-discounting practices, which bias choices against long-term outcomes.

[45] See A Renda, 'European Union' in CA Dunlop and CM Radaelli (eds), *The Edward Elgar Handbook of Regulatory Impact Assessment* (Cheltenham, Edward Elgar, 2016).

[46] See A Renda, 'From Impact Assessment to the Policy Cycle: Drawing Lessons from the EU'S Better-Regulation Agenda' (2016) 9(33) University of Calgary School of Public Policy Technical Paper.

and for a subset of the policy initiatives. In most cases, other methods will be preferable.

Second, the EU Impact Assessment system is explicitly designed to achieve consistency with the Commission's priorities or medium-term goals (currently, Juncker's 10 priorities in the future the 2030 Agenda for Sustainable Development).[47] This means that the major initiatives that undergo Impact Assessment will most likely have far-reaching social and environmental impacts, as well as impacts on fundamental rights. The need to test the new initiatives for policy coherence and consistency with medium-term goals in turn determines a need to emphasise the role of policy objectives in the IA. This is clearly reflected in the need to specify the general, specific and operational objectives of all new initiatives, and to pre-select alternative policy options based on their ability to achieve such objectives rather than based on the likelihood that they will solve the market or regulatory failures identified in the section on problem definition.

Third, since 2009, the Commission has advocated the combined use of *ex ante* Impact Assessment and *ex post* evaluation to enable a more complete appraisal of policy outcomes and impacts during the policy cycle. After the introduction of the 'evaluate first' principle, which mandated that an *ex post* evaluation be carried out before any new Impact Assessment, in October 2010 the Communication on 'Smart Regulation' reinforced and relaunched the importance of Better Regulation throughout the policy cycle. Still, since then the methodologies for *ex ante* Impact Assessment and *ex post* evaluation have remained different, and are still subject to rather different sections of the Better Regulation guidelines. However, since the European Commission is moving away from the use of CBA or other specific methods in its *ex ante* IAs, such divergence might be reconsidered to achieve more consistency between the *ex ante* and *ex post* analysis. In particular, to borrow language from a (still-pending) bipartisan proposed bill presented in the US Congress last year,[48] the *ex ante* Impact Assessment could more explicitly be transformed into a 'prospective retrospective review', which anticipated and facilitates *ex post* evaluation. Were this to be the case, the Commission services would then be called to already specify during the *ex ante* phase the main elements of effectiveness, efficiency (including CBA where appropriate), relevance, coherence and EU added value of new major initiatives. On that basis, both monitoring and evaluation could enable more direct policy learning effects by facilitating the comparison between the *ex ante* Impact Assessment and the *ex post* evaluation.

Fourth, such a partial move away from methods like CBA could also facilitate the Commission in embracing so-called adaptive regulation, in particular

[47] See Commission Communication, 'Better Regulation for Better Results', May 2015; for a comment, see A Renda, 'Too Good to Be True? A Quick Assessment of the European Commission's New Better Regulation Package' 108 (2015) CEPS Special Report. Available at SSRN http://ssrn.com/abstract=2613343.

[48] https://www.congress.gov/bill/114th-congress/senate-bill/1817.

when it comes to emerging technologies for which it is difficult to provide a fully informed prospective assessment. Technologies like artificial intelligence and the Internet of Things are so rapidly evolving that policy-makers are placed in a state of continual adaptive IA, or constant ongoing market monitoring, rather than being able to rely on an *ex ante* and *ex post* phase. This is even truer in the case of EU institutions.

Finally, other EU institutions are not primarily relying on CBA to assess their major amendments or the Commission's initial proposals. The European Parliamentary Research Services (EPRS) is producing a significant amount of *ex ante* Impact Assessment and *ex post* evaluation, but most of these documents do not contain a complete CBA. As a matter of fact, as already observed by Ashford and Renda,[49] the EPRS could increase its impact on the work of the Members of the European Parliament if it adopted a more coherence-oriented approach to policy evaluation. And the Council of the EU could rely on such an approach to more usefully inform the decisions of the various Council formations.

TOWARDS CONVERGENCE BETWEEN *EX ANTE* IMPACT ASSESSMENT AND *EX POST* EVALUATION METHODS IN THE EU?

Some scholars would argue that having a RIA system based on CBA is ideal, whereas others argue that it is at least better than having no system at all. In the case of the European Commission, it seems that the adoption of CBA has been partial, and the use of CBA has been patchy and *sui generis* during the 15 years that have elapsed since the first completed Impact Assessment. Meanwhile, the EU Better Regulation toolbox has become much richer and articulate, bringing a more *nuanced* approach to the identification of positive and negative impacts of regulation, without necessarily requiring or even recommending the monetisation of all impacts or the direct calculation of the net present value of policy alternatives.

This chapter argued that this is a welcome feature of the EU system, well aligned with its peculiarities, and that further clarifications and more explicit methodological guidance in this direction would make the EU Better Regulation Agenda even more attractive and world-class than it is today. At the very least, the adoption of consistent methods for the *ex ante* and *ex post* evaluation of policy initiatives would at once enable more direct policy learning, more adaptive regulation and more accountability for the Commission and other EU institutions. More specifically, working with a common monitoring and evaluation scheme and engaging in prospective retrospective review may strengthen accountability by facilitating

[49] N Ashford and A Renda, *Aligning Policies for Low-Carbon Systemic Innovation in Europe*, Report for the European Climate Foundation's Institute for Industrial Innovation and Competitiveness (i24c), November 2016.

the identification of policy changes (including amendments and implementation measures by Member States and local governments) that have generated positive or negative impacts.

Furthermore, stronger emphasis on coherence with medium-term goals would help EU institutions stay away from ill-advised deregulatory approaches, enabling a more direct focus on the achievement of the 2030 goals. A closer look reveals a number of outstanding challenges for the Better Regulation Agenda to really embrace in relation to the sustainable development goals included in the Europe 2030 Agenda. As a matter of fact, the EU Better Regulation guidelines could guide the Commission services (and the EPRS) in measuring policy impacts in terms of Sustainable Development Goals (SDGs), and the distance from the goals set for 2030. This would end up involving several phases of the Commission's *ex ante* Impact Assessment work, from problem definition to the monitoring and evaluation strategy.

Finally, explicitly departing from CBA would not mean that EU institutions would cease to identify and where possible quantify the positive and negative impacts of policy alternatives. Rather, it implies that quantification and monetisation are no longer imposed on services that have to handle non-market, hard-to-quantify impacts such as impacts on fundamental rights. Such a move may strengthen the ownership of the Better Regulation Agenda and its integration with other pillars of policy-making in all EU institutions. It would occur at a time in which academics increasingly ask for an improvement (when not a complete replacement) of the standard CBA framework; and government experiment with more specific screens such as cost reduction strategies and targets. And it would make the EU Better Regulation Agenda even more unique and more tailored to the needs of a project that needs consistency and salience in order to be successfully relaunched.

5

The Better Regulation Agenda and the Deactivation of EU Competences

Limits and Opportunities

ROBERT ZBÍRAL*

INTRODUCTION: THE PREVALENT NOTION OF 'EVER CLOSER UNION'?

THE BETTER REGULATION Agenda is often viewed as a somewhat technical endeavour that at best only indirectly touches on the destiny of the integration process. I do not contest that opinion—it is easily supported by empirical evidence. While other EU-related topics such as the threat of the collapse of the eurozone or the boom in the influx of immigrants have dominated the public discourse for the last couple of years, debate on Better Regulation seems to be reserved for connoisseurs of EU legislative process. However, the principal thesis of my contribution is that Better Regulation Agenda might also serve as an instrument affecting one of the core issues of EU framework: the division of competences between the EU and its Member States. Specifically, the main goal of the chapter is explore the link between the Better Regulation Agenda and the process of deactivation of EU competences.

Since the founding of the European Community almost 70 years ago, the integration process has largely succumbed to the mindset of deepening cooperation, entrenched in primary law with the famous phrase of 'ever closer Union'. There were obviously also periods of slowdown, but these were dealt as mere temporary *obstacles en route* to a common (federal) goal. The situation has changed in the new millennium. EU membership has grown to 28 states with very diverse characteristics and ensuing distinct interests—most agreements become very

* Robert Zbíral is Assistant Professor, Faculty of Law, Masaryk University, Brno, Czech Republic.
Support from the Czech Grant Agency is acknowledged (Grant No 17-03806S).

costly. On the other hand, the EU has been asked to tackle an ever-expanding list of crises. These two diverging vectors stretch the EU's resources to the limits and question its ability to meet the demands of both Member States and EU citizens, which consequently undermines the legitimacy of the EU. The result of the British referendum brought about a shocking collapse of the ever closer Union narrative. There is no space to discuss in detail the reasons behind this unfortunate outcome, but one of the most prevalent drivers was a feeling that 'the EU meddles too much with too many issues with too little efficiency'. Indeed, requests 'for doing less better' and an accompanying restoration of some competences to the Member States formed the cornerstone of demands from numerous British politicians as a condition for continuing membership of the EU.[1]

Obviously it is impossible to make a causal claim that the dominance of one dimensional transfer of competences within the EU contributed to the withdrawal of the UK. But, contrarily, given that the notion of 'ever closer Union' did not persuade a Member State from leaving, maybe it is no longer sustainable to assume that any renationalisation endangers the fate of the integration process? In the end, the integration is hardly a pure natural force with a predetermined course. Many theories of federalism acknowledge that due to changing external and internal pressures, the allocation of competences between the centre and the states in federations is in constant flux. While centralisation prevails in the majority of federations, the restoration of tasks to lower levels has quite often occurred in practice as well without any disruptive effects.[2] Also within the EU, the idea of renationalisation was floated in the past, for example, by Jacques Delors during the prolonged ratification of the Maastricht Treaty.[3] Currently it forms part of the discourse of many mainstream political forces in the EU and has noticeable support among a considerable number of EU citizens. Last but definitely not least, as the next section will elaborate upon in more detail, restoration is legally imprinted into the fabric of primary law after the Lisbon Treaty reforms.

This chapter's first section conceptualises the framework of restoration of competences and due to the nature of Better Regulation, the concept of deactivation deserves most attention. The next section assesses the position of the concept within the Better Regulation framework—in other words, it assesses how and why the agenda's instruments might contribute to the deactivation of EU competences. The penultimate section presents and evaluates the empirical outcomes of the Better Regulation Agenda, including the data from the latest legislative outputs of EU institutions. The final section provides a conclusion.

[1] One must admit that the requests were usually only general, without any specific proposals: see, eg, D Cameron, 'David Cameron's EU Speech—Full Text' *The Guardian* (23 January 2013).

[2] eg, the new federalism movement in the US or the educational reforms in Germany in 2006.

[3] See D Obdradovic, 'Repatriation of Powers in the European Community' (1997) 34 *Common Market Law Review* 59, 76–77.

RESTORING TASKS TO MEMBER STATES: THE CONCEPTUAL FRAMEWORK WITH THE EMPHASIS ON THE DEACTIVATION OF COMPETENCES

Despite the intensity of debate on EU competences, the term itself remains ambiguous, even if one leaves aside the confusing distinction between power/competence in the EU law doctrine.[4] Primary law does not define what the competence means.[5] In my view it is useful to distinguish between EU competence based on primary law (area of competences, legal basis, such as transport in Article 91 TFEU) and the exercise of EU competence through acts of secondary law (concrete measures, such as the duty to use tachographs for certain vehicles according to Regulation No 165/2014).

I conceptualise renationalisation as a process in which the competences previously transferred or exercised by the EU are restored to the Member States. I emphasise the word 'restore', the applied concept therefore excludes mechanisms such as opt-outs or negative competences (eg, Article 344 of the Treaty on the Functioning of the European Union (TFEU)) because they instead guard the state(s) against future EU action. In light of the presented concepts, there are in principle two options of how to renationalise. The first has a constitutional dimension and occurs when a part of or the whole legal basis is removed from primary law (see Article 48 of the Treaty on European Union (TEU)) and due to the principle of conferral (Article 4/1 TEU) is therefore reallocated to the Member States. I call this possibility the repatriation (retrieval) of competence. The second option has a legislative dimension and takes place when the EU stops exercising its competence(s)/concrete measure(s). The competence itself (legal basis) is not returned; the EU only decides to discontinue regulating a matter within the given field. This situation is labelled deactivation in my framework.[6]

As the scope of the Better Regulation Agenda encompasses the realm of secondary legislation, I will further deal solely with the process of deactivation. Primary law empowers the EU institutions to intervene in a number of fields, which the Lisbon Treaty helpfully (albeit imperfectly) categorised into three categories. Deactivation does not have any effect in the case of exclusive competences, because the Member States are precluded from seizing these fields even if the EU stops exercising its competences (see implicitly Article 2/1 TFEU). Similarly irrelevant for our analysis is deactivation in case of supporting competences, as Member States could continue to regulate these fields concurrently and independently from the EU (see Article 2(5) TFEU). That leaves us with shared competences, by far the largest category of EU intervention.

[4] See, eg, F Mayer, 'The Debate on European Powers and Competencies: Seeing Trees But Not the Forest?' (2003) *WHI Paper* 1, 3–4.

[5] See L Azoulai (ed), *The Question of Competence in the European Union* (Oxford, Oxford University Press, 2014), particularly the contributions by Beaud and Tusseau.

[6] See the detailed account of the concepts in R Zbíral, 'Restoring Tasks from the European Union to Member States: A Bumpy Road to an Unclear Destination?' (2015) 52 *CMLR* 51, 55–60.

The following rules control the category under Article 2(2) TFEU: 'When the Treaties confer on the Union a competence shared with the Member States in a specific area, the Union and the Member States may legislate and adopt legally binding acts in that area. The Member States shall exercise their competence to the extent that the Union has not exercised its competence. The Member States shall again exercise their competence to the extent that the Union has decided to cease exercising its competence.' The provision's interpretation seems unambiguous: once the EU decides to legislate on and regulate a certain issue, the Member States have to retreat. Conversely, if the EU opts to no longer regulate the given issue and the competence is deactivated, the Member States may step in again. In practice the situation is often not so clear-cut as the question of the scope of EU intervention might arise. In order to limit the pre-emption of EU action, representatives of the Member States at the 2007 Intergovernmental Conference adopted Protocol No 25, which states that 'when the Union has taken action in a certain area, the scope of this exercise of competence only covers those elements governed by the Union act in question and therefore does not cover the whole area'.[7] However, this provision merely serves as an interpretative tool in borderline cases—the actual scope is always delineated by the relevant legislative act.

Primary law indicates what procedure the EU should follow in order 'to cease exercising its competence'. The cleanest option is to repeal the secondary legislative act on which the EU measure is based. Consequently, the EU (properly) retreats and the 'elements governed by the Union act in question' might be regulated by the Member States again. Repeals correspond to the wording of Article 2(2) TFEU and are expressly highlighted as the most suitable tools for this purpose in Declaration No 18.[8] Obviously, the repeal of the whole legislative act does not represent the only scenario of deactivation; the same logic applies if the EU institutions decide to repeal just a certain part of the act backing the EU intervention. Because the Founding Treaties do not contain any specific provisions for repealing secondary legislation, the repeal shall follow the same procedural requirements as the adoption of the original act.

I have to again emphasise here the rather narrow definition of 'deactivation' in this chapter. In this sense it shall be distinguished from wider concepts such as dismantling, which is defined as 'cutting, diminution or removal of existing policy'.[9] While dismantling at the EU level formally covers deactivation as well, it chiefly encompasses the scaling back of the scope or density of action regardless of the intervening subject, thus limiting both the EU and the Member States.[10]

[7] Sole article of Protocol (No 25) on exercise of Shared Competence [2010] OJ C83/207.

[8] Declaration (No 18) in relation to the delimitation of competences [2010] OJ C83/344.

[9] A Jordan, MW Bauer and C Green-Pedersen, 'Policy Dismantling' (2013) 20 *Journal of European Public Policy* 795, 795.

[10] V Gravey and A Jordan, 'Does the European Union Have a Reverse Gear? Policy Dismantling in a Hyperconsensual Polity' (2016) 23 *Journal of European Public Policy* 1180, 1181–82.

Other authors would probably call this latter process deregulation. Deactivation will also not be mixed with reverse delegation, a situation in which the EU, acting within a conferred competence, instructs the Member States to regulate selected issues. While the national administrations are awarded a certain (sometimes even quite wide) amount of discretion, they still play the role of mere EU agents.[11]

THE POSITION OF DEACTIVATION IN THE FRAMEWORK OF THE BETTER REGULATION AGENDA

Deactivation as enshrined in Article 2(2) TFEU aims to repeal secondary legislation on which EU intervention is based and to open the vacated space to the discretion of the Member States. A decision to proceed along the described path may result from a political (subjective) will of the EU institutions that some matter shall no longer be exercised at the EU level and rather will be returned to the national level. But the reasons behind deactivation may be objective as well. Because of changing external or internal conditions, even a well-meant measure (or its part) may gradually become ineffective, irrelevant or onerous, or will simply not address the initial objective. This section describes how the Better Regulation Agenda seeks to evaluate the impact of legislation and while deactivation is not the only option in terms of how to react to 'problematic' legislation, the concept shall be taken as a feasible one.

Other chapters in this book explore various aspects of the Better Regulation Agenda and demonstrate its multi-dimensional nature. One of the core elements of the programme treats the legislative process as an ongoing exercise that does not end with the publication of the act in the Official Journal. The later phases of the policy cycle (implementation and application) are as vital as the earlier ones (preparation and adoption). Reflecting this, the Commission states unequivocally: 'it is important that every single measure in the EU's rulebook is fit for purpose, modern, effective, proportionate, operational and as simple as possible'.[12] In order to ascertain the continuing fulfilment of these (objective) criteria, an *ex post* review of legislation controlling the measure needs to be performed.

The basic idea of *ex post* evaluation is to gather evidence on how the given EU action has performed in practice, namely in comparison with initiate predictions. The importance of the practice was first emphasised in the Maldenkern Report in 2001[13] and was consequently embraced by the Commission in its various Better Regulation initiatives that have been implemented ever since. In 2012, the Regulatory Fitness and Performance Programme (REFIT) was launched with the objective to continuously review the whole stock of the *acquis* and ensure that it

[11] See Case 239/86 *Ireland v Commission* [1987] ECR 554, para 13.

[12] Commission, 'Better Regulation for Better Results—An EU Agenda' COM (2015) 215 final, 4.

[13] Commission, 'Mandelkern Group on Better Regulation: Final Report', 13 November 2001, 12.

was 'fit for purpose'.[14] This goal is accomplished either through review of single legislative acts or so-called fitness checks that comprehensively evaluate an interconnected set of measures within the wider policy area (eg, the protection of EU fresh water resources). The growing prominence of *ex post* evaluations of existing legislation was confirmed in the 2016 Interinstitutional Agreement on Better Law-Making, which contains the following obligation: 'In the context of the legislative cycle, evaluations of existing legislation and policy, based on efficiency, effectiveness, relevance, coherence and value added, should provide the basis for impact assessments of options for further action.'[15] All the main EU legislative actors therefore pledged to support the objective reviews of the existing EU interventions (legislation).

The above-mentioned statement from the Commission and the Interinstitutional Agreement indicates the criteria on which the review shall focus. If we elaborate on the delineation in the latter document, effectiveness explores whether and to what extent the original aims of the activity were met, efficiency weights the cost against the benefits, coherence asks how the activity interacts with other EU interventions and goals, and finally relevance reviews if the activity is still necessary and required. Because of the diverging impact of the activity on affected subjects and their interests, evaluation needs to be independent, transparent and based on sound empirical evidence in order to be persuasive.[16] Overall, given the variance of the monitored criteria, it is not hard to imagine an outcome of *ex post* review that will mark the intervention as 'not fit for purpose'.

I left the 'value added' criterion for separate discussion. Its aim is to investigate if the continuing EU action is preferable to intervention at the lower levels, namely by the Member States.[17] Obviously, the EU added value largely represents only a different language label for what is commonly known as the principle of subsidiarity. While the review of previous criteria may equally result in deactivation, subsidiarity links directly with the core of the concept. The attitude of the Commission to the evaluation of subsidiarity in *ex post* reviews of EU legislation used to be somewhat cautious, particularly if we compare it to the high level of attention dedicated to the evaluation of subsidiarity in the initial parts of the policy cycle. Even nowadays the hesitant approach resurfaces: notice the omission of subsidiarity in the list of criteria in the Commission's statement above and, in addition, the discussion on the EU added value only tiptoes around the subsidiarity principle. The current consensus is that subsidiarity does not end with a one-off exercise performed before the legislative proposal is adopted; all EU activities must meet the principle's requirements throughout their whole lifetime.

[14] See Commission, 'EU Regulatory Fitness' COM (2012) 746 final.

[15] Interinstitutional Agreement between the European Parliament, the Council of the European Union and the European Commission on Better Law-Making [2016] OJ L123/1, para 22.

[16] See in detail Commission, 'Better Regulation Guidelines' SWD (2015) 111 final, 53–61.

[17] ibid 3.

Indeed, Declaration No 18 expressly states that a legislative act that no longer respects subsidiarity shall be deactivated[18] and the importance of the principle in *ex post* reviews is also emphasised by academic sources.[19]

Any thorough *ex post* evaluation of a legislative act (or a policy field) is a demanding and costly task. The evaluating subject, usually represented by the Commission, might therefore review only a limited amount of legislation at any given time. The selection may have important political repercussions, but at the same time shall be backed by some objective criteria. The process would make little sense if acts (probably) no longer fit for purpose survive by being omitted from evaluation. The arbitrariness of choice can be prevented by the incorporation of special clauses into the legislative act that is targeted for review. A more radical version—the sunset clause—represents a provision in an act stipulating that the act becomes invalid after a given period of time unless the legislature agrees to prolong its effect.[20] One might expect that any extension of validity will be accompanied by an Impact Assessment of the previous intervention. A less strict instrument—the review clause—may take different forms, but basically demands evaluation of the effectiveness and impact of the intervention after a certain time period following the act's adoption.[21] Both types of clauses are commonly used in democracies around the world;[22] however, at the same time, it must be admitted that their application suffers from certain disadvantages and they shall not be incorporated into all legislation.[23] Both instruments have been linked with *ex post* evaluations from the beginning of the Better Regulation Agenda; already in 2003, the Commission promised that 'review or sunset clauses will be proposed in new legal acts wherever appropriate'.[24] The reference to the latter clauses gradually disappeared,[25] but the commitment to review clauses has remained firm—the Commission pledged to 'include systematically in every new act provisions to allow monitoring and future evaluation'[26] and similarly a positive obligation was expressed by all EU institutions in the Interinstitutional Agreement.[27]

[18] See above, n 7.

[19] eg, A Meuwese and P Popelier, 'Legal Implications of Better Regulation: A Special Issue' (2013) 17 *European Public Law* 455, 459.

[20] See, eg, S Ranchordas, *Constitutional Sunsets and Experimental Legislation* (Cheltenham, Edward Elgar, 2015).

[21] Different types of review clauses are discussed in K Weigrich et al, *Wirksamkeit von Sunset Legislation and Evaluationsklauseln* (Gürtersloh, Bertelsmann Stiftung, 2005) 8–9; see also the discussion in I Anglmayer, 'Evaluation and *Ex-post* Impact Assessment at EU Level' (2016) *European Parliament Study PE 581.415*.

[22] Apart from Ranchordas (above n 20), see also B Jantz and S Veit, *Sunset Legislation and Better Regulation: Empirical Evidence from Four Countries* (Güntersloh, Bertelsmann Stiftung, 2010).

[23] See R Kysar, 'Lasting Legislation' (2011) 159 *University of Pennsylvania Law Review* 1007.

[24] Commission, 'Updating and Simplifying the Community Acquis' COM (2003) 71 final, 19.

[25] The Commission concluded that 'review clauses serve a similar purpose whilst presenting a lower risk of legal lacunae'. See Commission, 'Implementing the Community Lisbon Programme: A Strategy for the Simplification of the Regulatory Environment' COM (2005) 535 final, 6.

[26] COM (2015) 215 final, 9.

[27] See above, n 15, para 23.

The analysis confirms the key position of *ex post* evaluations within the Better Regulation Agenda as well as the wider EU framework. All EU measures are continuously required to meet various objective criteria in order to substantiate their validity and existence. If the review finds that the intervention (act) is not fit for purpose, there are four (formal) options in terms of how to proceed:

1) The EU measure in question continues, but is amended in order to address identified deficiencies. This would be the most common option—the scope and aim of the change might vary extensively and could range from small alterations or simplification to a complete recalibration of the original intention.
2) The EU measure in question is deactivated (repealed) at the EU level, but new legislation is adopted that generally precludes the same intervention at the national level. An example would be the current regulation of quantities of products in pre-packed goods. When the original directives from the 1970s on which the EU action was based were repealed in 2007, it was simultaneously determined that neither the EU nor the Member States could set limits on the quantities of these products introduced to the market.[28] Some authors call the results of such a process *les compétences abolies.*[29]
3) The EU measure in question is deactivated (repealed), but other part of the *acquis* continue to affect the exercise of EU competence (the fall-back option). The EU intervention in policy fields is usually multi-layered: there are general measures mixed with more specific ones. Even if certain acts are repealed, it does not always mean that the Member States are free to regulate the issue because there may be constrained by other EU legislative acts that still apply.[30]
4) The EU measure in question is deactivated (repealed) and Member States may regain the space vacated by the deactivated intervention. Only this last alternative represents 'pure' deactivation as conceptualised in this chapter.

All four scenarios represent ideal models and it is probable that a comprehensive review of the whole field (fitness check) or elaborate individual act will lead to the utilisation of a combination or even all options at the same time. Consequently, the formal legislative effect of the reform could be rather difficult to disentangle. Nonetheless, the categorisation verifies that at least formally, the deactivation within the meaning of Article 2(2) TFEU shall be treated as normatively sensible

[28] Directive 2007/45 of the European Parliament and of the Council of 5 September 2007, laying down rules on nominal quantities for prepacked products, repealing Council Directives 75/106/EEC and 80/232/EEC, and amending Council Directive 76/211/EEC [2007] OJ L247/17.

[29] *cf* D Simon, *Le système juridique communautaire*, 3rd edn (Paris, Presses Universitaires de France, 2001) 136–37.

[30] I do not want to complicate the framework further, but we should not forget that the scope of EU influence is wider than the *acquis*—membership of the EU obliged Member States to follow certain principles that restrain all their activities, including those without any link to integration.

and as the anticipated outcome of the Better Regulation Agenda. The next section analyses if this is applied in practice.

THE BETTER REGULATION AGENDA AND THE DEACTIVATION OF EU COMPETENCES: EMPIRICAL EVIDENCE

The deactivation of EU competences shall form a natural part of the Better Regulation Agenda, if only due to the obligation of continuing observance of the subsidiarity principle for all EU interventions. However, if we review the Agenda's documents since its inception in 2002, we see out that deactivation has never really been discussed as a viable objective. Not even the adoption of the Lisbon Treaty with its explicit recognition of the concept changed anything. On the contrary, one may find hints that such a course of action is considered undesirable. In its 2015 communication, the Commission stated that 'Better regulation is not about "more" or "less" EU legislation; nor is it about deregulating' and, still more emphatically, the aim of *ex post* review is described as 'looking back … at the impact the policy actually had on specific sectors, and suggesting ways to lighten the load without reducing the policy ambition'.[31] Similarly, the European Parliament in its report on REFIT stressed out that the 'REFIT programme does not call into question existing policy objectives'.[32] Put simply, the underlying strategy is primarily adjustment, not the discontinuation of EU intervention. On the other hand, it must be admitted that the Commission has consistently promoted *ex post* evaluations and while the endeavour encountered numerous difficulties in practice,[33] the efforts have steadily intensified and currently cover many important policy areas.[34] A question is thus in order: what if deactivation has for some reason not found its way into the stated goals of the Better Regulation Agenda, but is nevertheless performed in practice? To test this assumption, I will present empirical observations on the use of repeals and review clauses in the remainder of this section.

Let us start with an evaluation of repeals as they are directly linked to the logic of deactivation. The Commission has viewed repeals primarily only in a narrow way as a tool for invalidating outdated or obsolete legislation. Nonetheless, initially the Commission was quite enthusiastic about the practice. It identified more than 880 suitable legislative acts by 2003, only to admit later that very few of these had actually been repealed and many departments within the Commission

[31] COM (2015) 215 final, 4, 9.

[32] European Parliament, 'Report on REFIT: State of Play and Outlook (Kaufmann Report)' *A8-0208/2015*, para H.

[33] See, eg, E Mastenbroek, S van Voorst and A Meuwese, 'Closing the Regulatory Cycle? A Meta Evaluation of *Ex-post* Legislative Evaluations by the European Commission' (2016) 23 *Journal of European Public Policy* 1329.

[34] See, eg, the results in Commission, 'Regulatory Fitness and Performance Programme REFIT and the 10 Priorities of the Commission' SWD (2016) 400 final part 2/2.

boycotted the action.[35] The subsequent development is very hard to follow: a report from 2009 suggested that the success of the plan would reduce the *acquis* by about 600 acts,[36] while another communication four years later suddenly surprisingly claimed that 5,590 acts had been repealed since 2005.[37] Unfortunately, none of these figures was backed by a list of repealed legislative acts and thus could not be verified.

Only since 2015 has the Commission started to identify concrete candidates for repeal in its annual Work Programmes. The lists contained nine legislative acts in 2015 (another 13 on a separate list)[38] and 27 acts in the 2016 Programme. Qualitative analysis of the sample together with a check on listed legislative acts in the EUR-Lex database expose interesting findings. Selected acts are unexpectedly mentioned, although they were formally (directly or implicitly) repealed years ago and therefore hardly require any further action. The lists also refer to acts with validity limited only to a certain time period in the past. Sometimes pure formal logic precludes an understanding of why certain other acts are (not) included.[39] In any case, consistently with the cited objective, all the acts on the lists represent 'dead' legislation that was largely temporary and does not currently have any real impact. Even if repealed, the situation would in most cases resemble the above-defined fall-back scenario when other EU legislation continues to regulate the issue. One might then wonder why even under these conditions the repeals are so challenging. Out of 49 targeted acts on the quoted lists, 26 (53 per cent) were still valid by May 2017 and only a couple of those invalidated were actually repealed as a result of deliberate direct action of the legislator.

The previous section discussed the prominent position of review clauses in the *ex post* evaluation process, so it is useful to analyse their use and objectives empirically. While the importance of clauses had been emphasised since the early days of the Better Regulation Agenda, there were even less data available on the practical use than in the case of repeals. Again a more systematic reporting has been implemented only recently, resulting in a study published by the European Parliament providing a list of all review clauses contained in legislative acts adopted under the ordinary legislative procedure between July 2014 and

[35] Commission, 'The Implementation of the Framework Action "Updating and Simplifying the Community Acquis"' COM (2004) 432 final, 5.

[36] Commission, 'Third Progress Report on the Strategy for Simplifying the Regulatory Environment' COM (2009) 17 final, 3.

[37] Commission, 'Regulatory Fitness and Performance (REFIT): Results and Next Steps' COM (2013) 685 final, 1.

[38] Which for some unexplained reason was published separately in Commission, 'Regulatory Fitness and Performance Programme (REFIT): State of Play and Outlook' SWD (2015) 110 final, 149.

[39] eg, in the case of regulations fixing the guide prices for fish. Only regulations for 2004, 2009 and 2012 are listed. As the same regulation is adopted annually, why are the regulations for other past years not included?

December 2016.[40] The results confirm that there has been a fairly widespread utilisation of the tool: 94 out of 147 (64 per cent) acts[41] include some type of review clause. The share is higher for directives (80 per cent) than regulations (58 per cent). No noticeable trend was recorded in distribution of review clauses in time and there were only slight variations across policy areas. Based on the Better Regulation Guidelines, the authors of the study differentiate between 'light' and 'core' review clauses: the former consist mainly of implementation and progress reports, and the latter of the real assessment of effectivity of the given legislative act compared to initial expectations. There were in total 37 regulations and 22 directives with core review clauses in the sample.[42]

However, the extensive application of review clauses does not have to correspond with their real content and impact. Do the clauses recognise the possibility of scaling back EU action and thus support the concept of deactivation? I manually reviewed the substance of all core review clauses listed in the study and coded them according to categories related to the scope of EU intervention.[43] Table 5.1 reveals that the clauses often demand general review of effectiveness of legislative acts (usually performed by the Commission), this task is almost always accompanied by a requirement to present a new legislative proposal or amend an existing one if the review finds that to be appropriate. Of course, when the result of evaluation is negative, one of the courses of action might be the formal repeal of the reviewed act through a 'new legislative proposal'. But the phrasing of clauses seems to prevent such scenarios in the case of general reviews; rather, it aims to adapt the legislation in light of the results of the reviews. This preference is in my opinion even more obvious in the case of repeated reviews.

Only a limited share of review clauses expressly acknowledge changes to the scope of EU action; moreover, most of these cases suggest a possible extension of scope (deepening of integration). No review clause explicitly admits the potential for the reverse process, either as any sort of reduction of scope of the reviewed act or its repeal. The closest to deactivation are therefore acts with review clauses that (implicitly) concede that changes could develop in both ways. For example, Article 68 of Regulation 2016/794 asks the Commission to undergo a full review of the effectiveness and efficiency of Europol, which may lead to addressing 'the possible need to modify the structure, operation, field of action and tasks of Europol'. Yet even these rare cases (five in total), almost exclusively reserved to the evaluation of newly established institutions (agencies), barely present examples of the concept of deactivation. The total lack of sunset clauses in the sample confirms their unpopularity within the EU framework.

[40] I Krišto and S Huber, 'Review Clauses in EU Legislation: A Rolling Check-List' (2017) *European Parliamentary Research Service PE 598.601*.

[41] I excluded decisions from the analysis.

[42] Krišto and S Huber, above n 40, 8–17.

[43] The goals of review clauses not related to my research topic were omitted.

Table 5.1: The content and goals of core review clauses (acts adopted under ordinary legislative procedure, July 2014 to December 2016)

	Regulations (n = 37)	Directives (n = 22)
General review of the legislative act	16	14
Repeated review of the legislative act	11	5
Possibility of new legislative proposal or amendment of the reviewed legislative act	20	16
Possibility of extending the scope of the legislative act	8	4
Possibility of modifying the scope of the legislative act	5	0
Possibility of reducing the scope of the legislative act	0	0
Possibility of repeal of the legislative act	0	0

Note: one review clause might contain several listed goals, so the sum does not equal the total number of reviewed legislative acts.

Empirical analysis of repeals and review clauses confirms that these instruments have not been utilised towards the deactivation of EU competences. The conclusion fittingly aligns with the normative strategy of the Commission expressed in the Better Regulation Agenda's documents. Yet in certain ways, the results are puzzling. Witness the findings from the repeals: for a long time, only confusing findings were published, currently the process proceeds at a glacial pace and even the acts targeted as being the most obsolete have been repealed from the *acquis* only partially. Compare this with the rather positive attitude of the Commission towards the withdrawal of its legislative proposals, where it has been willing to abandon even flagship initiatives. What is the driver behind such a deep-rooted preference for status quo, with a pinch of salt almost resembling Stalin's 'Not one step back!' order during the Great Patriotic War? The reasons would surely be multi-faceted and their detailed elaboration is beyond the scope of this chapter. In my view, the most important obstacles to deactivation are decision-making rules. Under ordinary legislative procedure, the active cooperation of both the Commission and the European Parliament is required. But as the analysis above also indicates, supranational institutions likely perceive deactivation as a loss of control over the given measure. It is then up to the Member States represented in inter-governmental institutions to guard the boundaries of EU competences,[44] yet breaking the opposition of supranational bodies might be very demanding,

[44] *cf* T Tridimas, 'Competence after Lisbon: The Elusive Search for Bright Lines' in D Ashiagbor (ed), *The European Union after the Treaty of Lisbon* (Cambridge, Cambridge University Press, 2012) 73.

moreover when the decision-making rules in the Council itself prefer status quo (joint-decision trap).[45] Again, states as masters of the Treaties tried to break the deadlock during the Lisbon Intergovernmental Conference and in Declaration No 18 instructed the Commission to devote attention to proposals for repealing legislative requested by the Council, but the provision does not bind the Commission and is in practice toothless.[46]

CONCLUSION

The deactivation of EU competences represents, at least in a legal and normative sense, a viable part of the EU fabric. The Better Regulation Agenda and its emphasis on *ex post* evaluation testing the fitness of EU intervention should naturally contribute to the facilitation of deactivation. However, the review of relevant documents revealed that deactivation was not one of the Agenda's priorities. This conclusion is mirrored in the empirical evidence, both from the investigation of repeals and the content of used review clauses.

Yet my analysis should be viewed as a neutral rather than a critical evaluation of the link between the Better Regulation Agenda and deactivation. It is a political responsibility of the Commission to normatively define objectives of the Agenda; if other actors such as Member States are not pleased with them, they certainly have numerous instruments through which voice their dissent and influence the Commission's position. It must be also acknowledged that even if the attitude of the Commission to deactivation becomes more welcoming, the concept would always be a minor one compared to changing or even extending the scope of EU action. On the other hand, I also do not believe that the current strategy is smart and sustainable in the long term. First, as already noted several times, the concept of deactivation is not an academic fantasy, but a basic constitutional rule expressly entrenched in primary law after the Lisbon Treaty reforms—it must have some meaning and value for the masters of the Treaties. Second, when we explore the scenario of future EU development, the Commission itself recognises in its recent White Paper on the Future of Europe that one of the possible paths is 'doing less more efficiently'.[47] Deactivation shall be treated as a standard instrument in balancing the relationship between the EU and the Member States rather than feared as an opening of Pandora's Box.

[45] See F Scharpf, 'The JDT Model: Context and Extensions!' in G Falkner (ed), *The EU's Decision Traps: Comparing Policies* (Oxford, Oxford University Press, 2011).

[46] See also D Phinnemore, *The Treaty of Lisbon: Origins and Negotiations* (Basingstoke, Palgrave Macmillan, 2013) 171–72.

[47] See Commission, *White Paper on the Future of Europe: Reflections and Scenarios for the EU27 by 2025* (Brussels, European Commission, 2017) 22–23.

Part III

Views from EU Institutional Practice

6

The European Commission and its Better Regulation Agenda

BEN SMULDERS* AND JEAN-ERIC PAQUET**

INTRODUCTION

YOU OR I would not buy a new house, a fridge or a holiday without some basic information to inform our decision. This is plain common sense. Evidence-based policy-making is no different. Politicians take decisions using the available evidence on what the problem is, what the alternative policy options are and what their impacts may be. Better regulation processes aim to ensure the best available evidence and analysis is made available to decision-makers in a timely fashion.

This evidence will inform but not predetermine politicians' choices. These will be influenced by many other legitimate factors such as their political programmes, their appreciation of the desirability of alternative mixes of impacts and, when relevant, their assessment of the relative likelihood of legislators' approval for different policy proposals. Better regulation processes are meant to bring sound evidence on the problems to be solved and solid estimations of the likely effects of potential solutions to the table of decision-making. This avoids political choices being taken solely on the basis of the strength of rhetorical arguments or, quite simply, raw political power. Similarly, it also forces politicians to justify choices in terms of evidence and expected impacts. Therefore, Better Regulation processes enhance accountability and increase the likelihood of effective and efficient policies.

Achieving the aims of Better Regulation is no easy task. Falling short of Better Regulation standards is thus not the rarest of occurrences. Of course, as people

* Ben Smulders is currently Head of the Cabinet of the European Commission's First-Vice President Mr Timmermans responsible for, inter alia, Better Regulation, Interinstitutional Relations, the Rule of Law and the Charter of Fundamental Rights.

** Jean-Eric Paquet is Deputy Secretary-General of the European Commission. Both would like to express their gratitude to their colleague Duncan Johnstone for his invaluable contribution to this chapter.

will always disagree on what to consider 'better' and on what bases, there will be a general tendency to complain about specific aspects of any Better Regulation analysis by those who do not subscribe to the ultimate political decision taken. These criticisms can be expected and, when valid as they sometimes may be, need to be acted upon by improving the Commission's processes and capacities.

However, this is different from the more radical criticisms sometimes levelled against the Commission Better Regulation processes, namely that they are *systematically* biased, favouring some stakeholders over others, ignoring important impacts and focusing too much on economic efficiency, leading to regulatory capture and deregulation etc. In this chapter we hope to show that there is no evidence to support such accusations of systematic biases. The fact that such alleged biases often point in opposite directions suggests that the underlying accusations are often self-serving. Paradoxically, they might well aim precisely at introducing a bias in the balance and comprehensive Better Regulation approach that the Commission is striving to preserve.

To do the above, the chapter sets out to explain the Commission's approach to Better Regulation from its early beginnings. It will also explain why we carry on with the policy and will debunk some of the ill-informed comments that continue to circulate about it. It will focus on three key pillars of Better Regulation: Impact Assessment, evaluation and stakeholder consultation.

THE ORIGINS OF EVIDENCE-BASED POLICY-MAKING AND THE THREE PILLARS OF BETTER REGULATION

According to certain views, Better Regulation suffers from the original sin of being born as a pro-business initiative, putting the focus on the burdens that legislation may put on businesses rather than on the benefits regulations may generate for society as a whole. Were this to be true, many could argue that Better Regulation has spectacularly failed, as legislative activity at the EU level has fortunately not ground to a halt over the last decade. But of course, this is certainly not true in the case of the European Commission Better Regulation system, the origins of which can be found in the White Paper on Governance from 2001[1] that followed on from the resignation of the Santer Commission and the need for more transparency and accountability. The White Paper was closely followed by other more specific Communications, including that from 2002 on better law-making.[2] An excerpt from the 2002 Communication is reproduced below:

> There are a lot of complex issues at stake now in enacting good European legislation which is mindful of the principles of subsidiarity and proportionality. People nowadays

[1] White Paper on European Governance COM (2001) 428: C 287, 12 October 2001, http://eur-lex.europa.eu/legal-content/EN/TXT/HTML/?uri=LEGISSUM:l10109&from=EN.

[2] Excerpt from the Communication, 'European Governance: Better Law-Making' COM (2002) 275, 5 June 2002, http://eur-lex.europa.eu/LexUriServ/LexUriServ.do?uri=COM:2002:0275:FIN:EN:PDF.

take an interest in the effectiveness of the rules handed down 'from Brussels' and the way they are drawn up. The advent of a democratic conscience is strengthening the need for accountability and proportionality in the way powers vested in the European institutions are exercised. This need is expressed more especially in transparency, clarity and the willingness to stand up to scrutiny. What we have here, then, is a veritable ethical requirement.

There was therefore an 'ethical' necessity for evidence-based policy-making at the root of Better Regulation in 2002 which is still relevant in today's world—arguably even more so. Take, for example, the worrying questioning of agreed basic science on climate change[3] and the lexicon of 'alternative facts'[4] in the US.

Better regulation provides a framework to deliver evidence-based policy-making—providing relevant information to those who take political decisions. It is therefore difficult to accept criticism that Better Regulation is somehow a means to de-democratise the legislative process in favour of technocratic decisions (influenced by business lobbies).[5] The aim is precisely the opposite.

The White Paper on Governance identified a need to engage more meaningfully with citizens, to bolster the transparency and accountability of the European institutions, and to inform decisions with analysis that stands up to scrutiny. These aims remain important foundations of the Commission's evidence-based policy-making process and are just as valid for the European legislators and national governments too. Why do we say that?

— First, legitimacy. Better regulation provides a range of tools to engage meaningfully with civil society. It is no secret that trust in the EU is in decline as

[3] The newly appointed Administrator for the US Environmental Protection Agency Scott Pruitt stated in March 2017 that: 'I think that measuring with precision human activity on the climate is something very challenging to do and there's tremendous disagreement about the degree of impact, so no, I would not agree that it's a primary contributor to the global warming that we see. But we don't know that yet. We need to continue the debate and continue the review and the analysis' (https://www.theguardian.com/environment/2017/mar/09/epa-scott-pruitt-carbon-dioxide-global-warming-climate-change). Take as a contrast the UN's International Panel on Climate Change (which represents the scientific consensus of the overwhelming majority of scientists), which stated in its 2014 report that: 'Anthropogenic greenhouse gas emissions have increased since the pre-industrial era, driven largely by economic and population growth, and are now higher than ever. This has led to atmospheric concentrations of carbon dioxide, methane and nitrous oxide that are unprecedented in at least the last 800,000 years. Their effects, together with those of other anthropogenic drivers, have been detected throughout the climate system and are extremely likely to have been the dominant cause of the observed warming since the mid-20th century' (https://www.ipcc.ch/pdf/assessment-report/ar5/syr/AR5_SYR_FINAL_SPM.pdf).

[4] Observations showed that the observed crowd at President Trump's inauguration was smaller than that of his predecessor, but this was disputed by President Trump's press team, who presented 'alternative facts' to the press. See www.nbcnews.com/meet-the-press/video/conway-press-secretary-gave-alternative-facts-860142147643.

[5] UNI Europa, the European services workers union: 'The [May 2015 Commission Better Regulation] package is aimed at improving the conditions for Europe's small and medium-sized companies by "cutting red tape" and "removing unnecessary burdens". UNI Europa has criticised the package for its lack of commitment to social conditions, for its favouritism of industry needs, and for the Commission's attempt to de-democratise the legislative process' (www.uni-europa.org/category/better-regulation).

well as in public authorities at all levels.[6] We have to rebuild that trust, and trust is built on transparency and engagement.

— Second, the policy challenges are too great and the problems too complex to think that we can find good solutions without looking first at the evidence in a structured and comprehensive way.
— Third, public and private budgets are under pressure and we have to be better at designing smarter policies that deliver what we want while avoiding unnecessary costs.

The Commission's approach to Better Regulation is built on three key pillars: Impact Assessment, evaluation and stakeholder consultation. These are complementary and intimately related. The three pillars have been built up at different speeds over the years translating into the peculiar institutional set up of the EU and international (and notably Organisation for Economic Co-operation and Development (OECD)) best practices and principles which stem from, and are largely thought for, national experiences. All three pillars aim to ensure a comprehensive approach looking at the economic, social and environmental fields across all relevant actors and Member States. This comprehensiveness was built into the EU system over time, admittedly starting first from the economic side. However, it now constitutes a fundamental element of the EU system. This comprehensiveness is a direct consequence of its governance-related origin and a guide for all possible evolutions since it fits the Treaty-based EU institutional system (a more focussed Better Regulation system can instead fit the case of a national government with an electoral mandate to prioritise certain impacts and actors over others).

Consulting stakeholders allows views and opinions to be expressed, but it also allows hard evidence to find its way into the preparation of new initiatives or the evaluation of existing policies. However, the role and value of stakeholder consultation goes much wider. Stakeholder acceptance of new policies and their commitment to implement them correctly are more likely if those most affected have been involved in an open and transparent process where their views and data have been considered seriously. This is so even where some stakeholders may have hoped for a different policy outcome. Analogies and support can be drawn from the research on procedural justice where people's attitudes are as much influenced by the processes they experience as they are by the outcomes they receive.[7] In the field of public policy-making, serious and systematic engagement with stakeholders, and citizens in particular, can only help improve trust in public authorities.

Evaluation and Impact Assessment depend on good-quality stakeholder consultation. They are also connected. The starting point for a good evaluation is to look back at the Impact Assessment and to see whether the changes that were expected to happen actually occurred. While forward-looking Impact Assessments fed by

[6] 'White Paper on the Future of Europe—Reflections and Scenarios for the EU27 by 2025' COM (2017) 2025, 12.

[7] See, eg, EA Lind and TR Tyler, *The Social Psychology of Procedural Justice* (Berlin, Springer Science, 1988).

stakeholder consultation can try to anticipate how policies will be implemented, they cannot anticipate everything. There will always be unexpected events or problems, particularly in fast-moving policy areas, and a mechanism is needed to correct policy implementation early on when we first become aware of problems. However, timely information about how a policy performs is absolutely necessary for evaluation, but is currently not always available; this is an issue we will return to later in the context of how to improve current approaches.

Impact Assessment in the Commission tries to ensure that a range of policy solutions is assessed that fit logically with the identified problems and their underlying causes. It also tries to ensure respect for Treaty principles (such as subsidiarity, proportionality and sustainable development) and to ensure that the most relevant and important impacts are identified and assessed particularly for important economic actors, such as small and medium-sized enterprises (SMEs). The assessment should also provide information about the views of the different stakeholders and in particular about who will be affected and how. Finally, an Impact Assessment should make the link to a future evaluation by identifying the benchmarks and arrangements to monitor the performance of the policy in practice. Such monitoring and evaluation will provide the crucial information for any subsequent revision of the policy and potential problems to be addressed by a future Impact Assessment.

THE PAST REVISITED

Those who worked in the European Commission before Better Regulation took root will confirm that Commission proposals were simpler to prepare. They were transmitted to the legislator with an explanatory memorandum and an explanation of the financial implications for the EU's budget. Early and meaningful collaboration between the Commission's decentralised departments was unstructured and variable. This is not the case today, but critics forget all too quickly the immense progress which has been made over the past 15 years.

The Commission produced its first Better Regulation action plan[8] in 2002, which set out new ways of working in many different areas.

First, it launched a new framework for *Impact Assessment*, building on and bringing together the various fragmented sectoral assessment practices (such as those on businesses and the environment) into a single integrated system under the auspices of the Secretariat General of the Commission.[9] This aimed to improve the quality and coherence of the policy development process, contribute

[8] 'Action Plan: Simplifying and Improving the Regulatory Environment' COM (2002) 278. This followed the mandate issued by the European Council at Lisbon and confirmed at the Stockholm, Laeken and Barcelona summits: http://eur-lex.europa.eu/LexUriServ/LexUriServ.do?uri=COM:2002:0278:FIN:en:PDF.

[9] Commission Communication, 'Impact Assessment' COM (2002) 276, http://eur-lex.europa.eu/LexUriServ/LexUriServ.do?uri=COM:2002:0276:FIN:EN:PDF.

to an effective and efficient regulatory environment, and deliver a more coherent implementation of the European strategy for sustainable development. New guidelines were prepared for the Commission's departments on how to prepare Impact Assessments in 2003 and these were updated and refined several times in the period up to 2009.[10] Interestingly, the Commission's Impact Assessment system is often criticised for not presenting sufficiently well the social and environmental impacts of policy proposals. Not all impacts are equally relevant for all Impact Assessments and it would be disproportionate to assess everything in all cases. This view was supported by the European Court of Auditors in a special report in 2010.[11]

A further innovation to the Commission's Impact Assessment system was implemented at the end of 2007. The Impact Assessment Board was established to scrutinise the quality of all Impact Assessments. Its members were drawn from a pool of senior officials across the Commission's departments. In principle, a positive opinion was required from the Board so that the associated proposal could be presented to the Commission for decision. The Impact Assessment Board has now been replaced by the Regulatory Scrutiny Board with a stronger independence and an enlarged mandate (see below).

Evaluation of projects and programme evaluation has been undertaken for several decades in the EU. It has focused on traditional expenditure policies, including the Common Agricultural Policy (CAP), the structural funds, research and technological development, and external action. The approach to evaluation varied across the Commission's departments. A more systematic approach emerged in the 1990s alongside the need for greater financial accountability. Evaluation became a central feature of budgetary allocations and the seven-year financial programming cycle. Evaluation standards were developed by the Commission's Directorate General for the Budget in 1999 (and revised in 2004)[12] to guide Directorates General in their evaluation work, particularly when outsourcing evaluation work to external consultants.

More recently, the Commission has tried to reorient its evaluation policy by embedding evaluation in the broader Better Regulation agenda as first set out in the 2007 Commission Communication 'Responding to Strategic Needs: Reinforcing the Use of Evaluation'.[13]

[10] 'Impact Assessment Guidelines' SEC (2009) 92, 15 January 2009, http://ec.europa.eu/smart-regulation/impact/commission_guidelines/docs/iag_2009_en.pdf.

[11] *Impact Assessments in the EU Institutions: Do They Support Decision-Making?* European Court of Auditors special report No 3 of 2010, http://ec.europa.eu/smart-regulation/impact/docs/coa_report_3_2010_en.pdf.

[12] Drafted by the Commission's Directorate General for the Budget as a 'Practical Guide for the Commission Services' by 'presenting practical solutions and good practices'.

[13] Commission Communication, 'Responding to Strategic Needs: Reinforcing the Use of Evaluation' SEC (2007) 2013, http://ec.europa.eu/smart-regulation/evaluation/docs/eval_comm_sec_2007_213_en.pdf.

The key idea was to place evaluation squarely in the policy-making process by linking it explicitly to the Impact Assessment of a new initiative. As a consequence, responsibility for evaluation policy shifted naturally in 2009 to the Secretariat General and to the same directorate that was responsible for Impact Assessment. This trend continued with the Commission's 2013 Communication 'Strengthening the Foundations of Smart Regulation—Improving Evaluation',[14] which introduced the 'evaluate first' principle and tried to promote an evaluation culture in the Commission. Progress was, however, limited (although the Commission has prepared close to 700 evaluations since 2010), but was given a new impetus with the new package of measures on Better Regulation in May 2015.

The Commission has also reinforced the culture of consultation of and dialogue in the EU, calling on stakeholders to make a direct contribution to its new approach towards Impact Assessments. The Commission's Communication entitled 'Towards a Reinforced Culture of Consultation and Dialogue'[15] gave effect to the White Paper and set out for the first time the general principles and minimum standards for consultation of interested parties by the Commission. The five minimum standards can be summarised as follows:

— All communications relating to consultation should be clear and concise, and should include all necessary information to facilitate responses.
— When defining the target group(s) in a consultation process, the Commission should ensure that relevant parties have an opportunity to express their opinions.
— The Commission should ensure adequate awareness-raising publicity and should adapt its communication channels to meet the needs of all target audiences. Without excluding other communication tools, open public consultations should be published on the Internet and announced at the 'single access point'.
— The Commission should provide sufficient time for planning and responses to invitations and written contributions. The Commission should strive to allow (at the time) at least eight weeks for the reception of responses to written public consultations and 20 working days' notice for meetings.
— Receipt of contributions should be acknowledged. Results of open public consultation should be displayed on websites linked to the single access point on the Internet.

[14] Commission Communication, 'Strengthening the Foundations of Smart Regulation—Improving Evaluation' COM (2013) 686 final, http://eur-lex.europa.eu/legal-content/EN/TXT/?uri=COM:2013:0686:FIN.

[15] 'Towards a Reinforced Culture of Consultation and Dialogue—General Principles and Minimum Standards for Consultation of Interested Parties by the Commission' COM (2002) 704, http://eur-lex.europa.eu/legal-content/EN/TXT/?uri=celex%3A52002DC0704.

From these beginnings, Better Regulation in the Commission has evolved. In doing so it has come to:

— provide a framework for evidence-based policy-making and helps deliver high-quality initiatives;
— support legislation and policies that deliver the EU's objectives efficiently—this means delivering societal objectives while avoiding unnecessary costs for businesses, public authorities and citizens;
— systematically invite the participation of all stakeholders in all aspects of the policy cycle from the earliest announcement of an initiative through to its implementation, monitoring, evaluation and subsequent modification;
— ensure common-sense collective working within the Commission services;
— help to ensure that political initiatives deliver as originally envisaged and remain fit for purpose over time;
— provide transparency about how policy is made and explain clearly why new rules are needed and who is affected in an effort to build greater democratic legitimacy.

A NEW IMPULSE FOR BETTER REGULATION: THE JUNCKER COMMISSION

A key objective of the Juncker Commission was to reinvigorate its Better Regulation policy as part of the President's political priority for democratic change.[16] A new series of measures was announced in May 2015 in its Communication on 'Better Regulation for Better Results'.[17] This package introduced and proposed some important changes that will deliver significant and long-lasting changes in terms of how the Commission and the other institutions make legislation. Better regulation is seen as supporting the President's priorities and making sure that these are done well.

These new elements covered profound improvements in transparency and stakeholder participation. They strengthened the commitment to evaluate existing policies in a systematic manner and strengthened the internal scrutiny of Better Regulation in the Commission. They also provided a greater focus on the regulatory fitness of existing legislation and made proposals to relaunch the cooperation between the institutions on better law-making. New comprehensive guidelines and associated tools were established to help the Commission services apply Better Regulation across the policy cycle.

It is clear that the Juncker Commission is firmly committed to its Better Regulation policy. The Juncker Commission is also focused on tackling a smaller number of political priorities and acting at the EU level only when necessary. This was

[16] https://ec.europa.eu/commission/priorities_en.

[17] Commission Communication, 'Better Regulation for Better Results—An EU Agenda' COM (2015) 215, http://ec.europa.eu/transparency/regdoc/rep/1/2015/EN/1-2015-215-EN-F1-1.PDF.

clearly set out at the time of President Juncker's endorsement by the European Parliament and the European Council. These are the President's *political* priorities. They are political choices about the areas in which the Commission intends to act. By definition, these choices cannot be influenced by Better Regulation which presents evidence about the possible *content* of such initiatives. The fact that the Commission does not prioritise action in a particular area is therefore not related to the application of Better Regulation.[18]

Interinstitutional Cooperation

In 2003, the European Parliament, the Council of the European Union and the European Commission entered into an Interinstitutional Agreement on Better Law-Making.[19] This was complemented by a common accord on Impact Assessment in 2005.[20] These agreements set out the commitment of the three institutions towards Impact Assessment in the legislative process.

However, these agreements have had mixed results at best. While the Commission has produced over 1,000 Impact Assessments since 2003, the Council has not assessed the impacts of a single substantial amendment. The European Parliament has made substantially greater efforts to assess substantial amendments as well as the Commission's own Impact Assessment. More generally, the aims of evidence-based policy-making cannot succeed if the Commission acts alone in applying Better Regulation. While the Commission has a right to initiate legislation, important changes are made during the legislative procedure which might entail significant impacts compared to the Commission's original proposal. Moreover, the way in which EU legislation is applied at the national level may also change the expected impacts significantly.

It is against this background that the Commission made proposals for a new interinstitutional agreement which was concluded in April 2016 and which replaces its predecessor from 2003 and the common accord on Impact Assessment.[21] The new agreement covers Impact Assessment, the monitoring and evaluation of legislation, stakeholder consultation, the 'gold-plating' of national transposing measures, the recast and codification of legal texts, the simplification of existing

[18] Better regulation watchdog network, July 2016, www.betterregwatch.eu/wp-content/uploads/2016/12/BRWN-Europe-needs-a-Strong-Safety-Net.pdf.

[19] Interinstitutional Agreement between the European Parliament, the Council of the European Union and the European Commission on Better Law-Making [2003] OJ C321, 31 December, 1, http://eur-lex.europa.eu/legal-content/EN/TXT/PDF/?uri=CELEX:32003Q1231(01)&from=EN.

[20] Interinstitutional Common Accord on Impact Assessment (IA) between the European Parliament, the Council of the European Union and the European Commission, 2005, http://ec.europa.eu/smart-regulation/impact/key_docs/docs/ii_common_approach_to_ia_en.pdf.

[21] Interinstitutional Agreement on Better Law-Making between the European Parliament, the Council of the European Union and the European Commission of 13 April 2016 [2016] OJ L123, 12 May, 1, http://eur-lex.europa.eu/legal-content/EN/TXT/?uri=OJ:L:2016:123:TOC.

legislation and the empowerment of the Commission to adopt delegated acts of EU law pursuant to Article 290 of the Treaty on the Functioning of the European Union (TFEU).

Under the new agreement, the role and importance of the Commission's Impact Assessment has grown. The European Parliament and the Council now commit to examine the Commission's assessment before starting to discuss their amendments. This in theory provides a common core of knowledge and provides an opportunity for the Commission to explain its choices and the pros and cons of these choices. This can only help the subsequent discussions with the legislator. The European Parliament and the Council have also restated their commitment to assess the impacts of their substantial amendments where they deem it appropriate in a given legislative procedure. The Council has until recently not given much effect to this commitment, but in April 2017 the Committee of Representatives of the Council decided to establish a pilot programme with the capacity to make assessments of substantial amendments. Perhaps the other key innovation is the joint commitment to consider the inclusion of monitoring and evaluation clauses in all new basic acts of EU law. This has the potential to greatly enhance the usefulness and quality of Commission evaluations.

The Practical Application of Better Regulation in the Commission

In May 2015, a new set of guidelines were introduced to guide the Commission services' work on Better Regulation.[22] They marked a significant departure from what had gone before. They now comprehensively cover the entire policy cycle which promotes greater thought and anticipation of the subsequent phases, such as how to ensure a good transposition, application, monitoring arrangements and evaluation. The new guidelines are substantially shorter and simpler to use than the previous version, but are complemented by a much larger 'toolbox'[23] which brought together existing (and added new) detailed and practical guidance on the many aspects of Better Regulation again across the policy cycle.

The guidelines are complemented by a range of training courses under a single banner in the Commission's training catalogue. These are currently being revamped with the help of the European Institute of Public Administration. The aim is to raise the general level of awareness about how to apply Better Regulation, starting with new recruits, but then offering increasingly specialised courses to those preparing specific Impact Assessments, evaluations and consultations. These training courses represent a substantial effort in capacity building when taken together with the frequent general presentations by Better Regulation experts in the Commission.

[22] https://ec.europa.eu/info/files/better-regulation-guidelines_en.
[23] https://ec.europa.eu/info/better-regulation-toolbox_en.

The Commission's Better Regulation policy requires all interested departments to participate in inter-service groups which prepare the consultations, Impact Assessments and evaluations collectively. These groups will include representatives of the Secretariat General who advise about the practical requirements of Better Regulation as well as experts from other departments who will advise about issues such as SMEs, innovation, digital issues, competitiveness etc. The strength of this collective approach is that all relevant issues can be identified early and addressed accordingly.

Transparency and Stakeholder Participation

An EU that is more transparent and accountable is an EU that will deliver better results for citizens. This has been the guiding philosophy since the White Paper on Governance and is still valid today. Over 700 open public consultations have been carried out since 2010.

The May 2015 package of measures delivered profound improvements in the transparency of the Commission's work. The aim was to open up policy-making to stakeholder participation at multiple points in the policy cycle while at the same time trying to improve the quality of the Commission's consultation activities and the evidence received from stakeholders.

The first important change requires an open public consultation lasting for 12 weeks to support all Impact Assessments, evaluations and Green Papers etc. This should be complemented with more bespoke activities that target the most relevant stakeholders and information so that for every initiative, there should now be a comprehensive consultation strategy. A ringing endorsement for this new approach was given by the evaluation of the EU's nature protection legislation with over 50,000 responses that informed a College of Commissioners discussion about its future development.

The second major innovation is the possibility to provide feedback at the very earliest point in the preparation of a new initiative. A roadmap or inception Impact Assessment[24] is published centrally by the Commission. This will describe the problems that the initiative aims to tackle, a justification from the perspective of subsidiarity, the kinds of policies the Commission is considering and a first indication of the impacts that might be expected in the case of the inception Impact Assessment. It will also alert stakeholders to the envisaged consultation activities so that they can prepare in advance, which hopefully will make their subsequent contribution of a higher quality.

A third change allows stakeholders to provide their feedback on the content of the Commission's proposal and any supporting Impact Assessment. The feedback

[24] Roadmaps are used where the initiative is not supported by an Impact Assessment. In this case, the roadmap should explain why no impact assessment is being prepared.

received is transmitted to the European Parliament and to the Council. Previously, there was no formal or transparent opportunity for the views of stakeholders to be made known as the other institutions do not systematically report stakeholder contacts or views received in the legislative process. The Legislator is not an enthusiastic supporter of this measure taken by the Commission, but it works. For example, over 25,000 responses were received on the Commission's proposals to make it harder legally to obtain high capacity firearms[25] and were duly considered by the legislator.

Finally, there has been a quiet revolution in the process of preparing implementing legislation and delegated acts. Subject to a strict set of well-justified exceptions, all acts, whether delegated acts (Article 290 TFEU) or implementing acts (Article 291 TFEU) of general application, are posted to the Commission's website for four weeks so that stakeholders can see and comment on a draft act before it is adopted into EU law. This represents a quantum leap in terms of transparency in what has traditionally been seen as a complex and opaque process involving experts and representatives of the Member States.[26]

Evaluate First

The Better Regulation guidelines presented in May 2015 signalled a further significant step in the strengthening of evaluation. A standard evaluation template was defined for spending programmes and regulatory interventions which must assess the same minimum five criteria of effectiveness, efficiency, relevance, coherence and EU added value. Evaluation was even more firmly embedded in the policy cycle with a stronger link made between evaluation and Impact Assessment. This link is strengthened by the reinforced mandate of the new Regulatory Scrutiny Board,[27] which now also scrutinises the draft evaluations it selects itself. The Board's predecessor did not look at draft evaluations at all. Also, the new Board is asking systematically whether an evaluation has been undertaken and whether the conclusions of that evaluation have been adequately reflected in the problem analysis of the Impact Assessment report. In 2016, the Regulatory Scrutiny Board reported[28] that just under half of the Impact Assessments it scrutinised were also supported by an evaluation. This is quite an achievement given the novelty of such a requirement introduced part way through a new Commission with a heavy policy agenda. This change in mandate further reinforces the structural link between evaluations and Impact Assessments.

[25] 'Proposal for a Directive of the European Parliament and of the Council Amending Council Directive 91/477/EEC on Control of the Acquisition and Possession of Weapons' COM (2015) 0750.

[26] A McLoughlin, 'A Dutch Man Lets in the Sunshine to EU Law Making' (2016), www.aaronmcloughlin.com/2035-2.

[27] See https://ec.europa.eu/info/law/law-making-process/regulatory-scrutiny-board_en.

[28] Regulatory Scrutiny Board annual report 2016, European Commission, Brussels, https://ec.europa.eu/info/sites/info/files/2016-rsb-report_en.pdf.

The new approach means that the expected changes and impacts reported in an Impact Assessment should now be checked in the subsequent evaluation. There should be a closer link between the initial monitoring arrangements and indicators described in the Impact Assessment and those actually put in place to underpin the subsequent evaluation. In addition, the new approach also relies on a strengthened approach to consultation that is similar to that for Impact Assessment where 12-week open public consultations must be performed as part of a wider consultation strategy that targets stakeholders and evidence. Evaluation will now be a tool to look systematically at the regulatory fitness of the EU's existing legislation and will have the potential to simplify and achieve policy objectives more efficiently.

The evaluation findings are presented to the Board in a working document of the Commission services. This short document of 50 pages or so allows the key conclusions and evidence to be presented and for the lead Commission department to take ownership of the findings; too often in the past, voluminous and expensive evaluation reports from external contractors have simply gathered dust on a shelf rather than being used in the policy development process.

This new approach is challenging. Commission departments in charge of spending programmes will have to adapt to the new standardised evaluation. Policy departments will have to learn to plan better in order to be better prepared to present timely evaluations that feed into new political initiatives. This represents a significant cultural change which will take several years to deliver if the experience of Impact Assessment is a guide.

However, it is possible. Most new initiatives proposed by the Commission are now amendments of existing legislation which have been supported by an Impact Assessment, which provides a ready baseline that an evaluation should check. The greatest obstacle is likely to be the lack of basic information about the actual impacts of EU policies on the ground in the Member States. The experience of the ABRplus programme[29] showed rather clearly the paucity of available information about how legislation works in practice. The relevance of this point for the whole purposes of Better Regulation can hardly be overestimated. This problem must then be solved, although it will not be immediately possible. Solving it requires that the European Legislator, and the Member States in particular, will have to make greater efforts to monitor legislation in line with the Interinstitutional Agreement on Better Law-Making, which envisages a more systematic incorporation of monitoring and evaluation provisions in basic acts of EU law.[30] The Commission will look to establish sensible monitoring arrangements more frequently in its proposals in line with the Interinstitutional Agreement. In addition, perhaps, monitoring work

[29] The Commission proposed an Administrative Burden Reduction programme with measures to deliver a 25 per cent reduction in administrative burdens. Twelve of the most important measures were followed up together with the Member States in the ABRplus programme. European Commission, *ABRplus Study Final Report*, 2015, http://bookshop.europa.eu/en/abrplus-pbKA0115190.

[30] Interinstitutional Agreement on Better Law-Making, above n 21, para 23.

could be undertaken jointly by the Commission and the Member States where surveys, consultations or evaluations have indicated particularly problematic legislation or have various impacts in key economic sectors.

CHALLENGES AND MYTHS

This section looks at a series of challenges which have been frequently raised against the European Commission Better Regulation system. Paradoxically for a discourse on Better Regulation, these challenges are often based on myths rather than evidence, the biggest myth being the belief that Better Regulation systems that are appropriate for national governments and bureaucracies can be applied in an unchanged manner to the peculiar institutional framework of the EU and the European Commission in particular. Noting this, of course, does not deny the recognition that all of these challenges do point to areas of crucial importance where further progress was needed and is still being worked at.

The Challenge of Quantification

The Commission is attacked at the same time for never quantifying (typically the costs of its proposals) and for being obsessed with quantification at the expense of the appreciation of non-quantifiable (social and environmental) benefits. Neither of these claims is correct, in guidance or in practice.

The Commission's Better Regulation guidelines are clear that quantification should be undertaken wherever possible, meaning where there is a sound methodology and the costs of presenting the quantified information are not disproportionate. The toolbox contains detailed descriptions of the types of costs and benefits to be assessed, as well as methods on how to estimate them. However, quantification is difficult and the Commission is often criticised for presenting insufficient quantified information about impacts. The Commission does however face some specific challenges:

First, the Commission's Impact Assessment aims to inform the decision about a range of possible policy options. The Impact Assessment is prepared well before the legislative proposal is drafted. As such, it is not an Impact Assessment covering the precise content and individual obligations of the legal proposal that the Commission presents to the legislator. The policy options considered in the Impact Assessment (and by the Regulatory Scrutiny Board) are by definition more general and high-level, which makes quantification more difficult. Member States systems with Impact Assessments only focusing on the specific content of a well-specified national measure therefore have a simpler task. There is limited appetite and little reason to argue the Commission's system should stop looking at a range of options (given the lack of a direct electoral mandate and the specificities of the EU legislative process).

Second, the Commission undertakes an integrated assessment of the economic, social and environmental impacts. This is also because the Commission's Impact Assessment system was also conceived as a response to the challenge to achieve sustainable development. This approach is ambitious compared to many national systems which may only focus on the assessment of costs. While costs are more straightforward to estimate, the social and environmental benefits are notoriously more difficult and may in fact be impossible to quantify. Many national Impact Assessment systems choose to ignore benefits because of this difficulty. Again, there is limited appetite and reason for the European system to move towards such a direction or towards the mandatory adoption of strict cost-benefit analysis (with its many theoretical limitations).

Third, estimating impacts at the national level is already difficult as Member States face challenges to collect relevant data at the national, regional and local levels. The challenge is even more difficult for the Commission, which is expected to make pan-European assessments for all Member States while still highlighting local and regional impacts. The data demands are substantially greater for the Commission, and greater cooperation will be needed between the Commission and the Member States.

Fourth, the costs and benefits of directives can hardly be estimated with great precision since the final balance will depend upon the way in which they are translated into national legislation. Similarly, key parameters for a quantitative definition of costs and benefits are at times left to later implementing measures to define. In these cases there is simply nothing that can be precisely quantified. Ranges will have to do.

Fifth, the weaknesses of certain quantification methods are magnified at the European level. Consider, for instance, the concept of average enterprise used for the most common calculation of compliance costs. What is the average enterprise in Europe? The exporting world champion or the small enterprise barely surviving in a backward area? Economic diversity is much higher at the EU level than at the national level. Any average calculation will hide very wide discrepancies in the actual impact across actual enterprises across different national policies. In such a situation, scarce resources would probably be better allocated to improving the estimates of impacts *across* regions than to the estimation of an individual figure. This would be of little purpose other than communication and would likely be perceived as deceptive more than anything by the affected individual entity.

Notwithstanding these challenges, the Commission is still presenting some quantified information in about half of its Impact Assessments and in almost all of those included in the REFIT programme.[31] This situation is expected to

[31] See p 21 of the 2016 report of the Regulatory Scrutiny Board: https://ec.europa.eu/info/sites/info/files/2016-rsb-report_en.pdf.

improve as the Commission services will be expected to make greater efforts to quantify impacts and to simplify existing legislation when they present amending proposals.[32]

Consultation on Draft Impact Assessments

Stakeholders frequently suggest that the Commission should consult on its draft Impact Assessments before it adopts its proposal. There are good reasons why the Commission does not do this that are connected to the Commission's constraints and institutional role, and the Commission does publish the Impact Assessment after it has adopted its proposal (and before it is turned into law). Impact Assessments are of course very useful for the legislator and stakeholders, and help build trust and confidence in what the EU does. But the Commission prepares Impact Assessments first and foremost to inform its own internal decision-making. This is recognised by the EU Court of Justice, which has decided that the Commission is not obliged to publish draft Impact Assessments prior to the adoption of a proposal.[33] The Commission needs time and space to reflect on its proposals. It would be inappropriate for the outside world to see the Impact Assessment and the policy choices before the College of Commissioners does so. Consultation of College-cleared draft Impact Assessments would most likely end up bringing forward the start of the legislative process with the Council and Parliament (and certainly Member States) providing a position on whatever the (draft) preferred policy position would be. Inevitably, then, the College would end up deciding its final position before publishing the draft Impact Assessment, thus undermining the whole purpose of the exercise.

To nevertheless reap the benefits of stakeholder input, the Commission consults on all aspects of an Impact Assessment and evaluations. It believes that stakeholder input is more useful early on in the policy development process when the problem and policy solutions are still being defined. The Commission has strengthened this early engagement with stakeholders by publishing an inception Impact Assessment which will set out in greater depth the problem, the possible policy options and an initial assessment of the impacts associated with these policy options. The Commission also provides stakeholders with the opportunity to provide feedback on its Impact Assessment and proposal once adopted by the College. This feedback is made available to the legislator in a transparent manner. This process has been criticised by the Members of the European Parliament (MEPs) in particular as it happens during the initial phase of the legislative procedure where the legislator is 'sovereign'. However, this process is the first ever attempt to capture stakeholders'

[32] See Commission Communication, 'Completing the Better Regulation Agenda: Better Solutions for Better Results', adopted on 24 October 2017.

[33] Judgment of the General Court of 13 November 2015 in Joined Cases T-424/14 and T-425/14 *ClientEarth v Commission*.

views on a Commission proposal in an open, transparent and objective manner. In many ways, this feedback process is no different from the operation of the subsidiarity mechanism (see below), where national parliaments can issue opinions on the Commission's proposal during an eight-week period following the adoption of the proposal by the Commission.

Clearly the Commission's proposal is only the start of a long and often complex negotiation with the European Parliament and the Council during which stakeholders can and do make their views known to the legislator.

Regulatory Scrutiny

The necessity for independent scrutiny of Impact Assessments was recognised in 2007 when the Impact Assessment Board was established and the Commission's working procedures adapted to require a positive opinion in order for the initiative to proceed. Such scrutiny ensures a minimum level of quality and provides credibility for the work of the Commission. But ever since its creation, Member States, parliamentarians and business organisations have repeatedly called on the Commission to create a fully externalised quality control body as if this was the only possible guarantee of full independence. Some simply don't trust the evidence we present.

The Commission has always resisted full externalisation—and for good reason. First, there is no systematic evidence of bias and poor quality. The OECD has ranked the Commission amongst the best performers in its 2015 Regulatory Outlook benchmarked review of regulatory practices of OECD countries.[34] Second, it is not appropriate to constrain the Commission's right of initiative under the Treaties. Third, quality control does not have to be situated outside of the Commission in order for it to be strong and independent. Indeed, the OECD has recommended that quality control bodies should be established close to the centre of government, with an independent mandate and in a way that is adapted to each institution's system of governance.[35] Finally, all Impact Assessments are public and stakeholders are free to comment on the Commission's Impact Assessment and to lobby the European institutions with their views during the legislative process. It is therefore a myth that the Commission has no interest in high-quality Impact Assessments as poor quality (or no Impact Assessment when there should be one) weakens the Commission's hand during the legislative process.

Nonetheless, the President of the Commission moved to strengthen the scrutiny of Impact Assessments in May 2015. The new Regulatory Scrutiny Board has seven

[34] OECD, *OECD Regulatory Policy Outlook 2015* (Paris, OECD Publishing, 2015), http://dx.doi.org/10.1787/9789264238770-en.

[35] Section 3.1 of the OECD Council Recommendation on Regulatory Policy and Governance, 2012, www.oecd.org/governance/regulatory-policy/2012-recommendation.htm. It is worth remembering that the American Office of Institutional Research and Assessment sits in the White House.

senior full-time officials[36] who are dedicated to scrutiny activities. Three of these have been recruited from outside of the EU's institutions and all will serve for a fixed period of three years. They are not involved in any policy development activity and work in a personal capacity, but are bound by the Commission's code of conduct and rules of ethics and conflicts of interest. This new Board represents a substantial reinforcement of its scrutiny capacity and independence.

However, Member States and business associations still argue that some issues should be systematically reported by the Board in its opinions. Most frequently this concerns impacts on SMEs, sectoral competitiveness, innovation or the digital environment. The Board must be guided by the principle of proportionate analysis and must ensure that the Impact Assessment or evaluation meets a minimum standard so that it can fulfil its purpose to inform political decisions. The Board does not generally refer to issues which are adequately addressed in the context of a specific Impact Assessment or evaluation. However, the Board itself recognises the weakness of the Impact Assessments it scrutinises and has set out areas where it will work with the Commission's departments to improve quality.[37]

Focus on Regulatory Fitness

Regulatory fitness is not about deregulation as often claimed with little supporting evidence. It is about regulation that continues to deliver efficiently in a changing world. There is no secret radical neoliberal agenda to repeal environmental and social protection. But the Commission does want to deliver simpler, modern and less costly legislation because that helps everybody, including those striving to grow a small business. The Commission must, however, have the right to make proposals to repeal when it finds that legislation is ineffective or no longer relevant, otherwise there is simply no point in wasting time, effort and financial resources on making evaluations of the EU's legislation.

Evaluations now systematically address the regulatory fitness of EU law from the point of view of the five mandatory evaluation criteria. This process has been complemented by a new stakeholder body (the REFIT Platform)[38] whose aim is to identify the most problematic or burdensome aspects of EU law. Stakeholders can submit suggestions to simplify and improve legislation via the website 'Lighten the Load',[39] which are then assessed by the Platform, which comprises representatives from a broad range of stakeholders and Member States. In 2016, the REFIT Platform issued 22 opinions which were then followed up in the Commission's work programme.

[36] See the Regulatory Scrutiny Board's website for details of its composition: https://ec.europa.eu/info/law/law-making-process/regulatory-scrutiny-board/members-regulatory-scrutiny-board-0_en.

[37] Regulatory Scrutiny Board annual report 2016, https://ec.europa.eu/info/files/regulatory-scrutiny-board-annual-report-2016_en.

[38] Commission Decision establishing the REFIT Platform; C(2015) 3261.

[39] 'Lighten the Load', http://ec.europa.eu/info/law/better-regulation/lighten-load_en.

Targets for Regulatory Burden Reduction

Several Member States have established targets to drive reductions in compliance costs for businesses. These include absolute financial reduction objectives as well as tools to reduce the flow of new legislative rules ('one-in-one-out', 'one-in-two-out' etc). The Council has also asked the Commission to establish targets for reducing regulatory costs.[40] The Commission is also committed to prepare an annual burden survey and to assess the feasibility of objectives for burden reduction in key sectors pursuant to the Interinstitutional Agreement on Better Law-Making.[41]

We cannot in this chapter prejudge in any manner what the Commission might decide in the future. It is, however, important to clarify a few issues and dispel a few myths in this area.

It is important to understand that burden reduction targets and Better Regulation are separate responses to different problems. As we have seen, Better Regulation processes aim to inform decision-makers' choices without determining them. There is clearly a wish to reduce costs unnecessarily imposed on businesses. *Ex ante* Impact Assessments highlight what the costs of alternative proposals are and *ex post* evaluations identify unnecessary costs that can be reduced. Consultations and mechanisms such as the REFIT Platform allow the public to flag which costs are thought to be excessive. Therefore, to the extent that excessive and unnecessary costs can be precisely identified, Better Regulation processes can already offer all the information needed for a political decision to reduce them.

Reduction targets aim instead to constrain the choices of decision-makers in the belief that, left to their own devices and independently of the information Better Regulation processes provided to them, they will systematically overregulate.

Some conclusions flow from this. First, Better Regulation should not be confused with reduction targets and vice versa. Second, with scarce administrative resources, there is a risk that any reduction target will tend to undermine the comprehensiveness of Better Regulation processes (as the targeted impact will be more important, this being after all the intended output). Third, the need for targets is a function of whether or not one believes in the existence of a regulatory bias and whether targets are the most efficient solution for such a bias. When assessing the latter, one should take into account several factors:

— Targets cannot be a Commission-only endeavour. The Commission makes proposals, the Legislator adopts legislation and the Member States transpose and implement it. A joint effort between the European Parliament, the Council, the Member States and the Commission would be needed if real

[40] Council conclusions of December 2014 (Doc 16000/14): 'call on the Commission to develop and put in place—on the basis of input from Member States and stakeholders—reduction targets in particularly burdensome areas, especially for SMEs, within the REFIT Programme, which would not require baseline measurement and should consider at the same time the costs and benefits of regulation'.

[41] Interinstitutional Agreement on Better Law-Making, above n 21, para 48.

benefits are to be delivered to businesses, SMEs and public authorities. In addition, what happens if the European Parliament or the Council denatures the Commission's proposal to simplify the burdensome legislation? Who is responsible for not delivering on the target?

— How can you be sure that the objective or target focuses effort on the most burdensome areas of law? How do we know that it is the EU's act that is problematic and not the way in which the Member State has implemented it? Member States very often 'gold-plate' their national legislation, but are seldom transparent about doing so—so that the EU is often, and incorrectly, blamed for imposing unnecessary burdens.
— Should we not verify the benefit of our efforts on the ground? The experience of the Commission in this sense is not encouraging. In the case of the Administrative Burden Reduction Programme implemented between 2007 and 2012, Member States could not provide meaningful data and evidence on the ground to prove that there had been a real effect on businesses. Without such data, any system of targets will remain an academic exercise.
— There is a risk that the application of targets or objectives leads inexorably to deregulation and the undermining of important societal objectives, such as those for environmental and social protection, or affects the flexibility with which emerging risks can be managed. Had a 'one in one out' system been in place at the EU level over the last couple of years, the response to the migration and security crises would have required giving up on solving other problems. Would there have been support for such a development? Should a formula dictate prioritisation to policy-makers? Could it, in any case, credibly do so? If not, would a target really change politicians' incentives?
— In an era of limited resources, would it not be more effective simply to identify the most problematic legislation through surveys and rigorous evaluation, to foresee lighter regimes for SMEs and to tackle the issues of unnecessary costs and legislative complexity directly? This is the path so far chosen by the Commission as it seems more practical and more likely to deliver tangible benefits to businesses, citizens and public authorities.[42]

Subsidiarity

The Commission is often criticised by national and regional authorities for overstepping the line on what should be done nationally and at the EU level. Indeed, if

[42] As of March 2017, 119 REFIT actions were included in the Commission Work Programmes for 2015 and 2016 and 93 proposals in the EU legislative procedure have been identified for withdrawal under the Juncker Commission. The Commission Work Programme 2017 lists an additional 34 legislative initiatives under REFIT, 19 withdrawals and 16 repeals. Initiatives to reduce regulatory burdens on SMEs: (the 'Think Small First' principle). Fifteen out of the 58 (26 per cent) legislative initiatives in the Scoreboard of the Regulatory Fitness programme (REFIT) include exemptions or lighter regimes for SMEs.

the UK electorate had voted to remain in the EU on 23 June 2016, the Commission would have been tasked with assessing the entire body of EU law from the perspective of subsidiarity.[43] But is there any evidence to support these criticisms?

The principle of subsidiarity is now a cornerstone of the Commission's legislative activity following its explicit introduction into the EU's legal order with the Single European Act of 1987. In 2007, the Lisbon Treaty (in Protocol No 2) enhanced the role of national parliaments in controlling the application of the subsidiarity principle, introducing the so-called 'yellow card' and 'amber card' procedures.

A national parliament can send a 'reasoned opinion' to the European Commission in the case of subsidiarity concerns about a legislative proposal.[44] If one-third of national parliaments think that a particular legislative matter should better be regulated at the national level (and not the EU level), the threshold for a yellow card is reached. More than half of national parliaments must raise subsidiarity concerns to surpass the threshold for an 'amber card'. In that case, a qualified majority in the Council or a simple majority in the European Parliament is sufficient to force the Commission to withdraw its proposal. In practice, a yellow card has only been triggered three times and the threshold for an 'amber card' has never been reached.

An independent analysis of the Review findings by the Centre of European Policy Studies[45] found that the principles of subsidiarity and proportionality are being taken increasingly seriously among Member States and the EU institutions, and that the appointment of the First Vice-President with responsibility for Better Regulation adds to the build-up of treaty-level safeguards.

IS BETTER REGULATION A LEFT-OVER FROM A BYGONE ERA?

We live in momentous times. Things not only change but seem to have become unmoored. It is a time of tectonic shifts in technology, economics and politics. And where there are tectonic shifts, earthquakes can happen, as has been seen repeatedly over the last couple of years. Yet, at the same time, this is also turning out to be the moment when we rediscover the fundamental reasons for what is being challenged. And this allows us to defend what needs to be defended and change what needs to be changed with renewed purpose. It is submitted that something similar might also be happening for Better Regulation and evidence-based policy-making. Let us begin with the doubt. Two developments have tested Better Regulation over the last few years—the return of politics and the emergence of a post-truth world:

[43] European Council Conclusions of 19 February 2016, EUCO 1/16, http://data.consilium.europa.eu/doc/document/ST-1-2016-INIT/en/pdf.

[44] Each national parliament has two votes and opinions must be submitted within an eight-week period after having received the Commission's proposal.

[45] M Emerson (ed), *Britain's Future in Europe: Reform, Renegotiation, Repatriation or Secession?* (London, Centre for European Policy Studies, Rowman & Littlefield International, 2015).

— What role is there for Better Regulation in a world where electoral majorities are seen as the sole source of authority across all policy fields? A world where governments can say 'stop whining about the rule of law—we have won the election so we can do whatever we like'.
— What role is there for scientific findings in a world where people 'have had enough of experts'? Where the head of the US Environmental Protection Agency does not 'believe' in the role played by CO_2 in global warming and says so publicly?
— What role is there for evidence-based policy-making in a world where it is increasingly claimed that politicians, media and bureaucrats not only tell lies—as they have always done at times—but also no longer care about being caught?

To put it bluntly, is Better Regulation perhaps becoming a left-over from a bygone era? An era of the end of history, all-powerful technocracies, and effectiveness and efficiency? Are we moving towards an era that dawned into the harsh reality of our daily present, a present of naked power politics, manipulation of emotions, fake news, strong men and illiberal democracies? We would argue that the answer is 'no'. To understand why, it is useful to return to the roots, to go back through the years, to cut through the pile of technicalities, measures and proposals accumulated over the years and once again consider the original raison d'etre of Better Regulation and appreciate its persisting relevance.

'People nowadays take an interest in the effectiveness of the rules handed down "from Brussels" and the way they are drawn up. The advent of a democratic conscience is strengthening the need for accountability and proportionality in the way powers vested in the European institutions are exercised. This need is expressed more especially in transparency, clarity and the willingness to stand up to scrutiny. What we have here, then, is a veritable ethical requirement.' This is not us speaking about the present now. It is us quoting the first Communication on Better Law-Making written 15 years ago. Is not such a statement relevant today? Is it not this 'ethical' necessity for evidence-based policy-making even more necessary today than it was in 2002?

Better regulation processes aim to ensure that the best available evidence and analysis is made available to decision-makers in a timely fashion. They inform politicians' choices. They do not, and should not, predetermine them. Final choices will be influenced by many other factors and legitimately so. It is therefore difficult to accept the view that Better Regulation is a project out of tune with the re-emergence of politics because it was a means to de-democratise the legislative process in favour of technocratic decisions. It is difficult because the aim was precisely the opposite from the very beginning. Better regulation does not hollow out political choices. On the contrary, it fills them with greater legitimacy and accountability for various reasons:

— It avoids political choices being taken solely on the basis of the strength of rhetorical arguments or, quite simply, raw political power. The world is too complex for good solutions to be found without looking first at the evidence in a structured and comprehensive way.

— Better regulation urges politicians to justify their choices in terms of evidence, expected impacts, benefits, costs and their distribution. Importantly, it also pushes stakeholders and lobbyists to argue in the same terms.
— Better regulation provides a range of tools to engage meaningfully with society in all its components. Stakeholder acceptance of new policies and their commitment to implement them correctly are more likely if those most affected have been involved in an open and transparent process where their views and data have been considered seriously (but not necessarily taken on board). Some may even claim that the lesson from the research on procedural justice applies here: people's attitudes are as much influenced by the processes they experience as they are by the outcomes they receive. In the field of public policy-making, serious and systematic engagement with stakeholders and citizens in particular can only help improve trust in public authorities.

But Better Regulation is also still relevant today for another reason. In the age of fake news, there is a fashionable belief laying waste to political discourse everywhere: the belief that all interpretations are equal, that the value of any narrative only rests in the numbers and power of its proponents, and not also on the soundness and coherence of its supporting arguments.

But some interpretations are better than others, and Better Regulation with its formal procedures, consultation mechanisms and independent scrutiny bodies is there to help us discriminate.

There is an intriguing parallelism here. Just as the core tenet of liberal democracies lies in the protection of minorities rather than in the power or majorities, so the core principle of Better Regulation rests in the consideration of alternatives rather than in the choice of a preferred option.

Hence, in today's world, Better Regulation is more, not less, relevant and explains why a key objective of the Juncker Commission has not simply been to reinvigorate the Commission's Better Regulation policy, but to do so:

— as part of the overall political priority to enhance democratic change; and
— under the responsibility of a First Vice-President also tasked with the Rule of Law, the Charter of Fundamental Rights and Interinstitutional Relations.

Of course, it is not enough to establish that Better Regulation still has a purpose (no matter how important it may be). When applying Better Regulation principles, one also has to make sure that the policy is fit for such a purpose. This is why, as explained earlier, in the very early days of the Juncker Commission, the challenges of the present as well as the successes and shortfalls of the past were looked at in order to identify what needed to be changed in the Commission Better Regulation policy. One of the conclusions was that Better Regulation must be about changing incentives and attitudes to ensure the system itself has changed and did not need constant policing. Another important conclusion was that Better Regulation at the EU level must be a joint agenda of all EU players.

A FEW CONCLUDING REMARKS

Changes We Hope to See

Evaluations now have a more prominent role to play in the policy-making processes of the Commission. They are structurally linked to Impact Assessments and have a much greater value in their own right. The quality of the evaluations should improve over time as the Commission services learn by doing under the scrutiny and direction of the Regulatory Scrutiny Board. This improvement is absolutely necessary if the Commission is to deliver on its wish to keep the existing stock of legislation fit for purpose.

Stakeholders have recently been given unprecedented opportunities to contribute to the Commission's Better Regulation activities. It is unlikely that all stakeholders are aware however. Greater outreach is envisaged so that stakeholders' contributions increase and for the Commission to show stakeholders that we listen seriously if they make the effort to contribute.

The Commission cannot deliver higher-quality legislation on its own. The new Interinstitutional Agreement on Better Law-Making provides opportunities to cooperate so that the legislative procedure is more transparent, has greater reliance on evidence, and that monitoring and evaluation are taken more seriously. There are even promising signs that the Council will have put into place the capacity to undertake Impact Assessments of substantial amendments at the start of 2018 in response to its commitment in the Better Law-Making Agreement.

The methodological guidance on how to apply Better Regulation is improving in the light of practical experience. The second editions of the Commission's guidelines and toolbox are now ready to be deployed and will hopefully lead to even better analyses.

The Importance of Evidence-Based Policy-Making

Better regulation is the means to deliver evidence-based policy-making. It provides tools to engage with stakeholders in processes that build trust and confidence in the work of the EU's institutions as well as helping to deliver better societal outcomes.

However, facts, studies and experts will not on their own counter recent populist trends. Politicians need to be convinced of the value of Better Regulation processes and to give the evidence its time and place in the decision-making process. Therefore, Better Regulation processes should not be overly complex, but should remain in the realm of common sense and of the possible; the dense and comprehensive Impact Assessment or evaluation does not talk particularly well to the sceptical citizen, MEP or SME. We need to find a better way to communicate about Better Regulation, but it is often hard to demonstrate tangibly the benefits it brings.

Better Regulation processes can help avoid further erosion of the public's faith in our systems and institutions. We have built an impressive array of tools to engage with stakeholders, but now we have to ensure they are used. This will take time, but habits will change as we make better use of social media and other online tools to raise awareness.

While the Commission has a very good and well-respected system for Better Regulation, we can still improve to meet better the needs of the policy-maker looking for feasible solutions and the expectations stakeholders wanting to be heard and of the entrepreneurs who want to understand why rules and regulations are needed. The Commission should be alive and respond to its critics, but let us not forget the progress the Commission has made while others lag a long way behind. Constructive dialogue about Better Regulation is always welcome, but not the negative ill-informed hyperbole.

Finally, Better Regulation is there to help us understand and to assist politicians in making informed decisions. A politics based on evidence is more likely to deliver more effective policies and safeguard our democratic traditions based on objective reality: 'Freedom is the freedom to say that two plus two make four. If that is granted, all else follows.'[46] The Juncker Commission has come into office at a very particular time in the history of European integration—a time of crisis and disillusionment in the tangible benefits of the European project. Only by delivering the results we can deliver at the EU level can we win back our citizens' trust in this unique project. This is the ultimate objective of the Juncker Commission. To achieve it, we certainly do not need to ditch evidence-based policy-making and the scrutiny and analytic framework that goes with it—quite the contrary.

[46] G Orwell, *Nineteen Eighty-Four* (London, Martin Secker & Warburg Ltd, 1949).

7

The European Parliament and the Better Law-Making Agenda

MARÍA JOSÉ MARTÍNEZ IGLESIAS*

FOR THE EUROPEAN Parliament, the Interinstitutional Agreement (IIA) on Better Law-Making constitutes its own contribution and commitment to the Better Legislation Agenda. This is the reason why I have chosen to focus in this chapter on the analysis of the IIA, the way it was framed by negotiation between the Institutions and its consequences for the interinstitutional balance from the point of view of the Parliament. This analysis is followed by a detailed examination of one of the most meaningful new elements of the IIA, legislative programming, which is of particular importance for the European Parliament.

WHAT IS IT ALL ABOUT?

As other contributors to this volume have recalled, the Juncker Commission's Better Regulation package, presented in 2015, constitutes yet another chapter in a long series of initiatives dating back to Jacques Delors' 1985 White Paper. That was a genuine effort to smooth the acceptance of the ambitious legislative and institutional programme aimed at building the Internal Market. The Better Legislation Agenda, in its various meanings and appellations (Good Governance, Better Regulation, Smart Regulation, Simplification, Better Law-Making, Fit Regulation, REFIT etc) has never since been abandoned.

I would like to mention a relevant stage in this journey, which was the addition, in 1999, of the Better Legislation aspects to the Annual Report on Subsidiarity and Proportionality. This addition may seem anecdotal, but it shifted the balance of the report towards the quality of legislation or, more specifically, the quality of the process of the production of law in the EU. This has resulted in a shift from an examination of legal requirements, which is how the principles of subsidiarity and proportionality appear under the Treaties, to a more complex and

* María José Martínez Iglesias is Director of Legislative Affairs, Legal Service, European Parliament.

ambiguous analysis, covering a series of more or less consensual parameters and instruments. Thanks to the Commission's annual reporting on the EU's legislative performance, which is followed each year by a European Parliament resolution, these aspects have become a recurring *leitmotiv* of the political debate.

Two distinct concepts are subsumed in the list of expressions I mentioned above: the first is eminently ideological in nature and refers to the outcome of the decision-making process and to the quality of the ensemble of norms. For some, 'Better Regulation' implies lightening the burden on companies and citizens, while for others, it means ensuring greater respect for the environment and so on. Certain political movements have traditionally identified Better Regulation as a force for the reduction of administrative burdens. Of course, no one wants regulations that impose excessive or unjustified burdens, but defining what is excessive or unjustified regulation is in itself an ideological exercise. In fact, it often forms the very core of the political debate and therefore should not be confused with a neutral institutional principle.

The second concept is related to the process of producing law. It is eminently procedural and refers to the mechanisms and instruments that contribute to the optimisation of the decision-making process, in order to ensure the quality of legislation without prejudging its content.

The European Parliament has been an eager partner of the Commission in embracing its recurrent initiatives. This is clearly expressed in the resolutions reacting to the Commission's annual reports, not only on subsidiarity, proportionality and better law-making, but also on the implementation of EU law. Besides these resolutions, the European Parliament has also entered into commitments of its own as legislator, in the form of two successive trilateral Interinstitutional Agreements[1] and the Framework Agreement with the Commission of 2010,[2] much of which is also devoted to instruments for better law-making.

The successive initiatives from the Commission have pursued the clear objective of strengthening legitimacy.[3] The purpose of the 2003 IIA was 'to win back the support and the trust of the citizens'. According to the 2015 Commission's proposal, the IIA was aimed at 'restoring citizens' and business confidence in our ability to deliver'. However, hidden behind this objective, and in some way justified by it, was the intention to resolve differences between the Institutions in the day-to-day exercise of their respective competences. Indeed, the IIA clearly reveals tensions between the three Institutions. It is an instrument not only to improve law-making procedures but also to resolve problems between the three political Institutions

[1] The 2003 Interinstitutional Agreement on Better Law-Making of 16 December 2003 [2003] OJ C321, 31 December and the recent Interinstitutional Agreement on Better Law-Making of 13 April 2016 [2016] OJ L123, 12 May.

[2] [2010] OJ L304, 20 November.

[3] Or, as Professor Kelemen rightly points out, it is a regular exercise in self-flagellation of the Institutions of the EU. 'Eurolegalism and the Better Regulation Agenda' paper prepared for the Workshop on 'The EU Better Regulation Agenda: Critical Reflections', College of Europe, Bruges, 10 October 2016.

of the EU, problems that arise because of their different and often contradictory vision of their roles and powers in the decision-making process of the EU and very often jeopardise the smooth running of the decision-making processes. This is the reason why, in blatant contradiction with the principles it advocates, the IIA redundantly reiterates provisions and principles already included in primary or secondary law, or clearly enshrined in European Court of Justice (ECJ) case law, in order for the three Institutions to reaffirm their respective rights and prerogatives but also to remind *the other two* what their duties are.

In fact, the real purpose of interinstitutional agreements is to resolve or prevent problems between the Institutions through cooperation. In a volatile constitutional environment, subject to constant change, as in the case of the EU, this kind of instrument has had particular importance, both before and after the Treaty of Lisbon, which introduced in Article 295 of the Treaty on the Functioning of the European Union (TFEU) a *sui generis* legal basis for this type of act. In the present case, as the object of the IIA concerns relations between the Institutions and commitments that could affect the exercise of their respective competences and the interinstitutional balance enshrined in the Treaties, we are in the presence of a kind of soft constitutional law. From the point of view of the European Parliament, being itself the direct representative of the citizens, this aspect of the IIA is undoubtedly just as relevant, if not more so, than the aforementioned reconquest of legitimacy and proximity to the people. Its own role in the decision-making process in the EU is more relevant for legitimacy enhancement purposes than the instruments of better law-making themselves.

As for the legal effect of the IIA, it seems to be generally acknowledged that its binding force derives from the intention expressed by the parties, as had already been established by the case law of the ECJ[4] even before Lisbon. This is the reason for the careful use of words and especially verbal forms throughout the document. If one compares the original proposal of the Commission with the final text, it is not difficult to appreciate the change of political intention through the subtle linguistic modifications made.

Except in revolutionary historical moments, it is uncommon for a parliament to find its own voice as an institutional entity with its own distinct personality. A parliament is a chessboard; it is the keeper of the rules of the game, while the protagonists of the action are parliamentary groups and political parties. The European Parliament is an exception in this regard. This is because it is keenly aware of the constant change that has characterised the EU and its institutional framework since its inception. The European Parliament has always been at the very centre of that change. The prerogatives of the Parliament have grown along

[4] Case C-41/95 *Council v Parliament* ECLI:EU:C:1995:431 and Case C-25/94 *Commission v Council* ECLI:EU:C:1996:114.

with the powers of the EU. A recurring theme in the narrative of the Institution is the defence of its own prerogatives as an instrument by which to acquire new powers that are not necessarily so clearly inferable from the Treaties in force at a particular historical moment. European history leads *inevitably* to European democracy and the European Parliament is the very key to that process.

One could recall the first informal 'conciliation procedure', which was the subject of an gentleman's agreement that, in the 1980s, afforded a Parliament, which was until then completely deprived of decision-making powers, the ability to influence legislation thanks to its—albeit very limited—budgetary powers. It gave the Parliament influence over the rules in areas relating to non-compulsory spending whereby it avoided the strong temptation to block budget decisions so as to pursue its political agenda. Since the first Delors Package of 1988, this has been the dynamic of successive interinstitutional agreements on the EU's financial perspectives. The need to obtain the Parliament's agreement on the Multiannual Financial Framework (to use the current terminology), which was meant to keep the budgetary peace for several years, served the Institution as a lever by which to assert its own power in defining the content of policies.

I use these anecdotes, which have been superseded by the evolution of the Treaties, to illustrate the importance that the Parliament, as an institution with this kind of historical memory, may attribute to the IIA and the legal-constitutional vision that characterises it. Indeed, as we shall see later, certain elements of the IIA address recurrent concerns of the Parliament.

THE IIA AND THE INTERINSTITUTIONAL BALANCE

The first pertinent issue when considering the Parliament's position in this exercise is the very title of the agreement: 'Better Law-Making'. Unlike the Commission's proposed title for the Agreement and its accompanying package of internal measures, 'Better Regulation', the result of the negotiations between the institutions emphasises the law production process, not its content or outcome, under the expression 'Better Law-Making', which was already the title of the 2003 IIA. Although, ultimately, the Agreement is one of voluntary self-limitation on the part of the legislator, which is more or less demanding depending on the issues at stake, the legislator cannot compromise its absolute freedom in decision-making, which is conditioned only by the principle of legality and the Rule of Law. Its commitment can only be extended to the instruments that will help it better to exercise its competences, but in no way can it renounce them. That is why the emphasis of the definitive title is placed not on the results of law-making, for which no guarantees can be given, but on the process.

This change in perspective between the initial draft and the final result is also visible in the way in which many elements of the IIA have been altered and others entirely deleted. Any evaluation of the final Agreement must of course take into account its content, but regard must also be had to those elements that are lacking[5] or those that were eliminated during negotiations. The style of the language is also relevant, particularly the change from the use of legalistic expressions to verb tenses with a conditional or tentative meaning.

Some examples can help to illustrate the change of perspective and ultimately, to interpret the scope and significance of the IIA.

The changes made to the 'Impact Assessment' mechanism are particularly important. In the 2003 IIA, the Commission appeared to regard this instrument as being inextricably linked to its privilege of legislative initiative. It was only on their insistence that the Council and the Parliament were recognised as having the right to carry out their own Impact Assessments of their own substantial amendments, using shared criteria and procedures. In fact, such criteria and procedures have never been defined: the Council has never carried out an Impact Assessment and the Parliament has done so only rarely.[6] The risk that it will be used as a tool of parliamentary filibustering, with the extension of deadlines that this could entail, should also be taken into account.

In its proposal for the IIA, the Commission appeared to have radically changed its position. Unlike in the 2003 IIA, the use of Impact Assessments is presented as an obligation for the legislator whenever an amendment could substantially modify the Commission's proposal. What is more, it was foreseen that an Impact Assessment carried out by the legislator would have to take the Commission's Impact Assessment as its starting point, thereby accepting its point of view and methodology.

The resulting final IIA was, predictably, profoundly modified. The legislators remain free to resort to an Impact Assessment in order to justify their substantial amendments (in that sense 'will' has simply been replaced by 'may'). It is up to them to define what constitutes a substantial amendment on a case-by-case basis. The Commission's assessment is still foreseen as the starting point for the exercise, but only as a 'general rule', from which the legislator may depart.

Another example of the change of perspective between the proposal and the final IIA is the fate of the independent panel charged with judging whether substantial amendments to a Commission proposal respected the principles of good legislation.[7] Needless to say, this interference would potentially have detracted from the democratic nature of the political decision-making process by interfering with the freedom of the legislator.

[5] The absence of any mention of soft law, which, by contrast, constituted one of the chapters of the 2003 IIA, is very significant.

[6] The European Parliament created in 2012 a new Directorate General, the European Parliament Research Service, with a special department dedicated to impact assessment. This has dramatically increased the activity of the Parliament in the production of Impact Assessments and the so-called added value studies, which are not necessarily limited to amendments.

[7] See point 12 of the Commission's proposal. These principles are now to be found in the second recital of the agreed text.

A third example that I believe is particularly relevant is the consultation of stakeholders after the adoption of the legislative proposal by the Commission, which, according to the initial proposal, was to be carried out in parallel with the consultation of national parliaments during the eight-week period in which they can express their views on respect for the principle of subsidiarity. Obviously, this new stakeholder consultation would have interfered with the role of the legislator, which is free to initiate consultations and acquire information on its own terms whenever it thinks fit after the Commission's proposal has been presented to it.

These examples illustrate the willingness of the Council and the Parliament to conserve their freedom as legislators in line with the institutional balance defined by the Treaties. The result is an agreement that is well suited to the political evolution of the EU: neither scientific nor economic justifications, nor arguments relating to technical suitability, can supersede the political responsibility of democratic institutions; decisions of a technical nature cannot replace political decisions taken by democratic institutions.

In short, it is the peculiarity of the EU's institutional system that had determined the existence and content of the IIA. The fact that the closest thing to an executive that the EU has, that is to say the Commission, is not directly associated with a stable majority in the legislative bodies constituted by the Council and the Parliament results in a deficit of trust and predictability. On top of this, the Commission has a monopoly on legislative initiative, thanks to which it participates in the decision-making process through the exorbitant power to modify majorities in the Council or to stop the adoption of an act by withdrawing the proposal. Although politically answerable to the Parliament, it is in a very different position from a national government, since political control is reduced at the end of the day to the extreme and unlikely recourse to a motion of censure. These are the reasons why, as we will see later, legislative programming in the EU takes on the importance reflected in the IIA.

Better Law-Making instruments, such as Impact Assessments or those aimed at improving oversight of the application of EU law, are factors of certainty and predictability. If such instruments are important in national frameworks, they are all the more so for the EU, whose law spans 28 legal environments. Consequently, it comes as no surprise that this new Agreement puts particular emphasis on instruments aimed at improving the application of EU law, in particular by seeking to curtail the practice of gold-plating by Member States. By the same token, it is important to emphasise the new prominence given to *ex post* evaluation, which means in fact that the legislature accepts to be judged by the effectiveness of the law it produces. In short, these are instruments designed to improve predictability, certainty and, ultimately, trust.

Two questions that are peripheral to the Better Law-Making Agenda and on which the Parliament has clearly failed to achieve its objectives also have significant repercussions for institutional balance and the position occupied by the Parliament.

First and foremost, there is the question of information about international agreements. The Parliament attempted to uphold the recent judgment on the right to be informed on the basis of Article 218(11) TFEU.[8] Point 40 of the IIA is one of the most flagrant examples of redundancy in the text insofar as it simply points out that the Treaties and the case law must be respected, and it merely establishes a rendezvous clause for negotiations on the modalities of cooperation and information sharing, six months after the entry into force of the Agreement. More than a year on, not even the slightest progress has been made in relation to this.

The same occurred with delegated acts. A rendezvous clause provides for the negotiation of criteria to facilitate the choice between delegated and implementing acts. So far, no progress has been made in this area either. However, unlike in the case of international agreements, where no concessions have been made, the Parliament in this case had agreed to support the Council's call for systematic consultation by the Commission of the Member States' national experts on delegated acts, in the hope that this would help facilitate their use. One year after the entry into force of the Agreement, it can be said with certainty that this concession by the Parliament has been to no avail. The Council continues to be reluctant to resort to delegated acts in many cases. This is certainly because, above and beyond the consultation of national experts (which the Commission already carried out in practice), the Council is uncomfortable with the qualified majority that would be needed to mount an objection to oppose a delegated act.

We could understand delegated acts as Better Law-Making instruments in that they would contribute to the simplification of legislative acts, leaving the more technical aspects, or those in need of rapid technical adaptation, to the Commission, albeit under the scrutiny of the legislator itself. In that sense, the IIA is intended to facilitate their use. However, unfortunately, in reality they constitute such a complicating factor, both for the readability of legislative acts themselves and in legislative negotiations, that in many cases more time is spent discussing whether or not certain issues should be the subject of a delegated act than the substantive content of the actual legislation.

INFLUENCING THE POLITICAL AGENDA: LEGISLATIVE PROGRAMMING

Among the most innovative aspects of the 2016 IIA compared to that of 2003 are its provisions on legislative programming. The incorporation of legislative programming in the Treaties, and the resulting evolution in the understanding and scope of the idea, led to its emergence as a central element of the Agreement. This evolution is also in part due to the dialogue developed between the Parliament

[8] Case C-658/11 *Parliament v Council* ECLI :EU:C:2014:2025 (Mauritius).

and the Commission in this area. From purely pragmatic beginnings, since 2010 this dialogue has been enshrined in the Framework Agreement between the two Institutions.

The European Parliament has been a pioneer in legislative programming. In the 1990s, after first acquiring its power as a legislator[9] with the Maastricht Treaty, the Parliament had to take the planning of its work more seriously, for two reasons.

First, a precise and, above all, predictable timetable was needed in order to secure the presence of the Members in the plenary session so that the qualified majority called for at the second reading under the newly established co-decision procedure could be achieved. This anticipated a problem—that of not being able to oppose or modify the common position of the Council owing to an insufficient turnout of Members of the European Parliament (MEPs)—which has, indeed, never occurred. In fact, the progressive increase in the Parliament's powers has been accompanied by a corresponding growth in the activity and attendance of its Members.

Second, along with the greater political importance it acquired during those years, the Parliament required a communication strategy to broaden its appeal and attract the attention of the media. A clearly structured political debate is an essential part of such a strategy.

Of course, the programming of the chamber's work could not be carried out effectively without the active collaboration of the Commission. This collaboration was consolidated through a series of annual interinstitutional discussions, which culminated in the 2010 Framework Agreement between the two Institutions. Indeed, the Agreement includes a procedure in the form of a detailed annual calendar, beginning in the spring with the 'structured dialogue' between each of the parliamentary committees and the Commissioners who answer to them, and ending with the presentation of the Commission's annual work programme in plenary, followed by the adoption of a resolution expressing the chamber's reaction. Meanwhile, in July the Parliament adopts a resolution containing the 'priorities' outlined by its committees and in September a second 'dialogue' is held between the committees and the Commissioners, with a meeting of the Parliamentary Committee Chairs and the College of Commissioners. Also in September, the Parliament plenary plays host to the debate on the state of the EU, in which the President of the Commission takes stock of the current year and announces the broad lines of the next work programme. One month later, the work programme for the next year is released. The procedure closes in December with a resolution reflecting the Parliament's reaction to the work programme for the following year.

[9] It should be borne in mind that in the pre-Lisbon Treaties, no legislative function whatsoever existed in the EU, nor did anything comparable to the concepts of separation of powers or hierarchy of norms. In fact, the words 'legislation' and 'legislator' are used in this chapter in a general way.

These are the broad lines of the procedure, which I am mentioning because I consider it extremely significant. It is a gruelling procedure that could have been thought up only by a parliamentary bureaucracy unsure of its own power. Whilst the whole process is intended to define 'priorities', the resolutions adopted each July have traditionally been long lists of requests that combine most of the wishes and priorities of all the parliamentary committees and groups, at least to the extent that they do not contradict one another. Clearly, under such conditions, there can be no real priorities, nor can the Commission seriously be asked to consider them all. The excessive number discredits the whole exercise.[10] The same has been happening, albeit to a lesser extent, with the December resolutions, and this despite repeated attempts by the Conference of the Presidents of the Political Groups to exercise some kind of restraint and discipline over their content. This is the reason behind the Joint Declaration of the Presidents of the three Institutions that should conclude the annual programming exercise[11] according to point 7 of the IIA and is to include only the *broad objectives and priorities* on which all of them can agree.

It is in this context that we must approach the new IIA, which, it must be emphasised, neither modifies nor replaces the procedure described, but overlaps with it, while making substantial additions to it. Three are of great importance: the Council now participates in legislative planning; the multi-annual programming referred to in Article 17 of the Treaty on European Union (TEU) has been included; and a new instrument of annual political programming has been created—the Joint Declaration of the Presidents of the three Institutions to which I have already adverted.

The introduction of these three elements should give an indication of the utility and institutional nature of legislative programming. Indeed, no other parliament attaches such importance to this issue. Of course, national parliaments do use programming tools, but their objective is limited to the orderly planning of work and coordination with the government and the other chamber, if there is one. Programming in the EU goes much further and it is no surprise that the Parliament was the institution that pioneered its development, as it has traditionally been the weakest institution in terms of its decision-making role.

For the Parliament, programming serves first of all to alleviate, at least to some extent, its lack of a genuine legislative initiative, which the Treaties reserve virtually entirely to the Commission. This monopoly is a determining factor in the design of our constitutional system. Programming enables the Parliament to compromise with the Commission on the use of its legislative initiative and, at the same time, to influence the choice of the legal basis and the type of legal act: two elements that determine the extent of the Parliament's power and that of the EU itself.

[10] Also, the Commission Work Programme used to set out a very long list of proposals, which very often were simply carried over from one year to the next.

[11] The first Joint Declaration was signed on 13 December 2016.

The principle of attribution of competences, which forms the basis of the system by which competences are distributed between the Member States and the EU, makes these two elements the key to the exercise of power, both within and by the EU.

Second, programming gives the Parliament a role in defining the political agenda of the EU. In a system where the parliament and the executive lack the degree of direct connection that exists in every traditional national parliamentary system, this exercise becomes all the more significant. The peculiar composition of the Commission, coupled with the weak and fragmented nature of the European political parties, means that in reality, the Parliament's political control over the Commission is restricted to the atomic bomb of the motion of censure. So, once again, it is the ability to compromise, to build the consensus that will later smooth the path for the adoption of the tabled initiatives that is vital for the Parliament and the EU. Nor should it be forgotten that programming, as a tool for defining and publicising political priorities, can be a formidable instrument for promoting transparency and communication between the Institutions and citizens.

The fact that the Council has joined in the exercise of programming is an important indicator of a shift in that Institution's self-perception; starting from a mostly intergovernmental mindset, it seems to have become aware of its role as a legislative chamber. Behind this shift, at least to a certain extent, there lies a desire to emulate the Parliament. The Framework Agreement between the Commission and Parliament had deeply troubled the Council, which received it with reluctance and serious doubts as to its compatibility with the institutional balance enshrined in the Treaties. In fact, during the negotiations on the new IIA, the mention of the Framework Agreement between the Parliament and the Commission was deleted and replaced by a reference to a joint, separately published declaration of the two Institutions. All this, in my opinion, gives strength to the view that change is taking place and that the Council is assuming its role as legislator, as I argued earlier.

The programming mechanism provided for in the Agreement consists, essentially, of a series of pre-established rendezvous designed to oblige the three Institutions to sit down together and discuss objectives, priorities and timetables.

The first rendezvous concerns multi-annual programming. Point 5 of the Agreement transposes the last phrase of Article 17(1) TEU by conferring on the Commission the initiative for multiannual and annual programming 'in order to reach interinstitutional agreements'.

The scope and motivation of the Agreement in this aspect cannot properly be understood without taking into account the *Spitzenkandidaten* phenomenon that characterised the last elections to the European Parliament. Thereby, a process aimed to enhance the democratic legitimacy of the election of the Commission President by the European Parliament was put in place; in a nutshell, the candidate from the political party which wins the European elections is given the nomination.

This is the unexpected result of two new elements introduced by the Lisbon Treaty into the process of appointing the President of the Commission. First, the European Council is now obliged to take into account the results of the European elections in designating the candidate to be voted on by the Parliament and, second, the parliamentary vote is no longer described as one of 'approval' of the presidential candidate, but as an 'election' in its own right. These two elements helped transform the political narrative over the months leading up to the electoral campaign and during the campaign itself. Once the electoral process had culminated in the nomination of Jean-Claude Juncker as the candidate for the Commission presidency, the presentation of the executive's programme was transformed into something resembling a genuine investiture debate, to use national terminology. The programme formed the basis of a pact for the legislative term between several political groups, which came together as a kind of 'grand coalition' to offer it their backing.

The IIA's multi-annual programming procedure sets out to complete this mechanism by taking those parts of the legislative programme that are seen as the most important as the basis for the *principal policy objectives and priorities* which are to form the content of the 'Joint Conclusions'[12] signed by the Presidents of the three institutions (in case of agreement, naturally). The IIA multiannual programming mechanism has the flavour of a political pact for the parliamentary term, but one that exceeds the traditional bilateral Parliament/Commission relationship enshrined in the Treaties, adding the Council to it: a deal between the two co-legislators and the Commission.

How that mechanism can be reconciled with the European Council's mission to define the EU's general political orientations and priorities is a question that only time can answer. In any case, it was because of a concern to preserve this prerogative of the Heads of State and governments that it was impossible to go further in the multi-annual programming.

As I have already mentioned, the regular discussions on annual programming provided for in the IIA overlap with those already provided for under the Framework Agreement between the Parliament and the Commission. So far, no amount of persuasion has convinced the Council to take part in or even simply to acknowledge 'the debate on the State of the Union', which is mentioned in the Agreement as a matter of fact. In fact, for the Council, participation would mean recognising the other co-legislator's leadership when it comes to the constitutional rituals of the EU. Nevertheless, the Council has agreed to be a party, together with the Commission and the Parliament, to the political commitment represented by the aforementioned Joint Declaration which concludes the annual programming exercise.

[12] See point 5 of the IIA.

As I said, programming is important for the Parliament because it allows it to influence the exercise of the legislative initiative by the Commission and the political agenda of the EU. This is the reason why the Annual Commission Work Programme should include the most complete information possible about the legal basis, the withdrawal of old proposals and the treatment of the Council and the Parliament's own legislative initiatives. The IIA also considers these issues in other specific sections.

Point 25 of the IIA, dealing with the choice of the legal basis, is another example of unnecessary reiteration. The obligation on the Commission to comply with the provisions of the Treaties and the case law when choosing the legal basis is obviously redundant. In fact, the only new provision is the third paragraph, which establishes the obligation for the three Institutions to engage in a dialogue before proceeding with any change to the legal basis that may involve moving from the ordinary legislative procedure to a special legislative or non-legislative procedure. In short, it refers to any situation in which a change in the legal basis implies the loss for the Parliament of its decision-making power.

In fact, legal bases are the source of numerous disputes between the Institutions, especially in the years following the entry into force of the Lisbon Treaty, because some of the legal bases modified by the Treaty have proved particularly controversial. In the litigation on legal basis, the Parliament finds itself always (alone or together with the Commission) in the position of the complainant. There are still many legal bases in the Treaties which attribute the decision-making responsibility to the Council alone within the framework of legislative or non-legislative procedures. This means that even where the Parliament or the Commission have a different opinion, the Council can adopt a controversial act, and this may be contested. The European Parliament has no such prerogative and thus cannot find itself in the position of being a defendant.

Sometimes the controversy about the legal basis does not culminate in a dispute before the Court of Justice, but in conflicts of a political nature, which can be extremely time-consuming. It is worth mentioning the conflict between the Council and the Parliament on the legal basis of the Schengen evaluation mechanism,[13] which was the reason why the 'Schengen' legislative package was blocked for more than a year.

Therefore, it is no surprise then that the new IIA provides for this mechanism designed to prevent interinstitutional conflicts about legal bases ending up in court or jeopardising the legislative procedures. It is simply a recognition of the need to engage in dialogue before entering into an open conflict that could eventually lead to litigation before the ECJ.

[13] Council Regulation (EU) No 1053/2013 of 7 October 2013 establishing a monitoring and evaluation mechanism to verify the application of the Schengen *acquis* is established, and repeals the Decision of the Executive Committee of 16 September 1998 on the establishment of a Standing Committee on the evaluation and implementation of Schengen.

Further to the Parliament's goal of influencing the EU's political agenda, point 10 of the IIA imposes a series of obligations on the Commission in response to legislative initiatives of the Council and the Parliament based on Articles 241 and 225 TFEU respectively. The Commission must respond within three months, devoting a specific communication to each response. With regard to this last requirement, the College itself, rather than the individual Commissioners or simply the Directorates General, is supposed to respond and thus assume full political responsibility. It should be noted that, up to now, legislative initiatives launched by the European Parliament have been answered by means of a document used by the Commission's various Directorates General to respond to all kinds of resolutions (including legislative resolutions) adopted by the Parliament.

Redundancy again crept into the IIA with regard to the withdrawal of Commission proposals. Point 9 reproduces the recent case law of the ECJ on the withdrawal of a legislative proposal by the Commission. It reflects the enthusiasm of the co-legislators at their victory in the ECJ in Case C-409/13.[14] It imposes on the Commission respect for the principle of sincere cooperation, the obligation to justify the withdrawal, to take into account and to respond to the co-legislators' positions.

COULD IT HAVE DONE LESS?

To conclude, I would like to emphasise what I pointed out earlier. For the European Parliament, the IIA on Better Law-Making has the significance of a constitutional pact, a sort of soft constitutional law. The redundant references to provisions of the Treaties and to the case law work as a guarantee that the interinstitutional balance and, in particular, the Parliament's role as co-legislator are not only respected but also *understood* in all their extension and implications. Many of the procedures established by the IIA are not binding and indeed cannot be binding, but neither are they useless. As EU history shows, the simple establishment of a procedure and the fixing of a rendezvous for dialogue afford means of achieving compromise and consensus, which have always been the basis for the functioning and the progress of the EU.

[14] Case C-409/13 *Council v Commission* ECLI:EU:C:2015:217.

8

The Council

Some Historical and Practical Aspects to the Better Regulation Agenda

JENŐ CZUCZAI*

INTRODUCTION

WHEN SOMEBODY IS addressing the notion of 'Better Regulation' within the EU from a historical point of view, then first of all he or she should recall the success of a Conference of the Asser Instituut, held on 23–25 April 1997 in The Hague, which addressed for the first time in its complex context the main problems and the daily difficulties with regard to the 'quality of legislation' initiatives and requirements in Europe, at that time specifically focusing on the Community internal market.[1]

At that Conference, the Council Rapporteur gave a very comprehensive and detailed summary about all Council (and European Council) policy approaches on better regulation, touching upon the issues of internal working methods (especially in the Council Legal Service), organisational modalities, legal drafting requirements and guidelines, control and coordination mechanisms of translations of legislative texts and of legal proofreadings etc, but also concerning the assurances of quality of Community legislation and its perspectives within the Council as well as in a wider inter-institutional context.[2] I think that this summary even today is to a large extent valid and shows very well the essence of our

* Jeno Czuczai is Legal Adviser at the Legal Service of the EU Council and Visiting Professor at the College of Europe, Bruges. All the views and opinions expressed in this chapter are exclusively those of the author and in no way represent the official or the formal position of either the Council of the EU or of its Legal Service. This chapter is based on an earlier presentation on the topic delivered in The Hague at the EU law symposium on 'Better Regulation in the EU Revisited: Benefiting Business and Citizens', organised by the TMC Asser Insituut on 23 April 2015, but has been updated and further developed.

[1] AE Kellermann et al (ed), *Improving the Quality of Legislation in Europe* (The Hague, Kluwer Law International, 1998).

[2] JC Piris, 'The Quality of Community Legislation: The Viewpoint of the Council Legal Service' in Kellermann et al, above n 1, 25–38.

daily work as legal advisers in relation to the EU legislative processes, although it is also true that since then, a lot of new challenges have emerged concerning better law-making in the EU, especially after the entry into force of the Lisbon Treaty, or stimulated otherwise, for example, by the global economic and financial crises or by the e-economy or digitalised global market and trade integration concepts, not to speak of the current migration crisis.

However, one should not forget that even if the work of the legal advisers in the Legal Services of the EU Institutions is of a high quality and the legal drafting patterns, devices and models are in practice standardised, there are a lot of other external elements (eg, political, institutional, complicated technical and/or scientific background-based), which have a significant impact on the quality of legislation in the EU and sometimes cause problems and difficulties in the law-making procedures. In 1997 at the above-mentioned Asser Conference on 'Improving the Quality of Legislation in Europe', AG Francis G Jacobs, for example, specifically drew attention to the following:

> Problems of legislative quality are difficult on the national level … But many of the difficulties seem to be aggravated on the Community level: to list some factors in no particular sequence:
>
> 1. There are often broad disagreements in the legislative process itself over the basic objectives of the legislation, and these are sometimes reflected in the final text …
> 3. The final shape of the legislation emerges from last-minute compromises, often papering over an agreement to disagree—or, in effect, an agreement to leave it to the Court to sort out …
> 6. Legislation is often, and perhaps inevitably, based on the use of legal concepts which have different meanings in the different legal systems. Regrettably the situation has not improved. If one compares the situation today with that 25 years ago—just before the first enlargement of the Community:
>   - The number of Member States has increased from six to fifteen, and the number of legal systems similarly.
>   - The number of official languages has increased from four (but for many practical purposes at that time only one—namely French) to eleven.
>   - The legislative process—or rather processes—have become far more complex, and political compromises perhaps more difficult.
>   - Legislation extends to many new fields, and therefore also has to be interpreted and applied by many different kind of courts and tribunals.
>   - Far greater detail is often required of the legislation, this will often make the task of interpretation even more difficult.[3]

[3] FG Jacobs, 'The Quality of Community Legislation: What is to Be Done?' in Kellermann et al, above n 1, 13–14. I should mention here that CWA Timmermans in his presentation at the conference on 'How to Improve the Quality of Community Legislation: The Viewpoint of the European Commission' also highlighted some other difficulties and even stated that: 'Là ou les juristes cherchent la précision, les diplomates pratiquent le non-dit et ne fuient pas l'ambiguité.' Nonetheless, he stressed that the clarity and consistency is the most crucial in relation to ensuring the quality of legislation. For more detail, see Kellermann et al, above n 1, 39–59, especially at 41–42.

But since 1997, more than 20 years have passed and certainly today we have a much more complex, more developed, deeper but also more fragmented legal order in the EU, which makes better law-making more and more difficult and, indeed, on a daily basis a real challenge. I would like just to recall that today the EU has 28 Member States, 23 official languages or after Lisbon the so-called ordinary legislative procedure (Article 289(1)–(3) of the Treaty on the Functioning of the European Union (TFEU)) has become the main rule concerning the adoption of legislative acts (so co-decision with the European Parliament),[4] a situation very different, of course, from the one in 1997. The Lisbon Treaty also introduced the distinction between delegated acts and implementing acts (Articles 290–91 TFEU), raising a lot of legal questions, but we now have a lot of new EU policy areas too, which did not exist at all in 1997 (eg, EU energy policy), not to speak of the enhanced transparency principle[5] and the increased role of the national parliaments in the EU decision-making process, which has been strengthened after Lisbon (together with the principle of subsidiarity and proportionality etc).[6] Moreover—although these are only examples—since the complete list of the developments in EU law is, of course, much longer, one could still think about the 'communautairisation' process of the former third pillar after 2010 and its impact on better law-making, the managing tasks of the eurozone crisis, and the bank insolvencies and their consolidation at the national level in order to save the euro at the EU level, or new enhanced cooperation initiatives (eg, the European Public Prosecutor's Office), but also not forgetting about the fact that the EU Charter of Fundamental Rights became legally binding and today has 'the same legal value as the Treaties' (Article 6(1) of the Treaty on European Union (TEU)), which certainly has important consequences on better law-making as well. All this has resulted in new and even more complex challenges as regards better law-making in the EU after Lisbon and finally in the reform of the EU better regulation agenda in 2015–16.

Following the above introduction, this chapter is divided into four section. First, I will give a short overview about the historical developments until the adoption of the first Interinstitutional Agreement (IIA) on Better Law-Making in 2003. Then I will explore some concrete examples from the post-Lisbon Council legal practice, when good inter-institutional cooperation for better law-making during the legislative processes has, in my view, proved its worth and contributed substantially to the good quality of a new, very complex and comprehensive regulatory framework, which closely affects the daily life of the citizens and the business

[4] See in more detail J Monar, 'The European Union's Institutional Balance of Power after the Treaty of Lisbon' in *The EU after the Treaty of Lisbon: Visions of Leading Policy-Makers, Academics and Journalists* (Luxembourg, Publications Office of the EU, 2011) 60–89, in particular as regards the increase of legislative and other powers of the European Parliament after Lisbon at 65 et seq, 74 et seq and 80 et seq.

[5] See in this respect Art 15 TFEU.

[6] See in particular Art 5 TEU and Art 12 TFEU, as well as Protocol (No 1) on the role of national parliaments in the EU and Protocol No 2 on the application of the principles of subsidiarity and proportionality, attached to the Lisbon Treaty [2012] OJ C326, 26 October, 203–09.

operators in the EU. I chose the most obvious EU policy field, namely the EU cohesion policy, which all EU citizens and business operators encounter on a daily basis. In the next section, I will focus on some practical legal innovations of the new IIA on Better Law-Making and I will give a brief summary of the state of play in terms of its implementation so far. Finally, I will draw some personal conclusions, following my research on this topic.

THE HISTORICAL ROAD TO THE ADOPTION OF THE 2003 INTERINSTITUTIONAL AGREEMENT ON BETTER LAW-MAKING[7] AND ITS HERITAGE

After the 1997[8] Asser Conference on 'Improving the Quality of Legislation in Europe', almost all the recommendations of the Conference[9] were implemented at the EU level in the following five years, showing very good inter-institutional cooperation between the European Parliament, the Council and the Commission. Just to mention a number of cornerstone elements of this fantastic development in the late 1990s and early 2000s, one should refer to the following documents:

— Declaration No 39 on the quality of the drafting of Community legislation adopted on 2 October 1997 by the Intergovernmental Conference and annexed to the Final Act of the Treaty of Amsterdam.
— The adoption of the Interinstitutional Agreement of 22 December 1998 on common guidelines for the quality of drafting Community legislation.[10]
— The adoption of Regulation (EC) No 1049/2001 of the European Parliament and of the Council of 30 May 2001 regarding public access to European Parliament, Council and Commission documents.[11]
— The adoption of the Interinstitutional Agreement of 28 November 2001 on a more structured use of the recasting technique for legal acts.[12]
— The adoption of the IIA on Better Law-Making in 2003.[13]

[7] See [2003] OJ C321, 31 December, 1.

[8] For the sake of historical correctness, it should be noted that the first element of Better Regulation developments was the adoption by the three main EU Institutions (the Parliament, the Council and the Commission) of the Interinstitutional Agreement on accelerated working method for official codification of legislative texts on 20 December 1994 [1996] OJ C 102/3, 4 April, 2–3. For more detail, see B Driessen, *Interinstitutional Conventions in EU law* (London, Cameron May, 2007), in particular the first three chapters.

[9] For more details, see Kellermann et al, above n 1, in particular at xxxii–lviii.

[10] See [1999] OJ C73, 17 March, 1.

[11] See [2001] OJ L145, 31 May, 43.

[12] See [2002] OJ C77, 28 March, 1.

[13] The new Interinstitutional Agreement on Better Law-Making, which entered into force on 13 April 2016 ([2016] OJ L123, 12 May, 1) also mentions yet more cornerstones in its Recital (9), such as the Joint Declaration on practical arrangements for the co-decision procedure from 2007 ([2007] OJ C145, 30 June, 5), or the Joint Political Declaration on Explanatory documents from 2011 ([2011] OJ C369, 17 December, 15), or, for example, in para 51, even the 2005 Interinstitutional Common Approach to Impact Assessment is referred to, but for the purposes of this contribution, the historical development until the adoption of the first IIA on Better Law-making is now relevant.

For the purposes of this chapter, I would like to recall some of the main requirements as regards better regulation first from the 1998 IIA on Common Legal Drafting Guidelines and then from the 2003 IIA on Better Law-Making, with the aim of showing how important these principles have been from the viewpoint of the examples that I will explore later on, as well as of seeing how these historically developed principles have been kept and to some extent even further developed in the new IIA on Better Law-Making in 2016:

1. From the 1998 IIA on Common Legal Drafting Guidelines one could highlight the following principles in particular:
   - Recital (1) reads as follows: '*clear, simple and precise drafting of Community legislative acts is essential* if they are to be transparent and *readily understandable by the public and economic operators.* It is also a prerequisite for the proper implementation and uniform application of Community legislation in the Member States'.
   - Recital (2) still adds: 'according to the case-law of the Court of Justice, the principle of legal certainty, which is part of the Community legal order, requires that Community legislation must be clear and precise and *its application foreseeable by individuals.* That requirement must be observed all the more *strictly in the case of an act liable to have financial consequences and imposing obligations on individuals* in order that those concerned may know precisely the extent of the obligations which it imposes on them'.
   - Point 6 stipulates that: '*The terminology used in a given act shall be consistent* both internally and with acts already in force, especially in the same field.'
   - Point 12 provides that: '*The enacting terms of a binding act shall not include provisions of a non-normative nature*, such as wishes or political declarations, or those which repeat or paraphrase passages or articles from the Treaties or those which restate legal provisions already in force' (emphasis added).
2. From the 2003 IIA on Better Law-Making the following requirements should be perhaps mentioned:
   - Point 2 states that: 'In exercising the powers and in compliance with the procedures laid down in the Treaty, and recalling the importance which they (the European Parliament, the Council and the Commission) attach to the Community method, *the three Institutions agree to observe general principles such as democratic legitimacy, subsidiarity and proportionality, and legal certainty.* They further agree *to promote simplicity, clarity and consistency in the drafting of laws* and the utmost transparency of the legislative process.'
   - Point 25 adds: '*The three Institutions*, exercising their respective powers, *will ensure that legislation is of good quality, namely that it is clear, simple and effective* … They are committed to the full application of the Interinstitutional Agreement of 22 December 1998 on common guidelines for the quality of drafting of Community legislation.'

— Point 35 provides that: '*In order to make Community law easier to read and to apply*, the three Institutions agree, firstly, to update and condense existing legislation and, secondly, *significantly to simplify it … The purpose of legislative simplification is to improve and adapt legislation by amending or replacing acts and provisions* which are too unwieldy and too complex to be applied. *Such simplification will be carried* out through the recasting of existing acts or *by means of new legislative proposals, whilst maintaining the substance of Community policies*' (emphasis added).

In the following section, I will explore in more detail some concrete examples showing how in practice all the above-mentioned law-making principles have been implemented since 2003.

SOME EXAMPLES FROM THE COUNCIL'S MOST RECENT LEGISLATIVE PRACTICE FOR BETTER REGULATION AFTER LISBON, DEMONSTRATING GOOD INTER-INSTITUTIONAL COOPERATION

Better Regulation is important not just on paper, but much more so in practice. That is why I turn now to present some concrete legislative solutions for better law-making and legislative simplification in the new *Cohesion Legislative Package*, which came into force on 1 January 2014[14] and provides excellent proof of this.

I have chosen the new cohesion legislative package because it relates the new legislative framework for the so-called European Investment and Structural Funds (hereinafter 'ESI Funds'), which covers the utilisation of *more than €400 billion for the seven years between 2014 and 2020* from the EU budget, for which reason it is of the utmost importance for business operators and citizens in the EU.[15]

Therefore, in the context of this chapter, it may be perhaps interesting and instructive to see how its legislative process has fulfilled the above-quoted better law-making principles and guidelines, though nobody states that such a complex and big legislative package (seven Regulations amounting to close to 400 Official Journal pages)[16] would be perfect, especially since this was the first time after the

[14] Regulation (EU) No 1303/2013 of the European Parliament and of the Council of 17 December 2013 laying down common provisions on the European Regional Development Fund, the European Social Fund, the Cohesion Fund, the European Agricultural Fund for Rural Development and the European Maritime and Fisheries Fund and laying down general provisions on the European Regional Development Fund, the European Social Fund, the Cohesion Fund and the European Maritime and Fisheries Fund and repealing Council Regulation (EC) No 1083/2006, [2013] OJ L347, 20 December, 320 (hereinafter the 'CPR'). The Regulation entered into force on 21 December 2013, but the provisions of a financial nature were only applicable from 1 January 2014 (Art 154).

[15] See in particular J Bachtler, C Mendez and F Wishlade, *EU Cohesion Policy and European Integration: The Dynamics of EU Budget and Regional Policy Reform* (Farnham, Ashgate, 2013) or S Piattoni and L Polverari (eds), *The Handbook on Cohesion Policy in the EU* (Cheltenham, Edward Elgar, 2017).

[16] It could be even added that with the related nine delegated acts and seven implementing acts adopted so far, the legislative framework consists of more than 1,000 Official Journal pages. For more detail, see http://ec.europa.eu/regional_policy/en/information/legislation/delegated-acts and implementing acts.

Lisbon Treaty entered into force that the European Parliament and the Council under the ordinary legislative procedure jointly adopted the new legislative framework for the ESI Funds.

When the European Commission submitted in September 2011 the seven legislative proposals to the EU legislature, it indicated inter alia that the proposals aimed to achieve on the one hand a *substantial legislative consolidation* (even 'codification', a uniform approach), but on the other hand a *significant legislative simplification* as well in order to help and assist European businesses (especially small and medium-sized enterprises (SMEs)), to promote investments, to create more jobs and growth, plus also to create better understanding and accessibility of the new rules, fully respecting the principles of subsidiarity and proportionality in the law-making process.[17]

The main aim of the Commission proposals was to set out a new legislative framework for all five Funds (the ERDF, the ESF, the CF, the EAFRD and the EMFF),[18] concerned with structural (social, economic and territorial cohesion) policies in a sort of 'codified manner', meaning the establishment of 'common provisions', which are binding on all five Funds in one single rule book together with general provisions on the so-called 'Structural Funds' (the ERDF and the ESF) and the so-called 'Funds' (the ERDF, the ESF and the CF), as well as, later on, certain general provisions for the so-called 'Funds and the EMFF', together with the set of the so-called Fund-specific Regulations in the same regulatory context. *Such a legislative approach aimed at providing more legal certainty, more legal clarity and better enforcement.* This legislative aim of the Commission also helped to bring an end to the previous legislative fragmentations, where, depending on the Fund in question, there had been different, very technical and diverging over-regulation, with a lot of legal uncertainties, unclarities and overlaps, which was not good for the European business operators and the citizens.

[17] Council Doc No 15243/11 on the Commission document for the proposal for a Regulation, as referred to in n 14, in particular its Explanatory Memorandum.

[18] Regulation (EU) No 1299/2013 of the European Parliament and of the Council of 17 December 2013 on specific provisions for the support from the European Regional Development Fund to the European Territorial Goal (ETC); Regulation (EU) No 1300/2013 of the European Parliament and of the Council of 17 December 2013 on the Cohesion Fund and repealing Council Regulation (EC) No 1084/2006 (CF); Regulation (EU) No 1301/2013 of the European Parliament and of the Council of 17 December 2013 on the European Regional Development Fund and on specific provisions concerning the Investment for growth and jobs goal and repealing Regulation (EC) No 1080/2006 (ERDF); Regulation (EU) No 1304/2013 of the European Parliament and of the Council of 17 December 2013 on the European Social Fund and repealing Council Regulation (EC) No 1081/2006 (ESF); Regulation (EU) No 1305/2013 of the European Parliament and of the Council on support for rural development by the European Agricultural Fund for Rural Development (EAFRD) and repealing Council Regulation (EC) No 1698/2005— all these Regulations can be found in [2013] OJ L347, 20 December, 259–548; and finally Regulation (EU) No 508/2014 of the European Parliament and of the Council of 15 May 2014 on the European Maritime and Fisheries Fund and repealing Council Regulations (EC) No 2328/2003, (EC) No 861/2006, (EC) No 1198/2006 and (EC) No 791/2007 and Regulation (EU) No 1255/2011 of the European Parliament and of the Council [2014] OJ L149, 20 May, 1–66 (EMFF).

Let us now see eight concrete examples in terms of how the above-mentioned objectives of the Commission's legislative proposals have been translated into the new legislative framework,[19] based on the principles of better regulation:

1. In order to establish a coherent and consistent legal framework (Article 1(5) CPR)

   Based on the classic principles of ensuring legislative quality, such as enacting general rules instead of furthering piecemeal regulations, respecting the standards of consistency and taking into account the high level of complexity of the new Cohesion policy-related legislative framework, the Commission in the course of the negotiations proposed having a special provision clarifying the relationship between the different regulatory levels and layers of the legislative package exactly, an idea that the EU co-legislators finally accepted in order to provide better legal clarity and legal certainty for the targeted business sectors and the citizens of the EU. The adopted relevant provision in Article 1 CPR reads as follows:

   > (5) Part Two of this Regulation *shall apply to all the ESI Funds except when it explicitly allows for derogations.*[20] Parts Three and Four of this Regulation shall establish complementary rules to Part Two that apply respectively to the Funds and to the Funds and the EMFF and may explicitly allow derogations in the Fund-specific Regulations concerned. The Fund-specific Regulations may establish complementary rules to Part Two of this Regulation for the ESI Funds, to Part Three of this Regulation for the Funds and to Part Four of this Regulation for the Funds and the EMFF. *The complementary rules in the Fund-specific Regulations shall not be in contradiction with Parts Two, Three and Four of this Regulation. In case of doubt about the application between provisions, Part Two of this Regulation shall prevail over the Fund-specific rules,*[21] *and Parts Two, Three and Four of this Regulation shall prevail over the Fund-specific Regulations.* (Emphasis added)

   This 'bridging' provision helps the EU citizens and the businesses to better understand the structure and the interconnection of the five different legislative acts creating one comprehensive new regulatory framework.
2. In order to ensure more legal certainty, a new provision on 'Calculation of time limits for Commission decisions' was also adopted.

[19] As regards the European Parliament's assessment on the whole Cohesion legislative package, see in more detail 'The EU Cohesion Policy 2014–2020: A Comprehensive Presentation of the Legislative Package and the Role of the European Parliament', Committee on Regional Development, Directorate General for Internal Policies and General Secretariat of the European Parliament, Brussels 2014, Doc PE532.425v01-00.

[20] See, as an example, for such explicit derogation from the Part Two rules Art 30(4) CPR (concerning the specific approval procedures of amendments of operational programmes as regards the EMFF).

[21] It should be noted that the ESI Funds 'Common Provision Regulation' contains in its Art 2 very detailed definitions on legal terms, used in that Regulation, including, for example, the definition on 'Fund-specific rules', which means 'the provisions laid down, or established on the basis of Part Three or Part Four of this Regulation or a Regulation governing one or more of the ESI Funds listed in the fourth paragraph of Article 1 ("Fund-specific Regulations")' (Art 2(4) CPR).

The right calculation of time limits for the Commission's decision-making had been a controversial issue for a long time and generated a huge amount of litigation before the EU courts.[22] Now it is clear how procedural deadlines are to be calculated, when in Article 3 CPR it is stipulated that:

> Where pursuant to Articles 16(2) and (3), 29(3), 30(2)–(3), 102(2), 107(2) and 108(3), a time limit is set for the Commission to adopt or amend a decision, by means of an implementing act, that time limit shall not include the period which starts on the date following the date on which the Commission sent its observations to the Member State and lasts until the Member State responds to the observations.

3. In order to involve all those stakeholders (civil society, business organisations, national, regional and local (urban) authorities, social and economic partners etc), which are the addressees, the actors and the potential beneficiaries of the ESI Funds in the application and implementation of the Regulation already from the programming phase, with due regard to the principles of proportionality and subsidiarity, a new model was adopted on partnership and multi-level governance under Article 5 CPR.

This is the greatest legal innovation of the package because it regulates the new multi-level governance consultation model in a way that at the same time respects all the forms of structural and cultural diversity in public administration and civic organisation structures in the different Member States.[23] The most important elements of the very long provision (Article 5 CPR) can be summarised as follows:

> 1. For the Partnership Agreement and each programme, *each Member State shall in accordance with its institutional and legal framework organise a partnership* with the competent regional and local authorities. The partnership shall also include the following partners:
>   (a) competent urban and other public authorities;
>   (b) economic and social partners; and
>   (c) relevant bodies representing civil society, including environmental partners, non-governmental organisations, and bodies responsible for promoting social inclusion, gender equality and non-discrimination.
> 2. In accordance with the multi-level governance approach, the partners referred to in paragraph 1 shall be involved by Member States in the preparation of Partnership Agreements and progress reports and throughout the preparation and implementation of programmes, including through participation in the monitoring committees for programmes in accordance with Article 48.
> 3. The Commission shall be empowered to adopt a delegated act in accordance with Article 149 to provide for a European code of conduct on partnership (the 'code of conduct') in order to support and facilitate Member States in

[22] See, for example, Case C-139/15 P *European Commission v Spain* ECLI:EU:C:2016:707 or Case C-513/13 P *Spain v European Commission* ECLI:EU:C:2014:2412.

[23] See in this respect Case T-529/13 *Izsàk Balàzs-Arpàd and Dabis Attila v European Commission* ECLI:EU:T:2016:282, in particular paras 68 et seq.

the organisation of partnership in accordance with paragraphs 1 and 2 of this Article. The code of conduct shall set out the framework within which the Member States, in accordance with their institutional and legal framework as well as their national and regional competences, shall pursue the implementation of partnership. The code of conduct, while fully respecting the principles of subsidiarity and proportionality, shall lay down the following elements: [and then seven elements are detailed laying down the good practices and more general expectations towards the participating organisations in the partnership].

The provisions of *the code of conduct shall not in any way contradict the relevant provisions of this Regulation or the Fund-specific rules.*

4. … That delegated act *shall not specify a date of application that is earlier than the date of its adoption.*[24]

…

6. *At least once a year, for each ESI Fund, the Commission shall consult the organisations* which represent the partners at Union level on the implementation of support from that ESI Fund and shall report to the European Parliament and the Council on the outcome. (Emphasis added)

4. In order to provide easier accessibility and better transparency to the EU citizens and businesses concerning the very complex new legislative framework, Article 13 CPR on 'Guidance for beneficiaries' makes it *expressis verbis* the Commission's obligation to issue a document that helps the citizens and business actors to better understand their opportunities and rights in the given new regulatory regime. This provision provides that:

(1) *The Commission shall prepare guidance on how to effectively access and use the ESI Funds*, and on how to exploit complementarities with other instruments of relevant Union policies.

(2) *The guidance* shall be drawn up by 30 June 2014 and *shall provide*, for each thematic objective, an overview of the available relevant instruments at Union level with detailed sources of information, examples of good practices for combining available funding instruments within and across policy areas, a description of relevant authorities and bodies, involved in the management of each instrument, a checklist for potential beneficiaries to help them to identify the most appropriate funding sources.

(3) *The guidance shall be made public on the websites* of the relevant Directorate Generals of the Commission and managing authorities, acting in

[24] See, further, Commission Delegated Regulation (EU) No 240/2014 of 7 January 2014 on the European Code of Conduct on Partnership in the framework of the European Structural and Investment Funds [2014] OJ L74, 14 March, 1 (it entered into force on 15 March 2014), as well as the Commission Staff Working Document on Best Practices as regards the implementation of the partnership principle in the European Structural and Investment Funds' programmes (accompanying the document of Commission Delegated Regulation on the European Code of Conduct on Partnership in the framework of the European Structural and Investment Funds), Brussels, 7 January 2014, SWD (2013) 540 final.

accordance with the Fund-specific rules, and in cooperation with the Committee of the Regions, shall ensure dissemination of the guidance to potential beneficiaries.[25] (Emphasis added)

5. In order to demonstrate the good quality of the cohesion legislative package and so that the prerogatives of the different EU Institutions can be fully respected in the decision-making processes regarding the suspension of commitments or of payments under the ESI Funds, when a Member State does not fulfil its obligations relating to EU economic governance rules, reference should be made to *Article 23 CPR on 'Measures linking effectiveness of ESI Funds to sound economic governance'*, which establishes a pragmatic and efficient framework for good interinstitutional cooperation even concerning such a sensitive issue as imposing 'sanctions' on a Member State.

Perhaps it is worth quoting from Article 23 CPR here only those elements that set out the so-called 'structured dialogue' requirements in the given EU decision-making process:

> 6. *Where the Member State fails to take effective action in response* to a request made in accordance with paragraph 1, within the deadlines set out in paragraphs 3 and 4, the *Commission may*, within three months following its observations under paragraph 3 or following the submission of the proposal of the Member State under paragraph 4, *propose to the Council that it suspends part or all of the payments for the programmes or priorities concerned … In making its proposal, the Commission* shall take account of all relevant information, and *shall give due consideration to any elements arising from and opinions expressed through the structured dialogue under paragraph 15.*
>
> 9. The Commission shall make a proposal to the Council to suspend part or all of the commitments or payments for the programmes of a Member State in the following cases: [and then five situations are described].
>
> *In making its proposal, the Commission shall* respect the provisions of paragraph 11 and shall take account of all relevant information in that regard, and it shall *give due consideration to any elements arising from* and opinions expressed through *the structured dialogue* under paragraph 15.
>
> 15. The Commission shall keep the European Parliament informed of the implementation of this Article. In particular the Commission shall, when one of the conditions set out in paragraph 6 or points (a) to (e) of the first subparagraph of paragraph 9 is fulfilled for a Member State, *immediately inform the European Parliament and provide details of the ESI Funds and programmes which could be subject to a suspension of commitments or payments.*

[25] It should be mentioned that pursuant to Art 54 CPR, the Commission is obliged to issue similar guidance on the preparation by Member States of the evaluations as far as the effective use of ESI Funds is concerned. The relevant Commission Guidance documents can be downloaded at DG Regio website of the Commission, http://ec.europa.eu/regional_policy/en/funding/.

> The European Parliament may invite the Commission for a structured dialogue on the application of this Article, having regard in particular to the transmission of the information referred to in the first sub-paragraph …
>
> 16. In 2017, the Commission shall carry out a review of the application of this Article. To this end, the Commission shall prepare a report which it shall transmit to the European Parliament and the Council, accompanied where necessary by a legislative proposal.
> 17. Where there are major changes in the social and economic situation in the Union, the Commission may submit a proposal to review the application of this Article, or the European Parliament or the Council, acting in accordance with Articles 225 or 241 TFEU respectively, may request the Commission to submit such a proposal. (Emphasis added)

6. In relation to legislative simplification, one should, for example, refer to the new legal drafting solution—which is fully in line with the principles of shared management and of subsidiarity—on a less onerous approval procedure of operational programmes in Article 96 CPR on 'Content, adoption and amendment of Operational Programmes under the Investment for growth and jobs goal', which reads as follows:

> (10) The Commission shall adopt a decision, by means of implementing acts, approving all the elements, including any of its future amendments, of the operational programme falling under this Article, except those falling under points … which remain under the responsibility of the Member States.
>
> (11) *The managing authority shall notify the Commission* of any decision amending the elements of the operational programme *not covered by the Commission decision*, referred to in paragraph 10, within *one month* of the date of that amending decision. The amending decision shall specify the date of its entry into force, which shall not be earlier than the date of its adoption. (Emphasis added)[26]

7. In the legislative process, due to the particular nature of this policy field,[27] special emphasis was certainly placed—fully in line with the above-mentioned

[26] There are plenty of other examples for legislative simplification—for example, in the given context, see Art 30(2)–(3) or 96(8) CPR.

[27] It should be noted here that, based on Art 4(2)(c) TFEU, the EU economic, social and territorial cohesion policy falls under shared competence; therefore, also in the context of shared management of the ESI Funds, Member States have substantive (remaining) legislative powers in the field—for example, what concerns the complaint procedure at the national level with regard to the use of the ESI Funds, or when establishing the eligibility criteria of expenditure, or when addressing the already-mentioned partnership principle and the multi-level governance of the ESI Funds. However, one could still refer to the support for public–private partnership (PPP) operations, the accreditation procedure of the national competent authorities, the information and communication strategies at the national level, or the issues of irregularities and financial corrections (see in particular Recitals (11)–(12), (36) and (72) and Arts 2(36), 6, 64(1), 85 and Annex XII.2.1(3) in the CPR, but the Fund-specific Regulations give still many other examples). Therefore, pursuant to Art 5 TEU and Protocol No 2 of the Lisbon Treaty, the principle of subsidiarity and the principle of proportionality must be respected by all means when legislating in this field at the EU level.

EU common legal drafting principles—on the principles of subsidiarity and proportionality, which are general and horizontal principles of the whole legislative framework (see Article 4(3)–(5) CPR).[28]

8. Finally, one should recall the fact that in relation to micro-enterprises and SMEs[29] and their more favourable access to the ESI Funds, there are plenty of special provisions in the CPR as well as in the Fund-specific Regulations that provide special legislative treatment for them, which is fully in line with the relevant EU policies and case law.[30]

Some other recent examples concerning *the enhanced Council contribution for better law-making at the EU level* (in many respects following the implementation of the Court's most recent jurisprudence in the field):

— the new Guidelines on methodological steps to be taken to check the fundamental rights' compatibility of Council legal acts in the working of the Council preparatory bodies;[31]
— the Indicative Guidance for Council Working Party Chairs on Impact Assessment;[32]
— or the Initiative to Complement the Common Understanding on delegated acts in relation to the consultation of Member States' experts and the

[28] See further the following concrete provisions concerning the principle of subsidiarity: Recitals (11), (61), (67) and (129) and Articles 4(3)–(4), 5(3), 10(3) and Annex I.5.1 in the CPR; for the principle of proportionality, see: Recitals (10)–(11), (14), (21)–(22), (57), (64), (72), (103), (117), (120) and (129) and Arts 4(5), 5(3), 19(1)–(3), 22(7), 26(3), 37(2), 75(2), 85(3), 116(1), 144(2) and Annex I.5.1 or Annex XIII.2 in the CPR. Obviously, the Fund-specific Regulations also still refer to both principles in many places. In the related jurisprudence, see, for example, Case T-145/15 *Romania v European Commission* ECLI:EU:T:2017:86.

[29] Commission Recommendation of 6 May 2003 concerning the definition of micro, small and medium-sized enterprises [2003] OJ L124, 20 May, 36; and Art 2(28) CPR.

[30] See, for example, Recitals (39)–(41), (58), (64), (74) and (126)–(127) and Arts 2(28), 9(3), 37(4), 39, 61(8) and 71, Annex I.2(2), 4.3.(1)–(2) and 7.2.(2), Annex III.2, Annex XI Part I, points (3) and (8) in the CPR Regulation, or in the ERDF Regulation, for example, see Recitals (5), (8), (11) and (14), Arts 3(1) and 5; or in the ESF Regulation, see, for example, Recital (10), Art 3, Annex I(2); or in the EAFRD Regulation, one could refer, for example, to Recitals (12)–(13), (17)–(18), (21), Arts 8, 14(2), 15 and 26–27; and finally in the ETC Regulation, see Recital (17). In the relevant jurisprudence, see, for example, Case T-124/14 *Finland v European Commission* ECLI:EU:T:2015:955.

[31] Council Doc 5377/15, 20 January 2015. This implements and is practically based on the Court's relevant jurisprudence, established inter alia in the following cases: judgment of 8 April 2014 in Joined Cases C-293/12 and C-594/12 *Digital Rights Ireland et Seitlinger ea* ECLI:EU:C:2014:238, in particular paras 47, 52–54; judgment of 9 November 2010 in Joined Cases C-92/09 and C-93/09 *Volker and Markus Schecke GbR et alts* ECLI:EU:C:2010:662; judgment of 5 September 2012 in Case C-355/10 *European Parliament v Council* ECLI:EU:C:2012:516; judgment of 16 December 2008 in Case C-73/07 *Tietosujavaltuutettu* ECLI:EU:C:2008:727, in particular paras 52–56; judgment of 7 November 2013 in Case C-473/12 *IPI* ECLI:EU:C:2013:715, in particular para 39; judgment of 13 May 2014 in Case C-131/12 *Google Spain and Google* ECLI:EU:C:2014:317.

[32] Council Doc 16024/14, dated 16 December 2014. However, it should be noted that this Indicative Guidance on Impact Assessments has been recently revised and updated in the light of the new IIA; see Council Doc 9790/16, dated 9 June 2016.

President of COREPER's letter of 19 February 2015, which was sent to the Presidents of the European Parliament and of the European Commission in this context.[33]

THE NEW IIA ON BETTER LAW-MAKING: THE CONTENT AND A FIRST BRIEF ASSESSMENT

As has already been mentioned, the new IIA on Better Law-making (hereinafter the new IIA) was signed by the Presidents of the European Parliament, the Council and the Commission on 13 April 2016, and it also entered into force on the same day.[34] The new IIA replaced the IIA on Better Law-Making from 2003 and the Interinstitutional Common Approach to Impact Assessment from 2005, while its Annex replaced the 2011 Common Understanding on Delegated Acts.[35] The legal basis for the adoption of the new IIA was Article 295 TFEU, which indicates that it is legally binding on all the three EU Institutions that signed it. The nature of the agreement is also demonstrated by the fact that it was published in the 'L' series of the Official Journal of the EU.[36]

The new IIA addresses all the main elements of interinstitutional cooperation at all stages of the legislative cycle and in practice it 'codifies' the existing good practices in this respect. It is composed of 10 successive chapters, which lay down provisions on common commitments and objectives, on interinstitutional (annual and multiannual) programming, on better law-making tools, on legislative instruments, on delegated and implementing acts, on transparency and coordination of the legislative process, on the implementation and application of EU legislation, on legislative simplification, on the implementation and monitoring of the Agreement and on final provisions. In addition, it contains a revised Understanding on Delegated and Implementing Acts and is accompanied by a Declaration of the Parliament and the Commission on their 2010 Framework Agreement.

As an overall assessment, I think that the new IIA is balanced; its precise and careful wording provides sufficient flexibility for the signing Institutions to properly interpret it. It clearly strengthens the transparency requirements of the EU's better law-making activities (via compulsory publication of impact assessments, better access to almost all documents concerning the legislative process, establishment of a joint functional register on delegated acts and of a joint database on the state of play of legislative files etc),[37] thus bringing the EU's better law-making

[33] Council Doc 6774/14, dated 21 February 2014, and Council Doc 6773/15, dated 3 March 2015, respectively.

[34] See its para 52.

[35] See its para 51.

[36] [2016] OJ L123, 12 May, 1.

[37] See further paras 13, 18, 29 and 38–39 of the new IIA.

closer to all EU citizens and business operators. The new IIA fully respects the autonomy of the signing Institutions while at the same time placing more emphasis on an even better level of cooperation among them in the process of EU law-making. The new IIA also contains some legal innovations, of which I would like now to highlight three because of their importance:

1. One of the positive procedural developments in the new IIA is that *now* it precisely regulates what the Commission must do when either the Parliament (based on Article 225 TFEU) or the Council (based on Article 241 TFEU) formally requests the Commission to submit a legislative proposal to the EU legislature. Paragraph 10 of the new IIA provides that:

   > The Commission will give prompt and detailed consideration to requests for proposals for Union acts made by the European Parliament or the Council pursuant to Article 225 or Article 241 TFEU respectively. *The Commission will reply to such requests within three months, stating the follow up it intends to give to them by adopting a specific communication. If the Commission decides not to submit a proposal in response to such a request, it will inform the institution concerned of the detailed reasons, and will provide, where appropriate, an analysis of possible alternatives* and respond to any issues raised by the co-legislators in relation to analyses concerning 'European added value' and concerning the 'cost of non-Europe'. If so requested, the Commission will present its reply in the European Parliament or in the Council. (Emphasis added)

   This new procedural rule is particularly important, since the Commission's right to initiative is well-protected by EU law, that is exactly why both Lisbon Treaty articles referred to above end up with the following: 'If the Commission does not submit a proposal, it shall inform the European Parliament (or under Article 241 TFEU the Council) of the reasons.' But now in the new IIA on Better Law-Making, it is further detailed how the Commission shall respond to the legislator, which strengthens the principle of loyal cooperation and of institutional balance in EU law-making.

   In addition, it should be recalled that such a 'legislative initiative' possibility for the EU co-legislators is also envisaged in EU secondary legislation, in which case the new paragraph 10 procedure obviously should also apply.[38]
2. Another good legal innovation of the new IIA is the very precise and careful drafting of those provisions addressing the preparation issues of Impact Assessments, especially when the need for the preparation of a new Impact Assessment is already raised in the process of the legislative negotiations taking place between the Council and the European Parliament. This is a sensitive but also a very practical issue, since it is well known that in practice legislative negotiations are sometimes concluded by virtue of agreeing on last-minute

[38] See, for example, Art 12 of the ESI Funds' known as 'Common Provision Regulation', referred to earlier in n 14.

new and substantial amendments (or rather compromise packages of such amendments), submitted at midnight at an informal trialogue, when there is simply no time left to have any Impact Assessment prepared based on these new last-minute compromise proposals for modifications, otherwise the deal is gone.

However, the new IIA has found the right legal wording for a balanced approach and also for ensuring the necessary flexibility, if justified, which can be demonstrated by the following provisions:

— Impact assessments *must not lead to undue delays* in the law-making process or prejudice the co-legislators' capacity to propose amendments (para 12).
— The European Parliament and the Council will, *when they consider this to be appropriate and necessary for the legislative process*, carry out impact assessments in relation to their *substantial amendments* to the Commission's proposal. The European Parliament and the Council will, as a general rule, take the Commission's impact assessment as the starting point for their further work.[39] *The definition of a 'substantial' amendment should be for the respective Institutions to determine.* (para 15)
— *Each of the three Institutions is responsible for determining how to organise its impact assessment work*, including internal organisational resources and quality control. (para 17) (Emphasis added)

In any case, in the context of the new IIA, the preparation of Impact Assessments is a central and focused tool for better law-making, which is exactly why since April 2016, in both wings of the EU legislature, and thus in the Council too, this issue has been given new impetus with a priority approach to properly address it in the light of the new IIA.

3. Third, I think that Chapter V of the new IIA is also carefully drafted, especially when the various issues in relation to delegated acts are addressed. In this respect, one might state that the following provisions in particular are forward-looking:
   — In paragraph 26, it is specifically underlined that: 'It is the competence of the legislator to decide whether and to what extent to use delegated or implementing acts, within the limits of the Treaties.'
   — For the Council, a special concern was the proper involvement of Member States' experts, prior to the adoption of delegated acts, at an early stage in the drafting phase of delegated acts in order to gather all the necessary expertise from them in the course of preparing the draft delegated acts. In paragraph 28, this is now sufficiently guaranteed.
   — After different legal interpretations and some controversies, paragraph 31 now clearly defines how to handle the so-called 'bundled' 'delegated acts' issue (namely when in one delegated act in fact there are many delegated

[39] It should be noted that at the request of any of the co-legislators, the Commission shall update and/or supplement its original Impact Assessment, submitted with a concrete legislative proposal (para 16).

acts (just 'put together') based on different empowerments in the same basic legislative act). The chosen solution fully respects the principle of institutional balance and the prerogatives of the EU co-legislators.

Finally, since the entry into force of the new IIA almost one and a half years have passed, is it thus perhaps justified to make a short summary about how its implementation has progressed in the Council?

Of course, there are already very good results, such as when, in December 2016, the three Presidents signed the Joint Declaration on Legislative Priorities 2017,[40] based on paragraphs 6 and 7 of the new IIA. The Council also adopted these practical arrangements, which define how the Council's early input to the Commission's Annual Work Programme for the upcoming year should be managed.[41] Based on paragraph 27 of the new IIA, the Council has started the examination of the so-called Commission RPS (Regulatory Procedure with Scrutiny) or PRAC Adaptation proposal, submitted on 16 December 2016, and this work is progressing well. Concerning the joint functional register on delegated acts (paragraph 29), good progress has been made and as planned it will be established by the end of 2017. Finally, concerning Impact Assessments, in April 2017 the Council launched a pilot project to establish the Council's own Impact Assessment Capability, which should be operational by January 2018.[42] In May 2017 COREPER also endorsed a procedure for triggering a request for an Impact Assessment on a 'substantial' amendment by the Council, and the Working Party on Competitiveness and Growth (Better Regulation) started working on designing a template for an Impact Assessment request, including the draft terms of reference for such a request.[43] With regard to all the other tasks stemming from the new IIA (namely the establishment of the joint database on the state of play of legislative files (paragraph 39), adopting delineation criteria for distinguishing between delegated acts and implementing acts (paragraph 28), and adopting practical arrangements for cooperation and information sharing in relation to international agreements (paragraph 40)), the joint work with the other two Institutions has started, but it is still a work in progress in each of them.[44]

CONCLUSIONS

In my view, the adoption of the new IIA is a good step forwards in terms of ensuring in reality the common objectives of the signing Institutions, namely enacting fewer but better rules for the benefit of EU citizens and business operators. The historical analysis of this contribution proved that the legal order of the EU in the last 20 years has changed significantly and has developed enormously, and

[40] Council Doc 15375/16, dated 9 December 2016.
[41] Council Doc 6879/16, dated 11 March 2016.
[42] Council Doc 7582/17, dated 3 April 2017.
[43] Council Doc 10006/17, dated 12 June 2017.
[44] Council Doc 15084/17, dated 1 December 2017 on the last progress report as regards the new iiA.

the legal drafting requirements (or in more general terms the law-making principles) must always be adapted to these changes and thus reformed. The practical examples I gave earlier could perhaps show that the good quality of a new and comprehensive legal framework for a very important EU policy area, like the cohesion policy, which directly relates to EU citizens and business operators, very much depends on good cooperation among the EU Institutions participating in the related law-making process. That is why it is welcomed that the new IIA places special emphasis on even more cooperation (including formal but also informal forms and channels) among Institutions in order to help the process of adopting fewer but better rules. 'Better' in this context means that those whom the rules address voluntarily implement them in practice, since they can understand that the rules make their life and the running of their businesses easier, protect them and provide a higher quality of life for them. I also welcome the strengthening of the principle of transparency, which is a real guarantee of better law-making, since it involves and listens to the voice of those who are the most affected by Better Regulation. Perhaps one element on which one could still give further thought to in the future is the use of alternative methods of regulation (co-regulation, self-regulation), which was more focused in the previous IIA, but not in the new IIA, and which regulatory tools can be still relevant in certain EU policy fields in the future (social policy, the environment, agriculture etc).

9

The Member States and the Better Regulation Agenda

The Case of Belgium/Flanders

JAN DE MULDER*

THIS CHAPTER ADDRESSES—FROM a practitioner's perspective—the role of Member States in the EU's Better Regulation Agenda development, follow-up, implementation and potential for improvement. The chapter also focuses on the 'Europeanisation' features of regulatory policy and management in Belgium and the Flanders region. The Belgian regulatory approaches reflect not only the particular characteristics of a federal state but may also assess and incorporate supra-national (OECD/EU) trends and innovations (eg Regulatory Impact Assessment (RIA)) differently. This chapter looks for the 'national' impact of the Better Regulation Agenda outcomes (Council conclusions, Interinstitutional Agreement (IIA) and Commission tools) and whether this also influences the Belgian participation in the fora where the Better Regulation Agenda is being discussed (eg, Council Working Parties, the Regulatory Fitness and Performance (REFIT) Platform, Directors and Experts on Better Regulation (DEBR) and the EU Public Administration Network (EUPAN)). Experiences from these participations might offer insights into possible improvements for the implementation of the Better Regulation Agenda.

INTRODUCTION: BETTER REGULATION INTENTIONS TOWARDS THE MEMBER STATES BY THE JUNCKER COMMISSION

If one searches for 'Better Regulation'[1] in the Political Guidelines for the current Commission and in the Opening Statement in the European Parliament by

* Jan de Mulder is Attaché at the Representation of the Flemish Government in the Permanent Representation of Belgium to the EU and lawyer with the Regulatory Management unit of the Flemish administration. He is also voluntary research fellow at the Department of International Public Law, University of Ghent. The observations and opinions in this contribution are strictly personal and do not represent any official position.

[1] Which is a popular label for the regulatory reform agenda according to CM Radaelli and ACM Meuwese, 'Better Regulation in Europe: Between Public Management and Regulatory Reform' (2009) 87 *Public Administration* 639.

President Jean-Claude Juncker, the results are rather disappointing. In the Political Guidelines 'Regulation' is linked to 'less', 'too prescriptive and too detailed' and 'burdensome'. In the Opening Statement in the European Parliament plenary session, one finds only 'bureaucratic over-Regulation'.[2] The next Statement ahead of the vote on the College avoided these negative connotations and sounded somehow more constructive.[3]

The appointment of a First Vice-President, Frans Timmermans, to coordinate Better Regulation in the Commission and ensure every proposal respects the principles of subsidiarity and proportionality is a novelty.[4] The Better Regulation policy is—without being mentioned as such in the Political Guidelines—part of the tenth priority 'A Union of Democratic Change', which also includes the intention by President Juncker to improve the interaction with national parliaments. The Political Guidelines also include the following clear message: 'I believe that Europe's policy agenda must be shaped in close partnership between the European Commission and the European Parliament, and in cooperation with the Member States. Political prioritisation as the basis for a better, more focused Union will only work if it is done in partnership between the Union institutions and the Member States, in line with the Community method.' Furthermore, President Juncker acknowledged that: 'We do not necessarily all have to move at the same speed.' The wording of these documents indicates the intention to strive for closer links and interaction between the Commission and the Member States, which presumably also incorporates Better Regulation policies.

But is this so new? Already in 2001 with its White Paper on Governance,[5] the Commission was searching for more legitimacy, looking for a governance 'network' approach including the introduction of appropriate instruments like impact analysis and consultation.[6] Although Commission-driven, the role of the Member

[2] J-C Juncker, 'A New Start for Europe: My Agenda for Jobs, Growth, Fairness and Democratic Change—Political Guidelines for the next European Commission/Opening Statement in the European Parliament Plenary Session Strasbourg', 15 July 2014, https://ec.europa.eu/priorities/publications/president-junckers-political-guidelines_en: 'This is why I intend to entrust the responsibility for Better Regulation to one of the Vice-Presidents in my Commission; and to give this Vice-President a mandate to identify, together with the Parliament and the Council, "red tape" both at European and at national level that could be swiftly removed as part of my Jobs, Growth and Investment Package.' These connotations reflect a rather widespread perception of regulation as a problem and no longer as a solution; see W Voermans, 'Legislation and Regulation' in H Xanthaki and U Karpen, *Handbook of Legislation: A Comprehensive Guide for Scholars and Practitioners* (Oxford, Hart Publishing, 2017).

[3] J-C Juncker, 'Time for Action', Statement in the European Parliament plenary session ahead of the vote on the College, Strasbourg, 22 October 2014: 'Mr Timmermans will oversee compliance with the principles of Better Regulation. This is a major task that will involve all the Commissioners, since they must all play their part in the effort to revitalise the European Union, its political responses, and its conduct.' Available at https://ec.europa.eu/priorities/publications/president-junckers-political-guidelines_en.

[4] See https://ec.europa.eu/priorities/democratic-change/Better-Regulation_en.

[5] COM (2001) 428, 25 July 2001.

[6] P Popelier, 'Governance and Better Regulation: Dealing with the Legitimacy Paradox' (2011) 17 *European Public Law* 519. This author also included a warning in her conclusion (at 532): 'Without marring the usefulness of governance and BR instruments as a strategy to compensate for democratic deficit problems of traditional lawmaking, the legitimacy paradox does remind us to keep a close and critical watch to the use and effects of these tools.'

States was not overlooked at all, as the White Paper contained phrases like 'there needs to be a stronger interaction with regional and local governments and civil society. Member States bear the principal responsibility for achieving this'. And concerning accountability—one of the five principles of good governance—it stated: 'Roles in the legislative and executive processes need to be clearer. Each of the EU Institutions must explain and take responsibility for what it does in Europe. But there is also a need for greater clarity and responsibility from Member States and all those involved in developing and implementing EU policy at whatever level.'

REALITY CHECK: MORE THAN ONE WAY?

The first major implementation signal of the Juncker Commission's intentions came with the adoption of the Better Regulation Agenda on 19 May 2015.[7] Although most elements of this package address the Commission, it also included the announcement to establish a permanent and inclusive platform for dialogue with stakeholders and Member States on how to improve EU laws in the context of REFIT.[8] The REFIT Platform—chaired by Vice-President Timmermans—consists of a Government Group, with one seat per Member State and a Stakeholder Group with 18 members and two representatives from the European Social and Economic Committee and the Committee of the Regions. The Government Group is of importance for Member States' regulatory policies—especially to give input and feedback to the Commission—and the members of this Group are expected to be high level experts and key players in their national administrations.[9]

Furthermore, the Commission's Better Regulation Agenda included a proposal for a new Interinstitutional Agreement (IIA) on Better Law-Making to the Parliament and Council. The proposal contained a number of relevant topics for Member States' regulatory policies, such as a common commitment to the REFIT

[7] 'Better Regulation for Better Results—An EU Agenda' COM (2015) 215 final, 4: 'The Commission commits to taking political responsibility for applying Better Regulation principles and processes in its work and calls on the other EU institutions and the Member States to do likewise.' Available at http://ec.europa.eu/info/law/law-making-process/Better-Regulation-why-and-how_en.

[8] REFIT is the European Commission's Regulatory Fitness and Performance programme. With REFIT, the Commission is taking action to make EU law 'fit for purpose': to simplify and reduce regulatory costs while maintaining benefits. REFIT is a key component of the Commission's Better Regulation Agenda. In 2015 REFIT was fully integrated into the Commission's annual work programme and the related political dialogue with the European Parliament and Council. See http://ec.europa.eu/info/law/law-making-process/overview-law-making-process/evaluating-and-improving-existing-laws/reducing-burdens-and-simplifying-law/refit-making-eu-law-simpler-and-less-costly_en. For an interim, critical assessment, see E Van den Abeele, '"Better Regulation": A Bureaucratic Simplification with a Political Agenda' (2015) Working Paper, European Trade Union Institute, 26, available at https://www.etui.org/Publications2/Working-Papers/Better-regulation-a-bureaucratic-simplification-with-a-political-agenda.

[9] See https://ec.europa.eu/info/law/law-making-process/overview-law-making-process/evaluating-and-improving-existing-laws/reducing-burdens-and-simplifying-law/refit-platform/refit-platform-members/refit-platform-members-government-group_en.

programme; Impact Assessment; continuous monitoring of the performance of EU Regulation and more thorough evaluations; as well as joint efforts to reduce unjustified 'gold-plating' of EU legislation by Member States. This IIA was politically agreed by the end of 2015[10] and was formally adopted on 16 April 2016.[11] Compared to the 2003 IIA, the new IIA mentions Member States twice as much, but given the trilateral institutional character of this agreement, one should not be surprised that the message towards the Member States is one of duties, focusing on implementing and applying EU legislation.[12] However, this message was also part of the 2003 IIA.[13] It is also striking that in Part III of the new IIA (on better law-making tools: Impact Assessment, consultation and *ex post* evaluation), Member States remain completely unmentioned. So concerning the shared responsibility of the Member States, the IIA has missed an opportunity.[14]

These elements at least illustrate that the role of Member States in the EU's current Better Regulation policies is getting some more—but still rather limited—attention. Of course, it is also up to the Member States to (further) enhance, develop and apply appropriate regulatory policies and practices that increase

[10] See www.politico.eu/article/eu-strikes-Better-Regulation-deal-timmermans.

[11] [2016] OJ L123/1, 12 May. The new IIA replaces the IIA on Better Law-Making of 16 December 2003 and the Interinstitutional Common Approach to Impact Assessment of November 2005.

[12] The annual Commission report on the monitoring of the application of European Union law (COM (2016) 463, 15 July 2016) states that monitoring and enhancing the application of EU law is a priority of the Juncker Commission and a key part of the Better Regulation Package. Furthermore, on 21 December 2016 the Commission published the Communication 'EU Law: Better Results through Better Application' (COM (2016) 8600 final), which also refers to the Better Regulation Package: 'That is why it is essential that certain aspects of the implementation and application of EU law are taken into account at the stage of policy development. The Commission's Better Regulation Guidelines (8) guide the Commission's services in how to prepare "implementation plans" to identify possible difficulties the Member States face in implementing EU law and suggest ways to mitigate these risks.' This communication seems to overlook the opportunities of using certain Better Regulation instruments at the national level, both in the EU policy development stage and in the transposition stages—eg, Impact Assessment (or RIA) is not mentioned in this communication.

[13] Compare paras 32–34 (old IIA) with the new paras 41–45 (ch VII) The issue of the implementation and application of EU legislation was particularly important during the negotiations. The three institutions recognised the need for more structured cooperation in order to assess the application and effectiveness of EU law. This involves three important practical 'innovations' (according to a briefing/information note from the European Parliament, available at www.europarl.europa.eu/RegData/etudes/BRIE/2016/579076/EPRS_BRI(2016)579076_EN.pdf). First, Member States (who are not a party to the agreement) are called upon to clearly communicate to the public measures that transpose or implement EU legislation. Second, when Member States choose to add elements that are in no way related to the EU legislation that they are transposing ('gold-plating'), then they should identify these additions in the transposing act or in an associated document. The use of correlation tables is also stressed. Third, in its annual report on the application of EU legislation, to be transmitted to the Parliament and Council, the Commission will include any 'gold-plating' information that Member States have transmitted. These provisions constitute a genuine improvement and should provide valuable assistance to the co-legislators in their overall effort of adopting ever more effective legislation.

[14] L Senden, 'Het Commissiepakket "betere regelgeving voor betere resultaten" en het nieuwe Interinstitutioneel Akkoord beter wetgeven: Too Little, Too Late?' (2016) *Nederlands Tijdschrift voor Europees recht* 211. See also Asser Institute, 'Conference Report: Better Regulation and EU Lawmaking: One Year on', May 2016, www.asser.nl/about-the-institute/asser-today/conference-report-better-regulation-and-eu-lawmaking-one-year-on.

the impact of their legislation. Positive comments on the appointment of Commissioner Timmermans[15] and the Better Regulation package did not neglect, inter alia, this weakness of the EU's Better Regulation ambitions, as Renda observed in a CEPS Report published shortly after the launch of the package.[16] Previously a report by the Dutch Clingendael Institute in collaboration with the Centre for European Policy Studies (CEPS) had clearly stated that Member States' governments and national parliaments have difficulties in becoming proactive in providing information to the Commission concerning the costs and benefits of new initiatives:

> [A] great deal of the success will depend on the ability of—in particular—the Member States (stakeholders, parliaments and administrations) to provide inputs into the decision-making processes. Making subsidiarity (broadly defined) work will require vigilance and investments from all concerned. It will involve further investments in the available procedures, for example in the form of Member States working together on impact assessments in early phases of the decision-making. Improving EU legislation will also have a price tag for national administrations.[17]

So the two-way traffic that has been observed by certain Better Regulation researchers is certainly not reflected everywhere, even in recent times.[18] It looks

[15] L Schrefler, A Renda and J Pelkmans, 'What Can the Better Regulation Commissioner Do for the EU?' *CEPS Commentary*, 29 September 2014, 3: 'Another interesting point of Timmerman's mandate is the combination of Better Regulation with inter-institutional relations. This should be interpreted both horizontally (ie relations with Parliament and Council) and vertically, by strengthening Better Regulation in the Member States. Better EU Regulation is a shared responsibility and far too little is happening at the Member State level. This is of utmost importance for the future of EU Better Regulation, since the Commission is often trapped into the impossibility to measure or anticipate the implementation costs of its proposed reforms, due to unpredictable patterns of implementation and transposition at national level.'

[16] A Renda, 'Too Good to Be True? A Quick Assessment of the European Commission's New Better Regulation Package' *CEPS Special Report* 108, May 2015, 8: 'Another weakness of the EU Better Regulation system in place until today is the lack of a real involvement of Member States. While some national governments have started to adopt sophisticated Better Regulation tools many years before the European Commission (in particular, the United Kingdom), and other have made significant steps in the development of methods for the assessment of regulatory costs (the Netherlands, Germany, and increasingly Sweden and the Czech Republic), in most Member States, despite the official adoption of Better Regulation tools, implementation remains poor or non-existent. This is not merely a problem for national governments, but also for the EU level.' This observation by Renda seems to reveal that during the last decade, the impact of the EU's Better Regulation efforts has not been that great as Radaelli and De Francesco already noted in 2007 in their conclusion 'that institutionalization and diffusion among stakeholders of Better Regulation policy are still limited across the EU'. see CM Radaelli and F De Francesco, *Regulatory Quality in Europe: Concepts, Measures and Policy Processes* (Manchester, Manchester University Press, 2007) 193.

[17] S Blockmans, J Hoevenaars, A Schout and JM Wiersma, 'From Subsidiarity to Better EU Governance: A Practical Reform Agenda for the EU' *Clingendael/CEPS Report*, March 2014, 13.

[18] CM Radaelli, 'Desperately Seeking Regulatory Impact Assessments: Diary of a Reflective Researcher' (2009) 15 *Evaluation* 32. See also JB Wiener, 'Better Regulation in Europe' in J Holder and D McGillivray (eds), *Taking Stock of Environmental Assessment, Law, Policy and Practice* (Abingdon, Routledge, 2007) 66: 'In a process of hybridization, European institutions are borrowing "Better Regulation" reforms from both the US approach to regulatory review using benefit-cost analysis and from European Member States' initiatives on administrative costs and simplification; in turn the European Commission is helping to spread these reforms among the Member States.'

like the EU is more concerned about downloading its Better Regulation policies whilst the Member States (as the 'intermediate' user)[19] remain reluctant to become engaged in more uploading actions.

MEMBER STATES AND THE 'ORIGIN' OF BETTER REGULATION

Although the prevailing perception[20] about the Better Regulation Agenda associates it with the Commission initiatives from the early 2000s,[21] literature reminds us that in the preceding decade, both at the EU level and in some Member States, ideas were floated and policies and tools were even developed to address particular regulatory problems.

The origins of Better Regulation as an item on the EU's policy agenda and those of its Member States lie in the 1990s, when the Edinburgh summit under the British Presidency (1992) expressed concern about the quality of legislation.[22] The Edinburgh outcome resulted in a number of reports and follow-up work.[23]

[19] The term 'end-user' appears in para 19 of the 2016 IIA: '19. Public and stakeholder consultation is integral to well-informed decision-making and to improving the quality of law-making. Without prejudice to the specific arrangements applying to the Commission's proposals under Article 155(2) of the Treaty on the Functioning of the European Union, the Commission will, before adopting a proposal, conduct public consultations in an open and transparent way, ensuring that the modalities and time-limits of those public consultations allow for the widest possible participation. The Commission will in particular encourage the direct participation of SMEs and other end-users in the consultations. This will include public internet-based consultations. The results of public and stakeholder consultations shall be communicated without delay to both co-legislators and made public.' The term 'user' of EU legislation seems not so appropriate here and given the Commission consultation practice that offers all stakeholders—including Member States' authorities (national, regional and local) opportunities to react, the wording of this paragraph is rather incomplete and unbalanced.

[20] JB Wiener, 'Better Regulation in Europe' (2006) 59 *Current Legal Problems* 447; see also E Degrave, '"Mieux légiférer"—La corégulation et l'autorégulation dans la politique législative européenne' (2007) 142 *JTDE* 232, available at www.crid.be/pdf/public/5554.pdf.

[21] TJA Van Golen, 'Better Regulation 2.0 in de Europese Unie: het nieuwe Interinstitutioneel Akkoord en de nieuwe Better Regulation-richtlijnen voor de Europese Commissie' (2016) 4 *RegelMaat* 295.

[22] CM Radaelli, 'Whither Better Regulation for the Lisbon Agenda?' (2007) 14 *Journal of European Public Policy* 190.

[23] The Sutherland Report ('The Internal Market after 1992: Meeting the Challenge') of 1992 (SEC (1992) 2044) sets out some basic requirements for EC legislation, holding that each Community legislative act should be assessed on the basis of five criteria, namely the need for action, the choice of the most effective course of action, proportionality of the measure, consistency with existing measures, and wider consultation of the circles concerned during the preparatory stages. The report of the Molitor Group included 18 recommendations (Report of the Group of Independent Experts on Simplification of Legislation and Administration, COM (1995) 288 final/2, 21 June 1995) and inspired the Dutch Presidency of the EU in 1996 to commission a working group to try and find more or less universal standards for legislation. The Koopmans Group came up with a set of standards that are derived from (or inspired by) the common legal cultures from the—then—10 EU Member States. Koopmans Report, 'The Quality of EC Legislation: Points for Consideration and Proposals', 1995. G Galli and J Pelkmans (2000) also refer to the UNICE and BEST reports. The former (1995) stressed, inter alia, the problem of the cumulative nature of the regulatory burden (ie, regional, national and EU regulation, a familiar issue in Belgium). The latter (1998), with a wider scope than regulation only, argued for a 'think small first' principle for regulatory reform.

Obviously this attention was rooted in policy initiatives in particular Member States, such as the UK, Germany and the Netherlands.[24] The attention at the EU level was preceded by an earlier regulatory reform wave in the 1980s that was characterized by its focus on liberalisation and privatisation in some countries.[25] In addition, the European Community had initiated the EC-1992 Programme,[26] a phase that can be labelled 'regulation for liberalisation'.[27]

The key role of the exploratory work by the OECD on regulatory policies has to be recognised too.[28] While in the first wave of Better Regulation work, Member States and business groups focused on the issue of simplification and overall improvement of legislation across Europe (as evidenced by the Molitor Report of 1995), the second wave of Better Regulation programmes in at least some Member States in the late 1990s revealed a common feature of anchorage to more open models of governance.[29] This reform wave was part of the attempt to modernise the state and its public administration in countries such as France, Germany and Italy. A review of the legislative policies of five Member States at the end of the 1990s (the Netherlands, Germany, the UK, Italy and France) revealed a number of 'cultural' differences, but also reform trends that included issues relating to Better Regulation.[30] These issues include items like simplification and the reduction of burdens, more use of evaluations both *ex ante and ex post*, and the introduction of consultation approaches.

THE MEMBER STATES IN THE MANDELKERN REPORT

The European Council introduced the Lisbon process in March 2000. The goal was to make the EU the most competitive and dynamic knowledge-based economy in the world by 2010, which required inter alia a clear, simple, functioning and effective regulatory environment. To prepare the corresponding recommendations in this area, the European Ministers for Public Administration appointed an expert

[24] W Voermans, 'Concern about the Quality of EU Legislation: What Kind of Problem, by What Kind of Standards?' (2009) 2 *Erasmus Law Review* 59. See also E Van den Abeele, 'L'agenda Mieux légiférer de l'Union européenne' (2009) Courier Hebdomadaire CRISP 5.

[25] Radaelli and Meuwese, above n 1, 641.

[26] R Dehousse, 'Integration v. Regulation? On the Dynamics of Regulation in the European Community' (1992) 30(4) *Journal of Common Market Studies* 383.

[27] G Galli and J Pelkmans, *Regulatory Reform and Competitiveness in Europe I: Horizontal issues* (Cheltenham, Edward Elgar, 2000) 461.

[28] OECD, Recommendation of the Council of the OECD on improving the quality of government Regulation, (OCDE/GD(95)95, adopted on 9 March 1995), available at www.oecd.org/officialdocuments/publicdisplaydocumentpdf/?doclanguage=en&cote=OCDE/GD(95)95. Voermans (above n 24, 63) mentions Belgium as being influenced by OECD work. For an analysis of the OECD work and its impact on regulatory policy innovation, see F De Francesco, *Transnational Policy Innovation: The OECD and the Diffusion of Regulatory Impact Analysis* (Colchester, European Consortium for Political Research Press, 2013).

[29] Radaelli, above n 22, 195.

[30] W Voermans, 'Wetgevingsbeleid in landen van de Europese Unie' (2000) 5 *RegelMaat* 193.

group consisting of representatives of the Member States and the European Commission, and chaired by the French Dieudonné Mandelkern, a former member of the Conseil d'Etat. The mandate of this group was to improve the quality of EU legislation and to promote collaboration between Member States. The Mandelkern Report,[31] presented in November 2001, contained a bundle of proposals with deadlines for qualitatively better and simpler laws and for measures for lasting legal reform. At the end of the Belgian EU Presidency, the European Council in Laeken (14–15 December 2001), welcomed the Mandelkern Report as an element of the Laeken Declaration on the future of the Union.[32]

The Member States and the EU were asked to implement the operational measures in the report as quickly as possible. In reference to the European institutions, the recommendations in the action plan provided for the following intentions which also expected the Member States to take up the challenge:

— As of 2003, the Commission should produce an annual report to the European Parliament and the European Council on developments in Better European law-making by the EU and each Member State.
— The Commission, the European Parliament, the Council and Member States should establish new or improve existing joint training programmes at the European level for officials on all aspects of Better Law-making, such as Impact Assessment, consideration of alternatives to regulation, consultation, simplification and codification (and other forms of consolidation).
— Within their respective responsibilities, the Commission, the European Parliament, the Council and Member States should take further practical steps to ensure their internal coordination and the coherence between European regulatory policies at different levels by June 2002.

This report had a fundamental impact on the subsequent work by the European Commission because for the first time all Member States agreed on a Better Regulation Agenda.[33] It is also striking how much the Member States were envisaged alongside the other entities:

> The Mandelkern Group on Better Regulation commends this Report and Action Plan to the European Parliament, to the Commission, to the Council and to the Member States

[31] Mandelkern Group on Better Regulation, Final Report, 13 November 2001, available at http://ec.europa.eu/smart-Regulation/Better_Regulation/documents/mandelkern_report.pdf.

[32] 'Finally, the European Council welcomes the final report by the High-Level Advisory Group ("Mandelkern Group") on the quality of regulatory arrangements and the Commission communication on regulatory simplification, which should lead to a practical plan of action in the first half of 2002.' This wording does not reflect the variety of issues addressed in the Mandelkern Report, which was added as an annex to the Laeken Declaration. See https://www.consilium.europa.eu/uedocs/cms_data/docs/pressdata/en/ec/68827.pdf. For the initial report, see www.thecre.com/eu-oira/oira.be.mg.initial.htm. According to Van den Abeele (above n 24, 30), the Competitiveness Council played a coordination and preparatory role.

[33] L Allio, 'Better Regulation and Impact Assessment in the European Commission' in CH Kirkpatrick and D Parker (eds), *Regulatory Impact Assessment: Towards Better Regulation?* (Cheltenham, Edward Elgar, 2007) 78.

of the EU. The Group considers that implementation of the programme described in this Report, in addition to other work underway or proposed, will make a significant contribution to increasing the competitiveness of the European economy and the welfare of its citizens and to improved credibility and legitimacy of government.

Furthermore, an annex to the Mandelkern Report describes the Member State context and experiences based on the answers to a questionnaire. Concerning the frameworks and principles, this annex reflects the history, the main visions and approaches:

> There seem to be two main frameworks used for work on Better Regulation in the Member States. One of these is modernisation of public administration, such as better quality and more responsive public services, easier access to information and forms by using new information and communication technology (ICT) and a greater sense of commitment to complying with the law. The other is economic reform—removing barriers to entrepreneurship, innovation and employment and improving the competitiveness of business. Of course, these two frameworks are not mutually exclusive, and many responses referred to both. However, ten responses had a greater accent on the former and four on the latter.

So this outcome of the questionnaire seems to indicate that the initial drive for Better Regulation practices was less rooted in competitiveness concerns than is generally perceived given the further development of the Better Regulation Agenda.[34]

Concerning the structures and driving forces for Better Regulation in the Member States, the Mandelkern Report stated that these also reflect the different two frameworks which in turn are often linked to the political force behind the Better Regulation programme. Those Member States with a greater emphasis on economic reform were more likely to have administrative or institutional arrangements based in the Economics Ministry and the political impetus coming from business and/or the Economics Minister. Those Member States working towards of a 'modernisation' approach were more organised around the Ministry of Public Administration or the Premier's office and to have the political impetus from the concerns of citizens as well as business. Whichever framework applies most in a Member State, in general the responses to the questionnaire indicated an awareness of the need for support from the whole government in order for the Better

[34] However the minority's competitiveness agenda managed to become dominant; see Radaelli, above n 22, 195: 'Since then, the re-definition of the Lisbon agenda has emphasised the economic dimension … In its 2005 communication to the Spring European Council on the "new start for Lisbon", the Commission highlighted the assessment of the impact of new legislation on competitiveness (mainly but not exclusively in the context of RIA), new initiatives on cumulative burdens (a controversial concept in its own right, as explained in the SQW report 2005).' See also I Lynch-Fannon, 'Legislative Policy, Law and Competitiveness: A Mysterious and Difficult Relationship in the EU' (2009) 15 *European Law Journal* 98. For a more outspoken opinion, see Van den Abeele, above n 8, 10: 'Reducing the administrative burden, and subsequently bureaucracy, has been a mantra tirelessly repeated by the Commission for around 20 years. Not one European institution text has failed to call for a reduction in the burden on business or for red tape to be cut.'

Regulation programme to succeed. One fairly common mechanism to secure this is the use of inter-ministerial committees or structures.[35]

Under the next EU Presidency, the European Council (Barcelona, 15–16 March 2002) adopted Presidency conclusions, including the following paragraph:

> 19. Efforts to simplify and improve the regulatory environment will be vigorously pursued at both national and Community level, including inter-institutional aspects, with particular emphasis on the need to reduce the administrative burden on SMEs. The European Council invites the Commission to submit, in time for its next session at Seville, the Commission's Action Plan, which should take into account in particular the recommendations of the Mandelkern Group on Better Regulation.[36]

These conclusions indicated clearly a greater economic focus that is further stressed in additional paragraphs in the third part of these conclusions as prepared by other Council formations.[37] The issue of the quality of public services was no longer linked to Better Regulation and remained restricted to the topics of services of general economic interest and state aid as addressed by the Commission.[38]

SUBSIDIARITY

The Mandelkern Report has also been important in reinforcing subsidiarity[39] as a key element of the Better Regulation policy in Europe, ensuring the balance between the democratic legitimacy and efficiency of European law-making. As Blockmans

[35] Mandelkern Group on Better Regulation, above n 31, 77.

[36] Presidency Conclusions, Barcelona, 15–16 March 2002, Document SN 100/1/02 REV 1, available at http://ec.europa.eu/invest-in-research/pdf/download_en/barcelona_european_council.pdf.

[37] From the Economic and Financial Affairs Council: 'Entrepreneurship should be encouraged by reducing administrative and legal barriers to the barest minimum. Benchmarks should be determined which shorten the time required for SME set-up, and an action plan will be laid down to improve and simplify the regulatory environment, in line with the conclusions of the Mandelkern Report. The European Charter for Small Enterprises should be further implemented. In addition, it is important to improve the tax environment for business.' From the Internal Market, Consumer Affairs and Tourism Council: 'In the light of the high priority which the Council and the Commission attach to simplifying and improving the regulatory environment, and taking into account the conclusions of the Laeken European Council, the Council urges the Commission to present its action plan as early as possible in the first half of 2002, taking into account in particular the report of the Mandelkern Group. The Community and the Member States should step up current efforts to simplify and modernise legislation and administrative procedures having an effect on business and consumers at Community, national and regional levels. In addition, legislative acts at both Community and national level should be preceded by a regulatory impact assessment.'

[38] See paras 18 and 42 of pt I of the Barcelona Presidency Conclusions.

[39] P Craig and G de Búrca, *EU Law: Text, Cases and Materials*, 4th edn (Oxford, Oxford University Press, 2008) 165: 'there has been a concerted emphasis in the EU over the past two decades in particular on the need to reform governance in ways which depart from traditional, hierarchical forms of law-making and policy-making ... broader governance-reform initiatives such as the better regulation strategy and the operationalization of subsidiarity and proportionality attest to this'.

et al observed: 'Subsidiarity is inherently connected to debates on smarter regulation, deregulation, improving the democratic accountability of EU policies and institutional equilibrium. In any case, the overall objective of better regulation is regarded as central whether that is achieved through subsidiarity, proportionality, the choice of the least disruptive instrument, deregulation or quality of output.'[40] The Commission has created a number of instruments to address the subsidiarity question as part of its regulation practices (eg, Impact Assessments,[41] roadmaps and explanatory memoranda) and in its Better Regulation Guidelines of 2015, the Commission called subsidiarity a 'general principle of better regulation'.[42] Tool #3 of the Commissions Better Regulation Toolbox also deals with the subsidiarity issue.[43]

In its opinion about the EU Agenda on Better Regulation, the Committee of the Regions sounded not only positive[44] but also regretted 'that the "better regulation" package does not appear to improve the assessment of the subsidiarity principle so as to ensure that decisions can be taken in the lowest tier of government as possible, in line with the Committee of the Regions subsidiarity assessment toolkit' (para 48).[45] So concerns about the effectiveness of these Better Regulation practices and tools remain and, in order to achieve real improvements, it has been stated that more resources and attention from national administrations are required.[46] Also, the European Economic and Social Committee in its opinion on the EU Better Regulation Agenda paid attention to the cultural dimension and the need for more engagement from Member States:

> 2.2 Europe is a common legal area, which must guarantee an effective, reliable and applicable legal framework. The concept of better regulation, which is intended to focus both on ex-ante measures at EU level and on the consistent transposition and application of EU law in the Member States, and which provides for better regulation measures throughout the entire life cycle of a legal act, will be of value to

[40] S Blockmans, J Hoevenaars, A Schout and JM Wiersma, 'From Subsidiarity to Better EU Governance: A Practical Reform Agenda for the EU' *CEPS Essay*, April 2014, 3.

[41] For an exploration of the usefulness of Impact Assessment in relation to subsidiarity, see W Vandenbruaene, 'What Scope for Subnational Autonomy: The Issue of the Legal Enforcement of the Principle of Subsidiarity' (2014) 6(2) *Perspectives on Federalism* 67.

[42] O Pimenova, 'Subsidiarity as a "Regulation Principle" in the EU' (2016) 4(3) *Journal of the Theory and Practice of Legislation* 381.

[43] Available at http://ec.europa.eu/smart-regulation/guidelines/tool_3_en.htm.

[44] eg, para 21: 'proposes that the Commission publish all ex ante impact assessments, even for initiatives that are not translated into legislative proposals, in the interests of transparency and strengthening accountability; the publication of the inception impact assessments at the start of the policy cycle is regarded as a good first step to provide feedback and bring forward concerns on subsidiarity'.

[45] Opinion of the European Committee of the Regions—EU agenda on better regulation (2015/C 423/08) [2015] OJ C423/41, 17 December.

[46] Blockmans et al, above n 40, 9. See also A Raccah, 'Les faux espoirs du principe de subsidiarité post-Lisbonne. Le principe de subsidiarité post-Lisbonne rationalise-t-il vraiment l'exercice des compétences de l'Union?', Colloque—ISPOLE, Louvain-la-Neuve, 13–14 October 2010, available at http://ot-ds.sipr.ucl.ac.be/cps/ucl/doc/spri/documents/Communication_raccah.pdf.

> European integration and to the public, as long as not only new technocratic procedures and instruments are introduced but in addition all European institutions and Member States commit to establishing a better regulation culture.[47]

MEMBER STATES' 'IMPLEMENTATION' OF BETTER REGULATION

Later research after the initial start of the Commission's Better Regulation work confirmed the variety of the Better Regulation policies carried out by the European Commission and the governments of the EU Member States. Radaelli and Meuwese listed the following elements in the Better Regulation toolkit(s):[48]

- RIA, including cost-benefit analysis and the assessment of administrative burdens via the so-called Standard Cost Model (SCM);
- simplification programmes;
- methods to foster market-based alternatives to traditional regulation;
- techniques for the choice of regulatory instruments;
- consultation standards (including notice and comment procedures);
- risk-based approaches to enforcement and inspections;
- *ex post* evaluation of regulations.

Obviously the application and implementation of these tools and instruments is done in various combinations and is characterised by different degrees of implementation in the Member States. The importance of national Better Regulation policies has been stressed continuously in the literature.[49]

Gaining an overview of the Better Regulation policies in the EU's Member States remains quite challenging. Given the initiative for the Mandelkern Report by the European Ministers for Public Administration, one might expect that EUPAN would cover this, but unfortunately that is not the case.[50] The Better Regulation

[47] Opinion of the European Economic and Social Committee (SC/41 Better Regulation) [2016] OJ C13/192, 15 January: '4.4.7 In the view of the EESC, one of the main weaknesses of the European better regulation agenda is that the Member States are not sufficiently involved. This is not only a problem for the Member States but also for the EU; it is therefore hardly surprising that the Member States, in the absence of careful, evidence-based transposition measures and plans, as well as measures for effective application, sometimes transpose legislation hesitantly, late or not at all.'

[48] Radaelli and Meuwese, above n 1, 640. Although this overview dates from almost a decade ago, all these elements are still in the current Better Regulation Toolbox of the Commission, available at https://ec.europa.eu/info/files/Better-Regulation-toolbox_en. This extensive set of methodological tools complements the Better Regulation Guidelines (document SWD (2015) 111), was gradually developed during the past decade and was updated in 2017. The various chapters containing individual tools are also available and are intended to be used as a series of Web tools which are downloadable from the Commission's Better Regulation website: http://ec.europa.eu/smart-Regulation/index_en.htm. This comprehensive array of guidance is available for practitioners in the application of Better Regulation in the Member States.

[49] See, eg, E Olovi, 'The EU Better Regulation Agenda' in S Weatherill (ed), *Better Regulation* (Oxford, Hart Publishing, 2007) 194: 'Let me stress that the regulatory environment can be improved only if the initiatives that we take at EU level are matched by equally ambitious programmes in Member States.'

[50] A look at the Better Regulation webpage of the EUPAN website offers a disappointing experience; see www.eupan.eu/en/thematic_areas/show/&tid=30.

element of the broader ambition to modernise the ambitions of the public administrations of the EU Member States seems to have been neglected, at least in this forum.

In order to achieve a view on developments in the EU's Member States, one has to turn to the OECD work on regulatory reform.[51] The OECD EU 15 project (2008–11)[52] confirmed the variety of national policies as well as the gaps and challenges for improvement. The EU 15 project assessed capacities for effective regulatory management across the EU, through individual reviews of 15 Member States, covering half the OECD membership. The first reviews offered some interesting initial findings,[53] such as the fact that 'Multilevel governance' has yet to take off as an integrated policy and 'Minding the gap' between principles and practice is important too. Some countries gave the impression of meeting the technical requirements for Better Regulation processes, but a closer examination suggested that their effective application in practice still had some way to go. On the interface between Member States and the EU, the review made clear that countries are anxious to influence EU policies for regulatory management in order to avoid problems further down the line with the creation of unnecessary burdens in transposition or the unhelpful consequences of new regulations. Countries also have a considerable interest in the Better Regulation policies being deployed at the EU level, from a range of actors—regulatory agencies as well as central ministries. In some cases considerable energy and resources are put into these issues. Another issue that required attention concerned securing a greater coherence in the timing of national and EU Impact Assessment processes on the same regulation.

The synthesis in 2011 highlighted a number of key emerging trends,[54] which included the following:

— The growing interest in a broader social/citizen dimension to regulatory policy, extending the scope beyond the business community. The reviews show, for example, the growth of citizen programmes, links with social welfare objectives and the emergence of sustainability Impact Assessments.
— The development of new forms of regulatory management based on networks, external oversight bodies and internal support units.
— The fundamental links between regulatory governance and other aspects of public governance, including e-government, civil service reform and budget processes.
— The challenges posed by complex modern societies for the effective management of public consultation, and the linked issue of how to make best use of new technologies.
— Growing acknowledgement of the importance of local or sub-national levels of government for effective regulatory management, as they are often the

[51] See www.oecd.org/regreform.
[52] See www.oecd.org/gov/regulatory-policy/Better-Regulation-in-europe-the-eu-15-project.htm.
[53] See www.oecd.org/gov/regulatory-policy/44983092.pdf.
[54] See www.oecd.org/gov/regulatory-policy/betterregulationineurope-progressandtrends.htm.

primary interface for SMEs and citizens in regulatory issues. This issue is important for unitary as well as federal states.

— The limited impact of *ex ante* Impact Assessment processes on the policy and rule-making process, despite a growing awareness that this is a key tool for improving regulatory quality, and the need for significant further culture change in this regard.
— The complex but crucial relationship between the national level and the institutions of the EU for regulatory management, which needs more attention and has some lessons for equivalent relationships outside the EU.
— The political and communication dimension—the reviews highlight that regulatory policy will only thrive if it has political support, civil service 'buy in' and if external stakeholders perceive it to be relevant.

In October 2015, the OECD published the Regulatory Policy Outlook.[55] This is the first evidence-based analysis of the progress made by countries to improve the way they regulate. Based on a survey (the OECD 2014 Regulatory Indicators Survey)[56] filled by all 34 OECD countries and the European Commission, the Regulatory Policy Outlook assesses progress in establishing the conditions for good regulation. It provides insights into the organisation and institutional settings in countries to design, enforce and revise regulations. It uncovers the areas of the regulatory cycle that receive too limited attention from policy-makers and identifies actors who have an important part to play in improving the way in which regulations are developed, implemented and evaluated. It reviews the use of three critical tools of regulatory policy (RIA, stakeholder engagement and *ex post* evaluation) and proposes options to use them in a more strategic manner to inform the development and delivery of regulations.

As this OECD Regulatory Policy Outlook covers 21 EU Member States,[57] its findings indicate relevant information on their current regulatory policies and trends concerning the future.

OECD countries have come a long way in improving regulatory quality over the past two decades. They have done this by taking a whole-of-government approach to regulatory policy and have made it a pillar of their public sector reform efforts: 33 countries have adopted an explicit regulatory policy; 29 countries have designated a minister or high-level official responsible for promoting government-wide progress on regulatory policy. A total of 33 countries have established a standing body charged with regulatory oversight. In all but one country, RIA and consultation have become formal requirements for the executive branch in the development of

[55] OECD, *OECD Regulatory Policy Outlook 2015* (Paris, OECD Publishing, 2015), available at www.oecd.org/gov/oecd-regulatory-policy-outlook-2015-9789264238770-en.htm.

[56] For the methodological background of the survey and analysis of this policy outlook, see C Arndt, AC Baker, T Querbach and R Schultz, '2015 Indicators of Regulatory Policy and Governance: Design, Methodology and Key Results' (2015) *OECD Regulatory Policy Working Papers*, No 1.

[57] Non-OECD, but EU Member States are: Romania, Bulgaria, Malta, Cyprus, Latvia, Lithuania and Croatia.

new regulations. Despite the strong commitment of OECD countries to regulatory quality, there is still a gap between the vision and the reality of regulation. Too often, countries regulate in the dark and do not use enough the leverage they have through Better Regulation to support growth, to restore trust and foster well-being. The indicators show that OECD countries have invested in developing the key elements of their RIA and stakeholder engagement systems. But only 14 OECD jurisdictions have the requirement to release RIA documents for consultation with the general public for subordinate regulation and only 12 jurisdictions in the case of primary regulations. OECD countries could also benefit more by exploiting information and communications technology (ICT) to strengthen the RIA process. There are a sizeable number of OECD jurisdictions which do not make RIAs publicly available online. Countries are less advanced in terms of *ex post* evaluation, where only a few countries systematically evaluate the impact of their regulations *ex post*. The practice of *ex post* evaluation has stagnated across OECD member countries. In the last three years, only seven countries have undertaken *ex post* evaluation frequently for primary and subordinate legislation. The majority of *ex post* evaluation exercises in the past 12 years have been confined to reducing administrative burdens, competition or compliance costs. Transparency and quality control remain underdeveloped in most countries. The impact of regulatory policy could be further improved by addressing shortcomings in the implementation and enforcement of regulations and by using new approaches to regulatory design and delivery such as those based on behavioural economics.

The following table offers an impression of the 'results' of the EU Member States in the OECD Regulatory Policy Outlook.[58]

Table 9.1: Regulatory policy performance

EU Member State	**Regulatory Impact Assessment**	**Stakeholder engagement**	***Ex post* analysis**	**Total**
Austria	A	<A	A	A
Belgium	A	A	>A	A
Czech Republic	A	A	<A	A
Denmark	A	A	A	A
Estonia	**>A**	**>A**	**A**	**>A**
Finland	A	A	<A	A

(continued)

[58] It is based on the 'totals'—and only taking into account the scores for primary laws—of Tables 1.1, 1.2 and 1.3 of the *Regulatory Policy Outlook 2015* at 31–33. The symbols used in the OECD tables have been transposed to < A (below average range), A (equal to average range) and > A (above average range). The four 'above-average' performing countries are Estonia, Germany, the UK and the EU Commission.

Table 9.1: ***(Continued)***

EU Member State	**Regulatory Impact Assessment**	**Stakeholder engagement**	***Ex post* analysis**	**Total**
France	A	A	A	A
Germany	**> A**	**A**	**> A**	**> A**
Greece	< A	A	< A	< A
Hungary	A	< A	A	A
Italy	A	< A	A	A
Ireland	A	< A	< A	< A
Luxembourg	A	< A	A	A
The Netherlands	< A	< A	A	< A
Poland	A	A	A	A
Portugal	< A	< A	A	< A
Slovak Republic	A	> A	< A	A
Slovenia	A	> A	A	A
Sweden	A	A	A	A
Spain	A	A	< A	A
UK	**> A**	**> A**	**> A**	**> A**
EU (Commission)	**> A**	**A**	**> A**	**> A**

As these results indicate, it is no surprise that in a follow-up OECD Working Paper, Arndt et al highlighted the key issue: 'a high potential for improvements to the institutional framework for regulatory policy in OECD countries to bridge the gap between formal requirements and implementation, which may help realise higher impacts of regulatory policy on economic and social outcomes'.[59]

REGULATORY POLICY IN BELGIUM

The OECD Regulatory Policy Outlook 2015 also included the publication of country profiles for all Member States. For Belgium, this two-page note started with the observation that: 'Belgium has made progress towards strengthening policies and institutions aimed at improving regulation at the federal level.' This statement revealed at the same time the limitation of the analysed information as

[59] C Arndt, S Hermanutz, C Kauffmann and R Schultz, 'Building Regulatory Policy Systems in OECD Countries' (2016) www.oecd-ilibrary.org/governance/building-regulatory-policy-systems-in-oecd-countries_dbb1a18f-en.

the Belgian regional regulatory policies had not been taken into account.[60] This is rather surprising given the fact that when Belgium was part of the OECD EU 15 project, the federalisation component was not neglected at all and the survey and analysis included information from the regions too.[61] Furthermore, the Belgium 2015 country profile gives a rather misleading picture about Belgium's national regulation policy as it also says that: 'Within the executive, since 2013 the Agency for Administrative Simplification (AAS) within the Prime Minister's Office, which was responsible for assessing administrative burdens, is also responsible for the whole better regulation policy.' A closer look at the responsibilities of AAS—which was established in 1998 as a Service for Administrative Simplification at the federal level as the first Better Regulation initiative within Belgium[62]—indicates that these are all linked to simplification initiatives and support the Impact Assessment system.[63]

The first policy intentions regarding better regulatory policies were incorporated in 1999 in both the federal Government Agreement (7 July 1999) and the Flemish Government Agreement (8 July 1999). The main focus at both levels concerned the reduction of administrative burdens and the simplification of legislation.

[60] It has to be stressed that the regional governments and parliaments in the Flemish Region, the Brussels-Capital Region and the Walloon Region each have the power to make primary and secondary legislation. Regional legislation is not subordinate to federal laws, as the Belgian state and the regions have different sets of powers and share the same level of authority.

[61] OECD, *Better Regulation in Europe: Belgium* (Paris, OECD Publishing, 2010). See the Executive Summary of the Belgium Report, 14: 'The federalisation process thus raises challenges for effective, efficient and timely policy and rule-making. Better Regulation is especially important in this context, as a means of controlling the bureaucratic effects of federalisation (including regulatory inflation). Officials in the federal state and in the regions and communities are especially conscious of this need. Better Regulation has close potential links with public sector efficiency and reform, which could usefully be exploited further.' See www.oecd.org/gov/regulatory-policy/45198474.pdf. This OECD report covered the federal as well as the regional Better Regulation policies and also highlighted some diversity of these policies, eg, on administrative burden-reduction programmes (Executive Summary at 27). Important initiatives have been taken by the federal government, and the Walloon and Flemish governments, to establish and develop administrative burden-reduction programmes. Different approaches have been used. The federal government and the Walloon Region have taken a selective approach, preferring to test and encourage a gradual evolution. The Flemish Region has opted for a more systematic approach. Variants on the SCM methodology are deployed to carry out measurements. At the same time, there is increasing adoption of a user-centric approach to improve the experience of citizens and businesses with the administration. The Brussels-Capital Region has been catching up, and in 2008 it launched a pilot for SCM, with a view to creating an SCM procedure. With the 'Brussels Plan for Administrative Simplification' launched in October 2009, this will be developed into a full programme, with the objective of a 25 per cent reduction in administrative burdens. From 2010 a selective measurement approach will be launched, the first target being Economy and Employment legislation (Executive Summary at 14–15).

[62] M Suykens, 'Administratieve vereenvoudiging: concept en praktijk' in B Hubeau and M Elst (eds), *Democratie in ademnood? Over legitimiteit, legitimatie en verfijning van de democratie* (Bruges, Die Keure, 2002) 397. The current Director General of the AAS (incorporated in the Chancellery of the Prime Minister) was also the Belgian delegate in the Mandelkern Group and leads a team of 12 people. For an overview of previous steps that could be considered as Better Regulation elements, see OECD, above n 61, 56.

[63] See www.vereenvoudiging.be/boek/over-de-dienst-administratieve-vereenvoudiging/over-de-dienst-administratieve-vereenvoudiging; see also www.simplification.be.

However, these ambitions were also linked to other instruments on evaluation and participatory approaches in order to address the growing concerns of citizens and societal stakeholders.[64]

At the federal level, the ambition was to realise a cutback of the overall burden of 10 per cent within two years and of 25 per cent by the end of the legislature (2003). In July 2000 the federal Council of Ministers decided on a two-way approach. The AAS took charge of the micro-economic approach to measure the administrative burdens of existing legislation that would be selected for specific aims. The results are published annually.[65] Furthermore, the federal Planning Bureau had to set up a biannual survey to a representative group of companies and small and medium-sized enterprises (SMEs). The latest survey results were published in 2016 and also include an aggregated figure of the reduction of administrative burdens for companies and self-employed entrepreneurs.[66]

So the initial task of AAS was to research and develop measures to tackle and reduce administrative complexities and the costs involved for companies, and from 2003 also for citizens. This federal approach was broadened through a cooperation agreement adopted on 10 December 2003 by all the Belgian governments.[67] The focus of this agreement was exclusively on administrative simplification and its objective was to realise joint results. It included the creation of a notification point at the AAS. In March 2004 a joint report with the initial experiences with the contact point was published.[68] No more publications were issued following this. The AAS also acted as a service desk for the Kafka-test aiming to prevent and reduce administrative burdens of regulations. This test was introduced at the federal level in October 2004 (and later also in Wallonia and in the Brussels capital region). Each note to the federal Council of Ministers that goes with a regulatory proposal had to be accompanied by a Kafka-test. A number of governmental initiatives were excluded, such as internal government regulations, budgetary regulations, regulations approving international and inter-regional conventions and agreements, and regulations without substantive impact or of a purely formal nature. In 2013 the Kafka-test became part of a more elaborate and integrated Impact Assessment approach that includes now four other issues for which separate tests existed: sustainable development, gender equality, policy coordination for development

[64] P Popelier, 'Naar een democratisch wetgeving(evaluatie)beleid' in Hubeau and Elst, above n 62, 363.

[65] The annual reports are available at www.vereenvoudiging.be/content/publicaties.

[66] 'En pour cent du PIB, le coût relatif total des charges administratives supportées par les entreprises et les indépendants diminue légèrement, atteignant 1,66 % en 2014 après 1,70 % en 2012, 1,79 % en 2010 et 3,48 % en 2000. En quatorze ans, le poids relatif des charges administratives a donc diminué de plus de moitié (1,82 point de pour cent).' The results of the 8th Survey (2014) were published on 8 March 2016 and are available at www.plan.be/admin/uploaded/201603080851210.CP_PP_charges_ad_20160307.pdf.

[67] See Press communication after the approval by the Flemish government on 10 June 2004, https://www.vlaanderen.be/nl/vlaamse-overheid/persberichten/administratieve-vereenvoudiging-vlaanderen-op-goedeweg.

[68] Available at https://www.vlaanderen.be/nl/publicaties/detail/eindrapport-meldpunt-voor-administratieve-lasten-december-2003-maart-2004. See also www.kafka.be; this website still exists, but seems not to have been updated since 2015.

cooperation, and SMEs.[69] The integration of these Impact Assessment tests may be considered as the result of observations and suggestions in the OECD 2010 Report.[70]

Representatives from the five involved administrations are members of the Impact Assessment Committee that has been established in the AAS that also steers this committee. The Impact Assessment Committee may be requested to evaluate *ex ante* the quality of the Impact Assessment and formulate proposals to improve the assessment. Furthermore, this committee reports annually, which include an *ex post* evaluation of the application of the legally required Impact Assessment system.[71] The report is published after it has been sent to the Council of Ministers. The OECD Belgium country profile also included some critical notes on the Impact Assessment system: 'While RIA can be shared with social partners during consultation, it is not released for consultation with the general public. Also, the scope and focus of the RIA is adapted depending on the theme of the proposed legislation, without however a more formal threshold test.' An initial review in 2014 and a more extensive review of 100 federal RIAs later on not only confirmed the low quality of these assessments (as acknowledged in the annual AAS report) but also questioned the usefulness of the AAS recommendations to improve the application of the existing RIA approach.[72] Poel et al considered the proposed improvements as not sufficient, as the current federal RIA system is not consistent with the six essential elements of a good Impact Assessment.[73] RIA has to be integrated within the policy process in order to be effective, but the feasibility of such an integration remains questionable given the governance culture in Belgium.[74]

[69] Law of 15 December 2013 and Royal Decree of 21 December 2013, both published in the Belgian OJ of 31 December 2013, 103694/ 103704.

[70] OECD, above n 61, 24: 'Another issue for attention is that the federal government now has two separate institutional anchors for impact assessment. The Sustainable Development impact assessment process is overseen by the FPS for Sustainable Development (one of the horizontal ministries), and the Kafka Test is overseen by the ASA in the Federal Chancellery. There is no formal link between the two processes, apart from the fact that the SDIA is (like the Kafka Test) attached to draft proposals going to the Council of Ministers. Both require the co-operation of (highly autonomous) other ministries. It does not make sense to continue, at least over the longer term, with two separate processes.' See also P Van Humbeeck, 'Regulatory Impact Analysis in Flanders and Belgium: Policy and Trends' (2012) Paper for the 2012 European Environmental Evaluators Network Forum, 9–10 February, HIVA–KU Leuven, Belgium, available at www.environmentalevaluators.net/wp-content/uploads/2012/04/Conference-paper_Peter-Van-Humbeek_-RIA-in-Flanders-and-Belgium.pdf.

[71] Although the annual reports contain critical observations about the Impact Assessment approach (eg, on the lack of quality of the assessments), one may question the usefulness of an exclusive 'in-house' evaluation. The new federal evaluation policy (launched in March 2017) could enhance improvements in the longer term; see https://bosa.belgium.be/nl/activiteiten/dg-begroting-en-beleidsevaluatie.

[72] K Poel and W Marneffe, 'De federale regelgevingsimpactanalyse: een stand van zaken na 6 maanden' (2014) *Tijdschrift voor Wetgeving* 185.

[73] K Poel, W Marneffe and P Van Humbeeck, 'De federale regelgevingsimpactanalyse: nood aan hervormingen?' (2016) *Tijdschrift voor Wetgeving* 196, 208.

[74] K Poel et al (ibid 208) state that in Belgium the relationship between politics and administration differs from many other countries given the hierarchical relationships of the political-ministerial cabinets versus the administration.

Its legal mandate requires the AAS to organise cooperation between federal administrations. It also has to organise consultations on administrative simplification with all government levels and with European and international institutions, as well as with representative partners from micro-businesses and SMEs. These tasks are foreseen in the cooperation agreement on administrative simplification of 10 December 2003. Better Regulation is mentioned only once in this cooperation agreement, where it states that the cooperation between the Belgian governments should also concern the work by international institutions like the EU and the OECD.

The impact of this cooperation agreement remained very limited and has not generated a real cooperation, as consultations with the regional level are still very infrequent and not systematically held.

With the exception of the still-infant Impact Assessment approach, the Belgian Better Regulation policy at the federal level has been and still is focused on administrative burden-reduction and simplification efforts, mainly—but not exclusively—addressing the business sector. The usefulness of other Better Regulation elements is also linked to these economic and efficiency objectives. This is confirmed in the federal Government Agreement (2014–18) of the current coalition.[75] This text also situates some responsibility for the administrative burdens at the EU level.[76] The General Policy Note[77] on administrative simplification of the responsible State Secretary contains a short section on qualitative legislation, mentioning four principles/criteria—legislation should be necessary, evidence-based, efficient and effective—but this part only refers to some existing practices (eg, Impact Assessment and the Parliamentary Committee on the evaluation of legislation

[75] Regeerakkoord—10 oktober 2014/Accord de gouvernement—10 octobre 2014, available at www.premier.be/sites/default/files/articles/Accord_de_Gouvernement_-_Regeerakkoord.pdf. eg, Regeerakkoord, 18: '1.10 … Le gouvernement doit encourager les gens qui entreprennent. Un gouvernement mince et efficace doit en première instance remplir un rôle de soutien. Il n'entre dès lors pas l'ambition du gouvernement d'entreprendre lui-même, mais de créer un cadre dans lequel toutes les opportunités sont données à l'entreprenariat. C'est pourquoi une diminution structurelle des charges administratives est prioritaire'; Regeerakkoord, 22: '1.11. Simplification administrative … L'objectif est de générer 30 per cent d'économies au bénéfice des entreprises. Le gouvernement élaborera et mettra en oeuvre un plan de simplification des charges administratives qui pèsent sur les entreprises. Il s'agira par exemple de généraliser la facturation électronique et de simplifier la mise en oeuvre des législations fiscales et sociales … Enfin, la complexité de la législation constitue une source importante de charges administratives pour les entreprises. Il est donc nécessaire de prévoir une analyse ex post des législations et des dispositions administratives'; Regeerakkoord, 170: 'Enfin, le gouvernement s'attachera à simplifier systématiquement la réglementation: l'orientation-usager, l'efficience des coûts et l'innovation sont en effet servies par des règles intelligentes, mais surtout moins nombreuses.'

[76] Regeerakkoord (2014) 186: 'Nous croyons également fortement au principe de subsidiarité lequel permet à l'Union de se concentrer sur des domaines et actions où elle a une valeur ajoutée. Il faut gouverner de manière efficace au niveau le plus approprié et le plus proche du citoyen. Il faut également attirer l'attention de l'Union sur les charges administratives parfois très lourdes que sa réglementation impose aux Etats membres, à leurs citoyens et à leurs entreprises. Tout cela est nécessaire pour rétablir la confiance du citoyen en l'Europe.'

[77] Algemene Beleidsnota Administratieve Vereenvoudiging, 28 November 2014, Belgische Kamer van Volksvertegenwoordigers, Document 54 0588/ (2014/2015).

established in 2007).[78] This policy note repeats the concern about the EU as a source of administrative burdens for Member States, citizens and companies, but also refers to the appointment of Vice-President Timmermans and the Better Regulation Agenda. It even says that Belgium will actively participate in the EU and internationally for Better Regulation. However, the largest part of this policy note is an overview of simplification projects, either ongoing or in the pipeline. A new federal action plan for administrative simplification is also announced for the period 2015–19. This is not a novelty as there was such a plan for the period 2012–15 under the previous federal government. The status of the current plan remains rather unclear as it is untraceable.[79] When questioned about it in Parliament in May 2015, the State Secretary promised continuity with the previous plan and in December 2015 he promised to present the new plan, which according to the conclusion of the policy note is the central element of his policy.[80] In any case, the basic objective of this policy is clear: 'Le mot d'ordre est la compétitivité.'[81] This is also the major concern regarding the transposition of EU legislation,[82] as the federal Government Agreement indicates that it not only wants to reduce the current delays but also to avoid 'gold-plating', except in cases where it might improve the international competitiveness of Belgium.

Finally, the federal policy intention—with reference to the agreement of 10 December 2003—to increase cooperation with the Belgian regions on administrative simplification remains unfulfilled. So the overall impression is that at the federal level, a whole-of-government approach concerning Better Regulation is hard to detect even after 15 years of EU signals and critical observations from, inter alia, academia.[83] However, as the latest state reform has created new legislative and implementation problems, a recent political initiative in the Belgian Senate addressed the coherence and coordination issue. Nevertheless, the outcome

[78] See www.comitewetsevaluatie.be/indexN.html. Its latest report (2013–14, Belgische Kamer van Volksvertegenwoordigers, Document 54 0435/002) dates from 12 March 2015 and contains an overview of legislation with problematic interpretation and application in the courts; available at www.dekamer.be/FLWB/PDF/54/0435/54K0435002.pdf.

[79] As of the time of writing (10 April 2017), there is no reference to this plan on the website of the AAS.

[80] Belgische Kamer van Volksvertegenwoordigers, Schriftelijke Vraag en antwoord nr 0142—zittingsperiode 54, Written request from member of Parliament K. Gabriëls, answer published on 29 June 2015; Belgische Kamer van Volksvertegenwoordigers, Verslag 8 December 2015, Document 54 1352 (2015/2016).

[81] Document 54 1352 (2015/2016), above n 80, 8: 'Le 21ème siècle est le siècle de la globalisation, les États rivalisant sans cesse pour réaliser des investissements et garantir leur croissance économique. Le mot d'ordre est la compétitivité. Des pouvoirs publics efficaces, simples et transparents, qui innovent et veillent à la qualité de la législation, ne sont dès lors pas un luxe, mais une nécessité absolue pour que le pays ait sa place sur l'échiquier économique.'

[82] The federal Government Agreement also announces an arrangement with the regions to share the financial sanctions imposed by the EU in the case of late or un-complete transpositions, but as of April 2017, this remains an intention for the time being.

[83] See, eg, Popelier, above n 64, 369; see also P Popelier, 'Politici, maak werk van degelijke wetgeving' *De Morgen* (9 January 2009).

did not include the proposal from one of the experts heard, who suggested the creation of a permanent coordination organ for regulatory policy.[84]

REGULATORY POLICY IN FLANDERS

As the existence of Flanders as a legislative region is quite recent in historical terms, its regulatory policy is young too compared to EU Member States or OECD countries. Thus, one might have expected that the creation of a new policy and administrative level that also envisaged modernisation inspired by New Public Management could probably entail a fresh regulatory approach.[85] In the 1980s and especially 1988–89 as a result of Belgian state reforms, the Flemish regulatory powers increased and resulted in a growing amount of regional legislation, inter alia as evidence for its autonomy. Already in the 1990s, concern and discomfort was growing in relation to the quantity and quality of regulations that had been created in that short period. The perception developed that legal quality was deteriorating and regulatory burdens were increasing so that the Flemish economy was becoming less competitive and the public policies less effective. Proposals from ad hoc working groups and research commissions did not result in structural and durable improvements. Building on the 1995 Recommendation of the OECD Council on Improving the Quality of Government Regulation, the Social and Economic Council of Flanders (SERV) published in 1997 and 1998 a series of reports and recommendations for the Flemish government to start a process of regulatory management.[86]

As already mentioned, the Flemish Government Agreement (8 July 1999) took these proposals up. On 25 July 2000, the Flemish government approved a 'general framework for the simplification of regulations, procedures and rules' containing 13 actions related to simplification and a plan to develop a central institution with a 'mission is to build and implement a regulatory management system'. This focus on institutional capacities was a real change compared to previous policies. The new approach led on the one hand to the adoption of a series of regulatory management action plans (2001–05), with many *ex post* projects for administrative simplification and codification of regulations. Furthermore, in 2001

[84] Belgische Senaat, Zitting 2016–17, 9 January 2017, Document 6-212/3: 'Het harmonieus samengaan van federale regelgeving en deelstaatregelgeving vergt een permanente bewaking. Daarom zou het goed zijn als er naast de voorbereidende commissie ad hoc ook een permanent coördinatieorgaan wordt uitgewerkt. Waarom geen interministeriële en/ of interparlementaire conferentie over regelgevingsbeleid.'

[85] M Brans, C De Visscher and D Vancoppenolle, 'Administrative Reform in Belgium: Maintenance or Modernisation?' (2006) 29 *West European Politics* 979. See also G Dierickx, 'Politicization in Belgian civil service' in BG Peters and J Pierre (eds), *The Politicization of the Civil Service in Comparative Perspective: The Quest for Control* (Abingdon, Routledge, 2004) 198.

[86] P Van Humbeeck, 'Best Practices in Regulatory Impact Analysis: A Review of the Flemish Region in Belgium', Social Economic Council of Flanders (SERV), Working Paper, February 2007.

the government created a Regulatory Management unit within its Coordination department ('Dienst Wetsmatiging' or 'Legislative Moderation Unit'). This unit had to build, promote, support and coordinate the regulatory policy, and it was launched in 2002.

The regulatory policy was developed along three tracks (administrative burden reduction, legal simplification/codification and regulatory impact analysis) and included actions covering different dimensions: improving the quality and reducing the quantity of existing regulation; reforming the legislative process and developing a structural regulatory policy, including the required management capacities and institutions. In November 2003 the Flemish government adopted eight Principles for Good Regulation.[87] These principles serve as guidance for designing, drafting and evaluating regulation. A major driving force for a Flemish Better Regulation policy has been (and still is) the SERV.[88] Over the years, it has formulated a range of advices as well as recommendations based on evaluations regarding all the different elements of Better Regulation.[89]

From 2004 onwards, the Regulatory Management unit developed tools such as the administrative burden measurement tool (based on the standard cost model and also including a compensation rule), a checklist for better forms and the RIA system that started in 2005.[90] Since 2005, RIA has been a mandatory step in the approval procedure of certain categories of regulations (decrees) at the initiative of the Government of Flanders.[91] In 2006 the government decided to establish regulatory quality units within the different policy areas of the Flemish administration. This decision was more formally reaffirmed in 2011 and these units had to serve

[87] Good-quality regulation now (April 2017) meets the following nine criteria: 1) necessary and effective; 2) appropriate and balanced; 3) implementable and enforceable; 4) lawful; 5) consistent; 6) simple, clear and accessible; 7) well-founded and well-discussed; and 8) relevant and up-to-date. This list has been supplemented with (9) the principle of digital-friendly regulation.

[88] The Social and Economic Council of Flanders (SERV) is the main advisory body to the Flemish government on Flemish socio-economic policy. It represents trade unions and employer associations. One of its fields of expertise concerns government and Better Regulation. The SERV's advisory reports are available to the public. The recommendations in these reports are not binding. The SERV houses many other organisations, including strategic advisory councils on mobility: welfare, health and family; agriculture and fishery. See https://www.serv.be/en/serv.

[89] eg, in 2009, the SERV published an evaluation of 10 years of Flemish regulatory policy and concluded that Flanders had to cope with five challenges: 1) maximising political support for Better Regulation; 2) placing Better Regulation at the core of the policy process and avoiding formalism; 3) assigning responsibilities for Better Regulation; 4) improving the quality of Better Regulation tools; and 5) putting priorities. See SERV, 'Wetgevingsprocedures, -structuren en—instrumenten in Vlaanderen: een evaluatie van 10 jaar wetgevingsbeleid in Vlaanderen. Achtergronddocument bij het SERV-advies 'Betere regelgeving voor een effectieve en efficiënte overheid en meer welvaart en welzijn' (2009), Report, October 2009, 84, available at https://overheid.vlaanderen.be/sites/default/files/SERV%20rapport%20evaluatie%20wetgevingsbeleid.pdf.

[90] The full range of policy intentions—although with a strong focus on administrative burden reduction and simplification—was announced in the Policy Note (2004–09) of the responsible Flemish Minister for Administrative Affairs, available at https://overheid.vlaanderen.be/sites/bz.vlaanderen.be/files/documenten/Beleidsnota_bestuurszaken_2004.pdf.

[91] See https://overheid.vlaanderen.be/reguleringsimpactanalyse.

as points of contact for the Regulatory Management unit and should facilitate cooperation for the application of the existing better regulation tools like drafting RIAs, measuring the administrative burdens, monitoring the action plans on simplification and drafting regulatory agendas. In line with the EU ambitions and actions to reduce administrative burdens by 25 per cent, in 2007 Flanders launched action plans for administrative simplification, including base-line measurements. In practice and particularly since the adoption of the strategic policy framework for smart regulation and administrative simplification in 2010, the rather ambitious Flemish Better Regulation policy has been declining.[92] This development is not that surprising as the Policy Note (2009–14) of the responsible Flemish Minister for Administrative Affairs focused not only on the better implementation of the tools and approaches introduced under the previous Flemish government, but also on reforming (in the sense of downgrading) some too, eg, the RIA. Concerns about the simplification and quality of regulation would be addressed as elements of more client-oriented policy approaches.[93] Efficiency and effectiveness were the overall priorities as the Flemish administration was also implementing a reform programme which reduced resources given the budgetary situation as a result of the economic crisis.[94]

Due to its processes, instruments and institutions, before 2010, Flanders was one of the better-performing countries in the OECD context. It was largely inspired by the Better Regulation developments regarding simplification, and RIA at the EU level and the OECD work in this field. However, in 2010 the OECD warned that:

> Flanders has opted for a different and broader approach to ex ante impact assessment. The Flemish government has established a 'comprehensive' ex ante impact assessment with some quantification and consideration of options, together with a quality control system, and a compensation rule for administrative burdens arising from new

[92] P Van Humbeeck, 'Betere regelgeving in Vlaanderen: quo vadis?' (2017) *Tijdschrift voor Wetgeving* 35. This author states that the Regulatory Management unit has disappeared from sight, which is correct as its (human) resources have been more or less halved and its duties broadened to more 'classical' legislative drafting projects over the course of the past decade. Meetings of the network of regulatory quality units are no longer held. The Regulatory Management unit only serves as some kind of basic helpdesk. P Van Humbeeck had already warned of the poor performance of the Flemish regulatory management in P Van Humbeeck, 'Wetgevingsbeleid in Vlaanderen op niveau van de uitvoerende macht: een update van de uitdagingen voor betere regelgeving' in P Popelier and J Van Nieuwenhove (eds), *Wie maakt de wet?* (Bruges, Die Keure, 2006) 137.

[93] Beleidsnota Bestuurszaken 2009–14, 38, available at http://docs.vlaamsparlement.be/docs/stukken/2009-2010/g184-1.pdf. In this policy note, the introduction of an Impact Assessment approach on new EU proposals was also announced, but was not developed later on, except for some research linked to a pilot project in the course of 2016–17 with some preliminary conclusions.

[94] D Verlet and G De Schepper, 'Over efficiëntie en effectiviteit van de Vlaamse overheid. Een stand van zaken uit de praktijk: over kiezen en keuzes beminnen' in D Verlet and C Devos (eds), *Efficiëntie en effectiviteit van de publieke sector in de weegschaal* (Brussels, Studiedienst Vlaamse Regering, 2010) 97. See also P Popelier, who even earlier stated that politicians will be mostly interested in a more rational decision-making process as it generates economic interests; P Popelier, *De wet juridisch bekeken* (Bruges, Die Keure, 2004) 385.

> regulations. The system has 'teething problems' typical of what is often encountered in other OECD countries. It is proving difficult to change attitudes and persuade officials (and ministerial cabinets) to take the assessment seriously and carry it out at a sufficiently early stage in the development of regulations (it is often treated more as an ex post note of justification for a decision which has already been taken). This initiative will only be effective if efforts to encourage the administration upstream to carry out higher quality and timely impact assessments are sustained over time. The review of RIA completed at the end of 2008 emphasised the need for stronger political support and further guidance to officials.

Under the current Flemish government, regulatory management is the responsibility of the Minister-President. At the level of the administration, the Regulatory Management unit has moved to the Chancellery and Public Governance department, which aims to become a Centre of Government inspired by this OECD concept. The concerned Policy Note 2014–19 continues the existing focus on simplification and burden reduction.[95] However, the practice focuses on pragmatic approaches and for that reason, for example, the compensation rule is no longer applied as it missed its objective. Inter alia, the experience with the already-mentioned action plans indicated that the quality of measuring burdens was problematic (the Standard Cost Model has its limits), resulting in misleading perceptions of the reality. Stakeholder involvement was also not easy and remains difficult with a view to formulating burden reduction targets. New Flemish legislation should be necessary, avoid useless details, be implemented easily and as cheap as possible. Existing legislation should only be amended if it is really necessary and 'regulatory rest' is an important concern. The newer policy intentions concern consultation, digitalisation and evaluation.[96]

Mainly to implement the basic line of the current Flemish government (trust, connect, progress), the Policy Note says that stakeholders and citizens should be consulted more systematically when regulatory initiatives are prepared.[97] Digitalisation opportunities should be explored, introduced and implemented as much as possible. The Policy Note also refers to the appointment of Vice-President Timmermans mainly focusing on the Better Regulation dimension of reducing the regulatory pressure and announces Flemish support for such an EU policy. Without referring to the Better Regulation Agenda, but definitely in line with it, are the policy objectives concerning a systematic evaluation of policies in order

[95] Beleidsnota Algemeen Regeringsbeleid 2014–19, 14–16, available at https://www.vlaanderen.be/nl/publicaties/detail/beleidsnota-2014-2019-algemeen-regeringsbeleid.

[96] These topics were further developed as elements of a Green Paper on Governance, published in October 2016 and the subject of public consultation afterwards. See: https://www.vlaanderen.be/nl/publicaties/detail/groenboek-bestuur. This resulted in a White Paper adopted by the Flemish government on 7 July 2017.

[97] Regeerakkoord Vlaamse Regering 2014–19, available at https://www.vlaanderen.be/nl/publicaties/detail/het-regeerakkoord-van-de-vlaamse-regering-2014-2019. However, L Huyse analysed this Government Agreement and missed a real participation objective: L Huyse, 'Doe-het-zelf-samenleving' *De Standaard* (2 August 2014) 44.

to gain a better view of the effects of Flemish policies and correct these where necessary.[98] RIA is mentioned in this context.

The RIA practice still exists, but its limited implementation raises questions. Good RIAs are exceptional and their effectiveness has been described as 'ritual rain dances'.[99] This observation about RIA has to be placed against the broader background of the current Flemish regulatory (management) policy. According to Van Humbeeck, this policy needs a new impetus and re-orientation focusing on better evidence-based decision-making, more and better consultations, and a greater level of transparency in policy and legislative processes.[100] Whilst the first two have been addressed in the last Policy Note, the latter remains the most difficult one, as it is linked to the existing governance culture with hardly any difference between the federal and the Flemish level. Already in 2010, the OECD gave a clear message:

> The sustainability of many Better Regulation institutions across the political cycles (and sometimes within them) is an issue, which is not unique to Belgium. There are few easily definable high-level political champions of Better Regulation. An issue of concern is that there is often weak political buy-in for Better Regulation.
>
> The difficulties of developing Better Regulation are aggravated by the often strong role of cabinets in rule-making processes. In all governments (federal, regions, communities), ministerial cabinets (referred to as 'strategic cells') are large, contain a mix of both civil servants and political nominees, and are often involved in law drafting (a task usually reserved for civil servants in other countries). A number of stakeholders voiced their concern to the team that this weakened the application of Better Regulation processes such as effective consultation, because the cabinets did not or could not (for example, under political pressure or in an emergency) automatically apply the processes when they drafted laws.[101]

Although the Flemish government signed a charter[102] with the College of high-level civil servants of the administration concerning their mutual responsibilities

[98] Beleidsnota Bestuurszaken 2014–19, above n 93, 32. See also B De Peuter Bart and V Pattyn, 'Waarom evalueren beleidsmakers? Een longitudinale analyse van motieven voor beleidsevaluatie in Vlaamse ministeriële beleidsnota's' (2016) *Bestuurskunde* 25, 32–45. Their research results revealed no particular development towards more evidence-based policies in Flanders, but in the legislature 2009–14 there was more attention for evaluation justification given the administrative reform context. This reform has established the tool of policy evaluation (eg, departments became responsible for evaluation), but its application varies widely within the Flemish administration according to these authors. So the situation seems to have been improved somehow compared to the observations in a previous research by F Varone et al: 'Both in Flanders (Dutch-speaking) and in the bilingual Brussels Region, evaluations are ordered unsystematically and outside any institutional framework regulating the practice.' See F Varone, S Jacob and L De Winter, 'Polity, Politics and Policy Evaluation in Belgium' (2005) *Evaluation* 253. These authors considered the existence of strong 'ministerial cabinets' as a major influence on the limited development of policy evaluation (at 261).

[99] Van Humbeeck, above n 92 (2017), 36.

[100] ibid 36.

[101] OECD, above n 61, 19.

[102] This happened under the previous Flemish government; the text is available at https://www.vlaanderen.be/nl/vlaamse-overheid/organisatie-van-de-vlaamse-overheid/charter-politiek-ambtelijke-samenwerking.

and cooperation, this particular 'ministerial cabinet' feature of the Belgian public governance model remains very strong.[103] Furthermore, not all stakeholders seem to consider this as a major concern as this issue was not incorporated into the recommendations of a study commissioned by the Belgian Federation of Enterprises to improve the quality of legislation.[104] The report was based on a benchmarking exercise (including the following Member States: Denmark, the Netherlands, the UK, France and Germany) and called inter alia for a better RIA approach, more regulatory coherence between the Belgian policy levels and also a more integrated regulatory policy.

On the other hand, the picture is also not that negative as the absence of very centralised Better Regulation approaches and monitoring[105]—or even a more general coordinated regulatory policy[106]—somehow obscure the view on implementation efforts in different sector policy domains, yet these efforts have to go beyond legalism and formalism.[107] Furthermore, institutionalised requirements remain important to generate legitimate, lasting and useful evaluation and regulatory outputs.[108] More recent institutional developments considered to be helpful to support the application of Better Regulation tools are, inter alia, the Circular Letters adopted in 2014.[109] Circular Letter 2014/4 on legislative techniques indicates the

[103] The umbrella NGO of the Flemish society stakeholders 'Verenigde Verenigingen' in 2011 published an interesting collection of interviews with key figures on the public governance culture and its need for reforms: *It's the culture stupid, Sporen naar een andere beleidscultuur* (Brussels, Verenigde Verenigingen, 2011); see also G Tegenbos, 'Goedbetaalde politieke pionnen en spionnen' *De Standaard* (21 December 2016); G Tegenbos, 'Vernieuwing of cosmetica?' *De Standaard* (14 June 2016); see also P Van Humbeeck, 'De politicus is al te overmoedig' *De Standaard* (27 February 2017). In February 2017 number of politically appointed cabinet staff members in the Flemish government was equal to the number under the previous government, despite the intention to reduce this number: *De Tijd* (10 February 2017).

[104] Idea Consult, De kwaliteit van de regelgeving in België: knelpunt of hefboom voor competitiviteit?, VBO, Brussels, 2015, available at www.vbo-feb.be/publicaties/de-kwaliteit-van-de-regelgeving-in-belgie-knelpunt-of-hefboom-voor-competitiviteit.

[105] See A Molenveld and K Verhoest, 'Coordinatie-arrangementen in internationaal perspectief: een blik vanuit de Vlaamse en buitenlandse overheidsorganisaties', SBOV-KU Leuven Instituut voor de Overheid, 2014.

[106] SERV, above n 89, 3; see also Popelier, above n 64, 369, who stated that the Belgian governments do not have a structured regulatory policy.

[107] See reports from the Policy Research Centre—Governmental Organization—Decisive Governance, eg, J Vandoninck, M Brans, E Wayenberg and E Fobé, 'Ex ante beleidsevaluatie voor beleidsinstrumentenkeuze Conclusies en pistes voor optimalisatie', SBOV-KU Leuven Instituut voor de Overheid, 2015; see also the thematic issue on policy evaluation published by the Flemish Journal for Public Management; and in particular E Desmedt, V Pattyn and P Van Humbeeck, 'Beleidsevaluatie vandaag: een voorzichtige balans' (2016) *Vlaams Tijdschrift voor Overheidsmanagement* 63. This issue contains a number of stocktaking contributions, collected within the framework of the Flemish Evaluation Platform; see www.evaluatieplatform.be/eng/index.htm.

[108] P Van Humbeeck, 'Maken we goede wetgeving? Benchmarking van Vlaanderen. Achtergronddocument bij de analyse gepubliceerd in SERA 2007' (2006) Sociaal-Economische Raad van Vlaanderen, October 2006, 29.

[109] Available at https://overheid.vlaanderen.be/omzendbrieven-wetsmatiging.

different responsibilities concerning the quality control of RIA.[110] It also clarifies the terminology of Green and White Papers as their use is growing. Circular Letter 2014/13 concerns the regulatory agenda, RIA and the compensation rule for administrative burdens.[111] Circular Letter 2014/11 regulates the cooperation between the Flemish administration and the Flemish Parliament. This document indicates the incorporation of the RIA in the legislative file more precisely as an element of the explanatory memorandum of a decree.[112]

Another, more recent Circular Letter (2016/41) adopted by the Flemish government in November 2016 concerns the coordination of the transposition of EU legislation. This document indicates clearly that the transposition challenges already start once the Commission has published a proposal as the concerned administration has to screen such a proposal in order to identify possible impact issues.[113] This new requirement reflects earlier announced policy intentions to develop an Impact Assessment approach about EU proposals.[114] Already in 2009, the Social and Economic Council of Flanders suggested using the political support for the EU's Better Regulation Agenda and the intention for a Flemish Impact Assessment about EU proposals as a catalyst for a more serious Flemish RIA practice.[115] This was also endorsed by the Interuniversity Centre for Legislation in its Memorandum for Better Regulation (2009).[116] Such an Impact Assessment would offer different advantages not only as an early, preparatory 'implementation device', but also in order to strengthen the Flemish position within the Belgian coordination and towards the EU negotiations. In December 2016 the Government of Flanders adopted a 'Vision on the Future of the European Union', which has to be considered as the general framework for assessing EU policy proposals and also includes a general position concerning Better Regulation issues.[117]

[110] Omzendbrief VR/2014/4: Wetgevingstechniek. This Circular Letter is regularly updated. See para 300 of this Circular Letter. These responsibilities differ as the Regulatory Management unit advises on RIA, the application of the compensation rule and the impact on local authorities. In the case of the application of the Youth and Children Impact Assessment, the Youth administration has to give its advice and when a poverty test was required, the Welfare and Society administration has to deliver an opinion.

[111] Omzendbrief VR 2014/13: Regelgevingsagenda, reguleringsimpactanalyse en compensatieregel administratieve lasten. This Circular Letter stipulates the procedure and contents of each tool. The regulatory agenda is an annex to each Policy Note (published by each Minister after the start of a new government) and each Policy Letter (annually by each Minister indicating more detailed policy objectives).

[112] Omzendbrief VR 2014/11: Samenwerking met het Vlaams Parlement; see point III.2.4 of this document.

[113] Article 3.1 of this Circular Letter.

[114] Beleidsnota 2014–2019 Buitenlands Beleid, Internationaal Ondernemen en Ontwikkelingssamenwerking, 20, available at https://www.vlaanderen.be/nl/publicaties/detail/beleidsnota-2014-2019-buitenlands-beleid.

[115] SERV, above n 89, 90.

[116] SERV, 'Externe reacties op het ontwerpadvies "Betere regelgeving voor een effectieve en efficiënte overheid en meer welvaart en welzijn"' (2010) Report, 69. The Interuniversity Centre for Legislation suggested, inter alia, making better use of the Commission's Impact Assessments.

[117] The text sets out the role of the EU in tackling the major challenges that European society faces. It also stipulates in which policy areas EU legislation provides added value for Flanders. See www.vlaanderen.be/int/en/vision-eu.

At the request of the Flemish government, in October 2016 the Social and Economic Council of Flanders adopted three advices concerning regulatory policies, of which one includes Better Regulation in its title.[118] Although the latter focuses mainly on a number of technical features (like simplification, digitalisation and innovation-minded), it also addresses issues like transparency, evidence-based, participation, consultation and evaluation. In a sense, this advice repeats ideas and suggestions that were already in previous opinions, advices and reports. Basically they consider the democratic quality of regulation or its legitimacy.[119]

Furthermore, the administration has drafted a Green Paper on public governance that was the subject of a public consultation at the end of 2016. The headlines of this Green Paper include similar aspirations as in the above-mentioned advices. They have been further developed in a White Paper and certain objectives should even become part of a decree on public governance.[120] This policy intention is included in the Policy Letter 2016–17 that also rather vaguely refers to the above-mentioned recent Better Regulation advice.[121] However, the expectations about the final outcome of the Green Paper process should be modest as another piece of advice from the Social and Economic Council of Flanders stated that this Green Paper misses important proposals for necessary cultural changes to reform the relationships between politics (cabinets) and the administration, to improve cooperation and to increase transparency, as well as evidence-based policies and Better Regulation.[122] As these kinds of observation are becoming repetitive, they also seem to be proof of a—quite strong—statement by Sottiaux about the immature democratic consciousness in Flanders.[123] But international rankings reveal similar indications, as in the 2016 Democracy Index of *The Economist*, Belgium only ranks at 35. This position is far behind its neighbouring states of Luxembourg (11), the Netherlands (12), Germany (13) and even France (24). This index is based on five categories: electoral process and pluralism; civil liberties; the functioning of government; political participation; and political culture. The Belgian scores for

[118] This advice concerned: 1) Better Regulation: priorities to reduce regulatory pressure, administrative simplification and improving the applicability of legislation; 2) experimental legislation; and 3) fixed moments of changing legislation. See https://www.serv.be/serv/publicatie/adviezen-betere-regelgeving.

[119] Popelier, above n 64, 369; see also Popelier, above n 6, 3: 'In order to qualify a decision as "legitimate" everyone affected by this decision should be able to participate in an effective deliberation concerning this decision, which makes it accountable towards everyone. Key principles are participation, transparency and justification.'

[120] This decree was already announced in the Policy Note 2014–19 at 6.

[121] Beleidsbrief Algemeen Regeringsbeleid 2016–17, 21 October 2016, 30, available at http://docs.vlaamsparlement.be/docs/stukken/2016-2017/g930-1.pdf.

[122] SERV, Advies Groenboek bestuur, Brussels, 19 December 2016, 11.

[123] S Sottiaux, 'Pleidooi voor een Vlaamse constitutionele cultuur' (2016) 349 *Nieuw Juridisch Weekblad* 705. In a kind of reply, the Flemish Minister-President did not really address this challenging statement; see www.knack.be/nieuws/belgie/integraal-de-constitutionele-agenda-van-geert-bourgeois/article-longread-675235.html.

'political participation' (5.00) and 'political culture' (6.88) are not impressive, so it now belongs to the group of 'flawed democracies'.[124] Also, Belgium's ranking in the 2016 edition of the Sustainable Governance Indicators (SGI) by the Bertelsmann Stiftung is not flattering. This report examines the OECD and EU Member States on the basis of our three indicators: policy performance (21), governance (19) and quality of democracy (20).[125]

The observation by the Social and Economic Council of Flanders about missing proposals to change the public governance culture in the Green Paper could also reflect a lack of ambition to implement the governance objectives of the Flemish Vision 2050 Strategy. This horizontal long-term sustainability strategy is inspired by transition management principles: focus on system innovation, taking into account a long-term perspective, involving stakeholders in the transition process and learning from experiments and innovative initiatives.[126] In its opinion on the Green Paper, the Flemish Advisory Council on Nature and the Environment linked its governance observations to this Strategy. This opinion mentioned not only opportunities for synergy between both, which is rather obvious from a coherence perspective, but also referred to possible critical regulatory issues, such as the balance between collective versus individual fundamental (constitutional) rights.[127] As this Advisory Council even found that the preparation process of the Green Paper could have been more transparent, it is clear that the basic policy framework and culture for the Flemish Better Regulation ambitions, as well as its contents and implementation, still face a number of challenges ahead.

THE ROLE OF MEMBER STATES IN THE EU'S BETTER REGULATION DEBATES

The EU's Better Regulation policy is predominantly associated with and steered by the Commission as the different tools and instruments are mainly applied in the policy formation stage when proposals are being prepared.[128] But obviously Member States can—next to developing and applying national or regional Better Regulation policies—voice their visions and opinions about Better Regulation. Some Member States are even reputed for their active engagement in the Better

[124] *The Economist* Intelligence Unit, 'Democracy Index 2016—Revenge of the "Deplorables"', 2016, available at www.eiu.com/topic/democracy-index.

[125] Bertelsmann Stiftung, 'Policy Performance and Governance Capacities in the OECD and EU—Sustainable Governance Indicators 2016', available at https://www.bertelsmann-stiftung.de/fileadmin/files/BSt/Publikationen/GrauePublikationen/Studie_NW_Policy_Performance_and_Governance_Capacities_in_the_OECD_and_EU_2016.pdf.

[126] See https://www.vlaanderen.be/nl/publicaties/detail/vision-2050.

[127] MINARaad, 'Advies inzake het Groenboek Bestuur', 15 December 2016, 10; available at https://www.minaraad.be.../bestuurskwaliteit/groenboek-bestuur.

[128] Impact Assessment Institute, 'A Year and a Half of the Better Regulation Agenda: What Happened?', 30 January 2017, 12, available at www.impactassessmentinstitute.org.

Regulation debates and for pushing for particular elements,[129] sometimes even more when they hold the EU Presidency.[130] A UK House of Commons Report is clear in this respect:

> I think it would be true to say we are probably quite experienced in the area of EU legislation. A lot of effort goes in jointly both through the UK permanent representation and from Defra officials back home and from the Better Regulation Executive in trying to influence the European agenda directly with director generals—and we have had commendable success, I think, in this part of the 2005 UK Presidency in getting regulating better on to the agenda.[131]

This is not surprising as we have already mentioned that the EU Better Regulation start-up was inspired by, inter alia, national initiatives. The Netherlands is probably one of the most prominent examples next to the UK.[132] Governments do not hesitate to send individual or joint letters[133] or position papers[134] to the Commission. Some Member States even cooperate to produce reports in order to influence the debate.[135] Positions in the debate of course depend on national policy practices, traditions, priorities and objectives.[136] Government officials and experts meet in formal and informal settings to discuss Better Regulation actions and developments at the EU and the national levels.

Probably the most important, informal but regularly organised forum is the ad hoc Group of Directors and Experts on Better Regulation (DEBR).[137]

[129] A Schout and J Sleifer, 'A Public Administration Take on Legitimacy: Better Regulation as Multilevel Governance Challenge' in M Ambrus, K Arts, E Hey and H Raulus (eds), *The Role of 'Experts' in International Decision-Making: Advisors, Decision-Makers or Irrelevant* (Cambridge, Cambridge University Press, 2014) 11: 'The Netherlands has been lobbying together with other lead-nations in BR such as Sweden, Denmark and the UK for simplification and cost reduction.'

[130] Van den Abeele, above n 24, 40.

[131] House of Commons, Regulatory Reform Committee, *Getting Results: The Better Regulation Executive and the Impact of the Regulatory Reform Agenda*, Volume 2 Fifth Report of the Session 2007–08, 103.

[132] Schout and Sleifer, above n 129, 11: 'Although the BR agendas have longer histories, the EU and the Dutch BR approaches have been converging in many ways over the past decade.' See also Lynch-Fannon, above n 34, 112.

[133] In relation to the letters sent in 2011–12, a group of 'like-minded' EU Member States that are putting pressure on the EU Commission and the European Council to prioritise growth and competitiveness: see www.nnr.se/nyheter/arkiv/nnr-newsletter-march-2012.html.

[134] eg, four European Better Regulation watchdogs—the Dutch Actal, the German Nationaler Normenkontrollrat, the Swedish Regelrådet and the British Regulatory Policy Committee—sent a joint position paper to the Commission in December 2011 setting out their recommendations on how to take forward the smart regulation agenda when the Action Programme ended in 2012.

[135] Schout and Sleifer, above n 129, 11. See also CH Montin, 'Smart Regulation in the European Union' in F Basilica and F Barazzoni, *Verso la smart regulation in Europa* (Santarcangelo di Romagna, Maggioli Editore, 2013) 110 about the Report 'Smart Regulation: A Cleaner, Fairer and More Competitive EU', published jointly by the UK, Denmark and the Netherlands in March 2010.

[136] See, eg, the description of the Member States' positions and their groupings in the Council when discussing the Better Regulation issues in the period 2008–09 given by Van den Abeele, above n 24, 40.

[137] For a description of its history up to 2010, see CH Montin, 'Better Regulation in Europe: The Work of the Group of Directors and Experts of Better Regulation (2002–2010)', available at www.montin.com/archive/documents/dbr_history.pdf.

This informal inter-governmental group of senior officials responsible for or engaged in regulatory policies in their home country usually meets twice a year. The meeting is chaired by the Member State that holds the EU Presidency. Commission officials also participate and external experts may be invited too. The DEBR participants exchange best practices and discuss Better Regulation developments. In the past—and not surprising given the Mandelkern background—the EU Public Administration Network also paid some attention to Better Regulation, although this seems to have ceased.[138] This development is regretful as Better Regulation cannot be considered as isolated from other elements and developments (eg, quality management and performance measurement) of the European administrative space where the Commission interacts with the Member States' public administrations.[139]

Some participants to the DEBR meetings are also regularly present at the meetings of the Better Regulation Working Party when these experts assist their national (Brussels-based) delegate. So there is definitely interaction between the informal and formal EU settings. The Better Regulation Working Party is one of the formations of the Working Party on Competitiveness and Growth.[140] The 2002 Decision of the Permanent Representatives Committee (Coreper Part 1) on streamlining and simplifying working group structures concerning the preparation of horizontal dossiers in relation to Competitiveness and Growth does not include a reference to (Better) Regulation.[141] This Working Party prepares legislation, Council conclusions and recommendations in the areas of EU growth strategy, single market, (smart) Better Regulation and industrial policy. The working party meets in various formations: single market, industry, including a sub-group on tourism, and Better Regulation. The latter has been established to address one

[138] G Konzendorf, P Wordelmann, S Bölck and S Veit, 'Milestones on the Way to Better Regulation at the European Union Level', Luxembourg, June 2005, www.eupan.eu/en/thematic_areas/show/&tid=30. Better Regulation is still a theme on the EUPAN website, but apart from the DEBR announcement under the Italian EU Presidency in 2014, there is nothing else noteworthy in relation to this. Another informal network is the Better Regulation Network, which should incorporate the former Standard Cost Model Network. The members of this platform are government experts in the field of Better Regulation and the goal of the network is 'to exchange and elaborate best practices of regulatory burden reduction in the aim of cutting unnecessary bureaucracy and red tape, as well as in other areas of Better Regulation'. The network communicates via the DIGIT-CIRCACB-system of the Commission. The most recent meeting was in Tallinn on 11 May 2017.

[139] E Heidbreder, 'Structuring the European Administrative Space: Policy Instruments of Multi-level Administration', Paper, European Group Public Administration Conference, 8–10 September 2010, Toulouse.

[140] The Working Party on Competitiveness and Growth is one of the 14 working parties for the Competitiveness (COMPET) Council and one of the more than 150 highly specialised working parties and committees, known as the 'Council preparatory bodies'. This Working Party belongs to the category of 'Committees and working parties set up by Coreper', which deal with very specific subjects and are chaired by the delegate of the country holding the rotating six-month presidency of the Council. General Secretariat of the Council, List of Council preparatory bodies, Document 5183/16, Brussels, 18 January 2016, available at www.consilium.europa.eu/en/council-eu/preparatory-bodies.

[141] Council Document 14818/02, Brussels, 26 November 2002, available at http://data.consilium.europa.eu/doc/document/ST-14818-2002-INIT/en/pdf.

of the particular tasks of the Working Party, namely 'creating an effective and smart regulatory framework'. The recommendations of the Working Party on Competitiveness and Growth are later dealt with in the Competitiveness Council.

Better Regulation has been on the agenda of the Competitiveness Council since 2004.[142] Apart from the General Affairs Council—especially when preparing European Council conclusions—other Council formations are not really engaged in discussions on Better Regulation.[143] During the past decade, the competitiveness objective has remained the dominant perspective in the Better Regulation debates, and the launch of the REFIT programme in 2012 has been considered to be an enhancement of this objective.[144] The position of Member States in the European and Competitiveness Councils is the outcome of previous and preliminary positions taken during the debates in the Working Party meetings and Coreper. These positions are ideally developed, discussed and agreed after internal coordination and consultation in the 'capitals'. In general, the agenda and the discussions in the Better Regulation Working Party are characterised by its follow-up approach of Commission work and this regularly leads to the adoption of Council conclusions. Most Presidencies include some lines—some are sometimes more ambitious[145]—on Better Regulation in their programmes and organise a couple of meetings of the Better Regulation Working Party. Obviously broader policy objectives or societal trends, like digitalisation and innovation in recent years, find their way into this forum too.

Unsurprisingly, the 2015 Better Regulation package inspired new Council conclusions. The European Council meeting of 18–19 February 2016 referred not only to Better Regulation in its conclusions, but the final document also contained two annexes dealing with particular elements and issues.[146] In the separate

[142] Radaelli, above n 22, 195; see also Van den Abeele, above n 24, 40.

[143] See ACM Meuwese, *Impact Assessment in EU Lawmaking* (Dordrecht, Kluwer, 2008) 128. This author refers to some involvement from Ecofin and the Environment Councils at that time.

[144] Van den Abeele, above n 8, 26. See also Renda, above n 16, 8 on REFIT in the 2015 Better Regulation package.

[145] Belgium had no ambition during its last Presidency (July–December 2010, where it was part of a trio with Spain and Hungary), although there was an indication that the Ministry of Foreign Affairs started paying more attention to the Better Regulation Agenda and the need for better Belgian coordination at the DGE level (see below).

[146] Council, EUCO 1/16, Brussels, 19 February 2016: 'The establishment of an internal market in which the free movement of goods, persons, services and capital is ensured is an essential objective of the Union. To secure this objective and to generate growth and jobs, the EU must enhance competitiveness, along the lines set out in the Declaration of the European Council on competitiveness. To this end, the relevant EU institutions and the Member States will make all efforts to fully implement and strengthen the internal market, as well as to adapt it to keep pace with the changing environment. At the same time, the relevant EU institutions and the Member States will take concrete steps towards better regulation, which is a key driver to deliver the above-mentioned objectives. This means lowering administrative burdens and compliance costs on economic operators, especially small and medium enterprises, and repealing unnecessary legislation as foreseen in the Declaration of the Commission on a subsidiarity implementation mechanism and a burden reduction implementation mechanism, while continuing to ensure high standards of consumer, employee, health and environmental

Declaration on competitiveness (Annex III of the Conclusions), the European Council 'urges all EU institutions and Member States to strive for better regulation and to repeal unnecessary legislation in order to enhance EU competitiveness while having due regard to the need to maintain high standards of consumer, employee, health and environmental protection'. This Declaration also mentions the IIA on Better Law-Making, the objective of which seems to be reduced to addressing the following concern: 'Effective cooperation in this framework is necessary in order to simplify Union legislation and to avoid overregulation and administrative burdens for citizens, administrations and businesses, including small and medium sized enterprises, while ensuring that the objectives of the legislation are met.' This declaration is also clear about the focus, which:

> [M]ust be on:
>
> — a strong commitment to regulatory simplification and burden reduction, including through withdrawal or repeal of legislation where appropriate, and a better use of impact assessment and ex-post evaluation throughout the legislative cycle, at the EU and national levels. This work should build on the progress already made with the Regulatory Fitness Programme (REFIT);
> — doing more to reduce the overall burden of EU regulation, especially on SMEs and micro- enterprises;
> — establishing where feasible burden reduction targets in key sectors, with commitments by EU institutions and Member States.

Next to the Competitiveness Council, the General Affairs Council is also expected to regularly evaluate progress on the various elements set out in this Declaration. The elaboration of the focus of the Competitiveness Declaration is the subject of Annex IV, the Declaration by the Commission on a subsidiarity implementation mechanism and a burden reduction implementation mechanism. The Commission announces that within the REFIT platform, it will work with Member States and stakeholders towards establishing specific targets at the EU and the national levels for reducing burden on business, particularly in the most onerous areas for companies, in particular SMEs.

Under the Dutch EU Presidency, on 26 May 2016the Competitiveness Council adopted (after Coreper endorsement on 11 May 2016) conclusions on 'Better regulation to strengthen competitiveness', which addressed four issues: future-proof and innovation-friendly legislation; Impact Assessment and quantification of costs and benefits; reduction targets; and Better Regulation and SMEs.[147] On 8 April 2016 the Presidency had presented the draft Council conclusions which were

protection.' Available at http://data.consilium.europa.eu/doc/document/ST-1-2016-INIT/en/pdf. The next European Council of 28 June 2016 committed itself in its conclusions just briefly 'to vigorously pursue efforts towards better regulation' (Council, EUCO 26/16, Brussels, 28 June 2016).

[147] Council Document 8849/16, Brussels, 18 May 2016, available at www.consilium.europa.eu/en/press/press-releases/2016/05/26-conclusions-better-regulation.

examined by the Better Regulation Working Party on 18 and 26 April and 4 May 2016. The contents of the draft conclusions had already been prepared in previous Working Party meetings on 9 February (on Better Regulation and innovation), on 15 March (on quantification) and on 1 April 2016 (on future-proof regulation and reduction targets/objectives). The discussions in the Working Party—the basic level of the inter-governmental arena[148]—were rather intense, especially on the issue of reduction targets. This issue had been the subject of letters sent to Vice-President Timmermans since 2015. A group of like-minded Member States, with the Netherlands clearly as one of the major driving forces, pleaded in favour of, inter alia, the introduction of burden reduction targets, and continue these efforts up to the present day.[149] This request was not that new as the Competitiveness Council conclusions on smart regulation of 4 December 2014 under the Italian EU Presidency included two paragraphs on regulatory burden reduction, which inter alia asked the Commission to develop and put in place—on the basis of input from Member States and stakeholders—reduction targets in particularly burdensome areas.[150] However, as Luxembourg, which occupied the EU Presidency at that time, had not signed the 'like-minded letter', it was not on the agenda of the Competitiveness Council on 30 November and 1 December 2015, as requested by the signatories. So the meeting report refers only briefly to the issue which was raised by some delegations.[151] But after the announcement in the above-mentioned European Council conclusions of establishing burden reduction targets, it was expected that the same topic would become an element in more specific Competitiveness Council conclusions. This outcome of the Council management by the Netherlands is hardly surprising, given the role of this Member State in the EU's Better Regulation developments based on its national experiences.[152]

[148] P Kaniok, 'In the Shadow of Consensus: Communication within Council Working Groups' (2016) 12 *Journal of Contemporary European Research* 881. This research article analyses how different actors acting in the Council working groups communicate in a formal way. Based upon analysis of non-participatory observation of interventions, it finds that working groups tend to be arenas for real bargaining where the actors enforce their interests. It also finds that even the Council Presidency focuses on the promotion of interests and that socialisation—which can be found at the Coreper level—does not take place in the working groups. Based on my personal participation in the Better Regulation Working Party, I find Kaniok's observations and analysis quite convincing.

[149] The first letter of 1 April 2015 was signed by 11 Member States, including the Netherlands. This letter contained four elements: quantification of regulatory burden reduction; independent regulatory scrutiny; future-proof legislation; and improved consultation. The shorter 26 November letter was signed by 19 Member States (but not the Netherlands) and is available at https://www.gov.uk/government/uploads/system/uploads/attachment_data/file/480401/eu-Better-Regulation-letter-timmermans.pdf.

[150] Council Document 16505/14, outcome of the 3353rd Council Competitiveness meeting, available at www.consilium.europa.eu/uedocs/cms_data/docs/pressdata/en/intm/146029.pdf.

[151] 'A number of delegations asked for the introduction of additional measures to the agenda, such as regulatory burden reduction targets in particularly burdensome areas'; see Council Document 14783/15, Outcome of the 3431st Council Competitiveness meeting, available at www.consilium.europa.eu/en/meetings/compet/2015/11/30-01.

[152] Schout and Sleifer, above n 129, 11. The Dutch work on Better Regulation during its Presidency (2016) was also not limited to the Competitiveness Council, achieving other outcomes like the Full Report of the High-Level Meeting 'Make it Work' of 4 April 2016 on 'Better Regulation for a Better

The fact that the Better Regulation debate remains rather exclusively within one Working Party which also functions as the provider for the sporadic European Council inputs could be questioned, given the objectives and potential horizontal impact of Better Regulation policies. It may sound remarkable, but whenever Council conclusions are debated, the inclusion of phrases like 'to always take into account a high level of protection of consumers, health, the environment and employees'[153] or 'to ensure high standards of consumer, employee, health and environmental protection'[154] is not superfluous. Certain Member States pay more attention to these broader policy objectives pursued by the Treaty on European Union than (most) others, which tend to focus on the more narrow objectives of competitiveness and business concerns.[155] As the impact of Working Party outcomes cannot be underestimated,[156] restricting the debate within one Working Group seems inappropriate as it risks becoming somehow path-dependent, and looking at the development of the EU's Better Regulation Agenda, it is hard to deny this feature.[157] This 'monopoly' could also be questioned from a legitimacy perspective[158] and even contradicts some of the objectives of Better Regulation: enhancing evidence-based policy-making and involving all stakeholders. Some delegations in the Better Regulation Working Party seem to have started feeling the narrowness of this setting and recently suggested also having this subject on the agendas of other Council Working Parties or organising joint meetings. So it looks acceptable and useful to engage other Working Parties in other Council formations in a more systematic way in the Better Regulation debate as they are also involved (or supposed to be) in applying Better Regulation objectives, eg, simplification requirements, REFIT proposals, evaluations or the confrontation with the Commission's Impact Assessment when a new proposal is tabled. Concerning the latter, in 2014, Coreper agreed on a procedure for examining Commission Impact Assessments on legislative proposals at the Working Party level with the help of an indicative checklist. Further to the new IIA on Better Law-Making which entered into force on 13 April 2016, the Council in June 2016 provided new indicative

Environment', available at https://english.eu2016.nl/documents/publications/2016/04/05/full-report-high-level-meeting-make-it-work-%E2%80%93-4-april-2016. The EU Urban Agenda agreed under the Dutch Presidency also includes a major focus on Better Regulation objectives; see 'The Urban Agenda for the EU: European Cities Get Their Say in EU Policy Making', press communication, 30 May 2016, available at http://europa.eu/rapid/press-release_IP-16-1924_en.htm.

[153] Competitiveness Council conclusions, 26 May 2016.

[154] European Council conclusions, 19 February 2016.

[155] Van den Abeele, above n 8, 37–38.

[156] I Olsen, 'The Council Working Groups: Advisors or De Facto Decision Makers?' (2010), paper presented at the Fifth Pan-European Conference on EU Politics, Porto, Portugal, 23–26 June 2010. Available at www.jhubc.it/ecpr-porto/virtualpaperroom/100.pdf.

[157] HC Hofmann and AH Türk (eds), *EU Administrative Governance* (Cheltenham, Edward Elgar, 2006) 28.

[158] T Larsson and J Trondal, 'Agenda Setting in the European Commission: How the European Commission Structure and Influence the EU Agenda' in FM Häge (ed), *Bureaucrats as Law-Makers: Committee Decision-Making in the EU Council of Ministers* (Abingdon, Routledge, 2013) 208.

guidance on Impact Assessment for Working Party chairs.[159] Given the almost complete lack of interest (or systemic reluctance?)[160] within the Council's daily work to implement this seriously, it is not surprising that the Impact Assessment Institute stated that: 'In the Council, there has not been any discernible progress and this is an ongoing vulnerability in the wider EU Better Regulation system.'[161]

The structural involvement of other Working Parties of other Council formations in the further Better Regulation policy development may of course question the current embedding of Better Regulation in the Competitiveness Council formation. However, this Council has no pure exclusivity as the General Affairs Council (GAC) is supposed to monitor the implementation of the new IIA on Better Law-Making as decided by the European Council on 18–19 February 2016. Furthermore, the General Affairs Council is responsible for a number of cross-cutting policy areas and the overall coordination of policies. Given the objectives of the Better Regulation Agenda[162]—and taking into account the more horizontal Commission approach where the Secretariat General plays a coordination role for Better Regulation—it seems obvious that Better Regulation deserves and needs a more balanced position and treatment in the Council setting, eg, via the GAC. But the question remains if the General Affairs Council would be the most desirable and effective solution in the light of this Council's reputation.[163] Furthermore, Better Regulation has already been addressed several times by the European Council and not only in the recent past.[164] So a more systematic follow-up by this Council could be an alternative and more constructive approach to support and endorse

[159] General Secretariat of the Council, Document 9790/16, 9 June 2016. The present Handbook provides practical advice for Working Party chairs and the General Secretariat of the Council (GSC) on handling Impact Assessments of legislative proposals. It should be used in a flexible way. It is subject to regular updates according to needs, as part of the annual report of Impact Assessment within the Council, and based on experience gained in this area. The Member State contribution to this report could be compiled on the basis of experiences of delegates in Working Parties. In 2013 the Council also agreed to monitor the implementation of its Impact Assessment commitments. The Presidency, with the assistance of the Council Secretariat, reports annually to Coreper. The first report was submitted in June 2014. Its recommendations were confirmed by the conclusions adopted by the Council (Competitiveness) on 4 December 2014 and were complemented by the conclusions adopted by the Council (Competitiveness) on 26 May 2016. Currently Coreper (the Mertens and Antici Groups) is discussing the Impact Assessment Council approach for substantive amendments.

[160] Renda, above n 16, 12: 'the Council, the most reluctant of all EU institutions when it comes to evidence-based decision-making'. This shortcoming was—once again—acknowledged in the Better Regulation Working Group meeting of 26 April 2017.

[161] Impact Assessment Institute, above n 128, 12.

[162] The Better Regulation Agenda is about designing and evaluating EU policies and laws transparently, with evidence, and backed up by the views of citizens and stakeholders. It covers all policy areas and aims for targeted regulation that goes no further than required, in order to achieve objectives and bring benefits at minimum cost. See https://ec.europa.eu/info/law/law-making-process/better-regulation-why-and-how_en#objectives.

[163] PM Kaczyński and A Byrne, 'The General Affairs Council: The Key to Political Influence of Rotating Presidencies' *CEPS Policy Brief* No 246, July 2011.

[164] eg, the European Council of June 2006 also addressed Better Regulation. In the debate, France stated its social concerns clearly: 'La France a eu l'occasion de s'exprimer sur les exigences auxquelles doivent répondre les analyses d'impact lors du débat du Conseil européen de juin 2006 sur l'avenir

Better Regulation more profoundly as far as its preparatory process (including the role of the General Affairs Council) assures comprehensiveness and coherence.[165]

Debating Better Regulation in many more Council Working Parties and formations would not only enrich the discussions, for example, with practical insights and experiences from other policy domains, but it would also offer Member States (representatives) more opportunities to participate and deliver contributions which go beyond the follow-up of the REFIT platform opinions as incorporated in new Commission policy proposals.[166] Such broadening might also correct and supplement the new interaction approach that has been created with the establishment of the REFIT platform with its Government and Stakeholder Groups.[167] This platform offers extra opportunities for Member States to influence the EU's Better Regulation policy. But this input is restricted to supporting the process of simplifying EU law and reducing regulatory burdens, for the benefit of civil society, business and public authorities, and making recommendations to the Commission, taking into account suggestions made by citizens and interested parties.[168] Furthermore, the REFIT work has to be clearly separated from the Working Party work, as was made clear by a number of delegations during the meeting of the Better Regulation Working Party on 26 April 2017. During this meeting, a representative of the REFIT platform Stakeholder Group was invited by the Maltese Presidency to present a draft opinion on how to improve the current consultation policy of the Commission. The debate that followed revealed a certain uneasiness as the draft opinion still had to be discussed by the REFIT platform in its plenary formation which includes the Government Group. Certain members of this group participate also in the Working Party, but others do not, which raises coordination

institutionnel de l'Union; elle a souhaité qu'à l'instar des travaux conduits dans la filière compétitivité du Conseil sur les études d'impact, la Commission et le Conseil dans toutes ses formations concernées, (s'engagent) à ce qu'aucun texte ne puisse être désormais adopté sans que ses incidences dans le domaine social n'aient été évaluées et publiquement présentées'; see C Dumont, 'De l'élaboration de la législation communautaire à mise en œuvre en droit national: contribution du Conseil économique et social à la réflexion sur "mieux légiférer"' (2007) *Avis et Raports du Conseil économique et social* 104, available at www.ladocumentationfrancaise.fr/var/storage/rapports-publics/074000531.pdf.

[165] U Puetter, *The European Council and the Council: New Intergovernmentalism and Institutional Change* (Oxford, Oxford University Press, 2014) 212.

[166] 'Delivering a Europe that Protects, Empowers and Defends' COM (2016) 710 final, Commission Work Programme 2017., Strasbourg, 25 October 2016.

[167] The REFIT platform initiative somehow reflects the EU's Better Regulation dual approach (bottom-up input and instrumentalism) as analysed by M Dawson, 'Better Regulation and the Future of EU Regulatory Law and Politics' (2016) 53 *Common Market Law Review* 1209.

[168] See https://ec.europa.eu/info/law/law-making-process/overview-law-making-process/evaluating-and-improving-existing-laws/reducing-burdens-and-simplifying-law/refit-platform/role-structure-and-working-methods-refit-platform_en. In his comment on the 2015 Better Regulation package, Renda (above n 16, 9) stated that 'it is probably true that the rhetoric of the Commission becomes focused much more on burdens and regulatory costs, rather than on the benefits of regulation: this is probably true of all sections of the new Communication that are dedicated to REFIT and member states'. More than half of the members of the Government Group of the REFIT platform represent the Economics/Business Ministry, while the others are mostly from a horizontal department (eg, the Prime Minister's office, the Better Regulation unit and the legal department).

challenges. In any case, a more cross-cutting and intensified handling of the Better Regulation Agenda in the Council formations would undoubtedly imply additional coherence and coordination challenges at the Member State level too.

THE FLEMISH/BELGIAN PARTICIPATION IN THE EU'S BETTER REGULATION DEBATES

The fact that the Competitiveness Council is responsible for Better Regulation also has an internal impact on the Belgian follow-up and participation in the relevant Council activities. More precisely, the Belgian participation in the EU's Better Regulation debate may be considered as an example of how EU policy developments maintain opportunities for the federal level to preserve a central role, at the least as a 'gatekeeper'. As Beyers and Bursens stated, the political authority of regions remains fairly bounded in national or federal arenas, despite the increased involvement of the Belgian regions in European policy-making and despite a large set of devolved competences.[169] This devolution affected foreign and EU policy-making as the constitutional reform of 1988 introduced the *in foro interno in foro externo* principle for Community competences and the 1993 constitutional reform expanded this principle to the competences of the Regions. This principle gave the Communities and Regions the powers to conduct foreign policy for those competences they had been granted by the Constitution. In other words, the 1993 Constitution created the full alignment between internal and external competences.

Due to this devolution, including the exclusive allocation of powers for a number of areas and because of the absence of a legal norm hierarchy within Belgium, the negotiation, transposition and implementation of numerous European regulations in many of these areas is the responsibility of the regions (and communities) and not of the central government. Furthermore, in many cases, so-called mixed competencies are at stake, which means that both the federal level and the regions have to participate and regulate. This also implies that the regions developed a huge and diverse regulatory framework and are important actors and stakeholders in the Belgian EU position formation, and consequently the national regulatory management. But as there is no overall national regulatory policy and governance framework, the current image of the Belgian regulatory practices resembles a patchwork which has a huge impact on the Belgian position, participation and implementation of the EU's Better Regulation Agenda.

Belgium's formal position on Better Regulation, including REFIT, is currently decided within two settings: the DGE meetings (at the federal Foreign Affairs Ministry) and the meetings of the Inter-ministerial Economic Commission (at the federal Economics Ministry).

[169] J Beyers and P Bursens, 'The European Rescue of the Federal State: How Europeanization Shapes the Belgian State' (2006) 29 *West European Politics* 1057.

In principle, the Belgian position on Better Regulation as an element of Council conclusions is discussed and adopted in a meeting organised by the Directorate of European Affairs (DGE) of the federal Ministry for Foreign Affairs. This body organises coordination meetings with representatives from a wide range of federal, regional and community ministries and ministerial cabinets. This federal body needs to reach unanimity to back negotiation positions; if not, the issue is referred to the Inter-ministerial Conference on Foreign Policy (ICFP) and eventually to the Concertation (Deliberation) Committee. This makes clear that, despite the *in foro interno in foro externo* principle, the role of the federal level remains more than substantial.[170]

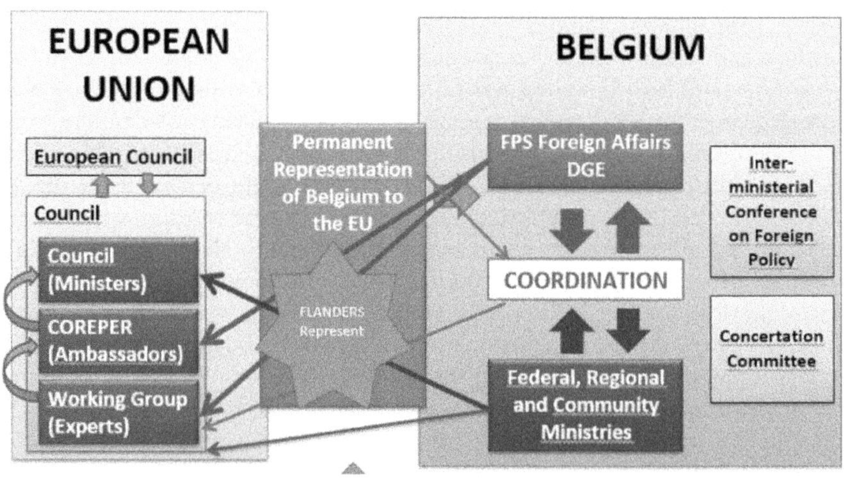

Figure 9.1: EU policy coordination in Belgium
Source: Federal Ministry for Foreign Affairs.

This approach is based on the Cooperation Agreement of 8 March 1994 between the regions, communities and the federal government. This Cooperation Agreement on EU policy-making outlines: (1) the internal arrangement for the coordination of common positions; and (2) the Belgian representation at the EU level. In practice, the coordination and representation of a specific subject or file at stake depend on its assignment and handling in a particular EU Council formation as well as on its embeddedness in the Belgian institutional and devolution setting as arranged according to categories in the Cooperation Agreement.

[170] S Van Hecke and P Bursens, 'How to Study the (Belgian) EU Presidency? A Framework for Analysis for the Research Network 2010 Belgian EU Presidency' (2010) Paper for Politicologenetmaal, Leuven, 27–28 May, available at https://soc.kuleuven.be/web/files/11/72/W04-108.pdf.

Table 9.2: Overview of the Belgian representation to EU Councils

Council configurations*	Category according to Belgian Cooperation Agreement**	Belgian representation	Possible assessor
General Affairs, Foreign Affairs, Ecofin, Budget, Telecom, Consumers, Development Cooperation, Civil Protection, Justice, Home Affairs	I—Exclusively federal competence (dominantly federal)	Federal Minister	
Internal Market, Public Health, Energy, Social Affairs, Transport	II—Mixed competence (shared, but more federal)	Federal Minister	Regional or Community Minister
Industry, Research, Environment	III—Mixed competence (shared, but more regional)	Regional or Community Minister	Federal Minister
Culture, Education, Youth, Sports, Tourism, Housing and Regional Planning	IV—Exclusively regional or Community competence (dominantly regional)	Regional or Community Minister	
Fisheries	V—Fisheries (exclusively regional)	Flemish Minister	
Agriculture	VI—Agriculture (dominantly regional)	Federal Minister	Two Regional Ministers

* The 1994 Cooperation Agreement uses the Council configurations as they existed before its number was reduced from 15 to nine in 2002. This Cooperation Agreement should be amended, given the outcome of the latest State Reform (2001–03), but negotations were put on hold under the current federal government[171].
** Description according to S Van Hecke and P Bursens[172].

This overview also gives a flavour of the regulatory diversity and its impact on the wider Better Regulation vision. This is reflected in the Belgian REFIT representation, for which the national delegate was appointed by a DGE meeting. Belgian REFIT positions are prepared at IEC meetings chaired by the national delegate. Only participants from the different regional and federal administrations and ministries (not from cabinets) participate and this participation is quite modest. Also at the Flemish level, the interest remains generally low, with the exception of a few policy fields in which the regulation might affect another (for example, the

[171] I De Coninck, 'De omzetting van Europese regelgeving' deel I (2015) *Rapport Steunpunt Bestuurlijke Organisatie*, KU Leuven, 26.
[172] Van Hecke and Bursens, above n 170, 12.

environment, industry and agriculture). The Flemish IEC participation is somehow coordinated by the Regulatory Management Unit, but as most REFIT work concerns particular legislation, experts may participate directly. The IEC coordination approach can be considered to be rather succesful apart from the limited interest.

In addition, the Belgian participation in the Better Regulation Working Party does not generate particular interest. Obviously, Belgium is always present at these Working Party meetings and is represented by the the federal competitiveness attaché at the federal Permanent Representation of Belgium to the EU.[173] The Flemish attaché participates regularly, but the other regions almost never do so.[174] This lack of interest also influences the Belgian interventions in the Working Party, which are partially based on the general lines developed in previous DGE meetings and sometimes include ad hoc reflections and exchanges. The absence of the other regions/communities in the position-making enforces the federal dominance. Although Better Regulation Working Party agendas are available in advance and coordination should be organised in principle, no such meetings are organised within the Permanent Prepresentation of Belgium to the EU. Only in the case of Better Regulation issues in draft Council conclusions is a DGE meeting held. In both cases (the Working Party and DGE meetings), there is no formalised Flemish coordination approach, but the Flemish attaché usually consults through an informal network (Flemish Representation at the EU, the Regulatory Management unit, contact persons in administrations and cabinet).

So it is hardly surprising that Belgium has no elaborate general position on Better Regulation due to its diverse range of internal regulatory policies and practices. In the case of a DGE meeting, participation remains very limited and the discussions are focused on particular issues at stake addressing specific Belgian concerns. However, in the course of 2015, the need for a Belgian position concerning the negotiations about the IIA on Better Law-Making also generated some more profound internal Belgian exchanges about the different Better Regulation components. There are two basic elements in that position that seem to dominate in general terms after more than 10 years of sporadic DGE meetings: in principle, Belgium supports the Better Regulation objectives, but it remains critical about elements that threaten the final say of politics. Historically, Belgium is among the

[173] The concerned attaché (who is detached from the federal Economics Ministry) is a long-term and active member of the Better Regulation Working Party and his particular insights and visions are reflected in his publications; see Van den Abeele, above n 8 and n 24 ('Better Regulation', 2015 and 'Mieux légiférer', 2009; these publications have been referred to during official contacts of the Belgian Permanent Representative). Given his experience and looking at the regularly critical but in general constructive Belgian positions in this Working Party, one might describe this participation as reflecting a variation in degrees of 'socialisation'; see AE Juncos and K Pomorska 'Playing the Brussels Game: Strategic Socialisation in the CFSP Council Working Groups' (2006) *European Integration Online Papers*, available at http://eiop.or.at/eiop/pdf/2006-011.pdf.

[174] The Permanent Representation of Belgium to the EU also includes four regional/community Representations to the EU, with a limited number of full-time and part-time attachés.

most pro-integration actors within the entire EU[175] and as such generally supports the Better Regulation Agenda with a view to an improved *acquis*. The *acquis* is not limited to internal market issues but also concerns—with equal importance—social, environmental and consumer protection issues.[176] So the Better Regulation Agenda should definitely not become an instrument to restrict or undermine EU policy objectives. In that sense, Belgium has been a critical observer of particular EU Better Regulation elements like Impact Assessment[177] and regulatory burden measurements.[178] Belgium supports REFIT as an element of Better Regulation insofar as its outcome supports the EU's policy objectives. An example of this approach is the Belgian participation in the debate about the Fitness Check of the Habitat and Birds Directives. Belgium did not sign a joint letter composed by Germany and eight other Member States to the Commission, but it sent a separate letter to the Commission.[179] Without questioning in principle the need for evidence in policy-making, and given the obvious knowledge that Impact Assessments only aim to inform the decision-making, Belgium remains concerned about the growing importance of the Impact Assessment tools, which it considers as possibly becoming 'bureaucratic governance' and a (too?) powerful instrument of the Commission.[180] Belgium is rather committed to opinion-based policy-making.[181] The fact that even the academic recommendation—in 2003—to start with a form

[175] De Coninck, above n 171, 6; see also Van Hecke and Bursens, above n 170, 14.

[176] A recent example concerns the Belgian position in the debate on the Innovation Principle—as incorporated in the Competitiveness Council conclusions of May 2016— where it strongly argued also referring to the Precautionary Principle (fn 3 of these conclusions). See also European Political Strategy Centre (EPSC), 'Towards an Innovation Principle Endorsed by Better Regulation' (2016) *EPSC Strategic Notes* 14.

[177] Belgium is suspicious about unbalanced and compartmentalised Impact Assessments and has continuously pleaded for integrated assessments that have to incorporate all relevant issues.

[178] Belgium never really agreed—due to internal differences—to subscribe the EU 25 per cent reduction target; see also K Wegrich, 'The Administrative Burden Reduction Policy Boom in Europe: Comparing Mechanisms of Policy Diffusion' (2009) LSE Centre for Analysis of Risk and Regulation, Discussion Paper No 52, 13: 'Two other countries are carrying out intensive measurement exercises, but have deliberately decided against adopting a fixed quantitative target (Belgium and Norway).' In that sense Belgium was also a critical observer of the functioning of the High-Level Group on Administrative Burdens, including comprehension for certain elements of the Dissenting Opinion in the final report of this HL Group; see *Cutting Red Tape in Europe, Legacy and Outlook*, Final Report, Brussels, 24 July 2014.

[179] Letter signed by Germany, France, Luxembourg, Spain, Poland, Croatia, Slovenia, Italy and Romania, available at www.birdlife.org/sites/default/files/attachments/fitness_check-letter_nine_ministers_to_vella_26.10.2015.pdf. Greece, Belgium, The Netherlands and Lithuania sent letters afterwards, see www.birdlife.org/europe-and-central-asia/news/real-european-union-emerges-back-nature.

[180] See CA Dunlop and CM Radaelli, 'Impact Assessment in the European Union: Lessons from a Research Project' (2015) 5 *European Journal of Risk Regulation* 41: 'Whilst it is customary to think of IA as control instrument, our research suggests that this instrument may strengthen the bureaucracy in Brussels.'

[181] In a recent DGE meeting (April 2017) concerning the Belgian position for Coreper on the introduction of a pilot exercise for the Impact Assessment approach on substantive amendments in the Council, observations were raised that were similar to the following from an Egmont paper: 'The proliferation of impact assessments cannot be overlooked in the Interinstitutional Agreement proposal. It indicates that impact assessments could be required in the case of "substantial amendments" tabled by the European Parliament or by the Council. The concept of "substantial" deserves a clear definition

of federal Impact Assessment about new EU propsals remained shelved is an indication of this Belgian attitude.[182] On burden-reduction exercises and in the light of the existence of activities of the Agency for Administrative Simplification and related efforts in the regions, Belgium also addresses this topic in a pragmatic, even critical and certainly non-ambitious way.[183] However, when questioning this reluctance, one definitely has to situate this against the background that neither at the federal level nor at the regional level is there an extensive policy practice to support the Belgian conservatism on these issues. But this lack of evidence is of course self-fulfilling—for example, the already mentioned criticism on the federal Impact Assessment and Flemish RIA practices. The dominating internal political-administrative culture as reflected in the cabinet systems at the federal level as well as at the regional levels,[184] which allow embedded policy preparations, can hardly be dismissed as a major underlying driver for this continued Belgian Janus vision, as was also stated in a paper by the national Royal Institute for International Relations:

> In this sense, we can only be sceptical vis-à-vis the aim of the Better Regulation Agenda. It appears to be a tool to rebuild trust in the eyes of EU citizens, but in many aspects it seems to limit the inherently political dimension of the EU decision-making process.[185]

The entrance of a dominating non-traditional political party in the Flemish and federal governments had raised expectations about change, certainly as the

by the Commission in order to avoid discussions, interpretations and its misapplication in practice. Together with the eight-week consultations with the stakeholders after the Commission adopted its proposal, it is likely that these additional impact assessments would burden the political process of law-making and eventually slow it down. Normally designed as tools of support for the legislative process, they should not overload or even substitute for the political character of the EU legislative mechanism. Moreover, impact assessments could be stripped of their necessity. The use of impact assessments by the Council could be used by some Member States as a tool for blocking or "indefinitely" postponing a proposal.' See F Willermain and A Cioriciu, 'The Better Regulation Package: Creating Better Regulations, But for What Kind of EU Politics?' (2015) *European Policy Brief*, No 39, Egmont Institute/Royal Institute for International Relations, available at www.egmontinstitute.be/wp-content/uploads/2015/10/Better-Regulation-package1.pdf.

[182] G Dierickx, P Bursens and S Helsen, *Omzetting, toepassing en toepassingscontrole van het Europees Beleid in België. Naar een structurele toepassing van de wijze waarop België zijn Europese verplichtingen nakomt*, (Federaal wetenschapsbeleid, Academia Press, 2003) 280.

[183] eg, Belgium was no signatory to the different letters that were sent to the Commission about this and related Better Regulation issues, as mentioned in n 133.

[184] A Hondeghem, C De Visscher, M Petit Jean and S Ruebens, 'Belgium' in M Van Wart, A Hondeghem, E Schwella and P Suino (eds), *Leadership and Culture: Comparative Models of Top Civil Servant Training* (London, Palgrave Macmillan, 2015).

[185] Willermain and Cioriciu, above n 181. These authors are less radical than the more critical vision on the (so-called) 'rational' policy cycle as applied by the EU institutions; see S Everett, 'The Policy Cycle: Democratic Process or Rational Paradigm Revisited?' (2003) 62(2) *Australian Journal Public Administration* 65, who writes: 'the policy cycle is not a substitute for the actual making of decisions but an administrative and bureaucratic mechanism for effectively setting in place a process once the difficult decisions have been made'. Sometimes these kinds of observation can even be heard in the Better Regulation Working Party when the Commission is being questioned why an Impact Assessment has not always been required or when certain policy options (alternatives) have not been included in the Impact Assessment.

Flemish Minister-President (in charge of regulatory management) and the federal Secretary of State (in charge of administrative simplification) attached to the Minister for Home Affairs all belong to this party.[186] The initial idea to apply the already mentioned 2003 Cooperation Agreement on Administrative Simplification and to establish an effective internal Belgian coordination mechanism at the level of the administrations has not yet materialised. This is regretful as this neglects the potential for at least a more profound input—based on mutual 'technical' exchanges—for DGE meetings and impact in Better Regulation Working Party discussions. Such a coordination mechanism should also be the platform where participation in the DEBR, the Better Regulation Network (BRN) and other fora (like EUPAN and the OECD Regulatory Policy Committee) is discussed and prepared, alongside the sporadic IEC meetings for REFIT. Apart from the latter, no arrangements are applied for coordinated Belgian participation as this participation occurs mainly on a personal opportunity and interest basis by the concerned—federal or sometimes regional—expert.

The most recent Flemish policy intentions (the already mentioned 'Vision on the Future of the European Union'[187] and the Policy Letter 2016–17) pay attention to EU Better Regulation elements (Impact Assessments, REFIT, consultation and avoiding gold-plating) and ideas such as 'low regulation zones'. On paper, Flanders seems less reluctant about Impact Assessments than the federal level and it even aims to introduce a kind of initial Impact Assessment of new Commission proposals.[188] The 'Vision' text also calls on the Commission to establish reduction targets, provided this can be achieved by implementing a mix of qualitative and quantitative methods on the basis of its own experiences, which revealed methodological limits.

SOME FINAL COMMENTS

The involvement and engagement of Member States in the EU's Better Regulation Agenda differ quite widely. Although the Commission's steering cannot be

[186] The Nieuw-Vlaamse Alliantie (N-VA, New Flemish Alliance). Its basic manifesto has a chapter on good governance, which includes ambitions on regulatory quality, evaluation of legislation and administrative simplification, as well as quality norms for a depoliticised administration. Concerning Europe, this party supports the EU and further European integration as far as the attribution of competences to the EU applies the subsidiarity principle and respects the cultural identities. As Eurorealists, the four N-VA MEPs in the European Parliament are members of the European Conservatives and Reformists Group, which also reflects its socio-economic positions. N-VA MEP A Van Bossuyt prepared the IMCO report for the European Parliament resolution of 12 April 2016 on 'Towards Improved Single Market Regulation' (Document P8_TA(2016)0105).

[187] See pages 30 and 35 of this text, available at www.vlaanderen.be/int/en/vision-eu.

[188] Recommendations from a pilot project in the course of 2016–17 included suggestions to improve the current approach (inspired by the Dutch BNC-fiche approach) through, inter alia, more data collection, analysis, coordination, capacity and multi-disciplinary work.

dismissed, future developments and implementation challenges will lie increasingly in the hands of the Member States not only as Council members—eg, by exporting the Better Regulation debate to other Council formations—but also internally. In the Better Regulation Working Party, the Commission keeps on spreading the positive messages of Better Regulation. The reactions of Member States are regularly critical, but only a small group of the (still) 28 (eg, Germany, the UK, the Netherlands, Denmark, Estonia, Italy, France and Poland)[189] can really refer to national (good) practices, mostly relating to specific elements of Better Regulation. An example concerns the call of the Maltese Presidency in early 2017 for reactions to a questionnaire about innovation-friendly legislation which only received 12 responses after two months. The Commission is aware of this diversity in national policies. However, in the light of the envisaged EU policy cycle approach,[190] the national and regional practices will have to become integral building blocks in this cycle, which deserves further improvements. One of the recommendations published by the Impact Assessment Institute in 2017 states that the Commission should use the views and experiences of the main beneficiaries of Better Regulation as the yardstick against which to measure progress:

> The focus has to be on the Member States and stakeholders that participate in policy development (and those that would like to, but are not able to). The Commission should develop clear outcome indicators for its Better Regulation Agenda, subject these to public consultation and use the intended positive effects for stakeholders to measure the success of the Better Regulation Agenda. The Commission should abandon the current approach in which its own interpretations of Better Regulation dominate the debate.[191]

This poses challenges for Belgium. Rhetorically it is an active participant in the Better Regulation Working Party. But its track record regarding the implementation of Better Regulation core elements and the development of appropriate national policies is not impressive. This is reflected in its limited and rather low-profile participation in less political Better Regulation fora and networks.

Almost two decades ago, some particular political interest instigated an institutionalisation of some elements of Better Regulation mainly focusing on simplification and burden reduction. This dominant perspective remained on the political agenda, but at the same time it has influenced the modest efforts for Impact Assessment, including RIA in Flanders. As this Better Regulation tool produces less short-term politically marketable—and even sometimes politically undesirable—effects, it does not receive much acclaim and is becoming rather marginal. This even signals contradictions: Flanders is reducing its RIA policy whilst it supports the

[189] The Session Reports of the Directors and Experts of Better Regulation Meeting (La Valletta, 20 January 2017) under the Maltese EU Presidency contain some examples from other Member States too.

[190] 'Better Regulation: Delivering Better Results for a Stronger Union' COM (2016) 615 final, 14 September 2016, 3: 'At any stage in the policy cycle, from legislative negotiations between Parliament and Council to transposition and implementation by the Member States and the Commission, better regulation should come into play.'

[191] Impact Assessment Institute, above n 128,.

EU's Impact Assessment, yet the federal level has some kind of Impact Assessment but is very reluctant about the Council's Impact Assessment approach. Without ignoring current good practices in particular fields[192] or organisations and some policy improvements and intentions, the different Belgian governments in general lack a profound and systemic learning willingness through, inter alia, information analysis, assessments and evaluations as a condition for long-term policy development and implementation.[193] Particular features of the Belgian system that could be labelled as consociationalism federalism[194] might perhaps explain this element of opinion-based 'belgitude'. But as the EU continues to look for improvements in its decision-making processes, Belgium should not stay with the laggards and even within its own model should look for innovation.

Culture and capacity were amongst the critical elements determined in earlier and more recent 'Europeanisation' studies of Belgium and Flanders.[195] As recommendations from this research have not really been materialised that much, they remain useful. This means that the first challenge should be to start establishing a real internal Belgian information exchange and coordination approach on regulatory policies and management with the available capacity in the concerned administrations. This would not only entail efficiency gains in times where public resources are under pressure but would also encourage some strategic thinking as Belgium is struggling with deficiencies in its regulatory policies, whether at the national or at the regional Flemish level, as indicated in the previously mentioned Senate report.[196] This report contains a straightforward but obvious suggestion; however, it remains doubtful if it will receive any further political attention.[197]

[192] eg, education; see Commission, *Support Mechanisms for Evidence-Based Policy-Making in Education* (2017) Eurydice Report, 16 (on Flanders), available at https://webgate.ec.europa.eu/fpfis/mwikis/eurydice/images/f/f4/206_EN_Evidence_based_policy_making.pdf.

[193] V Smet, 'Evidence-Based Policy en de doorwerking van sociaalwetenschappelijk onderzoek: Are We There Yet?' (2013) *Beleidsonderzoek Online*, December 2013, available at www.beleidsonderzoekonline.nl/tijdschrift/bso/2013/12/Beleidsonderzoek-D-12-00031.pdf; see also B Tieleman and P Van Humbeeck, 'Evolutie in de evaluatie? Analyse van de Vlaamse Milieubeleidsevaluatiepraktijk' (2007) MIRA-BE, Vlaamse Milieumaatschappij, 12, on the need for strategic intelligence, available at www.milieurapport.be/Upload/main/docs/Administrators/MIRA-BE/BE_rapport-2007.pdf.

[194] K Deschouwer, *The Politics of Belgium: Governing a Divided Society* (Basingstoke, Palgrave Macmillan, 2012) 11; K Deschouwer, 'And the Peace Goes on? Consociational Democracy and Belgian Politics in the Twenty-First Century' (2006) 29 *West European Politics* 895; see also D Caluwaerts and M Reuchamps, 'Combining Federalism with Consociationalism: Is Belgian Consociational Federalism Digging its Own Grave?' (2014) 14 *Ethnopolitics* 277.

[195] Dierickx et al, above n 182, 271; M Baetens and P Bursens, 'De Europeanisering van de bestuurlijke cultuur. Europese opinies, expertise en aandacht van Vlaamse ambtenaren en politici' in Steunpunt Bestuurlijke Organisatie Vlaanderen, *Vlaanderen en/in Europa: omgaan met de Unie en vergelijkend leren—Jaarboek 2004* (Bruges, Die Keure, 2005) 223; M Baetens and P Bursens, *De Europeanisering van de bestuurlijke structuur en cultuur in Vlaanderen en België* (2005) Report KU Leuven 129; De Coninck, above n 171, 100.

[196] Belgische Senaat, Zitting 2016–17, 9 January 2017, Document 6-212/3.

[197] Which would be regrettable, given the status of the concerned expert (Jeroen Van Nieuwenhove) not only as an academic (inter alia, as a member of the Interuniversity Centre for Regulatory Policy; see www.associatie-antwerpen.be/main.aspx?c=*ICW&n=20685), but also as State Counsellor with extensive direct legislative experiences and oversight.

In any case, recent administrative reforms and policy intentions both at the federal level and at the Flemish level (eg, the current ambition to develop a Centre of Government approach along the lines of the OECD concept, more stakeholder involvement) suffice to justify efforts to establish such a permanent coordination platform. Given the federal endorsement of the 2003 Cooperation Agreement and the current policy work on governance in Flanders, such an initiative could be jointly agreed by the concerned administrations and services without additional political approval.[198] Referring to the EU REFIT platform, one might also consider a dual-track approach and engage stakeholders more directly. Furthermore, the platform should also function as a knowledge centre, including the expertise from the Council of State, the only central institution, given its advisory role in the legislative processes of all Belgian government.[199]

Such a cooperation platform will require willingness, transparency and inter-organisational trust, which is already a challenge within the Flemish administration,[200] but was also acknowledged by the Commission during a Better Regulation Working Party meeting in April 2017 when asked about the use of the Better Regulation 'Toolbox' by the different Directorates General. However, as the concept of trust towards citizens, companies and other stakeholders is central in the Flemish and federal government agreements and is also a crucial concern in the Commission's White Paper on the future of Europe,[201] there is no excuse for further delay. This trust-building will inevitably require additional capacity in the concerned administrations at all levels in order to ensure the improved quality of Belgian legislation.

A Dutch expert once described law-making 'like steering in the mist',[202] a comparison to which I can subscribe based on my past experiences. So in order to navigate as well as possible and avoid accidents, it is evident that constructing future-proof legislation should at least incorporate efforts to take advantage of available guiding and enlightening tools. The complexity of the EU's multi-level governance setting means there are different drivers and as the mist is everywhere, the drivers as well as the target groups of the regulatory outcomes should be able to rely on 'trustworthy' instruments. The Better Regulation Agenda offers such opportunities and the national and regional administrations should provide for their appropriate use. This would also allow Belgian participants to the European Better Regulation fora to speak with evidence-based voices.

[198] This would not only overcome the lack of political interest (Baetens and Bursens, above n 195; Popelier, above n 83) but would also prove the increased independence that high-level civil servants claim when accused of being too politicised, even since the introduction of more objective selection tools, whilst the final selection of top (public) managers has remained political.

[199] Popelier (above nn 64 and 94) already clearly suggested the need for an enhanced and central role of the Council of State in the Belgian regulatory policies.

[200] P Oomsels, 'Interorganisationeel vertrouwen in Vlaamse horizontale departementen: naar een managementmodel' (2016) *Vlaams Tijdschrift voor Overheidsmanagement* 85.

[201] COM (2017)2025 of 1 March 2017, available at https://ec.europa.eu/commission/sites/beta-political/files/white_paper_on_the_future_of_europe_en.pdf.

[202] GJ Veerman, 'De paradox van wetsevaluatie' in *Wetgeven en evalueren* (Justitiële Verkenningen, WODC-Ministerie Justitie, 1991) 5, 19.

10

From Better Regulation to Better Adjudication?

Impact Assessment and the Court of Justice's Review

JULIAN NOWAG* AND XAVIER GROUSSOT**

INTRODUCTION

SINCE THE INCEPTION of Impact Assessments (IAs) in the Better Regulation Agenda, these are seen as the flagship tool of this new policy.[1] The use of IAs is not specific to the European Union (EU), but can be found both at the national level and within international organisations such as the Organisation for Economic Co-operation and Development (OECD) or the World Bank.[2] It is, in that sense, that they can be described as a 'global standard'. However, it is worth noting that the relevance of EU IAs and, more generally, of the Better Regulation Agenda 'received a boost, at least in terms of attention from major actors, after the failure of the constitutional project'.[3] In the last few years, following the elaboration of Guidelines in 2005, 2009 and 2015,[4] the evidence-base of law-making has become increasingly significant and IA is clearly the method to attain it.[5]

* Julian Nowag is Senior Lecturer at Lund University.
** Xavier Groussot is Pro Dean and Professor of EU Law at Lund University.

[1] The EU Commission announced its desire in 2002 to rely on IA as a 'general purpose impact analysis tool' in the preparation of proposals; see 'Communication from the Commission on Impact Assessments' COM (2002) 276 final. On 19 May 2015, it adopted its Better Regulation Agenda. This package of reforms covers the entire policy cycle and is aimed at boosting openness and transparency in the EU decision-making process, improving the quality of new laws through better IAs of draft legislation and amendments, and promoting constant and consistent review of existing EU laws, so that EU policies achieve their objectives in the most effective and efficient way.

[2] S Jacobs, 'Current Trends in Regulatory Impact Analysis: The Challenges of Mainstreaming RIA into Policy-Making', 2006, 5.

[3] A Meuwese, *Impact Assessment in EU Lawmaking* (Dordrecht, Kluwer Law, 2008) 274. The author here makes reference to the failure of the Constitutional Treaty.

[4] 'Impact Assessment Guidelines' COM (2005) 791, COM (2009) 92, and COM (2015) 215 final.

[5] Meuwese, above n 3, 174.

In this chapter, we will study specifically the use of IAs by the European Court of Justice (ECJ) as adjudicative tools in assessing the regulatory fitness of EU legislation and whether this practice brings more quality to the process of judicial review. The IAs are essential here because—according the 2015 Guidelines—they are used to 'collect evidence to assess if future legislative or non-legislative EU action is justified and how such action can best be designed to achieve desired policy objectives. An impact assessment must identify and describe the problem to be tackled, establish objectives and formulate policy options'.[6] This chapter explores the relevance of IAs in the ECJ's review, in particular, with a view to proportionality and subsidiarity. It first examines the relationship between the Better Regulation Agenda and the 2015 Guidelines with the rule of law principles: proportionality and subsidiarity. In the second section, it turns to study the increasing role of IAs in the ECJ's case law. This examination shows how the ECJ uses the IAs in order to help and bolster its assessment of the proportionality/subsidiarity of the EU's legislative measure viewed as a procedural tool of adjudication. We argue that while IAs have the potential to bring more evidence/rationality to the core reasoning of the ECJ, the current light touch judicial review may appear problematic. The next section focuses on comparing the EU IAs with their US counterparts and suggests ways to improve the use of IAs by the ECJ. Such improvements have the potential to lead to a more serious review of proportionality and subsidiarity, as well as of the numerous clauses calling on the EU to integrate, for example, environmental protection.[7] Moreover, this increased review might in turn lead to pressure for more meaningful IAs. We conclude with a section on issues surrounding the broader issue of juridification, the use of IA in adjudication, and the important constitutional limits which are related to the core issues of EU competence and institutional balance.

IMPACT ASSESSMENT, THE RULE OF LAW AND THE BETTER REGULATION AGENDA

The recent case law of the ECJ on subsidiarity and proportionality is paradigmatic in defining the contours of judicial review in the EU. It shows that a variety of principles are gravitating around subsidiarity and proportionality, and seem to establish a substantive and a procedural review of subsidiarity. Within this context, the new formal tool of IA has gained further traction. In light of the 2015

[6] Available at http://ec.europa.eu/smart-regulation/guidelines/docs/br_toolbox_en.pdf; see 2015 Guidelines, above n 4, 8.

[7] See Art 11 of the Treaty on the Functioning of the European Union (TFEU); on the integration of environmental consideration in competition, free movement and state aid, see J Nowag, *Environmental Integration in Competition and Free Movement Laws* (Oxford, Oxford University Press, 2016).

Guidelines on Better Regulation, it is not wrong to state that 'Impact Assessment' has become the new buzzword. The reinforcement of procedural requirements in Protocol 2 of the Lisbon Treaty is also connected to this new trend, which sees an increase focus on the 'how'.[8]

But what is the constitutional impact of IAs in EU (case) law after the adoption of the Better Regulation Agenda and, in particular, after the adoption of the 2015 Guidelines? The formal tool of IA builds on the idea of impact studies which the EU occasionally used within the legislative context. An IA is different from impact studies: while impact studies were previously used on an ad hoc basis, the IA is a formal tool. In 2015, the Commission as part of the REFIT programme[9] adopted Better Regulation Guidelines[10] together with the Better Regulation 'Toolbox'.[11] These set out that an IA would be necessary for all 'Commission initiatives that are likely to have significant economic, environmental or social impacts'. The Commission also defined standards for consultation and substantive standards for the IA. As put clearly by the 2015 Guidelines, Better Regulation means designing EU policies and laws so that they achieve their objectives at the lowest cost. Better Regulation is not about regulating or deregulating. It is a way of working to ensure that political decisions are prepared in an open, transparent manner, informed by the best available evidence and backed by the comprehensive involvement of stakeholders.[12] Therefore, and as lucidly argued by Dawson: 'Better regulation is not better because it meets with popular or political approval but because it meets procedural and technical standards of better law making.'[13]

The 2015 Guidelines establish a strong link between subsidiarity and proportionality (the so-called Better Regulation principles which are also defined as overarching principles)[14] and IAs (defined in details by Chapter 3 of the Guidelines and structured around the IA process and the following IA report).[15] As made clear by Chapter 3 of the Guidelines, 'IAs must set out the logical reasoning that links the problem (including subsidiarity issues), its underlying drivers, the objectives and a range of policy options to tackle the problem. They must present the likely impacts of the options, who will be affected by them and how'. The IA process, according to the Guidelines, should have allowed for the identification

[8] M Finck, 'Challenging the Subnational Dimension of Subsidiarity in EU Law' (2015) 8 *European Journal of Legal Studies* 6.

[9] The Regulatory Fitness and Performance (REFIT) programme is a rolling programme to keep the entire stock of EU legislation under review and ensure that it is 'fit for purpose', that regulatory burdens are minimised and that all simplification options are identified and applied.

[10] See n 4.

[11] Available at http://ec.europa.eu/smart-regulation/guidelines/docs/br_toolbox_en.pdf.

[12] 2015 Guidelines, above n 4, 5.

[13] M Dawson, 'Better Regulation and the Future of EU Regulatory Law and Politics' (2016) 53 *Common Market Law Review* 1230.

[14] ibid.

[15] Case T-424/14 *Client Earth v Commission* ECLI:EU:T:2015:848, in particular paras 86, 91 and 92.

of one (or more) preferred options. When developing the proposal, it is useful to double-check a number of key questions to ensure that the final proposal linked to the IA is fit for purpose and in line with the Better Regulation principles, ie, subsidiarity and proportionality.[16] The IA report, then, presents the final results of the IA process and accompanies the draft proposal through the Commission decision-making process. The Commission's Regulatory Scrutiny Board (RSB) scrutinises the quality of all draft IAs and issues an opinion on the draft IA report. A positive opinion by the RSB is required before an initiative can proceed.[17] It is also worth underlining that the Guidelines are complemented by the Better Regulation Toolbox, which also heavily insist on the respect of subsidiarity and proportionality. In this respect, the Toolbox highlights that the IA Report must describe the appropriate legal basis for action derived from the Treaty. For IAs, the choice of legal basis must be based upon the nature of the main/predominant objective, eg, health, the environment and the internal market.[18]

In our view, the new Guidelines and the Toolbox reinforce the 'rule of law' commitments. Answering previous criticism, they also bring about broader control by extending IAs to earlier and later moments of the EU policy-making cycle.[19] Yet, the IAs of the Commission are not binding on the other EU institutions. The Interinstitutional Agreement of 13 April 2016 signed by the European Commission, the European Council and the European Parliament considers that the IAs of the Commission can be used as a starting point for the work of the other institutions, but that each institution should remain responsible for conducting its own IAs.[20] The Interinstitutional Agreement thus confirmed the *Afton Chemical* case of 2010, where it was held that the IA was not binding on the Council and the Parliament, and that they were entitled to make amendments to the Commission's proposal based on a specific IA.[21] In the light of this case and the agreement, it appears evident to us that the principle of institutional balance constitutes a clear limit to the establishment of binding IAs between EU institutions.[22]

[16] 2015 Guidelines, above n 4, 31–32. Verifying regulatory fitness for a proposal requires checking issues, some of which will have already been touched upon during the IA process: does the draft (legal) text fully comply with subsidiarity?; is the proposal proportionate?; is it in line with the Charter of Fundamental Rights?

[17] ibid 18.

[18] See Tool #3: Legal Basis, Subsidiarity and Proportionality.

[19] 2015 Guidelines, above n 4, 7.

[20] Interinstitutional Agreement of 13 April 2016 on Better Law-Making [2016] OJ L123/1. See in particular paras 12 and 15 of the Agreement. The Commission asked for a common process of IAs.

[21] Case C-342/09 *Afton Chemical* ECLI:EU:C:2010:419, para 57.

[22] ibid, AG Kokott; see in particular paras 82–86. The Advocate General stressed that the Commission's IA is not binding on other institutions and that the other institutions can draw different conclusions. The Advocate General pointed out that the broad discretion of the legislature is not restricted to the Commission, but is conferred on all the institutions participating in the legislative procedure and their members. As put by the Advocate General at para 86: 'The relevant procedure in each case determines which assessment is decisive. In the present case the co-decision procedure under Article 251 EC was applied. It embodies the principle of democracy which was expressly enshrined in Article 6(1) EU as one of the foundations of the European Union. While the democratic decision-making process

Such a binding Commission IA would alter the democratic nature of the co-decision procedure.

IMPACT ASSESSMENT IN THE COURT'S REVIEW: THE RISE OF PROCEDURAL PROPORTIONALITY

Only in the last decade, IAs made their way into the ECJ. After the entry into force of the Lisbon Treaty, *Vodafone and Others* is the first preliminary ruling procedure in which the Court relied on an IA report when examining the alleged infringement of the principle of proportionality.[23] The focus on the procedural aspects of proportionality suggests that the EU institutions must show that they took 'all the relevant factors and circumstances of the situation the act was intended to regulate'[24] into account before exercising their discretion to adopt the relevant legislative act. The direct advantage of this approach is that it does not require the Court to second-guess the policy choices adopted by the EU legislature, as these will be clearly listed. The ECJ followed the same approach in *Luxembourg v Parliament and Council*.[25] Indeed, just like in *Vodafone*, the Court recited its mantra on the broad discretion accorded to the legislature and reviewed the IA report, finding that the Commission's review of several regulatory options satisfied the burden imposed by the regulatory action.[26] The *Philip Morris* case is revolutionary in relation to the issue of IAs. Even if it follows the logic of *Vodafone*, it refers for the first time to Article 5 of Protocol 2 of the Lisbon Treaty.[27] Also, the ECJ relied on IA not only in relation to the assessment of proportionality but also in relation to the principle of subsidiarity. There is thus a spill-over of IAs within the adjudicative principles applied by the ECJ. The use of IA provides additional information/evidence to the EU judges and thus leads to an increase in the rationality of judicial decision-making. Therefore, it may be said that IAs are not only interesting for creating Better Regulation but also for creating better adjudication.[28] The Court's

it provides for requires first a Commission proposal, for the adoption of Directive 2009/30 it required a qualified majority in the Council and the absolute majority of votes cast in the Parliament. Those majorities clearly took a different view from the Commission. Such differences of opinion cannot, as such, be criticised by the courts, as the institutional balance in the relevant legislative procedure would otherwise be called into question.'

[23] Case C-58/08 *Vodafone* ECLI:EU:C:2010:321. The ECJ referred to the findings set out in the IA report on six occasions and to the explanatory memorandum on five occasions. See D Keyaerts, 'Ex Ante Evaluation of EU Legislation Intertwined with Judicial Review?' (2010) 35 *European Law Review* 869.

[24] Case C-310/04 *Spain v Council* ECLI:EU:C:2006:521, para 122.

[25] Case C-176/09 *Luxembourg v Parliament and Council*, ECLI:EU:C:2011:290.

[26] ibid paras 60–65.

[27] In *Vodafone*, above n 23, the ECJ only refers to Arts 6 and 7 of Protocol 2 of the Lisbon Treaty.

[28] A Alemanno, 'Courts and Regulatory Impact Assessment' in C Dunlop and C Radaelli (eds), *Handbook of Regulatory Impact Assessment* (Cheltenham, Edward Elgar, 2016) 127, 131–32.

current use of the IAs in the proportionality analysis can also be observed in the Tobacco Directive cases—*Philip Morris*,[29] *Pillbox 38*[30] and *Poland v Parliament and Council*[31]—as well as in *Estonia v Parliament and Council*.[32]

However, even before these cases which directly address the formal tool of IA in the context of the legislative process, the Court used impact studies in its assessment, for example, in *Spain v Council*.[33] This case concerned the Common Agricultural Policy or more specifically rules concerning aid measures for cotton production. The Council had adopted a new aid system with the aim of decoupling aid from actual production while similarly ensuring the continued production of cotton. The new rules adopted by the Council changed the system so that the majority of aid would be paid as income support irrespective of the actual production of cotton. Only around one-third of the aid would continue to be paid for the actual production of cotton. In this case, the Court found that the proportionality principle had been breached. While in other areas an impact study of the effects of the decoupling of aid had been carried out, such a study was not carried out regarding the economic viability of cotton production under the new scheme. The Council had therefore not been able to show that it taken 'into consideration … all the relevant factors and circumstances … [which were] necessary to take into account for assessing the profitability of that crop'.[34] Thus, because the Council had not taken into account 'the relevant factors and circumstances of the situation the act was intended to regulate',[35] the principle of proportionality was infringed.[36] Thus, the case of *Spain v Council* suggests a focus on procedural aspects of proportionality and, in particular, the duty to establish basic facts. This establishing of basic facts, if necessary, must be done by means of an impact study.[37]

This procedural element of IA was further highlighted in *Vodafone and Others*. In this case the IA is used by the Court first to show that the Commission had gathered all necessary evidence[38] or, in the words of *Spain v Council*, that it was able to take 'into consideration all the relevant factors and circumstances'.[39] However, the IA in *Vodafone and Others* is also used in another way. The Court uses the findings of the IA to further substantiate that the roaming regulation was

[29] Case C-547/14 *Philip Morris Brands and Others* ECLI:EU:C:2016:325.
[30] Case C-477/14 *Pillbox 38* ECLI:EU:C:2016:324.
[31] Case C-358/14 *Poland v Parliament and Council* ECLI:EU:C:2016:323.
[32] Case C-508/13 *Estonia v Parliament and Council* ECLI:EU:C:2015:403.
[33] *Spain v Council*, above n 24.
[34] ibid para 133.
[35] ibid para 122.
[36] ibid para 135.
[37] See X Groussot and J Nowag in Festskrift till Christina Moëll, 'New Directions in Judicial Review? Proportionality, Subsidiarity and Impact Assessment in the Tobacco Product Directive Case', (Juristförlaget i Lund, 2017) 83–101.
[38] *Vodafone*, above n 23, paras 52–55.
[39] *Spain v Council*, above n 24, para 133.

proportional.[40] A similar approach can be observed in *Luxembourg v Parliament and Council* as well as the subsequent case *Estonia v Parliament and Council* and in the so-called Tobacco Directive cases.[41] In all these cases the IA has a similar function; it provided the Court with additional arguments to support the conclusion that the measure in question was compliant with the proportionality requirement. Looking at the use of IA in these cases, it might be argued that the consequence of an IA is that the measure is presumed to be compliant with the proportionality principle. Where an IA has been performed, the Court seems to show even greater deference than under its already deferential approach to proportionality.[42] Additionally, the Court has, so far, not subjected the IA to any further requirements, so that one might even argue that an IA provides immunity to a measure, insofar as the EU institutions do not act deliberately against the findings of the IA. To conclude, the IA in the context of the proportionality requirement can be said to have two functions. First, it is used in the context of the gathering of facts and evidence, and thus as a procedural element. Second, it is used for the substantive assessment of proportionality. In this context, the IA provides additional material and arguments for examining and justifying why the measure is proportional. And in the current state of affairs, it seems to establish a presumption of legality or, as Dawson highlights, it 'provides a "shield against judicial review" with the danger of becoming a box ticking exercise'.[43]

BETTER REGULATION AS BETTER ADJUDICATION? COMPARING AND IMPROVING THE USE OF IAS

While the current use of IA in the Court's jurisprudence may give rise to concern, this section aims to provide some ideas on how the EU's Better Regulation might be used to provide better adjudication by the Court. In this sense, it is a truism to say that the focus on scholarship has often been on the meaning and scope of the 'better' in regulation. But can Better Regulation also mean better adjudication? And is it possible to improve adjudication of EU legislation and non-legislative acts with the help of IAs? There is perhaps a need of a more clearly delineated and juridified IA in the EU. A brief comparison with the US shows that IAs or what they call on the other side of the pond cost-benefit analysis (CBA) are more

[40] ibid paras 64–70.

[41] *Luxembourg v Parliament and Council*, above n 25; and *Estonia v Parliament and Council*, above n 32.

[42] On deference in the EU Courts' proportionality assessment, see, eg, G De Búrca 'The Principle of Proportionality and its Application in EC Law' (1993) 13 *Yearbook of European Law* 105; W Sauter, 'Proportionality in EU Law: A Balancing Act?' (2013) 15 *Cambridge Yearbook of European Legal Studies* 439.

[43] Dawson, above n 13, 1230.

structured and more entrenched within judicial practice.[44] This is perhaps not surprising given the history of CBA in the US, a history that started in the 1970s and gained momentum during the Reagan administration in the 1980s, where CBA was used by federal agencies in a systematic way and by courts in reviewing executive regulations.[45] In the US, CBA has been used mainly for controlling agencies.[46]

In a recent article, Petrin compares the US and EU models of IAs.[47] In this study he considers that:

> In the US … the analyses that many agencies are required to conduct may be referred to as 'Impact Statements' or 'Regulatory Impact Analyses'. In the EU … the official expression for the method of evaluating the consequences of regulatory policies is now 'Impact Assessment'. These concepts may include the balancing of costs and benefits, but are different in substance from what is traditionally called CBA. They generally allow for a broader view that goes far beyond the balancing of costs and benefits. Notably, such analyses also tend to place greater weight on qualitative considerations and may also focus on factors such as sustainability, environmental, and humanitarian or societal effects. They are therefore different from rigid cost-benefit balancing and purely net benefit-focused methodologies.

This analysis is confirmed by the 2015 Guidelines, which make clear that the Commission's IA system follows an integrated approach that assesses the environmental, social and economic impacts of a range of policy options, thereby mainstreaming sustainability into EU policy-making.[48] At a more general and theoretical level, it is not possible to deny the fact that IAs can be difficult to rely on in practice. This is due, in our view, to three main interrelated elements: their complexity, cost and methodology. A good IA analysis should be comprehensive, balanced and 'forward looking'. This is not an easy task to realise since risks interact with many (if not endless) parameters, ie, economic and social parameters. Moreover, such an assessment is difficult because, for example, the costs of environmental regulations are often overestimated and the benefits tend to be higher after implementation.[49] The useful IA is therefore difficult to realise. The Evaluating Integrated Impact Assessments (EVIA) report[50] on the situation in the

[44] A Meuwese and S van Voorst, 'Regulatory Impact Assessment in Legal Studies' in Dunlop and Radaelli, above n 28, 21.

[45] ibid.

[46] See E Posner, 'Controlling Agencies with Cost-Benefit Analysis: A Positive Political Theory Perspective' (2002) 68 *University of Chicago Law Review* 1137, 1182–86 (discussing the inefficiency of regulations); R Hahn and C Sunstein, 'A New Executive Order for Improving Federal Regulation? Deeper and Wider Cost-Benefit Analysis' (2002) 150 *University of Pennsylvania Law Review* 1489, 1498–99.

[47] M Petrin, 'Regulatory Analysis in Corporate Law' (2016) 79 *MLR* 573.

[48] 2015Guidelines, above n 4, 8.

[49] ibid.

[50] Evaluating Integrated Impact Assessments, available at http://cordis.europa.eu/publication/rcn/11716_en.html.

EU Member States, underlined that there was a substantive gap between practice and the requirements set out in official documents. It is in the light of this document that Jacobs criticised the 'ticking box mentality' in the IA analysis.[51] He explained that even in countries with a lot of experience in mandatory IA, quality of analysis continues to be uneven. There is a lack of investment in skills and incentives and in attention to key constraints on good-quality analysis.[52] Other methodological drawbacks can be identified. For instance, IA should be the *ex ante* evaluation of how the policy intervention will work in practice. This is often overridden by the second question: do the benefits outweigh the cost? And, as rightly put by Macrae, the question should be: *will* the benefits outweigh the costs?[53] This 'forward-looking' analysis together with the need of comprehensiveness and reasoned balancing render the costs of a proper IA analysis very high. This is the price to pay for ensuring a balance of the goals of efficiency and democracy enshrined within the core of IA analysis.[54]

Though it is perfectly apt to argue that the integrated approach as to IAs is broader than a traditional CBA, the recent case law of the ECJ has relied on IAs mainly in the balancing part of the EU proportionality assessment. This point is salient if one looks at the recent *Philip Morris* case and the use of IAs in the last part of the proportionality test, ie, proportionality in the strict sense,[55] which might also be viewed as a judicial form of CBA. In this context, the *Philip Morris* case is a milestone in defining the forthcoming contours of judicial review in the EU. It clearly shows that a variety of principles are gravitating around proportionality. As discussed above, it is a very 'structured judgment' which clarifies the relationship between proportionality and subsidiarity in judicial review. Notably, the subsidiarity review is divided into substantive and procedural review. The decision is of importance since it explicitly confirms the use of IA in the judicial review of acts of the EU legislature. In that respect, it is worth underlying again that it is the first case of the ECJ making reference to Article 5 of Protocol 2 of the Lisbon Treaty. Yet, as highlighted in the previous section, this greater importance of IA in the case does not mean that there is a requirement to carry out an IA. Rather, at the current stage, it seems to support the view that as soon as an IA has been carried out, the measure will in all likelihood comply with the said principles of proportionality and subsidiarity.

51 S Jacobs, 'Towards a Simpler and Practical Approach' in Dunlop and Radaelli, above n 28, 80.

52 ibid. See also S Blockmans et al, 'From Subsidiarity to Better EU Governance: A Practical Reform Agenda for the EU', *CEPS Essay*, No 10, 8 April 2014.

53 D Macrae, 'Compliance and Delivery Analysis' in Dunlop and Radaelli, above n 28, 66. This point makes sense particularly when taking into consideration the fact that the costs of environmental regulation are often overestimated in IA. After implementation, net benefits turn out to be higher. See A Meuwese and S van Voorst, 'Regulatory Impact Assessment in Legal Studies' in Dunlop and Radaelli, above n 28, 23.

54 J Schwartz, 'Approaches to Cost-Benefit Analysis' in Dunlop and Radaelli, above n 28, 32, 34.

55 This is the last part of the three-pronged test of proportionality. See X Groussot, *General Principles of Community Law* (Groningen, Europa Law Publishing, 2006).

However, how could IA become a meaningful tool within the Court's assessment, bringing more evidence/rationality to its core reasoning? The light-touch review of subsidiarity[56] both in political as well as legal assessment, in terms of substantive and procedural review, could be improved by taking the requirements for and within IA more serious. This development can be based on the EU Courts' case law on the relevance of guidelines in other areas. The Courts have held the EU's institutions to their standards expressed in guidelines and soft law more generally. This has two consequences: on the one hand, the institution is required to use its guidelines when they are applicable; on the other hand, the content of the guidelines binds the relevant institution of the EU. While Article 288 TFEU highlights that recommendations, options and other forms of soft law such as guidelines do not have binding force, the Court in *CIRFS* already made an exception. It held that it was not possible to implicitly amend certain guidelines, which the Member States had also accepted, by means of an individual decision due to the principles of equal treatment and legitimate expectations.[57] In *Dansk Rørindustri A/S*, the Court explicitly held that guidelines and other forms of soft law can limit an institution's scope of action. For the institution, such guidelines 'imposes a limit on the exercise of its discretion and cannot depart from those rules under pain of being found, where appropriate, to be in breach of the general principles of law, such as equal treatment or the protection of legitimate expectations'.[58] The guidelines may therefore become the standard of review for annulment proceedings.[59]

In other areas, in particular the competition context,[60] the Court therefore has held the Commission to its standards.[61] There seems to be no reason why the Court could not insist that the Commission meets its own consultation and substantive standards for IA as provided in the Guidelines and the Tool-kit. The Court should therefore clearly embrace the Commission's commitment to carry out an IA whenever 'the expected economic, environmental or social impacts of EU action are likely to be significant'.[62] Taking the Commission up on its commitment

[56] See P Craig, 'Subsidiarity: A Political and Legal Analysis' (2012) 50(1) *Journal of Common Market Studies* 72.

[57] Case C-313/90 *CIRFS v Commission* ECLI:EU:C:1993:111, paras 32–52.

[58] Joined Cases C-189/02 P, C-202/02 P, C-205/02 P–C-208/02 P and C-213/02 P *Dansk Rørindustri and Others v Commission* ECLI:EU:C:2005:408, para 211.

[59] ibid para 212.

[60] See N Petit and M Rato, 'From Hard to Soft Enforcement of EC Competition Law: A Bestiary of Sunshine Enforcement Instruments' in C Gheur and N Petit (eds), *Alternative Enforcement Techniques in EC Competition Law* (Brussels, Bruylant, 2009); H Hofmann, 'Negotiated and Non-negotiated Administrative Rule-Making: The Example of EC Competition Policy' (2006) 43 *Common Market Law Review* 153; L Senden, *Soft Law in European Community Law* (Oxford, Hart Publishing, 2004).

[61] See also Case C-171/00 P *Libéros v Commission* ECLI:EU:C:2002:17, para 35; Case C-397/03 P *Archer Daniels Midland Co and Archer Daniels v Commission* ECLI:EU:C:2006:328, paras 89–90; Case C-226/11 *Expedia Inc v Autorité de law concurrence and Others* ECLI:EU:C:2012:795, para 28; and Case *T–446/05 Amann & Söhne GmbH v Commission* ECLI:EU:T:2010:165, paras 137–39.

[62] See in particular the Better Regulation Toolbox, Tool #5: When is an IA Necessary?

made in the Better Regulation Guidelines, it becomes clear that a formal IA seems required for the majority of legislative proposals because significant, economic, environmental or social impacts can typically be expected.

As the Commission explains, any IA should be 'comprehensive, proportionate, evidence-based, open to stakeholders' views, unbiased, prepared collectively with relevant Commission services, embedded in the policy cycle, transparent and of a high quality'.[63] In particular, the following question needs to be answered: 'what are the impacts of the different policy options and who will be affected?'[64] From Chapter 2 of the Better Regulation Toolbox, it becomes clear that the Commission commits to: 1) identifying the impacts of the policy options; 2) singling out likely significant impacts; and 3) assessing these quantitatively and, if this is not possible, qualitatively.[65] The range of impacts to be screened for is wide-ranging and is grouped under economic, social and environmental impacts.[66]

Moreover, a second aspect of the EU Courts' case law on guidelines needs to be considered. Guidelines cannot conflict with EU law and in particular with primary EU law. Hence, the Courts would need to ensure that the Better Regulation Guidelines as well as the actual IA need to be compliant with the requirements of the EU Treaties. In this context, it might be useful to remember the general consistency clause of Article 7 and the numerous integration clauses.[67] Judicial review of these clauses has so far been rather weak.[68] The Better Regulation Agenda and in particular the IA may, possibly to the surprise of some, provide the opportunity for an improvement in this regard. The broad range of issues which an IA according to the Guidelines should cover provides the Court with a means to police such clauses. Based on the Guidelines, the Commission could now be held accountable where such an IA has been omitted or certain aspects have not been considered contrary to the IA Guidelines.

The Guidelines also seem to improve the situation because of the structured approach they provide for the IA process. Previously, compliance with all integration clauses might have been considered to be a tedious exercise. From a practical

[63] 'Better Regulation Guidelines' COM (2015) 215 final 18.

[64] ibid 24.

[65] Chapter 2 of the Better Regulation Toolbox.

[66] These include impacts on sectoral competitiveness; research and innovation; small and medium-sized companies; competition; the internal market; external trade and investment; the digital economy and society; fundamental and human rights; employment, working conditions, income distribution and inequality; education, culture and youth; health; consumers; territorial impacts; developing countries and resource efficiency. For a more detailed overview of key impacts to be screened, see pages 99–100 of the Better Regulation Toolbox.

[67] Beyond Art 7 TFEU, these are Art 8 TFEU (equality between men and women); Art 10 TFEU (discrimination); Art 12 TFEU (consumer protection); Art 13 TFEU (animal welfare); Arts 147(2) and 9 TFEU (employment, social protection and exclusion); Art 167(4) TFEU (culture); Art 168(1) TFEU (public health); Art 173(3) TFEU (industrial policy); Art 175 TFEU (regional policy); Art 208(1) TFEU, second sentence of the second subpara (development cooperation).

[68] See, eg, J Nowag, 'Article 11 TFEU and Environmental Rights' in S Bogojević and R Rayfuse (eds), *Environmental Rights in Europe and Beyond* (Oxford, Hart Publishing, forthcoming).

point of view, it might therefore not have been surprising that these were not always considered. Yet, such practical considerations should not lead to ignoring the legal requirements imposed by the Treaty. Instead, the Guidelines provide for a structured process[69] that is iterative, in that it 'starts with a wide reach and then focusses, and deepens, the analysis on the most relevant impacts, being ready to go back and improve the retained options before finalizing'.[70] The focus is placed upon significant impacts which are assessed by means of taking account of the 'expected overall magnitude; relevance for specific stakeholders ... importance for Commission horizontal objectives and policies'.[71] For the Court's review of the Treaties' integration clauses, these statements provide a valuable starting point. In cases where the compliance with such clauses is at issue, the case law would already advance if the Court would add a statement like the following to its judgment:

> 'The plaintiff did not plead omissions in the impact assessment' or 'such an omission is not relevant because the plaintive did not show that the expected overall magnitude; relevance for specific stakeholders ... or importance for Commission horizontal objectives and policies would require the inclusion'.

Such steps would also intensify the procedural elements of the Courts' review of subsidiarity. However, it would not impose any particularly new, revolutionary or overly burdensome requirements upon the Commission, because the Commission would only be taken up on its commitment to the Better Regulation Agenda. Moreover, while it might only be a small change in terms of the procedural review, it would be a substantial move in terms of the review of subsidiary and the integration clauses. The intensified review would increase the relevance of the IA in the legislative as well as the judicial process. One could expect that with increased focus on the IA by the Court, the Commission's IA would become more sophisticated, with an increase in terms of transparency and an intensified political review in particular with regard to the integration clauses and subsidiarity. In this way, a feedback loop could be created. The Courts' improved use of IA would lead to improved and more frequent use of IA—in other words, 'better regulation'—which in turn would allow for more evidence/rationality in the core reasoning of the ECJ in the review—that is, 'better adjudication'.[72]

JURIDIFICATION AND CONSTITUTIONAL LIMITS

However, despite these options for improvement, IAs may also be viewed as a catalyst for the changing relations between institutions. This is all the more true in

[69] See the Better Regulation Toolbox, Tool #16.

[70] 2015 Guidelines, above n 4, 25.

[71] ibid 26–27; see also 27ff. and Better Regulation Toolbox, Tool #16ff.

[72] See X Groussot and S Bogojevic, 'Subsidiarity as a Procedural Safeguard of Federalism' in L Azoulai (ed), *The Question of EU Competence* (Oxford, Oxford University Press, 2014) 234.

the EU context, where they can modify the relationship between the political institutions and the ECJ, fostering a culture of Better Regulation even when the IAs are not legal requirements.[73] As discussed before, the ECJ case law has recognised the importance of impact studies even before the entry into force of the Lisbon Treaty. In *Spain v Council*, it may be said that the non-respect of a course of conduct[74] is apt to lead to a breach of the general principle of proportionality if it constitutes a basic fact or essential factor that should have been taken into consideration by the EU legislature.[75] The trace of the increased importance of IAs can also be found in recent cases such as *Philip Morris*. This case concerned the interpretation and validity of a number of provisions of the Directive dealing with the manufacture, presentation and sale of tobacco and related products, the so-called Tobacco Product Directive.[76] Two companies, Philip Morris and British American Tobacco brought proceedings against the Secretary of State for Health regarding the legality of the 'intention and/or obligation' of the UK government to implement Directive 2014/40. Seven questions were asked by the national court to the ECJ, but the Court decided to declare some of the questions inadmissible. In the end, only four questions were answered by the ECJ, mainly focusing on the issues of the legal basis, proportionality and subsidiarity of the Tobacco Product Directive.

The last question (Question 7) is the most relevant for this chapter. It concerns the issue of the validity of Article 7 of Directive 2014/40 in the light of the principle of subsidiarity (the Court has already checked the proportionality of Article 7 in Question 3(a)). The claimant argued that the EU legislature merely asserted, using a standard formula, that the principle of subsidiarity was complied with, without showing that the internal market benefits deriving from that prohibition are sufficient to justify action on the part of the EU. It was also argued that public health protection could have been sufficiently achieved at the Member State level. Quoting Article 5(2) of the Treaty on European Union (TEU) and Article 5 of Protocol No 2 on the application of the principles of subsidiarity and proportionality, the Court considered that after an initial review of compliance at the political level, the EU judicature must verify both compliance with the substantive conditions set out in Article 5(3) TEU and compliance with the procedural safeguards provided for by Protocol No 2.[77] Concerning the judicial review of compliance with the substantive conditions, the ECJ must determine whether the EU legislature was entitled to consider, on the basis of a detailed statement, that the objective of the proposed action could be better achieved at the EU level.[78] According to the Court, the inter-dependence between the two objectives (facilitating the smooth functioning of the internal market while ensuring a high level of protection of

[73] *Spain v Council*, above n 24.

[74] A non-compulsory impact study had been carried out in relation to other support systems such as in the tobacco sector.

[75] *Spain v Council*, above n 24, paras 122–23.

[76] [2014] OJ L127, 1.

[77] *Spain v Council*, above n 24, paras 214–17.

[78] ibid paras 218–19.

human health, especially for young people) pursued by the Directive means that the EU legislature could legitimately take the view that it had to establish a set of rules for the placing on the EU market of tobacco products with characterising flavours and that, because of this inter-dependence, these two objectives could best be achieved at the EU level even if the second objective might be better achieved at the national level.[79]

As to the judicial review of compliance with the procedural conditions, it is observed by the Court that the obligation to state reasons must be evaluated not only by reference to the wording of the contested act, but also by reference to its context and the circumstances of the individual case.[80] In the present case, it is undisputed that the Commission's proposal for a directive and its IA include sufficient information showing clearly and unequivocally the advantages of taking action at the EU level rather than at the Member State level.[81] According to the Court, in the political process, this information has enabled the EU legislature and the national parliaments to determine whether the proposal complied with the principle of subsidiarity. Therefore, Article 7 of the Tobacco Product Directive is valid in the light of the principle of subsidiarity.[82]

The principle of subsidiarity, as enshrined in Article 5 TEU and Protocol 2 of the Lisbon Treaty, can be seen as both a political and a judicial safeguard.[83] It is often, but not always, connected to proportionality[84] and as having a modest role when taking the form of judicial review.[85] In any event, it is a truism to say that the difficulties in defining subsidiarity are without doubt related to 'its lack of conceptual contours'.[86] However, the recent case law of the ECJ such as *Vodafone*, *Luxembourg v Parliament and Council* and *Philip Morris* seem to structuralise the application of the principle of subsidiarity using Protocol No 2 as a tool. In these cases, the ECJ assessed, in the first place, a breach of the principle of proportionality and, in the second place, the breach of the principle of subsidiarity. This structured application is also visible in *Estonia v Parliament and Council*,[87] a case delivered a few months before *Philip Morris.*

In *Estonia v Parliament and Council*, the ECJ had to rule on the validity of Directive 2013/34 on annual financial statements. Estonia advanced three claims based on proportionality, subsidiarity and lack of statement of reasons. Similarly

[79] ibid paras 220–22. See, by analogy, *Vodafone*, above n 23, para 78; and *Estonia v Parliament and Council*, above n 32, para 48.

[80] *Spain v Council*, above n 24, para 225. See also *Estonia v Parliament and Council*, above n 32, para 61.

[81] *Spain v Council*, above n 24, para 226.

[82] ibid paras 227–28.

[83] See, eg, Finck, above n 8.

[84] The political aspect of subsidiarity enshrines in Arts 6 and 7 (the so-called 'yellow card system') is not directly connected to proportionality.

[85] See I Maletic, 'The Role of the Principle of Subsidiarity in EU Lifestyle Risk Policy' in A Alemanno and A Garde (eds), *Regulating Life Style Risks* (Cambridge, Cambridge University Press, 2015) 197.

[86] R Schütze, *European Constitutional Law* (Cambridge, Cambridge University Press, 2012) 178.

[87] *Estonia v Parliament and Council*, above n 32.

to *Philip Morris*, the objectives of the Directive are twofold, ie, harmonising the financial information of EU undertakings so that addressees of the financial information have comparable data, but also of doing so by taking into account through a special scheme (itself also largely harmonised) of the particular situation of small undertakings on which the application of accounting requirements laid down for medium and large undertakings would impose an excessive administrative burden.[88] Estonia claimed that the pursuit of the second objective would be better achieved by action at the Member State level. The Court disagreed with this contention and stated that the inter-dependence of the two objectives pursued by the Directive means that the EU legislature could legitimately take the view that it had to include a special scheme for small undertakings and that, because of that inter-dependence, this twofold objective could best be achieved at the EU level.[89] As to the alleged defective way in which the EU legislature ensured compliance with the subsidiarity principle prior to taking action, the Court considered that the EU legislature had rightly concluded on the basis of 'detailed evidence' and without committing any error of assessment that the general interests of the EU could be better served by action at that level.[90]

The ECJ adopted a similar reasoning in *Philip Morris*, but even went further in terms of the 'structured application' of the principle of subsidiarity. In this case, the Court looked both at substantive subsidiarity and procedural subsidiarity. As to substantive subsidiarity, the Court found these two objectives could best be achieved at the EU level even if the second objective might be better achieved at the national level.[91] With regard to procedural subsidiarity, it ruled that the Commission's proposal for a directive and its IA should include sufficient information showing clearly and unequivocally the advantages of taking action at the EU level rather than at the Member State level.[92] In both *Philip Morris* and *Estonia v Parliament and Council*, 'detailed evidence' or IA is important to assess a potential breach of procedural subsidiarity. So it seems that the EU judge finally enforced 'with particular rigour'[93] the obligation to state reasons within the subsidiarity framework.

Wyatt has criticised with virulence the ECJ's approach in subsidiarity cases for being undemanding, uncritical and resulting in a judicial dead letter.[94] It is true

88 ibid paras 12–13 and 46.
89 ibid para 48.
90 ibid para 54.
91 *Philip Morris*, above n 29, paras 220–22.
92 ibid para 226.
93 See AG Léger in Case C-233/94 *Germany v Parliament and Council* EU:C:1996:478, para 87. According to AG Léger, 'on a more general level, I should point out how useful I consider it could be, for the purpose of ensuring proper application of the principle of subsidiarity, for the obligation to state reasons laid down in Article 190 of the Treaty to be enforced with particular rigour whenever the Community legislature takes action to lay down new rules'.
94 D Wyatt, 'Does the European Court of Justice Need a New Judicial Approach for the 21st Century?', 2015 lecture at the Bingham Centre, 12, available at https://www.biicl.org/documents/760_derrick_wyatts_paper.pdf?showdocument=1.

that the approach taken in *Philip Morris* as to substantive subsidiarity and the so-called 'interdependence of the objectives' is clearly tautological and, irremediably, leads to a non-questioning of the potential best achievement of the objective at the local level. The choice of the legislature is obviously not challenged. It is also true that another more proactive approach (often described as 'federal proportionality') would inevitably question the choice of the legislature and put into jeopardy the system of qualified majority voting within the EU.[95] This is the reason why the Court does not follow a 'broad interpretation', but rather a 'narrow interpretation' of substantive subsidiarity.[96]

Thus, it is not surprising that critical voices against this reconceptualisation and proceduralisation of the principle of proportionality are now growing. Many authors are condemning the 'box-ticking approach'[97] of the ECJ and are arguing for an increased control of the substantive merits.[98] For instance, Dawson has considered that 'IAs could act as a shield against judicial review, allowing the Commission to immunize it proposals against judicial scrutiny through checking the boxes of stakeholder consultation and impact assessment. Judicial emphasis on process review places even more pressure on the adequacy of IAs, ie on the question of whether they are sufficiently serious and an adequate methodological basis'.[99] At the broader level, this move towards an EU style of 'adversarial legalism'[100] fits the spread of what has been called 'Eurolegalism'. Indeed, for Kelemen, the EU encourages the development of this mode of governance that relies on detailed rules containing strict transparency and disclosure requirements; legalistic and adversarial approaches to regulatory enforcement and dispute resolution.[101] This mode of governance alters *in fine* the character of the democracy in Europe.

Some have also recently tried to defend this significant move towards the proceduralisation of proportionality.[102] In a recent article in the *Yearbook of European Law*, Öberg shows not only the close relationship between substantive review and procedural review[103] but also argues that a more intense procedural review would address some of the concerns related to the issue of competence and the

[95] See Groussot and Bogojevic, above n 72, 234.

[96] See AG Kokott in *Philip Morris*, above n 29, discussing the issue of partial harmonisation and subsidiarity.

[97] Dawson, above n 13. See also D Harvey, 'Towards Process-Oriented Proportionality Review in the European Union' (2017) 23 *European Public Law* 93.

[98] Harvey, above n 97.

[99] Dawson, above n 13, 1230.

[100] See R Kagan, *Adversarial Legalism: The American Way of Law* (Cambridge, MA, Harvard University Press, 2001).

[101] D Kelemen, 'Eurolegalism and Democracy' (2012) 50 *Journal of Common Market Studies* 55. The central argument of this article is that judicialisation and the rise of Eurolegalism are not undermining democracy in Europe.

[102] J Öberg, 'The Rise of the Procedural Empire: Judicial Review of EU Legislation' (2017) 36 *Yearbook of European Law* 248.

[103] See also M Shapiro, 'The Giving Reasons Requirement' [1992] *University of Chicago Legal Forum* 179.

application of the principle of proportionality and subsidiarity in areas of wide discretion. He argues that procedural review poses a lesser challenge to democratic political theory and the principle of institutional balance, since its aim is not to frustrate democratic decision-making.[104] Öberg concludes that the ECJ must change its current deferential approach and construct new limits to the exercise of EU powers by reviewing the EU legislation with more rigour and thus leading to the application of a strict procedural review. This is an interesting proposal which perhaps could be backed up by the text of the 2015 Guidelines of the Better Regulation Agenda and the emphasis on IAs.[105]

The constitutional implications may be viewed as adjudicative tools fostering a 'space for constitutional discourse'[106] through 'adversarial legalism' or the proceduralisation of subsidiarity and proportionality.[107] This rise of proceduralism should also be analysed in light of the broader context of the juridification of EU (soft) law in order to grasp its full constitutional meaning. Indeed, we see a move in the ECJ case law towards an increased significance of non-binding instruments such as IAs or technical standards. For instance, in the recent *James Elliot* judgment, the ECJ had to decide whether a harmonised technical standard (HTS) developed in response to the Commission's mandate was a provision of EU Law. The judgment followed the Opinion of the Advocate General, resulting in the finding that an HTS is a part of EU law: 'The fact that a *measure of EU law* has no binding effect does not preclude the Court from ruling on its interpretation in proceedings for a preliminary ruling under Article 267 TFEU.'[108] In the IA context more specifically, the juridification of non-binding instruments brings about increased litigation related to core constitutional issues such as transparency. In the pending appeal case *Client Earth*, the ECJ must rule on a decision of the General Court, which considered that the Commission is entitled to presume, without carrying out a specific and individual examination of each of the documents drawn up in the context of preparing an IA, that the disclosure of those documents would, in principle, seriously undermine its decision-making process for developing a policy proposal.[109] This case of the General Court highlights that though an IA contributes to ensuring that the Commission's decision-making process for the

[104] ibid.

[105] Dawson, above n 13.

[106] Meuwese, above n 3, at 282.

[107] ibid; as lucidly put by one author, 'IA seems to encourage decision-makers to become entrenched in their chosen option early on. Paradoxically the only way to let EU IA succeed as a tool of proceduralization is to find a way to get actors focused on the content'.

[108] Case C-613/14 *James Elliot* ECLI:EU:C:2016:821, para 35. See M Medzmariashvvili, 'A Harmonisied (Technical) Standard-Provision of EU Law' (2016) *European Law Blog*; and R van Gestel and HW Micklitz, 'European Integration through Standardization: How Judicial Review is Breaking Down the Club House of Private Standardization Bodies' (2013) 50 *Common Market Law Review* 145.

[109] Case C-57/16 *Client Earth v Commission* (pending) and Case T-414/14 *Client Earth v Commission*, paras 96–7.

preparation and development of policy proposals is transparent and open, and to ensuring the objective of having interested parties participate in that process, its disclosure in the name of transparency is not totally unbridled.[110]

CONCLUSION

This last point takes us to the issue of the constitutional limits of IAs in the adjudicative process of the ECJ. This chapter has shown that it would be wrong to think that the use of IAs is unlimited when it comes to the judicial review of EU legislation. On the contrary, we find strong constitutional and institutional limitations which are related to the overarching issue of competence in EU law and the division/conferral of powers not only between the institutions inter se (an issue related to the horizontal division of powers in EU law), but also between the EU institutions and Member States (an issue related to the vertical division of powers in EU law). As to the horizontal division of power, this chapter has shown that the use of IAs is clearly limited by the principle of institutional balance. In fact, as it stems from the ECJ case law and the Interinstitutional Agreement of 13 April 2016, the Commission IAs cannot be made binding on the Parliament and the Council. As to the vertical division of power, it is apparent that the scope of evidence-based judicial review is not indefinite. Many scholars have argued for putting an end to the box-ticking approach of the ECJ, and thus extend the adjudicative scope of subsidiarity and proportionality to a more substantive review of the merits. However, we do find it extremely difficult to put into practice this suggestion without undermining the margin of discretion granted to the EU institutions in adopting legislation and the system of qualified majority voting. The IAs are creatures of the manifest test of proportionality/subsidiarity and of its light-touch judicial review. A shift from procedural review to substantive review would therefore go against the very reasons of their existence in EU law adjudication. Instead, we suggest taking the Commission's commitment to IA more seriously and hold the Commission to account with regard to this commitment, thereby starting a feedback loop where Better Regulation leads to better adjudication and vice versa.

[110] *Client Earth v Commission*, above n 109, para 93.

Part IV

Broader Perspectives on the Better Regulation Agenda

11

Eurolegalism and the Better Regulation Agenda

R DANIEL KELEMEN*

INTRODUCTION

THERE ARE FEW certainties in the increasingly tumultuous world of EU politics. But one thing you can count on is that each new Commission will launch some sort of Better Regulation initiative. As Anand Menon and I put it a decade ago in a volume on Better Regulation, 'at least since the Delors Commission's *relance* of the Single Market, policy-makers have coupled their regulatory initiatives with ceremonial self-flagellation concerning the inflexibility of EC regulation and the need to "simplify" and "improve" it'.[1] In the mid-1980s, the Delors Commission announced that its Single Market programme would shift away from the traditional total harmonisation approach and would adopt a 'new approach' to regulation, allowing for greater flexibility and national discretion. In 1996, the Santer Commission promised to 'do less in order to do it better' through its regulatory simplification initiative (SLIM).[2] In 2002, the Prodi Commission announced its 'Simplifying and Improving the Regulatory Environment' plan as a lynchpin of its efforts to enhance the competitiveness of the European economy.[3] In 2005, the Barroso Commission embraced a high-profile 'Better Regulation' initiative, promising to slash red tape and simplify EU regulation,[4] and the second Barroso Commission re-emphasised its commitment, launching the Regulatory Fitness and Performance Programme (REFIT)[5] in 2012 to review the entire

* R Daniel Kelemen is Professor of Political Science and Law, Jean Monnet Chair in European Union Politics at Rutgers University.

[1] RD Kelemen and A Menon, 'The Politics of EC Regulation' in S Weatherill (ed), *Better Regulation* (Oxford, Hart Publishing, 2007) 183. See also S Weatherill, 'The Challenge of Better Regulation' in S Weatherill (ed), *Better Regulation* (Oxford, Hart Publishing, 2007).

[2] Commission of the European Communities, 'Communication on Simpler Legislation for the Internal Market', COM (1996) 204 final, 8 May 1996.

[3] Commission of the European Communities, 'Action Plan "Simplifying and Improving the Regulatory Environment"' COM (2002) 278 final, 5 June 2002.

[4] Commission of the European Communities, 'Communication on Better Regulation for Growth and Jobs in the European Union' COM (2005) 97 final, 16 March 2005.

[5] Commission of the European Union, 'Communication from the Commission: Regulatory Fitness' COM (2012) 746 final, 12 December 2012.

body of EU legislation and to propose action to reduce unwarranted burdens, inconsistencies and ineffective measures. Most recently, the Juncker Commission in 2015 announced a new EU agenda labelled 'Better Regulation for Better Results' and a new set of Guidelines on Better Regulation.[6] More generally, the slew of initiatives over the past two decades gathered under the labels of the Open Method of Coordination (OMC) and 'new modes of governance' should be understood as part of this same impulse, in that they aim to rely on more informal, flexible approaches than traditional EU regulation.

Yet for all the time and effort that the European Commission has put into Better Regulation initiatives, their impact has been somewhere between modest and undetectable. They have not changed the prevailing style of EU regulation by simplifying it or making it more flexible. Despite a series of such initiatives, EU regulation continues to be characterised by 'Eurolegalism',[7] a mode of governance that relies on detailed rules containing strict transparency and disclosure requirements, legalistic and adversarial approaches to regulatory enforcement and dispute resolution, slow, costly legal contestation, active judicial review of administrative action, and the empowerment of private actors to enforce legal norms. Indeed, Eurolegalism has been spreading, emerging as the EU's predominant mode of governance in an ever-wider range of areas of regulatory policy over the past three decades.

Better Regulation initiatives may produce some marginal benefits, but for the most part they are destined to fail. At their core, they have two sets of objectives and they will fail on both counts. First, they will fail substantively in their efforts to render EU regulation simpler and more flexible, because these characteristics of EU regulation are deeply rooted in the project of continent-wide market integration and in the EU's fragmented institutional structure. Second, they will fail as public relations exercises. All of these initiatives are motivated by the Commission's desire to combat criticisms that the EU produces too much red tape—inflexible, onerous regulations that strangle European businesses. But Better Regulation initiatives, no matter what their substantive impacts, will never reduce criticisms of excessive red tape from Brussels. Such critiques are ultimately grounded in Eurosceptic and sometimes anti-government ideologies, and cannot be swayed even by successful reforms. Those who believe that the European economy is being strangled by red tape from Brussels cannot be appeased by promises of 'doing less, but doing it better'. On the contrary, they are likely to take such initiatives as an admission of guilt and a show of weakness, and to press ahead with their campaign against 'Brussels'.

The remainder of this chapter is divided into three section. The first section explains why Eurolegalism has remained the EU's predominant mode of regulation despite all the initiatives to promote regulatory simplification and flexibility.

[6] Commission of the European Union, 'Communication from the Commission: Better Regulation for Better Results—An EU Agenda' COM (2015) 215 final, 19 May 2015.

[7] RD Kelemen, *Eurolegalism: The Transformation of Law and Regulation in the European Union* (Cambridge, MA, Harvard University Press, 2011).

The second section evaluates Better Regulation initiatives as a public relations exercise and argues why they are likely to fail in this regard. The third section concludes.

WHY EU REGULATION IS DETAILED AND PRESCRIPTIVE

The failure of Better Regulation initiatives to change the predominant character of EU regulation should not be taken as a sign of insincerity or a lack of zeal on the part of Better Regulation advocates. Rather, the EU's penchant for Eurolegalism has resisted change, despite all manner of Better Regulation initiatives, because it is so deeply rooted in the dynamics of market integration and in the very institutional structure of the EU. Together, the EU's institutional structure and its project of integrating the European market generate political incentives and functional pressures that lead the EU to produce detailed, prescriptive regulation, often involving strict procedural requirements and transparency provisions, and to back this regulation with a judicialised approach to enforcement.

First, establishing the EU's Single Market has prompted a dynamic familiar to scholars of regulation in which establishing 'freer markets' actually requires 'more rules'.[8] In the EU context, as in other polities, deregulation and reregulation are intertwined. Economic liberalisation and deregulation at the national level associated with the drive to complete the Single Market are coupled with reregulation at the EU level. However, EU regulation differs from the national regulatory regimes it replaces. It tends to be more formal, inflexible and juridified; indeed, it has to be. When national regulators were dealing with small, sheltered national markets, they could develop trust-based relationships with the limited number of repeat market players and could rely on informal flexible modes of regulation. But as efforts to integrate the single European market open previously closed national markets to a wider diversity of players, it becomes difficult to employ such informal, flexible approaches. Indeed, traditionally informal, flexible and often opaque regulatory practices at the national level are attacked by new market entrants as barriers to entry and distortions of the Single Market. As disparate national regulatory regimes are dismantled, the EU steps in to reregulate at the EU level in order to promote modes of governance better suited to the liberalised environment. In a liberalised environment, where regulators will confront a wide variety of unfamiliar market actors (many of them foreign), law-makers must put in place more detailed, uniform and judicially enforceable forms of regulation in order to ensure a level playing field. Ironically, many Better Regulation initiatives have a 'back to the future' character, with their supposedly 'new modes of governance' aping techniques that had predominated at the national level years ago, but that had been rendered obsolete in the context of the Single Market.

[8] S Vogel, *Freer Markets, More Rules: Regulatory Reform in Advanced Industrialized Countries* (Ithaca, Cornell University Press, 1996).

Second, when EU policy-makers reregulate at the European level, they do so within the EU's fragmented institutional structure that generates political incentives for policy-makers to rely on precisely the sort of detailed, prescriptive, judicially enforceable regulation that many 'Better Regulation' initiatives rail against. Political power in the EU is fragmented both horizontally (between the Council, the Parliament, the Commission and the Court of Justice) and vertically (between EU-level institutions and Member State governments). This fragmentation encourages legislative gridlock, which makes it difficult for EU law-makers in the Council and Parliament to control the bureaucratic agents to whom they delegate authority (that is, the Commission and national administrations). At the same time, political fragmentation encourages judicial independence and the willingness of courts to enforce legal norms against bureaucratic agents who may violate them. In this institutional context, law-makers have an incentive to draft laws that specify with detailed substantive and procedural requirements just what bureaucratic agents must do and to encourage litigation to enforce these norms before European or national courts.

Likewise, the EU's limited administrative capacity also encourages this mode of prescriptive, judicialised governance. Despite all the rhetoric about bureaucracy in Brussels, the EU in fact has a small administration, with a central executive (the Commission) with a staff the size of a typical mid-sized European city, supplemented by a network of over 30 decentralised EU agencies with a few thousand staff members between them.[9] Given the EU's limited administrative capacity, EU law-makers rely primarily on national administrations to implement EU policy, but law-makers recognise that these administrations may have incentives to shirk their obligations. Therefore, EU law-makers in the Council and Parliament seek to craft detailed, judicially enforceable laws that will limit national discretion in implementation to ensure that all states fulfil their obligations. Moreover, while the EU has limited administrative capacity, it has a powerful judicial order. Therefore, law-makers have an incentive to judicialise the policy process—drafting detailed laws that specify what states must do and inviting EU and national courts to enforce these norms. This helps explain why EU law-makers so often frame policies as rights and encourage private parties to enforce them through national courts acting as the decentralised enforcers of the EU judicial order.

The inclination of law-makers in the European Parliament to draft transparent, legally enforceable directives and regulations is further enhanced by their concern over criticisms of the EU's supposed democratic deficit. To address such criticisms, they seek to ensure that laws require transparent processes of implementation and afford ample opportunities for the public to participate in regulatory processes

[9] RD Kelemen, 'European Union Agencies' in E Jones, A Menon and S Weatherill (eds), *Oxford Handbook of the European Union* (Oxford, Oxford University Press, 2012); RD Kelemen and G Majone, 'Managing Europeanization: The European Agencies' in J Peterson and M Shackleton (eds), *The Institutions of the European Union* (Oxford, Oxford University Press, 2012); J Trondal, *An Emergent European Executive Order* (Oxford, Oxford University Press, 2010).

and enforce their rights. Such procedural requirements may add to the regulatory burden, but they are the price of regulating in a large, politically fragmented democracy.

Thus, it is hardly surprising that the Commission found in its recent review of Better Regulation that 'the European Parliament and the Council have at times been hesitant to agree to measures that would reduce administrative burdens'. The Commission emphasised that the 'European Parliament and the Council should, therefore, mirror the Commission's commitment to better regulation, as should Member States when transposing and implementing EU law' and lamented the fact that they did not do so in practice.[10] On the contrary, empirical studies have repeatedly demonstrated that EU law-makers in the Parliament and Commission consistently craft legislation that has many of the attributes that 'Better Regulation' initiatives are designed to eliminate. For instance, Franchino discusses the European Parliament's 'ongoing and relentless activity of specifying policy instructions in greater detail and precision, revealing the systematic desire of the Parliament to reduce [Member State] discretion'.[11] Detailed, prescriptive and justiciable regulation provides substantive and procedural causes of action that law-makers want to put in place, so that the Commission and private litigants can turn to the EU's powerful judicial order to promote the enforcement of EU regulation. In short, the Commission's latest Better Regulation initiative is unlikely to be any more successful than its predecessors, because a tendency to adopt inflexible, detailed, action-forcing regulation backed by judicial enforcement is baked into the very DNA of the EU's institutional structure and its project of market integration.

BETTER REGULATION AS A FAILED PUBLIC RELATIONS EXERCISE

Though advocates of Better Regulation initiatives may be sincerely motivated by their belief in the need to improve the quality of EU regulation, we must recognise that all Better Regulation initiatives are at the same time public relations exercises designed to allay criticism of the EU's supposedly excessive and inflexible regulation and red tape.[12] Indeed, it would be fair to assume that is their main purpose. Evaluated as public relations exercises, previous Better Regulation initiatives have been abject failures, and the latest one is likely to be as well. The presumption behind Better Regulation initiatives, from the public relations perspective, seems to have been that if the European Commission engaged in enough public self-flagellation and recited enough *mea culpas* regarding the flaws and excesses of EU regulation, and promised to do better in the future, this would appease critics.

[10] Commission of the European Union, above n 6, 8.

[11] F Franchino, *The Powers of the Union: Delegation in the EU* (New York, Cambridge University Press, 2007) 264.

[12] T Idema and RD Kelemen, 'New Modes of Governance, the Open Method of Coordination and other Fashionable Red Herring' (2006) 7(1) *Perspectives on European Politics and Society* 108.

However, there is no evidence that these initiatives did anything to reduce criticism of EU regulation. Ironically, Better Regulation initiatives may have inadvertently done more to harm the EU's image than to mend it by implicitly validating highly misleading Eurosceptic tropes about supposedly excessive regulation by so-called 'Brussels bureaucrats'. This section first explores why Better Regulation initiatives have failed to improve the EU's image and then suggests how the EU could better target its public relations activities to improve the EU's image as a regulator.

For Eurosceptics, the idea that EU is a regulatory leviathan strangling Europe in red tape is an article of faith. Attacking unelected, 'faceless' Brussels bureaucrats for producing costly, needless regulations has been part of the Eurosceptic catechism in a number of Member States for decades. Eurosceptics have never been very discerning in their attacks on EU regulation: alongside criticising actual EU regulations, they have frequently attacked the EU for regulations that do not actually exist. Indeed, the European Commission has catalogued hundreds of these fabricated 'Euromyths',[13] ranging from imagined bans on curved cucumbers and bagpipes to a requirement that producers rename the snack 'Bombay mix' as 'Mumbai mix', to the existence of a 26,911-word regulation on cabbage, to a ban barmaids from showing cleavage. The fact that so many attacks on EU regulation are based on Euromyths, or 'fake news' as it might be referred to today, should alert us to a crucial fact: making actual EU regulation 'better' is unlikely to appease critics, since much of their opposition to EU regulation is based on myths. A related article of faith for Eurosceptics is the idea that the EU is a massive regulatory bureaucracy. The National Front's candidate for the French Presidency, Marine Le Pen, expressed the views of Eurosceptics across Europe when she said: 'Il faut en finir avec ce monstre bureaucratique.'[14] As with other Euromyths, this belief is impervious to empirical disconfirmation: the fact that the EU has a small administration will not dissuade Eurosceptics from their belief that it is a massive bureaucracy.

In short, any sober assessment of the efficacy of Better Regulation initiatives for improving the EU's public image must begin by recognising that most vocal critics of EU regulation simply cannot be appeased. Even the most effective 'Better Regulation' initiative cannot hope to win over critics for whom attacks on EU regulation form part of a Eurosceptic ideology that cannot be shaken by even the most concrete evidence that the EU is making its regulation less burdensome.

If one accepts this conclusion, it suggests that the EU should adopt a very different public relations strategy with regard to EU regulation. While the Commission should of course seek to make EU regulation 'better' (who could oppose that?), for

[13] See the European Commission's catalogue of Euromyths at http://blogs.ec.europa.eu/ECintheUK/euromyths-a-z-index. For a summary of some of the most famous Euromyths, see K Lyons, 'The 10 Best Euro Myths—From Custard Creams to Condoms' *The Guardian* (23 June 2016), https://www.theguardian.com/politics/2016/jun/23/10-best-euro-myths-from-custard-creams-to-condoms.

[14] The phrase translates as: 'We must get rid of this bureaucratic monster' (translation by the author); see 'Marine Le Pen veut "en finir" avec l'UE', *Le Figaro* (23 February 2017), http://www.lefigaro.fr/flash-actu/2017/02/23/97001-20170223FILWWW00384-marine-le-pen-veut-en-finir-avec-l-ue.php.

public relations purposes the Commission would do better to challenge Eurosceptic tropes about EU regulation and to emphasise the many benefits of EU regulation for European citizens. Also, the EU should throw the blame for failures of EU regulation back on the Member State governments, critiquing them for needlessly 'gold-plating' many EU regulations and even more importantly for their failure to implement and enforce many others effectively. In short, the EU should cease its public self-flagellation, promote a positive narrative about EU regulation to counter Euromyths and call out Member State governments for their deficient implementation of EU rules. Such an approach is likely to improve the image of the EU as a regulator far more than all the Better Regulation initiatives pursued to date.

Rather than engaging in Maoist-style self-criticism about the shortcomings of EU regulation, the Commission should celebrate and claim credit for the strengths and benefits of EU regulation. The EU should emphasise in its public pronouncements that its style of regulation—when compared to many of the opaque national regulatory regimes it supplants—enhances legal certainty, individual rights and access to justice, transparency and accountability of government.[15] To be sure, the EU has undertaken a number of initiatives in this spirit. To take just one prominent example in the field of passenger rights regulation, the EU has been aggressive in highlighting the benefits of EU regulations for individual citizens. As any air traveller in Europe will have noticed, with posters and notices on monitors in airport lobbies, the EU has worked to alert passengers of their EU passenger rights—including rights to compensation—which has been a more effective public relations exercise than all the Better Regulation initiatives put together. Such positive initiatives promise to do more to improve the image of EU regulation than any self-critical 'Better Regulation' programme ever could. The EU should press ahead with many more such initiatives. For instance, in the field of banking regulation, the EU might require every bank in Europe to display on its entry door a sign with an EU flag and a statement to the effect of: 'The European Union ensures that your deposits in this bank are insured by a deposit guarantee scheme that meets the requirements of Directive 2014/49/EU including deposit protection of at least €100,000.' Likewise, the EU might encourage employers across Europe to display in their staffrooms posters that remind workers of their EU rights, including rights to protection against discrimination under the Equal Treatment Framework Directive (2000/78/EC), health and safety protections under Directive 89/391/EC and other worker safety rules.

In addition to claiming the credit for popular regulations, the European Commission needs to be more aggressive in shifting blame for problems with EU regulation to where it rightly resides—above all, to the Member States. Thus, it was refreshing to see the Commission, in introducing its latest Better Regulation agenda (COM (2015) 215 final), plainly point out that national governments in the Council—and also the European Parliament—bear most of the blame for

[15] RD Kelemen, 'Eurolegalism and Democracy' (2012) 50(S1) *Journal of Common Market Studies* 55.

instances where EU regulation imposes unnecessary costs on businesses and public authorities. The Commission should go further, highlighting the practice of gold-plating, in which Member States go beyond the requirements of EU law, adding burdensome provisions to those required under a directive or in other ways extending its scope. The Commission might then press national governments to undertake 'Better Regulation' initiatives to reduce unnecessary 'red tape' not required by the EU.

Most importantly, however, the EU must do more to name and shame Member State governments that fail to enforce EU regulations—many of them ones that serve popular regulatory objectives. This can be done in part through various scoreboards, but it must also be done through a reinvigoration of the infringement procedure. With regard to scoreboards, there has been much talk in EU policy-making circles in recent years (for instance, with regard to the OMC) about benchmarking, the sharing of best practices and peer pressure. Yet, in practice, Member States are reluctant to publicise explicit rankings of the sort one might think were integral to such modes of governance because they do not want to name and shame their peers (and risk being named and shamed themselves).[16] The Commission should become more aggressive in this regard. The EU's regular ranking of bathing water quality at European beaches serves as a good model in this regard.[17] Every summer, EU evaluations of water quality at European beaches attracts considerable press attention, both highlighting the fact that EU regulations keep bathing water at most European beaches clean and noting which Member States have the most beaches that fall below EU standards.[18] Likewise, the EU should publish many more rankings of Member State compliance with EU regulations and achievement of EU regulatory objectives.

But rankings and shaming alone are insufficient; to do more to improve the image of EU regulation, the EU must aggressively enforce its rules (many of which actually enjoy considerable public support) against recalcitrant Member States and publicise this enforcement. While general support for the EU sank to an all-time low in the wake of the eurozone crisis, European citizens continue to support the EU, playing a leading role in many specific areas of regulation, including environmental protection, financial market regulation and immigration.[19] Indeed, EU citizens want the EU to play a much more prominent, aggressive role in some areas of regulation where national governments have prevented it from taking on

[16] Idema and Kelemen, above n 12; European Parliament 'The Lisbon Strategy 2000–2010: An Analysis and Evaluation of the Methods Used and Results Achieved' *Final Report, Directorate General for Internal Policies* IP/A/EMPL/ST/2008-07, PE 440.285 (2010) 92.

[17] See, for instance, 'European Bathing Water Quality in 2015', European Environment Agency Report No 9/2016 (2016).

[18] See, for instance, I Johnston, 'Britain's Beaches Rated the Worst in the EU for Levels of Poor Quality Bathing Water' *The Independent* (25 May 2016), http://www.independent.co.uk/environment/britains-beaches-rated-the-worst-in-eu-for-levels-of-poor-quality-bathing-water-a7048286.html.

[19] A Marziliano, 'Tolerating Europe: Integration without Identification', Dissertation, Rutgers University, 2016, on file with the university.

greater authority. For instance, recent surveys reveal that 75 per cent of Europeans want the EU to 'intervene more than at present' in regulating tax fraud, 74 per cent favour more EU intervention in migration policy and 67 per cent favour more EU intervention in environmental protection regulation, to name but a few areas.[20]

And yet, while the public continues to want the EU to intervene more in many areas of regulation, the EU has in fact been backing off in terms of enforcing its existing rules. Shockingly, since the start of the global financial crisis in 2008, the number of infringement cases brought by the Commission before the ECJ has decreased by over 72 per cent.[21] This precipitous decline is likely due to the fact that the Commission was focusing its limited resources on addressing the eurozone crisis and perhaps due to the fact that the Commission was wary of antagonising Member State governments, whose cooperation it needed to address the crisis. But whatever the cause for this decline in enforcement, the time has come to reverse it and to reinvigorate the enforcement of EU law. The European Commission should lead the charge in shifting the spotlight from the supposed excesses of EU regulation to the actual derelictions of duty by Member State governments that fail to enforce EU law—often to the great detriment of their own citizens.

In short, the EU should seek to 'flip the script' within discussions of Better Regulation, redirecting the blame from Brussels to national capitals. For decades, the EU has mostly been the victim in the blame game of EU politics: national leaders have been content to agree to policies in the Council and then to blame 'Brussels' for any costly consequences these policies might have.[22] Rather than reinforcing this narrative by criticising its own regulations—as all previous 'Better Regulation' initiatives have done—the EU should highlight the benefits of EU regulations and criticise national governments for denying these benefits to their citizens through inadequate enforcement. Brexit presents a historic opportunity for such a change in the EU's rhetoric regarding 'Better Regulation'. While critiques of excessive EU red tape have emanated from many quarters, by far the primary and loudest source of such critiques has always been the UK. The overwhelming majority of the Euromyths catalogued by the EU[23] were propagated by the UK's tabloid press. While Brexit may be a tragedy in many respects for both the UK and the EU, it will provide a welcome relief from decades of attacks on EU regulation by Britain's tabloid press. Quite simply, EU leaders should feel less compelled to respond to Euromyths propagated by the British press because as a third country, the UK will no longer have a voice in EU policy-making.

[20] European Parliament, 'Public Opinion and EU Policies: Exploring the Expectations Gap', July, PE 586.596, (2016) 19, 23, 35.

[21] M Blauberger and RD Kelemen, 'Can Courts Rescue National Democracy? Judicial Safeguards against Democratic Backsliding in the EU' (2017) 24(3) *Journal of European Public Policy* 317.

[22] On Jean-Claude Juncker's comments about this blame game, see J Rankin, '"Stop Bashing the EU" Jean-Claude Juncker tells European Leaders' *The Guardian* (1 March 2017), https://www.theguardian.com/world/2017/mar/01/stop-bashing-the-eu-jean-claude-juncker-tells-european-leaders.

[23] See above, n 13.

Brexit also presents an opportunity to change the 'Better Regulation' narrative because it will finally put the lie to British Eurosceptics' claims about EU regulation. The recent headline in *The Telegraph*, 'Cut the EU Red Tape Choking Britain after Brexit to Set the Country Free from the Shackles of Brussels',[24] reflects the promise held out by leaders of the Brexit campaign: that EU regulation was stifling the British economy and that freed from Brussels red tape, the British economy could finally thrive. As one of the leaders of the Leave campaign, former Lord Chancellor Michael Gove, (falsely) claimed: 'Outside the EU we wouldn't have all the EU regulations which cost our economy £600 million a week.'[25] Likewise, another colourful Leave leader, former London mayor Boris Johnson, spread Euromyths during the referendum campaign, such as the claim that the EU would only allow bananas to be sold in bunches of two or three,[26] and promised Brexit would be 'an opportunity for this country to get rid of some of the burdensome regulation that has accreted over the last 44 years'.[27] Of course, in reality, British voters will likely soon discover that 'freedom' from the EU's supposedly onerous regulations is no panacea and that in fact they may prefer their government not to repeal many EU regulations that protect things like environmental quality and that safeguard the rights of everyone from bank depositors to workers, consumers and the disabled.[28]

CONCLUSION

The EU has a wonderful 'product' but terrible marketing. As the Nobel Committee that awarded the EU the Peace Prize recognised, the EU has played a crucial role in bringing peace, stability and prosperity to Europe. For all its faults, the EU is clearly the most successful example of supra-national cooperation and integration in human history. Nevertheless, support for the EU amongst its citizens hit

[24] R Gordon and C Hope, 'Cut the EU Red Tape Choking Britain after Brexit to Set the Country Free from the Shackles of Brussels' *The Telegraph* (28 March 2017), http://www.telegraph.co.uk/news/2017/03/27/cut-eu-red-tape-choking-britain-brexit-set-country-free-shackles. See also 'Brexit is a Golden Chance to Throw Some EU Regulations on a Bonfire' *The Telegraph* (28 March 2017), http://www.telegraph.co.uk/opinion/2017/03/28/brexit-golden-chance-throw-eu-regulations-bonfire.

[25] A McSmith, '15 EU Laws and Regulations We Will Miss in post-Brexit Britain' *The Independent* (25 June 2016), http://www.independent.co.uk/news/uk/politics/brexit-15-eu-laws-we-will-miss-in-britain-a7103031.html.

[26] 'Reality Check: Does the EU Limit the Number of Bananas in a Bunch?' *BBC News* (17 May 2016), http://www.bbc.com/news/uk-politics-eu-referendum-36316094.

[27] S Swinford, 'Boris Johnson Backs Telegraph Campaign to Cut EU Red Tape that is Choking Britain after Brexit' *The Telegraph* (28 March 2017), http://www.telegraph.co.uk/news/2017/03/28/boris-johnson-backs-telegraph-campaign-cut-eu-red-tape-choking.

[28] McSmith, above n 25; C Thomas, 'Don't Call it Red Tape: Disabled People Will Miss EU protection When it is Gone' *The Guardian* (2 February 2017), https://www.theguardian.com/commentisfree/2017/feb/02/eu-red-tape-disabled-people-care-jobs-education; P Walker, 'Tory Voters Want Environmental Regulations Maintained after Brexit' *The Guardian* (4 April 2017), https://www.theguardian.com/politics/2017/apr/04/tory-environmental-regulations-brexit-renewable-energy.

an all-time low over the last two years in the wake of the eurozone and refugee crises,[29] and voters in one of its Member States recently chose to exit the Union. Clearly something needs to be done to improve the EU's image, to make its policies more attractive to citizens and to recapture their enthusiasm for the Union. Elsewhere, I have offered my own thoughts on a range of policies that might help achieve this.[30] EU initiatives and rhetoric in the regulatory domain constitute just one element in an overall effort to improve the EU's image. But the EU's current approach is not working. However valuable they may be on their merits, Better Regulation initiatives that focus on self-criticism and promises of reform will do little or nothing to win over public support for the EU. The EU needs to stop apologizing for its regulations. Instead, it should highlight their many benefits for European citizens, criticise Member State governments for their failure to implement them properly, and step up enforcement actions against Member States for those shortcomings.

[29] I Traynor, 'Crisis for Europe as Trust Hits Record Low' *The Guardian* (24 April 2017), https://www.theguardian.com/world/2013/apr/24/trust-eu-falls-record-low.

[30] M Matthijs and RD Kelemen, 'Europe Reborn: How to Save the European Union from Irrelevance' (2015) 94(1) *Foreign Affairs* 96.

12

An 'Impact Assessment' of EU Better Regulation

SACHA GARBEN*

INTRODUCTION

AS WILL HAVE become clear from the preceding chapters, Better Regulation is not a passing fad and is much more than an inconspicuous soft law policy initiative. Over the past few decades, it has become a semi-permanent feature of the EU legal and political landscape. It has become increasingly institutionalised by means of the creation of independent bodies such as the Regulatory Scrutiny Board, interinstitutional agreements and as an instrument of the judicial review of the Court of Justice of the European Union (CJEU). The EU legislative process is increasingly conditioned by it, through Better Regulation's requirements of *ex ante* and *ex post* evaluation, the way it structures and informs the Commission's exercise of its monopoly on legislative initiative, and in its application to the Parliament and Council in their capacity as the European Legislator. This raises an array of constitutional questions of how Better Regulation impacts on, inter alia, the 'competence principles' of conferral, subsidiarity, proportionality and national identity, the principle of legal certainty, democracy and the Rule of Law. As such, it is curious that in terms of general EU legal scholarship, Better Regulation is still somewhat overlooked[1] and seems to remain largely the purview of scholars of 'regulation'. This is regrettable, because without an understanding of Better Regulation's intricacies, one cannot fully understand the contemporary EU legislative process, and without an analysis of its position in (and impact on) the EU legal and political order, one cannot fully understand the merits and risks of Better Regulation.

* Professor of EU Law, College of Europe, Bruges, and on leave from the European Commission. The views expressed in this chapter are entirely personal and do not represent those of the European Commission. Many thanks to Susi Forderer for her valuable comments and editorial assistance.

[1] There are, of course, notable exceptions, such as (non-exhaustively) M Dawson, 'Better Regulation and the Future of EU Regulatory Law and Politics' (2016) 53 *Common Market Law Review* 1209; the various contributions in the special issue on Better Regulation in (2011) 17 *European Public Law*; and S Weatherill, *Better Regulation* (Oxford, Hart Publishing, 2007).

Together with the other contributions to this book, this chapter hopes to provide some meaningful input into this research area. In particular, it aims to provide an improved conceptual understanding of the various aims underlying EU Better Regulation. It will become clear that while Better Regulation may be seeking to address certain important problems in EU decision-making, it operates on the basis of several unproven assumptions, it does not effectively deliver on many of its objectives because of its inherent limitations or because it has ignored better alternatives, and that while it may have certain benefits, its significant costs are often overlooked. In terms of its more general impact on the EU constitutional order, it will be argued that by displacing the EU legislative process at least to a certain extent, the EU Better Regulation Agenda as it currently stands carries the risk of aggravating two of the central legitimacy problems of the EU, namely the regulatory asymmetry that underlies European integration[2] and 'covert integration' or 'harmonisation by stealth'.[3] As such, this chapter subjects Better Regulation itself to a critical 'Impact Assessment'[4] by considering whether there is a clear definition of the problems it seeks to address and what the evidence is for the existence of these problems, whether Better Regulation more effectively responds to those problems than any alternative options, and what the costs, benefits and broader impacts are.

DEFINITION OF THE PROBLEM(S)

A general starting point in the analytical framework of Impact Assessments and evaluations is the clear definition of the problem(s) that the proposed or existing EU action aims to address. What is/are the problem(s) that EU Better Regulation seeks to solve? The EU Better Regulation Agenda itself does not contain a rigorous analysis of the problems and the underlying factors and behaviours (so-called 'problem drivers'). This leaves us to deduce Better Regulation's problem definitions from the Agenda's various aspects and manifestations. It must have already become clear to the reader of this book that the Agenda is highly multi-faceted and

[2] Building on the work of Fritz Scharpf, such as 'The Asymmetry of European Integration, or Why the EU Cannot be a "Social Market Economy"' (2010) 8 *Socio-Economic Review* 211; 'De-constitutionalisation and Majority Rules: A Democratic Vision for Europe' in S Garben and I Govaere (eds), *The Division of Competences in the EU Legal Order: Reflections on the Past, the Present and the Future* (Oxford, Hart Publishing, 2017); and 'After the Crash: A Perspective on Multilevel European Democracy' (2015) 21(3) *European Law Journal* 384, 389.

[3] See also S Garben, 'Restating the Problem of Competence Creep, Tackling Harmonization by Stealth and Reinstating the Legislator' in Garben and Govaere, above n 2; S Garben, 'Competence Creep Revisited' *Journal of Common Market Studies* (forthcoming, 2018).

[4] According to the Impact Assessment Guidelines: 'IAs must set out the logical reasoning that links the problem (including subsidiarity issues), its underlying drivers, the objectives and a range of policy options to tackle the problem. They must present the likely impacts of the options, who will be affected by them and how.' See http://ec.europa.eu/smart-regulation/guidelines/ug_chap3_en.htm.

complex, and seems to pursue a range of objectives that are loosely collected in the mixed bag of 'Better Regulation'. From this, we can distill at least five different assumed problem definitions.

Poor Legislative Quality

A first objective of EU Better Regulation is the improvement of the quality of EU legislation, as was discussed by Helen Xanthaki in Chapter 3. The Interinstitutional Agreement on Better Law-Making of 2016 states under 'common commitments and objectives' that the Institutions 'agree to promote simplicity, clarity and consistency in the drafting of Union legislation'. According to the Interinstitutional Style Guide 2015,[5] EU acts must be clear, simple, precise, concise and with homogeneous content. They must be formulated appropriately for their intended audience, terminology must be consistent, the title of the act must give a full indication of the subject matter and the legal basis, and the main objectives must be clearly identified. It is hard to object to these stipulations. Clear, accessible and enforceable rules are central requirements of the Rule of Law. But, unfortunately, as anyone who has ever handled EU legislation will probably confirm, the quality of EU legislation in this sense often leaves something to be desired, which thus clearly poses a problem.

A first often-encountered problem is that of contradictory provisions in, and between different pieces of, EU legislation. As an example, we could mention the Temporary Agency Work Directive 2008/104/EC, which in most of its provisions provides protection for temporary agency workers against this precarious form of employment. As such, it is a labour law directive, adopted on the basis of Article 153 of the Treaty on the Functioning of the European Union (TFEU), which sets minimum standards of protection for workers across the Member States. But at the same time, the Directive contains in its Article 4 a rather ambiguous provision that encourages the use of this precarious form of employment and seems to impose a ceiling of protection that Member States can provide for temporary agency workers ('prohibitions or restrictions on the use of temporary agency work shall be justified only on grounds of general interest relating in particular to the protection of temporary agency workers, the requirements of health and safety at work or the need to ensure that the labour market functions properly and abuses are prevented'), which if interpreted literally would not only be inconsistent with the Directive overall but also with its legal basis. The CJEU has resolved this contradiction in its *AKT* judgment by denying Article 4 its direct effect.[6] However, while

[5] http://publications.europa.eu/code/en/en-000500.htm.

[6] Case C-533/13 *Auto- ja Kuljetusalan Työntekijäliitto AKT ry v Öljytuote ry and Shell Aviation Finland Oy* ECLI:EU:C:2015:173.

consistent with the Directive's legal basis and overall objectives, this interpretation is not clear from the provision's wording. This means that legally, the problem is resolved, but one needs to consult the law as well as the case law to know what the meaning of the law really is.

A second persistent problem is that EU legislation often contains undefined crucial notions and concepts. As these notions may determine the very nature of the right or obligation in question, such legal uncertainty is highly undesirable for everyone concerned. For instance, in Regulation 261/2004 concerning air passenger rights, no definition is given as to what constitutes 'delays' and what constitutes 'cancellations', which matters because for the latter, monetary compensation is provided (in Article 7), while for the former, it is not. Nor does the Regulation contain any precise description as to what 'extraordinary circumstances' are, even though this absolves the airlines of having to pay any compensation at all. Again, it has fallen to the CJEU to give the necessary clarifications, but this means that individuals and companies need to consult both the case law as well as the law to know what their rights and obligations are.[7] Furthermore, because judgments are by their nature situation-specific, it is difficult to obtain any firm guidance on how the rules are supposed to apply in slightly different circumstances. This necessitates further litigation and results in a dense body of case law, making the legal situation even more unclear and complex.

Another often-encountered problem with EU legislation is that it can consist of a complex mix of general rules accompanied by long lists of exceptions, exceptions to exceptions, and further exceptions thereto. For instance, Article 5 of the Working Time Directive 2003/88/EC provides that all workers have the right to a minimum weekly rest period of 24 consecutive hours per seven days. Article 16 provides a derogation to this, in that Member States may provide a reference period of 14 days to calculate whether on average 24 hours rest was given per seven-day period. Article 17 in turn provides a derogation to the limit of this exception, allowing a longer reference period, for activities where continuity of service is required. In Article 19, a limit to that derogation to the limit of the original derogation to the initial rule is provided, stipulating that the reference period shall not exceed six months. The following paragraph of that same article provides an exception to its own first paragraph allowing Member States to lay down a reference period of up to 12 months.

A final problem, which does not relate so much to the quality of drafting as to the enforceability of the text as well as its overall coherence, thus impacting on legal certainty and uniform application of the law, is that much of EU law depends on the national level for its enforcement. In line with the principle of national procedural autonomy, Member States are primarily responsible for making EU rights

[7] See Joined Cases C-402/07 and C-432/07 *Christopher Sturgeon, Gabriel Sturgeon and Alana Sturgeon v Condor Flugdienst GmbH and Stefan Böck and Cornelia Lepuschitz v Air France SA* ECLI:EU:C:2009:716; and Case C-549/07 *Friederike Wallentin-Hermann v Alitalia—Linee Aeree Italiane SpA* ECLI:EU:C:2008:771.

a reality for citizens, and the conditions will vary from Member State to Member State, making it easier or more difficult to procure rights from one country to the next. Even if we are seeing an increasing tendency to establish specific enforcement mechanisms at the EU level for this reason, the majority of the rules still at least partially depend on Member State enforcement within the specificities of national systems of remedies and judicial protection. These national variations are even more pronounced when the EU rules in question are laid down in the form of directives or Framework Directives, which are specifically intended to leave as much scope for the national level as possible in terms of implementation.

So, there are indeed some important problems with EU legislation, particularly from a perspective of the requirements of the Rule of Law. Apart from being problematic in itself, this also creates the conditions for 'judicial activism', as the CJEU has to mediate the contradictions, fill in the lacunae, and is thus invited to provide its own definitions and their interpretation, which can quickly lead to (accusations of) judicial legislation and thereby poses its own problems from a constitutional and democratic perspective.

(Perceived) Over-regulation

Second, corresponding to the 'roots' of Better Regulation in the Thatcher and Reagan era as explained by Colin Scott in Chapter 2, the Better Regulation Agenda is informed by a concern about the quantity of legislation and its impact on businesses, economic growth and competitiveness. Admittedly, this particular aspect of Better Regulation was more pronounced under the Barrosso Presidency, and the current Commission has stressed that the Agenda is not about more or less regulation, but about better regulation.[8] Nevertheless, this objective can still be detected in various aspects of how the Agenda continues to operate.[9] This approach does not disqualify regulation as such and instead conditions it on being limited to what is 'necessary' and 'proportionate', but this still generates a certain deregulatory impulse. It implicitly adheres to an economically liberal analytical framework that considers 'no regulation/state intervention' to be the most desirable default situation and that demands high levels of justification for any change in that situation through the adoption of binding rules, usually limited to situations where 'the market' cannot provide the public goods in question. It has a tendency to conceptualise rules as 'burdens' that are assumed to be harmful for the creation, functioning and growth of businesses and, as such, the economy at large, and that therefore constantly need to be suspiciously scrutinised and justified. At the same time, this

[8] European Commission Communication, 'Better Regulation for Better Results: An EU Agenda' COM (2015) 215 final; European Commission Staff Working Document of 19 May 2015, 'Better Regulation Guidelines' SWD (2015) 111 final.

[9] See to this effect Dawson, above n 1.

partisan approach is bolstered by a more general, cross-spectrum concern about the EU's 'bureaucracy' and its perceived EU over-regulation: some figures show that 74 per cent of Europeans believe that the EU generates too much red tape.[10]

The difficulty with this particular problem definition is that it does not clearly distinguish between objective and subjective considerations, and between different underlying concerns with rules and 'over-regulation' that are lumped together in the problem definition and its current solution, but that may actually merit very different responses. Is the problem that, objectively speaking, there is too much (unnecessary) regulation? And is this negatively affecting Europe's economy? Who has determined this and on what basis? Or is the problem that there is a *perception* of over-regulation with European citizens and businesses? In that latter case, the question remains what precisely citizens and businesses would consider to be such 'red tape', and how this consideration is different from some people/businesses simply disagreeing with certain rules because it inconveniences them somehow, as is bound to happen in any system of government. The EU Better Regulation Agenda does not appear to make these nuanced distinctions, but instead hurls one and the same stone at the issue, hoping it will kill all birds at once. On the one hand, EU Better Regulation is, as R Daniel Kelemen discusses in Chapter 11, a public relations exercise. At the same time, it presents itself as an objective, fact- and evidence-based assessment that aims to fairly determine what rules are necessary and what rules are not, in order to address or prevent over-regulation.

While the public relations problems of the EU can be objectively established, the evidence supporting Better Regulation's implicit assumption that there is indeed a problem of (a tendency to produce) over-regulation in the EU system, and thus a need to assess every piece of legislation to try and prevent or address this, is less evident. The 2013 'Top 10' exercise,[11] in which small and medium-sized enterprises (SMEs) could identify the pieces of EU legislation that they found most 'burdensome' (or simply undesirable?) cannot be considered an example of the objective, evidence-based policy-making that Better Regulation itself tries to promote, and instead qualifies as evidence for 'perceived' over-regulation at best. One could argue that Better Regulation *itself* is about objectively establishing whether or not there is indeed a problem of over-regulation in the EU, through its Impact Assessments and evaluations that determine what rules are justified and what (parts) constitute(s) unnecessary red tape. But there is an element of path-dependency and self-fulfilling prophecy in such an undertaking: when an initiative of this scale is mounted to look for something, it is of course bound to find it. It would be highly unlikely that, after spending enormous administrative and financial resources on organising hundreds of evaluations and assessments, the

[10] Eurobarometer Question QA 16.4 on p 59: http://ec.europa.eu/commfrontoffice/publicopinion/archives/eb/eb79/eb79_anx_en.pdf.

[11] COM (2013) 446, 18 June 2013.

conclusion would be that they simply proved that there was not a single instance of potential over-regulation and that therefore nothing was amended, repealed or withdrawn. And, furthermore, one could question how objective Better Regulation's assessments are from a methodological perspective. Cost-benefit analysis is one of the dominant elements of EU Better Regulation and, as Andrea Renda explored in Chapter 4, this carries a risk of bias through a range of its assumptions and because of its over-reliance on quantification. Furthermore, subsidiarity is operationalised in Impact Assessment in a default preference for 'non-regulatory alternatives', and the REFIT exercise has evaluated the *acquis* with the explicit aim to consider the repeal or amendment of regulation considered too burdensome for businesses.[12] This leaves the distinct impression that this second aim is not based on evidence of a real problem, but on evidence on perceptions of a problem and on political choices.[13]

Indeed, the narrative of an over-regulating EU stands in stark contrast to competing accounts of the EU's regulatory asymmetry, said to lead to an overall deregulatory bias in European integration.[14] The EU's capacity to deregulate national standards, as also argued by Kelemen, is very strong. The EU has liberalised a range of sectors and integrates national legal systems directly through the free movement provisions and more indirectly through regulatory competition, as well as more recently through economic policy coordination. The CJEU's case law, which has constitutionalised the free movement provisions and has defined 'restrictions' to these freedoms exceedingly widely, plays a crucial role in this dynamic.[15] Striking down national standards that do not pass the strict proportionality test significantly limits Member States' regulatory powers (negative integration). The EU in turn does not possess equal capacities to reregulate by setting European standards (positive integration). It can lack the competence to directly reregulate the issue, meaning that it has to rely on the internal market legal bases, which may not fully cover the issue and/or lead to an economic bias by demanding that the measure serves the functioning of the internal market.[16] The EU legislator is subject to high consensus requirements that it has to fulfil

[12] Dawson, above n 1, 1225.

[13] The fact that this aspect of Better Regulation would be a political choice of course in itself does not make it illegitimate. As also discussed in ch 1 to this book, especially since the use of *Spitzenkandidaten* in European elections, it could be argued that the European Commission has stronger political legitimacy, and then so would a deliberate policy choice such as the Better Regulation Agenda—at least to the extent that the Commission applies it to its own activities. However, as Mark Dawson discusses, EU Better Regulation does not clearly present itself as such: as a political commitment to reduce EU regulation in the interest of economic actors. Instead, it tends to present itself as the evidence-based, politically neutral policy that it itself purports to promote. See Dawson, above n 1.

[14] Most authoritatively advocated by Scharpf, above n 2.

[15] See S Garben, 'The Constitutional (Im)Balance between "the Market" and "the Social" in the European Union' (2017) 13 *European Constitutional Law Review* 23.

[16] See G Davies, 'Democracy and Legitimacy in the Shadow of Purposive Competence' (2015) 21 *European Law Journal* 2.

in the context of a very diverse EU28, with national parliaments posing an additional hurdle. The effect of the case law on the bargaining conditions in the Council which favour the status quo makes it difficult for the legislator to deviate from that case law in practical terms.[17] Moreover, a fundamental deviation is also difficult in legal terms, as the Court's interpretations of the internal market provisions are of constitutional nature. The legislative process is powerless in that case to alter the interpretation given by the CJEU; only a Treaty revision would suffice. This imbalance results in a regulatory gap, potentially eroding regulatory standards across Europe. Whether or not one accepts this account of European integration, it is clear that there is sufficient ground to challenge the implicit assumptions of EU Better Regulation concerning an over-regulating EU and that the Agenda would therefore need to be more convincingly justified in light of these counter-arguments.

Lack of Democratic Legitimacy

The EU is often said to suffer from a democratic deficit. This debate comprises a wide range of observations and claims.[18] A first group is mainly concerned about a decrease in representative democracy, or 'input legitimacy', in that EU governance displaces the national legislative process. The European Institutions are seen as less democratically legitimate than their national 'equivalents' and, as such, whenever the EU legislates (or more generally acts) instead of the national level, this implies a loss of democratic control. A second group of claims about the EU's democratic deficit focuses on output legitimacy, positing that perhaps because of the preceding problems with input legitimacy, EU rules and policies are not in accordance with the preferences of the (majority of) European citizens. A third group is instead about participatory or deliberative democracy,[19] and about what Schmidt has called 'throughput legitimacy', consisting of 'governance processes with the people, analyzed in terms of their efficacy, accountability, transparency, inclusiveness and openness to interest consultation'.[20] It is tied to the need for 'reflexive governance' as set out in further detail by Colin Scott in Chapter 2, which 'involves engagement with those affected by a regime, sometimes targeted at collecting the views of those affected, and sometimes oriented towards a more

[17] See to this effect Scharpf, above n 2.

[18] See for a comprehensive discussion A Føllesdal and S Hix, 'Why There is a Democratic Deficit in the EU: A Response to Majone and Moravcsik' (2006) 44 *Journal of Common Market Studies* 533.

[19] P Magnette, 'European Governance and Civic Participation: Beyond Elitist Citizenship?' (2003) 51 *Political Studies*; B Kohler-Koch, 'Post-Maastricht Civil Society and Participatory Democracy' (2012) 34(7) *Journal of European Integration* 809.

[20] V Schmidt, 'Democracy and Legitimacy in the European Union Revisited: Input, Output and "Throughput"' (2013) 61 *Political Studies* 2.

radical ambition to engage participants in thinking not only about solutions to pre-defined problems but also about the nature of the problems faced'.[21]

EU Better Regulation 'sets out to ensure that decision-making is open and transparent and that citizens and stakeholders can contribute throughout the policy and law-making process'.[22] As such, it can be considered a commitment to participatory, deliberative democracy, 'throughput legitimacy' and reflexive governance, thus apparently assuming that there is currently a lack thereof in EU decision-making. Indeed, scholars seem generally to be in agreement that there is a problem.[23] The complexity of the legislative process and the use of informal trilogues[24] are identified as important challenges, as well as 'lobbying' or skewed interest-representation.[25] The latter concern is explicitly recognised by the EU Better Regulation Guidelines, stating that the Commission has a duty to promote in its policy proposals the general public interest of the EU as opposed to special interests of particular Member States or groups of society.[26] However, it should also be noted that these problems are perhaps more persistent in some areas than in others. For instance, in the area of social law and policy, the Social Title of the TFEU provides important possibilities for self-regulation by the European Social Partners[27] and for the structured involvement (in so-called two-phase consultations) of these key stakeholders in the legislative process. As such, there is already a strong guarantee of participatory and reflexive governance in that area, meaning that the implicit problem definition of Better Regulation is unsubstantiated and unconvincing in this respect. In several other policy areas, however, this concern would seem to be a legitimate one.

[21] C Brown and C Scott, 'Regulation, Public Law and Better Regulation' (2011) 17 *European Public Law* 467, 476–77.

[22] https://ec.europa.eu/info/law/law-making-process/better-regulation-why-and-how_en#objectives.

[23] Although some influential scholars such as A Moravcsik have presented counter-arguments, pointing out that EU policy-making process is now more transparent than most domestic systems of government, that transparency and access to documents rules have made it far easier for citizens to obtain information about EU policy-making, and that the European Parliament and national parliaments have increased scrutiny powers, including as regards the latter through the Early Warning System. See A Moravcsik, 'In Defence of the "Democratic Deficit": Reassessing the Legitimacy of the European Union' (2002) 40 *Journal of Common Market Studies* 603.

[24] See, eg, C Lord, 'The Democratic Legitimacy of Codecision' (2013) 20 *Journal of European Public Policy* 1056, 1063; K Huber and M Shackleton, 'Codecision: A Practitioner's View from Inside the Parliament' (2013) 20 *Journal of European Public Policy* 1040; C Burns, 'Consensus and Compromise Become Ordinary—But at What Cost?' (2013) 20 *Journal of European Public Policy* 988.

[25] See, eg, S Saurugger, 'Interest Groups and Democracy in the European Union' (2008) 31 *West European Politics* 1274; W Streeck and P Schmitter, 'From National Corporatism to Transnational Pluralism: Organized Interests in the Single European Market' (1991) 19 *Politics and Society* 133.

[26] European Commission Staff Working Document, 'Better Regulation Guidelines', above n 8, 74.

[27] Article 155 TFEU provides: '1. Should management and labour so desire, the dialogue between them at Union level may lead to contractual relations, including agreements. 2. Agreements concluded at Union level shall be implemented either in accordance with the procedures and practices specific to management and labour and the Member States or, in matters covered by Article 153, at the joint request of the signatory parties, by a Council decision on a proposal from the Commission. The European Parliament shall be informed.'

Insufficient Respect for Subsidiarity and Proportionality

Furthermore, EU Better Regulation aims to enforce the principle of subsidiarity. The implicit problem definition is that the EU does not sufficiently respect this principle in its decision-making, which is indeed an often-heard accusation. As this principle first and foremost relates to the vertical division of competences between the EU and the Member States, it expresses a 'Federal' concern about over-centralisation and a lack of respect for the powers, and identities of the constituent jurisdictions. As such, it is closely related to the discussion on 'competence creep', following which it is argued that regardless of the principle of conferral, the EU encroaches on areas of national autonomy through an (overly) expansive interpretation and use of its powers.[28] The principle of subsidiarity was introduced in the Maastricht Treaty as a way to address these concerns, but has itself triggered criticism for being ineffective and insufficiently adhered to.[29] As a primarily political principle, it is difficult for the CJEU to rigorously apply, all the more because the legal bases in the Treaties are often formulated in a way that if their requirements are complied with (eg, contributing to the functioning of the internal market in the sense of Article 114 TFEU), it will be difficult to posit that the Member States are better placed to do this. As such, it is perhaps not surprising that the CJEU has yet to strike down an EU act for breach of subsidiarity. The political control of subsidiarity by national parliaments through the Early Warning System introduced by the Lisbon Treaty has arguably been more successful in this respect, with three 'yellow cards' issued to date.[30] Still, some national governments have felt the need to conduct 'balance of competences'[31] reviews or 'subsidiarity exercises',[32] and a problem with 'competence creep' indeed remains. Regardless of the Lisbon Treaty's stipulations of national autonomy, conferral, and classification of competences, it remains possible for the EU to act in virtually any policy area, on the basis of its broad, functional and non-legislative powers.[33]

The principle of proportionality is a well-established general principle of EU law, which is applied 'against' the Member States (most notably in the context

[28] For discussion, see the various contributions in Garben and Govaere, above n 3.

[29] See G Davies, 'Subsidiarity, the Wrong Idea, in the Wrong Place, at the Wrong Time' (2006) 43 *Common Market Law Review* 63.

[30] For the so-called Monti II initiative on the right to strike and the internal market freedoms, for the European Public Prosecutor's initiative and for the proposal to revise the Posting of Workers Directive.

[31] The UK, before the referendum on the EU. See V Miller, 'Repatriating EU Powers to Member States' (2011) Standard Note SN/IA/6153, House of Commons Library.

[32] The Netherlands. See the letter of (then) Minister of Foreign Affairs Frans Timmermans to the Dutch Tweede Kamer, and the accompanying document, identifying a range of specific EU measures that are considered at odds with subsidiarity: https://www.rijksoverheid.nl/documenten/kamerstukken/2013/06/21/kamerbrief-inzake-uitkomsten-subsidiariteitsexercitie.

[33] Garben, 'Restating the Problem of Competence Creep', above n 3; Garben, 'Competence Creep Revisited', above n 3.

of the free movement provisions, when Member States seek to justify national restrictions by reference to the general public interest) as well as the EU Institutions. While the CJEU, in its enforcement of proportionality, is noticeably stricter towards the national legislator compared to the European level, it has nevertheless on occasion also struck down EU legislation for a breach of proportionality.[34] In addition to such judicial review, the proportionality principle is also policed alongside the subsidiarity principle by national parliaments through the Early Warning System. A concern for proportionality is omnipresent in the Better Regulation Agenda. In many ways, Impact Assessments and evaluations could be conceptualised as overall proportionality tests of EU legislation. Apparently, therefore, EU Better Regulation implicitly assumes that there is a fundamental problem with the respect for the proportionality principle in the EU. However, it is not clear what the factual basis for that assumption would be. It would seem to be linked to the discussion on EU 'over-regulation', for which we have already established that there is little objective evidence above. While the implicit problem assumption as regards lack of respect for the subsidiarity principle can thus be accepted, as regards proportionality it cannot.

Lack of Evidence-Based Policy-Making

As Ben Smulders and Jean-Eric Paquet have argued in Chapter 6:

> [A]n 'ethical' necessity for evidence-based policy-making [was] at the root of Better Regulation in 2002 which is still relevant in today's world—arguably even more so. Take, for example, the worrying questioning of agreed basic science on climate change and the lexicon of 'alternative facts' in the US.
>
> Better regulation provides a framework to deliver evidence-based policy-making—providing relevant information to those who take political decisions.

Indeed, EU Better Regulation places emphasis on (preferably quantifiable) proof for postulated problems and to what extent the proposed or existing policy will address these. Impact Assessments and evaluations aim to provide a rational analytical framework for policy-making, in order to limit political discretion and to provide the decision-makers with a structured assessment to help them make informed decisions. Thus, an implicit problem definition of Better Regulation appears to be that left to its own devices (ie, without a Better Regulation Agenda), the EU legislative and decision-making process would be prone to regulate in an unscientific or irrational manner, responding to imaginary problems or opting for

[34] eg, Joined Cases C-293/12 and C-594/12 *Digital Rights Ireland Ltd v Minister for Communications, Marine and Natural Resources and Others and Kärntner Landesregierung and Others* ECLI:EU:C:2014:238 concerning the data retention directive.

costly solutions instead of more effective and efficient alternatives, and ignoring certain important issues that actually need regulation.

Whether Better Regulation as it currently operates indeed guarantees evidence-based governance in this sense will be discussed below. At this stage, it may be pointed out that this very problem definition in itself seems to warrant some further evidence. What are the examples of unscientific law-making that Better Regulation is supposed to filter out? The hairdresser's collective agreement, a high-profile withdrawal of 'bad regulation' in the context of the Better Regulation Agenda,[35] can be fully defended on the basis of scientific evidence concerning the health and safety risks of workers in the sector. The olive oil regulation that the media widely cited as an example of the EU's rule-sickness[36] and that was hastily withdrawn in response to the media controversy could probably similarly be defended on evidence-based grounds of consumer protection (referring to the high incidence of fraud in olive oil serving) and public health (referring to the high incidence of expired oils served in restaurants in unlabelled containers). As Alberto Alemanno has pointed out,[37] no Impact Assessment had been conducted for this proposal, so it is difficult to establish whether it would have made a difference. But it seems likely that if data would indeed have proven the above consumer and health risks, the proposal would have passed the Impact Assessment and would have been tabled all the same, and would have encountered the identical level of media outcry in certain Member States. It is doubtful that being able to cite exact percentages about health risks and frauds would have appeased these reactions. It is equally doubtful that because of that hypothetical Impact Assessment, the Commission in that case would have decided to maintain the proposal.

Indeed, a more recent example also shows how evidence-based policy does nothing to dispel fact-free claims about over-regulation: the EU's alleged ban on Belgian *frites*. The issue is with acrylamide, a chemical that naturally forms in

[35] This Agreement, aimed at improving the health and safety of workers in the hairdressing sector concluded by workers and employers, was publicly denounced by the European Commission as an example of bad regulation and was not put forward to the Council. See '"REFIT—Fit for Growth": Examples How EU Law is Becoming Lighter, Simpler and Cheaper', http://europa.eu/rapid/press-release_MEMO-13-833_en.htm. As Schindler notes, former Commission President Barroso polemically declared in a TV interview that Europe does need to regulate hairdressers' 'high heels', even though the agreement primarily concerns the use of chemicals in the sector where workers are most at risk of work related skin disease. Interview by D Krause, *Tagesschau* (2 October 2013), https://www.tagesschau.de/ausland/interview130.html, as reported by S Schindler, 'The Social Chimera of the Economic and Monetary Union: Social Policy in the Context of European Economic Governance' (2014) *LUP Student Papers*, available at https://lup.lub.lu.se/student-papers/search/publication/4460811.

[36] See, eg, J Ramsden, 'Dishes of Olive Oil to Be Banned from Restaurants? The EU's Gone Mad' *The Guardian* (22 May 2013), https://www.theguardian.com/lifeandstyle/wordofmouth/2013/may/22/dishes-olive-oil-banned-restaurants-eu.

[37] A Alemanno, 'Stop Bashing the EU with Olive Oil' *EUtopia Law* (30 May 2013), https://eutopialaw.com/2013/05/30/stop-bashing-the-eu-with-olive-oil/.

starchy food products during high-temperature cooking, including frying, baking, roasting at +120°C and low moisture. Acrylamide is found in products such as potato crisps, fries, bread, biscuits and coffee. It was first detected in foods in April 2002, although it is likely that it has been present in food since cooking began. Acrylamide is furthermore present in tobacco smoke. On 4 June 2015, the European Food Safety Authority published its first full risk assessment of acrylamide in food. Experts reconfirmed previous evaluations that acrylamide in food potentially increases the risk of developing cancer for consumers in all age groups.[38] As a result, the Commission has proposed a new draft Regulation,[39] updating its existing measures in this area, suggesting, inter alia, that fries are cooked first before being fried. It is a highly politicised issue, with food activists arguing for stricter standards and the industry and some national governments (like Belgium) opposing any further binding or non-binding EU actions. Despite the scientific evidence, several media outlets have derided this proposal as another incident of ludicrous EU over-reach.[40]

These examples do not prove that there is a structural problem with the evidence base of EU regulation, but rather that such evidence does nothing to dispel accusations of over-regulation and that such 'technical' proposals are perhaps particularly prone to misrepresentation in the media. In fact, the problem (if any) with the initiatives that have met with most 'bad regulation' accusations instead seems to be that they were (presented as) *too* scientific and were not politically savvy. Indeed, Better Regulation's implicit critique that EU decision-making would not be sufficiently evidence-based does not sit well with the many accounts over the years qualifying the EU as a 'regulatory state' very much characterised by science-driven governance, which allegedly serves to alleviate claims about its democratic deficit, since the merit of a regulatory approach is to insulate certain areas of decision-making from politics and instead to deliver sound output legitimacy in the form of evidence-based policy.[41] To the extent that Better Regulation aims to guarantee evidence-based policy, it therefore seems to operate on the basis of a faulty, unproven problem definition.

[38] EFSA, 'Scientific Opinion on Acrylamide in Food' (2015) 13 *EFSA Journal* 4104.

[39] Proposal for a Commission regulation establishing mitigation measures and benchmark levels for the reduction of the presence of acrylamide in food, Ares (2017)2895100.

[40] See, eg, D Boffey, 'Chips are Down for Belgian Frites as EU Acts on "Unsafe Compound"' *The Guardian* (20 June 2017), https://www.theguardian.com/world/2017/jun/20/chips-are-down-for-belgian-frites-as-eu-acts-on-chemical.

[41] M Everson and G Majone, 'Institutional Reform: Independent Agencies, Oversight, Coordination and Procedural Control' in O de Schutter et al, *Governance in the European Union* (Brussels, Office for Official Publications of the European Communities, 2001).

THE EFFECTIVENESS OF BETTER REGULATION IN SOLVING THE IDENTIFIED PROBLEM(S) COMPARED TO ALTERNATIVE POLICY OPTIONS

The second analytical step in our evaluation of Better Regulation is to consider to what extent it actually helps to address the problems that have been identified as underlying objectives of the Agenda, and whether it is likely to be more effective and efficient than alternative policy options (which include 'no action').

Improving Legislative Quality

It is impossible to exhaustively regulate the future, and legislation is almost invariably the product of negotiations and political comprise, so the problems of legislative quality set out previously can be expected to present themselves in all legal systems. However, they do tend to be more pronounced in the EU, due to a variety of causes that are all, ultimately, linked to its multi-lingual and multicultural nature. As R Daniel Kelemen explained in Chapter 11, the EU's diversity implies relatively low levels of inter-Member State trust and thereby increases the need for a legalistic approach, where agreements are laid down in a clear, binding and enforceable way. He has called this 'Eurolegalism',[42] a mode of governance that relies on detailed rules containing strict transparency and disclosure requirements, legalistic and adversarial approaches to regulatory enforcement and dispute resolution, slow, costly legal contestation, active judicial review of administrative action, and the empowerment of private actors to enforce legal norms. In principle, Eurolegalism should be conducive to 'quality legislation', as it demands clear, precise, coherent and enforceable rules. However, the same linguistic/cultural diversity and plurality of legal systems that pushes juridification as posited by Kelemen also makes it more difficult to reach the common understandings and unequivocal agreements that are necessary for this type of governance to function correctly. Furthermore, diversity combined with the high consensus requirements of the EU legislative process (in themselves the consequence of low inter-Member State trust) leads to compromises—the nemesis of quality legislative drafting—and makes it difficult to amend/update/repeal legislation as discussed by Robert Zbíral in Chapter 5, thus 'locking in' potentially low-quality rules. Finally, this diversity warrants respect for subsidiarity and national (procedural) autonomy, arguing for framework rules and directives, and to leave as many details of implementation up to the Member States, which does not work in favour of a coherent, comprehensive and enforceable legal act.

The slightly disconcerting upshot is that because of the EU's diversity, we tend to end up with a need for more law, but which is likely to be of low quality.

[42] RD Kelemen, *Eurolegalism: The Transformation of Law and Regulation in the European Union* (Cambridge, MA, Harvard University Press, 2011).

Even more disheartening is the realisation that since diversity as the root cause of the problem—the 'problem driver' to use Better Regulation language—cannot realistically be resolved, Better Regulation is fighting an unwinnable battle, at least to the extent that it aims to drastically improve the quality of EU legislation rather than tinker at the margins. While the directions contained in the style guides amount to more than mere cosmetics, and Impact Assessments may provide some analytical structure to the legislative initiative which could ultimately translate in more coherent legislation, the fact remains that ultimately the adoption of legislation remains a political, democratic exercise, which will therefore inevitably result in ambiguities and contradictions, especially in the EU's pluralistic context. In the above-mentioned example of the Temporary Agency Work Directive, which was the hard-fought result of two decades of debate and negotiations,[43] Article 4 was the necessary concession to the political right to make its adoption possible. Similarly, in the example of the Passenger Rights Regulation, the decision to not provide compensation in cases of delay, although difficult to justify in light of equal treatment since the inconvenience suffered could be equal to that in cases of cancellations, was a deliberate political strategy of the Commission as a compromise towards the industry that strongly opposed the measure.[44] And the various derogations and exceptions of the Working Time Directive are clearly the result of compromises and negotiations between Member States, employers, trade unions and the EU. Non-derogatable rules would have been easier to apply, but are considered too rigid. However, too wide derogations would have been considered to undermine the goals of the Directive. The result is a complex system that works substantively to accommodate most concerns, except those of legal clarity. No style guide or Impact Assessment could realistically bring about much improvement in these cases.

These concerns apply with most force to the ordinary co-legislative process. What about other types of regulation—for instance, implementing or delegated measures—which are often more technical and less political in nature? On the one hand, political compromises may play a less important role in these areas, making it easier to agree on clear, substantive standards. On the other hand, the technical nature of these issues makes the regulation thereof inevitably complex and difficult to understand for the ordinary citizen. For example, limit values for substances only scientists have ever heard of will probably never be easy or appealing to explain. While it would perhaps not be impossible to try and draft some of these measures in a more user-friendly way—for instance, by clearly stating the overall benefits that the measure aims to achieve in the interests of citizens as Helen Xanthaki proposes in Chapter 3—this also risks making the exercise more political and thus undermining the 'regulatory' rationale of the measure and the procedure for its adoption.

[43] N Countouris and R Horton, 'The Temporary Agency Work Directive: Another Broken Promise?' (2009) 38 *Industrial Law Journal* 329.

[44] S Garben, 'Sky-High Controversy and High-Flying Claims? The Sturgeon Case Law in Light of Judicial Activism, Euroscepticism and Eurolegalism' (2013) 50 *Common Market Law Review* 15.

By being unable to tackle the 'problem drivers', it seems that initiatives such as EU Better Regulation to improve the quality of EU rules are bound to disappoint. What are the alternatives? Considering the significant costs of EU Better Regulation as set out below and the limited benefits it can be expected to bring in terms of legislative quality, 'no action' may in fact be a viable option. Alternatively, and more ambitiously, it would seem that the best solution lies in improving citizens' capacity to understand, and engage with, these inevitably imperfect texts. This calls for interpretative guidance by the European Commission (which indeed it already increasingly produces) in the form of Communications and Guidelines, as well as other communications tools. But it also relies, to perhaps an even greater extent, on the Member States taking responsibility in this regard. At the most fundamental level, investments should be made in civic education at all levels of society with an important component of 'European literacy', improving individuals' understanding of how the EU works and the general framework of its body of rules. Member States should furthermore provide systematic and accessible information on how EU rules apply in their country by reference to the way in which EU Directives have been transposed into national law and what national actors/issues are specifically affected by EU Regulations. Finally, access to national courts is crucial, meaning that Member States would have to invest in their judicial systems, keeping any court fees to an absolute minimum, and ensuring that judicial proceedings are expedient and effective.

Tackling (Perceptions of) Over-regulation

As regards the objective to 'combat criticisms that the EU produces too much red tape—inflexible, onerous regulations that strangle European businesses', R Daniel Kelemen has argued in Chapter 11 that:

> Better Regulation initiatives, no matter what their substantive impacts, will never reduce criticisms of excessive red tape from Brussels. Such critiques are ultimately grounded in Eurosceptic and sometimes anti-government ideologies, and cannot be swayed even by successful reforms. Those who believe that the European economy is being strangled by red tape from Brussels cannot be appeased by promises of 'doing less, but doing it better'. On the contrary, they are likely to take such initiatives as an admission of guilt and a show of weakness, and to press ahead with their campaign against 'Brussels'.

The crucial point is that the Better Regulation Agenda, by implicitly or explicitly formulating 'EU over-regulation' as a part of the problem definition that it is aimed at addressing, confirms these perceptions and thereby feeds the existence of the very problem that it intends to solve. It is thus a counterproductive policy.

As Kelemen explains, it would have been (and would still be) more effective to engage in a positive public relations exercise instead:

> 'Rather than engaging in Maoist-style self-criticism about the shortcomings of EU regulation, the Commission should celebrate and claim credit for the strengths and benefits

> of EU regulation ...To be sure, the EU has undertaken a number of initiatives in this spirit. To take just one prominent example in the field of passenger rights regulation, the EU has been aggressive in highlighting the benefits of EU regulations for individual citizens. As any air traveller in Europe will have noticed, with posters and notices on monitors in airport lobbies, the EU has worked to alert passengers of their EU passenger rights—including rights to compensation—which has been a more effective public relations exercise than all the Better Regulation initiatives put together. Such positive initiatives promise to do more to improve the image of EU regulation than any self-critical 'Better Regulation' programme ever could. The EU should press ahead with many more such initiatives.

Beyond the question of public perception, another issue altogether is whether, if tackling over-regulation itself is an explicit goal of the EU Better Regulation Agenda, it is (capable of) achieving this aim. Robert Zbíral's analysis in Chapter 5 has found that only a few proposals or existing pieces of legislation have been withdrawn following the application of the EU Better Regulation Agenda, and most of these qualify as the repeal of 'low-hanging fruit' of obsolete provisions or self-evident consolidations and recasts. While others would argue that Better Regulation 'victims' such as the hairdresser's agreement and initiatives on musculoskeletal disorders and carcinogens and mutagens in the workplace[45] are in themselves highly significant, in terms of sheer numbers it is indeed true that EU Better Regulation has not led to the Grand Repeal of the *acquis* that some hoped and others feared it would be. This can be explained by a variety of legal and political factors.

First of all, as Zbíral points out, for legislation, the same procedure that is followed for the adoption of an act is necessary for its repeal, which means that the high consensus requirements that make the adoption of EU legislation difficult equally make the repeal of successfully adopted legislation very hard. Second, there objectively is a high need to regulate in the EU, as R Daniel Kelemen also explained in his work on Eurolegalism and as is confirmed from a different perspective by the above-cited work of Scharpf. Because of the EU's market-making actions, in the form of liberalisation and integration, it deregulates pre-existing national governance structures and standards, and thus needs to replace them at the European level. Whether or not the EU succeeds in equivalent levels of reregulation remains an open question, but the need and pressure to do so is clear. And the very adoption of EU reregulation in the interest of market-making tends to lead to a need for further EU regulation. Especially where Member States have become excluded from regulating in the public interest such as health, consumer and environmental protection because of EU internal market measures that 'fully harmonise' a particular part of the market, it becomes necessary for the EU to take over the regulation of these interests in a proactive way, regulating emerging risks and newly developing situations on a rolling basis. If this is considered undesirable, the alternative would

[45] Discussed in further detail below.

be to reconsider the EU's market-making ambitions altogether. If there were a less ambitious interpretation of the internal market, and fewer instances of liberalisation, there would also be less need for reregulation at the EU level. However, it is highly doubtful that such an alternative would meet the approval of precisely those who currently advocate 'less regulation' most vehemently.

Increasing Democratic Legitimacy

Better Regulation's efforts to bolster the EU's deliberative and participative democratic credentials fit well with Schmidt's general finding that 'attention to the mechanisms of "throughput" legitimacy, that is, to the efficacy, accountability, openness and inclusiveness of the governance processes, has not only been increasing among scholars but has long been among the central ways in which EU-level institutional players have sought to counter claims about the poverty of input legitimacy and to reinforce claims to output legitimacy'.[46] The current EU Better Regulation Agenda indeed strengthens public consultation and stakeholder involvement commitments, such as by broadening the range of acts for which a full 12-week online consultation is required (including all proposals subject to Impact Assessment, fitness checks of existing legislation and Green Papers)[47] and giving a four-week consultation period for many delegated and implementing acts.[48]

However, as Dawson has pointed out, some recurrent problems remain. First, consultations tend to involve the usual suspects of industry associations, EU-funded transnational non-governmental organisation (NGOs) and those with existing privileged access to the political process.[49] While they are open to all citizens, such genuine public participation does not seem to take place on a large scale, which may be due to the fact that the only people who know about the public consultation are those who are already in the know about the respective initiative in the first place. Too many consultations running in parallel may also result in lower participation rates of average citizens. As the main thrust of contributions is thus from the traditional interlocutors, the added value of the responses in terms of policy input is at times very limited, as the positions are predictable and usually along pre-determined political lines, of which the Commission is already well aware. Second, many consultations ask participants to comment on a defined set of questions set by the lead Directorate General and 'there thus remains significant scope simply to remove key aspects of a given initiative from the political table through how the terms of reference for consultation are defined'.[50] This risks

[46] Schmidt, above n 20, 3.
[47] Better Regulation Guidelines, above n 8, 52.
[48] ibid 77.
[49] Dawson, above n 1, 1219.
[50] ibid 1220.

amounting to a 'thin' notion of reflexive governance,[51] where instead of policy being developed on the basis of constructive, open dialogue with the public and stakeholders, consultation is conceived as a narrowly framed window-dressing exercise. Third, there are no clear commitments as to what is done with the results of the consultations, further feeding that latter criticism.

Fourth, in highly politicised areas, there have been problems with 'stakeholder campaigns', where industry associations, NGOs and trade unions have encouraged members to send hundreds of almost identical contributions on the basis of a template. Apart from processing issues, this raises the more general problem of 'weighing' contributions in public consultations: does every reply carry equal weight or should the reply of an organisation representing more than 1,000 members count for more? And what do they count towards? Are the consultations to be seen and used as a gauge of public opinion, like a mini-referendum on the specific issue, or instead simply intended to receive policy input? This also links to a specific problem with public consultation in the area of social policy, where the Treaties accord a privileged role for the European Social Partners. They should first and foremost be consulted and included in the decision-making process through the two-stage consultation provided in the Social Policy Title. The added value of additional public consultation is not entirely clear in this case. Moreover, against the background of Better Regulation's commitment to reflexive and participatory governance, it is remarkable that one of the few high-profile Better Regulation actions has been the Commission's refusal to submit the collective agreement in the hairdressing sector for adoption to the Council.[52] Finally, there is a clear tension between the idea of Better Regulation as a vehicle for more participatory, democratic decision-making on the one hand, and Better Regulation as a guarantee for evidence-based, efficient and effective governance on the other. What if the public consultation clearly shows a majority preference for a policy option that is not based on any sound facts? Which of Better Regulation's various aims takes precedence?

Apart from the fact that the way in which EU Better Regulation organises public consultation and stakeholder involvement is perhaps not fully effective, one could also question whether the Agenda is not misdirecting its efforts, spending disproportionate amounts of resources on public consultations with limited added value, while doing little to tackle the more problematic features of the current legislative process, such as trilogues. These informal negotiations taking place behind closed doors and foreclosing the normal interinstitutional debates and negotiations were applied to 80 per cent of legislation during the last European Parliament term of office.[53] The Interinstitutional Agreement on Better Law-Making does state that

[51] Brown and Scott, above n 21.

[52] For discussion of the legal implications, see ch 1 of this book.

[53] Opinion of the European Economic and Social Committee on the communication from the Commission to the European Parliament, the Council, the European Economic and Social Committee and the Committee of the Regions, 'Better Regulation for Better Results: An EU Agenda' COM (2015) 215 final.

the 'three Institutions will ensure the transparency of legislative procedures, on the basis of relevant legislation and case-law, including an appropriate handling of trilateral negotiations', but neglects to indicate any further concrete measures in this regard and as such may be considered a rather hollow promise. The European Economic and Social Committee has called for trilogues to be reserved for particular emergencies and for the majority of legislation to be decided via the ordinary legislative procedure, considering that 'only this will ensure full democratic legitimacy and participation'.[54] The Ombudsman has proposed that the Institutions make the following documentation and information publicly available: 'trilogue dates, initial positions of the three institutions, general trilogue agendas, "four-column" documents, final compromise texts, trilogue notes that have been made public, lists of the political decision makers involved and as far as possible a list of other documents tabled during the negotiations. All of these should be made available on an easy-to-use and easy-to-understand joint database'.[55] It would seem that EU Better Regulation would need to invest more in these alternative types of action if it effectively wants to improve the EU's throughput legitimacy.

Finally, there is another way in which EU Better Regulation could be said to fail on democratic legitimacy grounds. While some might argue that to the extent that Better Regulation seeks to limit EU action to what is necessary and proportionate, it serves 'input' or representative democracy by leaving as much space for the national legislative process as possible, other strands of the Better Regulation Agenda do not sit easily with such a narrative. For one thing, its rather hostile stance on 'gold-plating' in the form of national rules that 'go beyond' the standards set in EU rules goes against any idea that Better Regulation would foster democracy by empowering the national legislator.[56] Furthermore, as was mentioned in the previous paragraph, EU Better Regulation does nothing to address the EU-induced deregulation on the national level that triggers the need for EU reregulation. Moreover, as will be discussed in more detail in the following paragraph, EU Better Regulation does not aim to limit all EU action, but is instead mainly directed at EU legislation, while promoting other forms of European integration

[54] ibid.

[55] Decision of the European Ombudsman setting out proposals following her strategic inquiry OI/8/2015/JAS concerning the transparency of trilogues.

[56] According to the European Commission: 'Member States also often go beyond what is strictly required by EU legislation when they implement it at national level ("gold plating"). This may enhance the benefits but can also add unnecessary costs for businesses and public authorities which are mistakenly associated with EU legislation.' It urges Member States to 'avoid unjustified "gold plating"' and that Member States should be invited to explain the reasons for any such gold-plating; Commission Communication, above n 8. The European Parliament has adopted a different line, stating that 'in the case of directives, it is the prerogative of the Member States to decide whether to adopt higher social, environmental and consumer protection standards at national level than those minimum standards of protection agreed upon at EU level, and welcomes any decision to do so; reaffirms that such higher standards must not be regarded as "gold plating"'. European Parliament, 'Report on Regulatory Fitness and Performance Programme (REFIT): State of Play and Outlook', 24 June 2015, 2014/2150(INI), para 44.

such as soft law processes. However, these pose a much greater democratic concern than EU legislation does.

Increasing Respect for Subsidiarity and Proportionality

It was mentioned above that there is a valid problem definition in that EU integration, especially in the area of Member State autonomy, is insufficiently contained, regardless of all the stipulations to the contrary in the Lisbon Treaty and despite the various mechanisms to enforce subsidiarity and proportionality, including through the Early Warning System. This problem of competence creep is most commonly associated with so-called 'indirect legislation', ie, legislation touching on policy areas in which the EU's direct competence is limited or even excluded, but which can be adopted on the basis of other Treaty provisions such as Article 114 TFEU on the internal market. On that point, the competence debate converges with the debate on Better Regulation. However, there is a range of other manifestations of the same problem: namely, negative integration through CJEU case law, international (trade) agreements, economic governance, soft law and parallel integration.[57] The main issue with competence creep, in all its various forms, is one of democratic legitimacy. All forms of competence creep, at least to a certain extent, displace the national legislative process, either through binding European or international norms, or through 'softer' European-level decision-making that constrains national regulatory autonomy. However, an often-overlooked point is that only competence creep in the form of indirect legislation can rely on an alternative form of democratic validation, in the form of the European legislative process, with the involvement of the European Parliament and all other checks and balances attached to it—imperfect as it may still be. Trade agreements, economic governance, soft law and parallel integration, on the other hand, displace not only the national but also the European legislator, to the benefit of executive or judicial decision-making, which poses much greater concerns in terms of input, throughput and output legitimacy.

The problem with the EU Better Regulation Agenda is that in the name of subsidiarity, it actually promotes and encourages these less democratic forms of European integration, especially soft law. As Dawson notes, in the Better Regulation Agenda 'there is a strong emphasis on conceptualizing subsidiarity in terms of a preference for the use of less harmonizing and hierarchical regulatory instruments'.[58] Furthermore, EU Better Regulation can be expected to have such an effect more indirectly, since policy-makers in the Commission may be tempted

[57] For a more extensive discussion of these issues, see S Garben, 'Competence Creep Revisited', above n 3.

[58] Dawson, above n 1, 1224.

to avoid having to engage in arduous Impact Assessments and being examined by the Regulatory Scrutiny Board by opting for a soft law initiative instead of a legislative one. It is open for debate whether soft law is more in line with the subsidiarity principle than legislation is. Especially compared to the most prescriptive forms of EU legislation, soft law obviously leaves much more room for manoeuvre at the national level in terms of how to achieve certain European-level goals and potentially even allows them to not comply with these non-binding norms, but one could ask how much such autonomy is worth if it nevertheless means being subjected by significant European-level pressures (including, in the case of economic governance, the possibility of financial sanctions). In any event, even if this is accepted to be so in a narrow sense, subsidiarity does not stand alone, but has to be considered hand-in-hand with the principle of democratic legitimacy, and, as stated, soft law is highly problematic from that perspective. While with EU Better Regulation the Commission seems to have departed from its original position on soft law in its White Paper on Governance,[59] where it stated that it should not be used when the Community Method is available, the European Parliament seems to remain committed to this view, and it is noteworthy that the Inter-Institutional Agreement indicates that '*recalling the importance which they attach to the Community method*, the three Institutions agree to observe general principles of Union law, such as democratic legitimacy, subsidiarity and proportionality, and legal certainty. They further agree to promote simplicity, clarity and consistency in the drafting of Union legislation and to promote the utmost transparency of the legislative process' (emphasis added). Taken seriously, this would necessitate a revision of the Commission's Impact Assessment approach as regards subsidiarity.

An alternative that would better serve both subsidiarity and democracy would be to subject all soft law initiatives to compulsory Impact Assessment. Currently, such Impact Assessment is foreseen for non-legislative initiatives which are expected to have significant economic, environmental or social impacts, but this does not seem to be adhered to. For instance, no such Impact Assessments are carried out for the annual country-specific recommendations (CSRs) issued in the context of the European Semester, the EU's annual cycle of economic policy coordination. Of course, as will be elaborated below, Impact Assessments and evaluations come at a significant price, and there are many arguments against applying EU Better Regulation to the CSRs. However, there is no particular reason why those arguments would not equally hold true for legislation, which is systematically subjected to these requirements. The point is that EU Better Regulation does not have a sufficient justification for targeting legislation with any more force than other forms of European integration, and it would thus make sense to either question the application of Better Regulation altogether or to argue for equal application to all forms of EU action.

[59] European Commission, 'European Governance—A White Paper' COM (2001) 428 final.

Finally, as regards the principle of proportionality, it was argued above that although respect for this principle seems to be an overarching aim of EU Better Regulation, it is based on a faulty problem assumption, since there is little evidence that there is a fundamental tendency to disrespect this principle in the legislative process. Furthermore, the Court has been willing to strike down EU legislation that does breach proportionality, and the Early Warning System adds political control of this principle to the Member States' toolbox. To the extent that EU Better Regulation is about ensuring proportionality, it therefore seems a rather disproportionate and unnecessary exercise. The remaining part of this problem assumption seems to coincide with concerns about (perceived) EU over-regulation, the discussion of which has taken place above.

Promoting Evidence-Based Policy-Making

It was argued above that the objective of promoting evidence-based policy-making appeared to be based on a poor problem assumption: it is unlikely that the EU will adopt unscientific regulation as this goes against part of its core 'regulatory' rationale, and so it is unclear why the Better Regulation exercise would be necessary to further ensure this. It was also mentioned above that some of the 'bad regulation' scapegoats in fact concerned initiatives that could be considered too scientific (but perhaps not politically savvy) and, to the extent that some of those have been withdrawn in light of EU Better Regulation, it thus seems that the Agenda is applied to the contrary of its own objective to foster evidence-based decision-making.

It could be added that genuine evidence-based policy-making would also require a more proactive commitment to initiate new legislation or other forms of EU action as expediently and effectively as possible whenever new risks or problems emerge. However, EU Better Regulation does not seem particularly conducive to such an approach that would stimulate and encourage the adoption of more regulation, although it should be mentioned that the Interinstitutional Agreement states that 'the Commission will duly take account of the views expressed by the European Parliament and the Council at each stage of the dialogue, including their requests for initiatives'. Yet, overall, EU Better Regulation acts instead as a deterrent for such proactive policy-making and has at times explicitly obstructed it. For example, the REFIT exercise held back important legislation on muscular skeletal disorders, the scientific need for which was recognised by the Commission in 2007,[60] as well as updates for legislation on carcinogens and mutagens, for over a decade.[61] Only after the European Parliament's Committee on Employment and

[60] See Second-Stage Consultation of the Social Partners on work-related musculoskeletal disorders.

[61] European Commission, 'REFIT: State of Play and Outlook—Questions and Answers', http://europa.eu/rapid/press-release_MEMO-14-426_nl.htm, stating that as a result of REFIT, 'the Commission … decided not to present a number of proposals on which it had already been working, for

Social Affairs in its opinion on REFIT 'called on the Commission to increase the protection of workers; calls on the Commission, in particular, to present a proposal on muscular skeletal disorders and environmental tobacco smoke, and to make necessary updates to the list of carcinogens and mutagens'[62] did the European Commission in 2017 finally move on some of these issues, in the form of a proposed Directive on carcinogens and mutagens.[63] For muscular skeletal disorders, it has refused to propose any new measures at this stage.[64]

THE COSTS AND BENEFITS OF EU BETTER REGULATION

It is impossible—and beyond the scope of this chapter—to exhaustively assess all the actual costs and benefits of the EU Better Regulation Agenda, let alone to quantify them. But for completeness of the argument, some of the main possible costs and benefits will be briefly postulated here. These notions will be used in a broad sense, encompassing more general impacts on society and the EU legal and political order.

Costs of EU Better Regulation

The first cost is that related to the 'bureaucracy of EU Better Regulation', ie, the actual running of Impact Assessments, evaluations and other Better Regulation activities. These should comprise: (i) the labour costs of the EU civil servants spending significant amounts of time on these activities, both in the Commission Secretariat General as in the policy Directorates General, as well as in the Parliament and the Council; and (ii) the price of expert studies contracted out to consultancies in the context of these activities. These actual costs could, on the basis of the necessary information, be determined with some reasonable accuracy and can be expected to amount to millions of euros each year.

The second cost is a more difficult-to-measure opportunity cost, in the sense of other important activities not being pursued because of: (i) the time available to

example in the areas of occupational safety and health for hairdressers, musculoskeletal disorders, environmental tobacco smoke and carcinogens and mutagens'. See also Euractiv, 'European Commission's "Better Regulation" Has Killed 100,000, Say Unions', 24 April 2015, http://www.euractiv.com/sections/health-consumers/european-commissions-better-regulation-has-killed-150000-says-etuc-314030.

[62] European Parliament, Opinion of the Committee on Employment and Social Affairs on Regulatory Fitness and Performance Programme (REFIT): State of Play and Outlook 2014/2150(INI), 28 May 2015, para 16.

[63] See Commission proposal for a Directive amending Directive 2004/37/EC on the protection of workers from the risks related to exposure to carcinogens or mutagens at work, 2017/0004 (COD).

[64] European Commission Communication, 'Safer and Healthier Work for All—Modernisation of the EU Occupational Safety and Health Legislation and Policy' COM (2017) 12 final.

the EU civil service being taken up by running EU Better Regulation exercises; and (ii) the deterrent effect of the administrative and economic burdens of new initiatives having to pass Impact Assessments. While it will be difficult to ever determine what initiatives might have been developed—or developed more expediently—without EU Better Regulation and to assess what costs and benefits those hypothetical initiatives would have brought, the point here is to recognise these costs of EU Better Regulation at least in theory.

Even more difficult to measure or quantify, but not unimportant to recognise as a negative impact, are the findings that have emerged from the previous paragraphs that: (i) EU Better Regulation risks aggravating the deregulatory asymmetry of European integration (with corresponding negative consequences on important non-economic interests such as consumer, health and environmental protection, and on fundamental (social) rights); and (ii) EU Better Regulation aggravates the EU democratic deficit by targeting the EU legislative process, but instead doing nothing to limit—and instead promoting—less legitimate forms of EU integration, such as soft law.

Benefits of EU Better Regulation

If the Better Regulation Agenda was right in its problem definitions and would be effective at addressing them all, the expected benefits would be significant, albeit difficult to quantify. They would include: (i) an increased respect for the Rule of Law through better-quality legislation; (ii) increased economic performance by reduced regulatory burdens on businesses and by reduced administrative burdens on public authorities; (iii) increased democratic legitimacy through enhanced participatory and reflexive governance, which would also lead to more enforceable legislation and thus would positively affect the Rule of Law; and (iv) increased legitimacy of the European integration process in the eyes of citizens, businesses and Member States alike through more effective, rational and proportionate rule-making. This of course coincides with the political narrative that is supposed to 'sell' the EU Better Regulation Agenda.

Unfortunately, as the foregoing assessment has shown, EU Better Regulation does not deliver all of these benefits. This is partly because it is shooting at enemies that are not there (over-regulation, unscientific regulation), partly because it targets the henchmen but not the bosses (public consultation instead of trilogues, EU legislation instead of soft law), partly because it engages in battles in already-lost wars (quality of EU legislation) and partly because it engages in counterproductive strategy (public perceptions of over-regulation). Of course, it is likely to have delivered some benefits: perhaps the drafting of legislation has slightly improved because of the style guidelines, perhaps some legislative initiatives have been better conceived because of the analytical framework of Impact Assessment, perhaps some costly or intrusive initiatives have not seen the light of day because of Better Regulation's deterrent effect or because a better alternative was chosen in light of the evidence-base, and perhaps its commitment to public consultation has somewhat improved the participatory image of the EU with informed citizens and certain interest organisations. But these benefits are likely to be marginal, especially compared to the aims, scope and costs of EU Better Regulation.

CONCLUSION

The present chapter has used the idea of subjecting Better Regulation to an Impact Assessment mainly as a rhetorical device. But it merits serious consideration. An official Impact Assessment (or *ex post* evaluation) of (each incarnation of) the EU Better Regulation Agenda itself would seem a good way to increase the legitimacy of a policy that is central to the legitimacy of European integration. Better Regulation generates an enormous administrative burden for the EU Institutions, has serious cost implications for the EU budget and can be expected to have certain negative constitutional, social and environmental impacts, if only because it throws up hurdles in the legislative process on which the protection of non-market interests depend more in the EU than the protection of market interests do. While on the basis of the foregoing analysis, it seems unlikely that the expected benefits—in terms of a clearer and simpler regulatory framework, more effective legislation and more throughput legitimacy through participatory governance—can be achieved to such a degree that they would outweigh the costs, a genuine Impact Assessment may obviously prove differently. The least that can be asked is for the very policy that trumpets evidence-based policy-making, proportionality and (cost-)effectiveness to be forced to live up to its own standards and thus: (i) to be clear about the evidence base for the postulated problems its tries to address and whether it is succeeding in doing so; (ii) to assess what the costs and the benefits and advantages and disadvantages are of the approach it takes at the expense of alternatives; and so (iii) to prove its own 'added value'. And if such an exercise would confirm the findings on the basis of the assessment conducted in this chapter, namely that the EU Better Regulation Agenda is currently 'unfit for purpose', the necessary conclusions must be drawn and actions should be taken accordingly, which would probably entail a fundamental overhaul of EU Better Regulation in its objectives, scope and content. There really is no good reason not to conduct such an assessment in all seriousness. For if its methodology is sound, what does EU Better Regulation have to fear in being judged by its own standards?

Index

adjudication *see* impact assessments (IAs), as ECJ adjudicative tool
Agency for Administrative Simplification (AAS) (Belgium) 153–6
Agenda for Europe 2020 41
Army Corps of Engineers (US) 51
Arndt, C 152
Asser Instituut Conference 1997 119–20, 120, 122

Barroso Commission 3–4, 205–6, 221
Belgium
  participation in EU's debates 175–81
    Better Regulation Working Party 178–9, 181
    Concertation (Deliberation) Committee 176
    Cooperation Agreement (1994), overview 176–7, 181
    devolution effect 175
    Directorate of European Affairs (DGE) 175–8
    formal position 175–6
    Habitat and Birds Directives, fitness check 179
    Inter-ministerial Conference on Foreign Policy (ICFP) 176
    opinion-based/pragmatic approach 179–80
    policy coordination role 176–7
    see also Flanders; participation in EU's debates
  regulatory policy 152–8
    administrative burden reduction/ simplification of legislation 153–4
    Agency for Administrative Simplification (AAS) 153–6
    consociationalism federalism 183
    cooperation agreement 156
    culture and capacity 183–4
    Democracy Index (*Economist*) rankings 165–6
    evaluation/participatory approaches, concerns 153–4
    federal ambition 152–3, 154, 157–8
    General Policy note 156–7
    Impact Assessment Committee 155, 156
    Kafka-test 154–5
    OECD profiles 152–3
    see also Flanders, regulatory policy
  see also member states' role

Bentham, Jeremy 50–1
Better Regulation
  aims of book 12
  contribution to debate 9–10
  democratic/constitutional legitimacy issues 4–8
  impact assessment *see* impact assessment of Better Regulation
  member states' role in origins 142–3
  narratives 8–9
  as semi-permanent/dynamic feature 3–4
  structure of book 10–12
  see also impact assessment of Better Regulation
Better Regulation Agenda 36–7, 41, 318–19
  see also under cost-benefit analysis (CBA)
Better Regulation for Better Results 206
Better Regulation Guidelines 2015 20–1, 24
Better Regulation Programme 2002 16
Better Regulation Working Party (Belgium/ Flanders) 178–9, 181
Beyers, J 175
bias against business 7–8
Blockmans, S 146–7
Bursens, P 175

Chicago School 53
Clingendael Institute report 141
Commission *see* European Commission
Committee of the Regions 147
competencies *see* deactification of EU competencies
cost per quality-adjusted-life-year (QALY) 54
cost-benefit analysis (CBA)
  assumptions 52–3
  Better Regulation Agenda 55–61
    adaptive regulation 60–1
    nuanced approach 56–8
    quantification 57
    reasons for departure from CBA 59–61
  cost per quality-adjusted-life-year (QALY) 54
  cost-effectiveness analysis (CEA) 54
  cost-focused stock-flow linkage rules 55
  debate on 49–50
  economic analysis of regulation 55
  feasibility analysis 54–5
  impact assessment system 56, 57 *Fig.*
    consistency with EC's priorities/ medium-term goals 60
    evidence of CBA use 58

ex ante/ex post assessment 60–2
scope wider than CBA 59–60
individual willingness to pay (WPT) 51–2
Kaldor-Hicks efficiency/Pareto superiority 53–4
key issues 50
net benefit concept 50–1
practical alternatives 54–5
preference-based approach 51–2
and public policy 50–5
regulatory budgeting 55
cost-effectiveness analysis (CEA) 54
cost-focused stock-flow linkage rules 55
Council *see* historical overview, Council perspective

Dawson, M 187
deactification of EU competencies
British referendum 64
ever closer Union 63–4
ex post evaluation 67–71
criteria 67, 68–9
fitness checks 68
formal options 70–1
goal 67–8
sunset/review clauses 69
value-added criterion 68–9
key issues/summary 63–4, 75
in practice/empirical evidence 71–5
repeals, evaluation/candidates 71–2
restoration to member states 65–7
constitutional dimension 65
dismantling/deregulation 66–7
exclusive/supporting competencies 65
legislative dimension 65
opt-outs/negative competencies, exclusion 65
procedure 66
reverse delegation 67
secondary legislation repeal 66, 67
shared competencies 65–6
review clauses 69, 72–4
content and goals 73, 74
preference for status quo 73–5
use and objectives 72–3, 74
delegated acts/legislation
European Commission, stakeholder consultation 90
European Parliament, and Interinstitutional Agreement (IIA), rendezvous clause 111
new IIA 2016 134–5
Delors Commission 205
Delors, Jacques 64, 105
Democracy Index (*Economist*) rankings 165–6
democratic legitimacy *see under* impact assessment of Better Regulation
Dupuit, Jules 51

ECJ adjudication *see* impact assessments (IAs), as ECJ adjudicative tool
Edinburgh summit 142
EU competencies *see* deactification of EU competencies
EU legislation, quality improvement
Agenda for Europe 2020 41
aims and objectives 34–5
'best possible' legislation aims 39–40
Better Regulation agenda 36–7, 41
Commission Guidelines and Principles 34–5
creative approach 42–3
drafting guidelines/process 35–7
effectiveness 31, 32–4, 35, 37–41, 42–5, 46–7
ex ante evaluation 38–9
external verification of draft legislation 43
future challenges 41–2
impact assessment 37
implementation improvement 39
Interinstitutional Agreements 35–6, 40
key issues/conclusions 29, 46–7
legislative mismatch 43
Member State evaluation/role 39, 44
regulatory tool, legislation as 36–7, 40–1
simplification programme 37–8
SMART Regulation Agenda 13, 36–7, 39–41, 60
theoretical definitions
clarity/clearness 33–4
effectiveness 31, 32–4, 35, 37–41, 42–5, 46–7
efficacy 31–2
functional definition 29–30
gender-neutral language 34
hierarchy of qualities 31
plain language 34
precision 34
regulation/legislation links 30–1
synergetic approach 31, 34
unambiguity 34
transposing legislation 44–6
EU treaties 5–6
Eurolegalism
Commission initiatives 205–6
definition 200, 206, 230
democratic deficit critique 208–9
European Parliament/Council legislation 209
fragmented institutional structure 208
key issues/conclusion 206–7, 214–15
limited administrative capacity 208
public relations initiatives 209–14, 215
Brexit effect 213–14
bureaucratic Euromyths 210
challenging Eurosceptic tropes 210–11
EU enforcement, re-emphasis 212–13

member states, ranking and shaming 211–12
positive narratives 211
presumption/failure 209–10
reasons for detailed/prescriptive regulation 207–9
Single Market dynamic 207
European Commission
action plan 2002 83–4
challenges 92–9
consultation *see* stakeholder consultation *below*
evaluation 82, 102
draft evaluation 90–2
framework development 84–5
evidence-based policy-making
aims 81–2
ethical necessity 81
importance 102–3
transparency/accountability need 80, 81
guidelines/training 88–9
impact assessments (IAs) 82–3
consultation on drafts 94–5
framework development 83–4
quantification 92–4
regulatory scrutiny 95–6
interinstitutional cooperation 87–8, 102
Juncker Commission *see under* Juncker Commission
key issues/conclusions 79–80, 102–3
past developments/evolution 83–6
pillars of Better Regulation 82–3
political choices in post-truth world 79, 99–101
political priorities/committment 79, 86–7
practical application 88–9
quantification issues 92–4
regulatory burden reduction targets 97–8
Regulatory Scrutiny Board 21–2, 24
regulatory scrutiny/fitness 95–6
Spitzenkandidaten 5, 114–15
stakeholder consultation 82–3, 102
consultation/feedback innovations 89–90
draft impact assessments 94–5
legislation/delegated acts, preparation/ implementation 90
minimum standards 85
subsidiarity 98–9
targets for regulatory burden reduction 97–8
transparency 89–90
European Council *see* historical overview, Council perspective
European Economic and Social Committee 147–8
European Investment and Structural (ESI) Funds 124
European Ministers for Public Administration (EUPAN) 143–4, 148–9
European Parliament, and Interinstitutional Agreement (IIA)
certainty/predictability, emphasis 110
Commission's role 110, 112
consensual parameters 105–6
delegated acts, rendezvous clause 111
first informal procedures 108
good legislation panel proposal 109
impact assessments 109
information about international agreements, rendezvous clause 111
interinstitutional balance 108–11
Juncker Commission *see under* Juncker Commission
key issues/conclusion 105, 117
law-making process 108–9
legal effect of IIA 107–8
legislative initiative 113–14
legislative programming 111–17
annual programming and Commission 114–16
as central element 111–12
Commission responses 117
Council's role 114, 115
joint conclusions 115
legal bases 116
legislative initiative 113–14
procedure 112–13, 115
reasons for 112
purpose of IIA 106–7
soft constitutional law 107, 117
Spitzenkandidaten 5, 114–15
stakeholder consultation 110
evidence-based policy-making
European Commission *see* European Commission
impact assessment *see* impact assessment of Better Regulation
ex post evaluation *see under* deactification of EU competencies

Flanders
participation in EU's debates 175–81
Better Regulation Working Party 181
devolution effect 175
Directorate of European Affairs (DGE), participation 175–8, 181
dominant non-traditional political party (New Flemish Alliance) 180–1
IEC meeting participation 177–8
opinion-based/pragmatic approach 179–80
Vision on the Future of the European Union 164–5, 181
see also Belgium, participation in EU's debates

regulatory policy 158–66
administrative tools, development 159–60
Circular Letters 163–4
culture and capacity 183–4
Flemish Vision 2050 Strategy 166
general framework (simplification/ development plan) approval/ development 158–9
Green Paper process 165–6
impact assessments 164, 183
ministerial cabinet approach 162–3
OECD context 160–1, 162–3
Policy Note 2014–19 161–2
process commencement (1997 and 1998) 158
RIAs (Regulatory Impact Assessments) 159–60, 162–4, 182
Social and Economic Council of Flanders (SERV), reports and recommendations 158, 165–6
see also Belgium, regulatory policy
see also member states' role
Franklin, Benjamin 50
Friedman, Milton 53

gold-plating critique 6–7
Gove, Michael 214

Heaton, Richard 31
historical overview, Council perspective
Asser Instituut Conference 1997 119, 120, 122
complexity, post Lisbon 121
Council approaches 119–20
factors in law-making 120
key issues/summary 121–2, 135–6
new IIA 2016 132–5
codification of existing good practice 132
Commission's right to initiative 133
delegated acts 134–5
impact assessments 133–4, 135
legal basis 132
overall assessment 132–3
post-Lisbon (IIA) practice
accessibility/transparency, example 128–9
certainty/clarity/better enforcement 125
coherent/consistent framework, example 126
Cohesion Legislative Package 124–5, 129–30
concrete examples 126–32
legal certainty, example 126–7
legislative simplification, example 130
micro-enterprises and SMEs, special provisions 131
recent examples 131–2
stakeholder involvement, example 127–8
subsidiarity/proportionality emphasis 130–1
substantial legislative consolidation/ significant legislative simplification 125
pre-2003 IIA
cornerstone documents 122
main requirements (IIA 1998) 123–4

IIA *see* Interinstitutional Agreement (IIA)
impact assessment of Better Regulation
background 217
benefits of Better Regulation 241–2
constitutional questions 217
costs of Better Regulation 240–1
definition of problem(s) 218–30
democratic legitimacy
lack of 224–5
national level 236–7
public consultation/stakeholder involvement 234–5
success in increasing 234–7
trilogues 235–6
effectiveness in problem solving 230–40
evidence-based policy-making
fact-free over-regulation claims 228–9
lack of 227–30
success in promoting 239–40
unscientific/irrational responses 227–8
key issues/conclusion 218, 242
legislative quality
complex mix of rules/exceptions 220
contradictory provisions 219–20
diversity/consensus requirements 230
effectiveness of solution 230–2
enforceability of text 220–1
improvement needed 219–21
problem drivers 231, 232
undefined notions/concepts 220
over-regulation
deregulatory bias 223–4
economically liberal analytical framework 221–2
effectiveness of tackling 232–4
legal political issues 233–4
objective/subjective considerations 222–3
perceptions 221–4
public perceptions 232–3
subsidiarity and proportionality
competence creep 237
Early Warning System 226, 237
insufficient respect for 226–7
soft law initiatives 237–8
success in increasing 237–9
see also Better Regulation

Impact Assessment Committee (Belgium) 155, 156
impact assessments (IAs)
cost-benefit analysis (CBA) *see under* cost-benefit analysis (CBA)
European Commission *see under* European Commission
European Parliament, and Interinstitutional Agreement (IIA) 109
Flanders 159–60, 162–4, 182–3
new IIA 2016 133–4, 135
impact assessments (IAs), as ECJ adjudicative tool 4
Afton Chemical case 188
Better Regulation
principles/Agenda 187, 201
Toolbox 187, 194–5
CIRFS case 194
Client Earth case 201–2
Commission's Regulatory Scrutiny Board 188
comparison and improvement of use 191–6
complexity/cost/methodology 192–3
constitutional limits 196–202
cost-benefit analysis (CBA) 191–3
Court's role 194–6
Dansk Rørindustri A/S 194
Estonia v Parliament and Council 190, 191, 198–9
EU legislation, quality improvement 37
Evaluating Integrated Impact Assessments (EVIA) report 192–3
evidence-base of lawmaking 185
global standard 185
Guidelines, 2015 185–9, 192, 195–6, 201
institutional balance 188–9
Interinstitutional Agreement 188
James Elliot case 201
key issues/conclusion 186, 202
Luxembourg v Parliament and Council 189, 191, 198
non-binding instruments 201–2
Philip Morris case 189, 190, 193, 197–9
Pillbox 38 190
Poland v Parliament and Council 190
practical difficulties 192–3
procedural proportionality 189–91, 193, 197–201
rule of law reinforcement 188
Spain v Council 190
subsidiarity and proportionality 186, 188, 189, 196–9
Tobacco Directive cases 191, 197–8
Treaty compliance 195–6
US, comparison with 191–2
Vodafone and Others 189, 190, 198
see also under European Commission

Interinstitutional Agreement (IIA)
Council perspective *see* historical overview, Council perspective
historical overview *see under* historical overview, Council perspective
Parliament perspective *see* European Parliament, and Interinstitutional Agreement (IIA)

Jacobs, S 193
Jenkins, I 33
Juncker Commission
European Commission 3–4, 14, 18, 20, 60, 86–92, 206
European Parliament, and Interinstitutional Agreement (IIA) 105, 115
member states' role 137–9

Kafka-test 154–5
Kaldor-Hicks efficiency 53–4
Kelemen, RD 200, 205

legislation *see* EU legislation, quality improvement
legislative programming *see under* European Parliament, and Interinstitutional Agreement (IIA)
legislative quality *see under* impact assessment of Better Regulation
Lisbon Treaty 64, 75, 143, 193, 197, 226

Maastricht Treaty 64, 112, 226
Macrae, D 193
Mader, L 32
Mandelkern Report *see under* member states' role
Marshall, Alfred 51
member states' role
Belgium *see* Belgium, participation in EU's debates; Belgium, regulatory policy
Clingendael Institute report 141
Committee of the Regions 147
current reality 139–42
Democracy Index (*Economist*) rankings 165–6
Edinburgh summit 142
emerging trends 149–50
European Economic and Social Committee 147–8
European Ministers for Public Administration (EUPAN) 143–4, 148–9
EU's debates 166–75
Competitiveness Council 169–71
Declaration on competitiveness 170
Directors and Experts on Better Regulation (DEBR) 167–8, 181
EU Public Administration Network 168

in more working parties 172–4
national initiatives 166–7
Working Party on Competitiveness and Growth 168–9, 172–3
see also Belgium, participation in EU's debates; Flanders, participation in EU's debates
Flanders *see* Flanders, participation in EU's debates; Flanders, regulatory policy
implementation actions 148–52
intentions 137–9
Juncker Commission *see under* Juncker Commission
key issues/conclusions 137, 181–4
Mandelkern Report 67, 143–6
context/experience 145
objectives/mandate 143–4
recommendations/impact 144–5
structures/driving forces 145–6
national good practices 181–2
new IIA 2016 139–40
OECD EU 15 project 149–50, 153
OECD Regulatory Policy Outlook 150–3
and origins of Better Regulation 142–3
proactivity issues 140–2
REFIT commitment 139
restoration to member states *see under* deactification of EU competencies
subsidiarity 146–8
tools and instruments 148
Menon, Anand 205
Meuwese, ACM 148
Michigan v EPA 54
Mousmouti, M 30
Muller, G 33

Öberg, J 200–1
OECD EU 15 project 149–50, 153
OECD Regulatory Policy Outlook 150–3
over-regulation *see under* impact assessment of Better Regulation

Pareto superiority 53–4
Petrin, M 192
Posner, Richard 53
Priestley, Joseph 50
procedural proportionality 189–91, 193, 197–201
Prodi Commission 205
proportionality
impact assessment *see under* impact assessment of Better Regulation
post-Lisbon (IIA) practice 130–1
procedural proportionality 189–91, 193, 197–201
public relations initiatives *see under* Eurolegalism

QALY (cost per quality-adjusted-life-year) 54

Radaelli, CM 148
Reagan government 10, 13, 14, 192, 221
REFIT (Regulatory Fitness and Performance Programme exercise) 5, 21, 24, 37, 67–8, 93, 96, 205–6, 239–40
member states' commitment 139, 169, 170, 172, 174, 175, 177, 178, 181
reflexive governance
approaches 20–4
categories 19
concept 19
ex ante/ex post evaluation 21–2
impact analysis 20–1
norm setting/monitoring/enforcement 17, 23
OECD role 15
oversight measures 21–2
and policy cycle 20, 22–4
policy reflection stage 22–3
principles of better regulations 14, 15
regulatory governance 14–18
regulatory trends 13–14
review and revision 24
rule-making focus 14–15, 17–19, 24–5
scholarly focus 16–17, 18, 25
stakeholder consultation 20–1
subsidiarity focus 15
summary 24–5
regulatory burden reduction targets *see under* European Commission
regulatory scrutiny/fitness *see under* European Commission
Renda, A 141
restoration to member states *see under* deactification of EU competencies
review clauses *see under* deactification of EU competencies
RIAs (Regulatory Impact Assessments) 159–60, 162–4, 182

Santer Commission 80, 205
Schmidt, V 224
SLIM (Simplification of Legislation in the Internal Market programme) 13, 15–16, 41, 205
SMART Regulation Agenda 13, 36–7, 39–41, 60
social partners 7
Sottiaux, S 165
Spitzenkandidaten 5, 114
stakeholder consultation
European Commission *see under* European Commission
European Parliament, and Interinstitutional Agreement (IIA) 110
impact assessment of Better Regulation 234–5

post-Lisbon (IIA) practice 127–8
reflexive governance 20–1
Stephanou, C 31, 37
subsidiarity
European Commission 98–9
historical overview, Council perspective 130–1
impact assessments (IAs)
as ECJ adjudicative tool 186, 188, 189, 196–9
see also under impact assessment of Better Regulation
member states' role 146–8
reflexive governance 15
sunset clauses *see under* deactification of EU competencies
Sunstein, CR 53
Sutherland, Peter 15

Teubner, G 32–3
Thatcher government 10, 13, 14, 221
Timmermans, Frans 20, 138, 139, 141, 157, 161, 171
transposing legislation *see under* EU legislation, quality improvement
Trump administration 55

Uhlmann, F 33

Voermans, W 30

Wyatt, D 199–200

www.ingramcontent.com/pod-product-compliance
Ingram Content Group UK Ltd.
Pitfield, Milton Keynes, MK11 3LW, UK
UKHW020805290926
15470UKWH00003B/971

9 781509 917334